Edge Computing - Technology, Management and Integration

Edited by Sam Goundar

Published in London, United Kingdom

Edge Computing - Technology, Management and Integration
http://dx.doi.org/10.5772/intechopen.105637
Edited by Sam Goundar

Contributors
C. Santhiya, S. Padmavathi, Syed Rizwan Hassan, Muhammad Rashad, Ruslan Smeliansky, Abhishek Mondal, Deepak Mishra, Ganesh Prasad, Ashraf Hossain, Lukas M. Broell, Christian Hanshans, Dominik Kimmerle, Jun Cai, You Shi, Yuye Yang, Changyan Yi, Bing Chen, Robert L. Drury, Justice Opara-Martins, Laisa Costa de Biase, Marcelo Zuffo, Pablo Calcina-Ccori, Roseli Lopes, Geovane Fedrecheski, Kofi Sarpong Adu-Manu, Gabriel Amponsa Koranteng, Samuel Nii Adotei Brown, Huanle Zhang, Xin Liu, Xueying Zhang, Lei Fu

First published in London, United Kingdom, 2023 by IntechOpen
IntechOpen is the global imprint of INTECHOPEN LIMITED, registered in England and Wales, registration number: 11086078, 5 Princes Gate Court, London, SW7 2QJ, United Kingdom

British Library Cataloguing-in-Publication Data
A catalogue record for this book is available from the British Library

Additional hard and PDF copies can be obtained from orders@intechopen.com

Edge Computing - Technology, Management and Integration
Edited by Sam Goundar
p. cm.
Print ISBN 978-1-83768-861-6
Online ISBN 978-1-83768-862-3
eBook (PDF) ISBN 978-1-83768-863-0

For EU product safety concerns:
IN TECH d.o.o., Prolaz Marije Krucifikse Kozulić 3, 51000 Rijeka, Croatia,
info@intechopen.com or visit our website at intechopen.com.

Meet the editor

Professor Dr. Sam Goundar is an international academic, having taught at twelve different universities in ten different countries. He is the editor-in-chief of the *International Journal of Blockchains and Cryptocurrencies* (IJBC), *International Journal of Fog Computing* (IJFC), *International Journal of Creative Computing* (IJCrC), and *International Journal of Cloud Applications and* Computing (IJCAC). He is the associate editor of *Tsinghua Science and Technology* and guest editor of the Special Issue on "Digital Banking and Financial Technology," *Journal of Risk and Financial Management* (JRFM). He is also on the editorial review board of more than twenty high-impact factor journals. Dr. Goundar has 126 publications in journals and book chapters to his credit. He has also written and edited fifteen books.

Contents

Preface

In today's rapidly evolving technological landscape, the concept of edge computing has emerged as a groundbreaking paradigm shift, revolutionizing the way we process and analyze data. As the traditional model of centralized cloud computing faces challenges related to latency, bandwidth limitations, and privacy concerns, edge computing offers a compelling alternative. At its core, edge computing brings computational power and data storage closer to the source of data generation, enabling real-time processing and analysis at the edge of the network. By distributing these tasks across a network of edge devices, such as routers, gateways, and Internet of Things (IoT) devices, edge computing enhances efficiency, reduces latency, and mitigates the strain on cloud infrastructure. This book delves into the multifaceted world of edge computing, offering a comprehensive exploration of its principles, applications, and implications, as well as its potential to reshape industries and empower emerging technologies.

Throughout the pages of this book, readers will embark on a fascinating journey that unravels the transformative potential of edge computing across various domains. From smart cities and autonomous vehicles to healthcare systems and industrial automation, the applications of edge computing are vast and far-reaching. By leveraging the proximity of computational resources to data sources, edge computing enables real-time decision-making, enhanced security and privacy, and improved reliability. Through insightful case studies and expert analysis, this book illuminates the ways in which edge computing is driving innovation and paving the way for the future of technology. It also delves into the challenges and considerations associated with implementing edge computing architectures, addressing topics such as edge device management, data orchestration, and edge-to-cloud integration.

Edge Computing Technologies

The utilization of edge computing technologies presents a multitude of benefits that have the potential to revolutionize various industries and enhance the overall digital ecosystem. Firstly, one of the key advantages lies in the significant reduction of latency. By processing and analyzing data closer to the source, edge computing minimizes the time it takes for data to travel to and from the cloud. This is particularly crucial for applications requiring real-time or near-real-time responses, such as autonomous vehicles, industrial automation, and immersive virtual reality experiences. The reduced latency not only improves the overall user experience but also enables time-sensitive decision-making, leading to increased efficiency and productivity.

Secondly, edge computing offers enhanced security and privacy. With traditional cloud computing, sensitive data often has to be transmitted and stored in remote data centers, raising concerns about potential security breaches or unauthorized access. Edge computing mitigates these risks by keeping data closer to its origin, reducing the exposure to external threats during transmission. Additionally, by enabling local processing, edge computing allows for data to be anonymized or encrypted at the edge devices themselves, further bolstering privacy protection. This capability is particularly relevant in industries handling sensitive data, such as health care and finance, where compliance with stringent data protection regulations is paramount. Whether you are an industry professional, an academic researcher, or simply curious about the cutting-edge advancements shaping our digital landscape, this book provides a comprehensive guide to understanding and harnessing the potential of edge computing.

Edge Computing Management

While edge computing offers numerous benefits, its implementation and management also present a set of challenges and issues that need to be addressed. One of the primary challenges is the complexity of managing a distributed network of edge devices. Unlike traditional centralized cloud computing, edge computing involves a multitude of devices located at various edge locations, often with different hardware capabilities and operating systems. This heterogeneity poses challenges in terms of device management, software updates, and ensuring consistent performance across the network. Coordinating and maintaining a large number of edge devices requires robust management frameworks that can handle tasks such as provisioning, monitoring, and troubleshooting in a scalable and efficient manner.

Another significant challenge is data governance and orchestration. Edge computing involves processing and storing data closer to its source, which means that data is distributed across multiple edge devices. This distributed nature raises concerns about data governance, security, and compliance. Organizations must establish robust policies and mechanisms to ensure data integrity, privacy protection, and regulatory compliance. Additionally, orchestrating data flows and managing the movement of data between edge devices and the cloud poses a challenge. Efficient data orchestration requires careful consideration of factors such as data priority, network bandwidth, and latency. Balancing the distribution of data processing and storage between the edge and the cloud while maintaining data consistency and minimizing data transfer costs is a complex task that requires intelligent data management strategies. Addressing these challenges and issues requires innovative solutions and frameworks for edge computing management. Efficient device management systems, centralized control planes, and automated provisioning mechanisms are essential to streamline the deployment and maintenance of edge devices.

Edge Computing Integration

The integration of edge computing with other emerging technologies holds immense potential to drive innovation and unlock new possibilities across various domains. One such synergy is the combination of edge computing with artificial intelligence (AI) and machine learning (ML). By bringing computational power and data processing closer to the source, edge computing facilitates real-time data analysis, enabling AI and ML algorithms to make informed and instantaneous decisions at the edge. This integration is particularly valuable in applications that require quick response times and autonomous decision-making, such as autonomous vehicles, smart surveillance systems, and predictive maintenance in industrial settings. The combination of edge computing and AI/ML also reduces the need for constant data transmission to the cloud, optimizing bandwidth usage and minimizing latency, which is critical for time-sensitive applications.

Another promising integration lies in the convergence of edge computing and the Internet of Things (IoT). The IoT ecosystem is characterized by a vast network of interconnected devices that generate and exchange large volumes of data. By integrating edge computing with IoT, data can be processed, filtered, and analyzed at the edge devices themselves, reducing the need for data transmission to centralized cloud servers. This enables faster response times, improved scalability, and enhanced reliability of IoT applications. For instance, in smart cities, edge computing can enable real-time analysis of sensor data to optimize traffic management, energy consumption, and waste management systems. Similarly, in health care, edge computing integrated with IoT devices can support remote patient monitoring, real-time diagnostics, and timely intervention, enhancing the delivery of healthcare services.

Organization of the Book

This edited book is organized into two sections with eleven chapters. The first section on "Edge Computing" looks generally at edge computing technologies like cloud, fog, network, and swarm computing. Chapter 1, "Cloud Computing to Fog Computing: A Paradigm Shift", provides an overview of healthcare services using cloud and fog computing. Chapter 2, "Perspective Chapter: A View – Cloud-Edge Computing Technology " looks at different types of cloud computing and edge computing services. Chapter 3, "Network Powered by Computing: Next Generation of Computational Infrastructure", deals with the convergence of data communications, cloud, and high-performance computing. Chapter 4, "Perspective Chapter: Cloud Lock-in Parameters – Service Adoption and Migration", highlights technical advancements that contribute to interoperable migration in heterogeneous cloud environments. The first section ends with Chapter 5, "Swarm Computing: The Emergence of a Collective Artificial Intelligence at the Edge of Internet", which provides a comprehensive vision of the key aspects of the swarm computing paradigm.

The next section is on "Edge Computing Applications". Edge computing has been applied to control unmanned aerial vehicles (UAVs), IoT, digital epidemiology, hyper-parameter tuning, 5G emerging technologies, and the Industrial Internet of Things (IIoT). In Chapter 6, "Optimal Unmanned Aerial Vehicle Control and Designs for Load Balancing in Intelligent Wireless Communication Systems", the authors propose a methodology to significantly improve the system's performance. Chapter 7, "IoT on an ESP32: Optimization Methods Regarding Battery Life and Write Speed to an SD-Card", deals with optimizing battery life methods for microcontrollers. Chapter 8, "Perspective Chapter: 5G Enabling Technologies – Revolutionizing Transport, Environment, and Health", examines how 5G technologies can revolutionize transport, health, and the environment. Chapter 9, "Federated Learning Hyper-Parameter Tuning for Edge Computing", proposes to facilitate the integration of federated learning and edge computing by optimizing federated learning hyper-parameters, which can significantly reduce training overhead and make it more affordable for edge computing Chapter 10, "Perspective Chapter: Edge Computing in Digital

Epidemiology and Global Health", looks at the application of edge computing in public health, critical medicine, and epidemiology. Finally, Chapter 11, "Perspective Chapter: Edge-Cloud Collaboration for Industrial IoT – An Online Approach", proposes how edge and cloud should converge for Industrial Internet of Things (IIoT) applications.

I am proud to present *Edge Computing – Technology, Management and Integration* and I would like to thank the staff at Intech Open, especially Ana Javor and Kristina Cvitan, who have ably supported me in getting this book to press and publication. I would also like to humbly thank all the authors who submitted chapters to this book. Without their tireless efforts and contributions, this book would not have been possible. I hope we can collaborate again in the future and publish more books together.

I hope everyone will enjoy reading and learning from this book and I hope it will inspire and encourage future research on edge computing. The adoption of edge computing technologies brings forth a host of benefits, including reduced latency, enhanced security and privacy, and improved reliability.

Any comments or questions can be emailed to sam.goundar@gmail.com

Sam Goundar
RMIT University,
Hanoi, Vietnam

Section 1

Edge Computing

Chapter 1

Cloud Computing to Fog Computing: A Paradigm Shift

Syed Rizwan Hassan and Muhammad Rashad

Abstract

Fog computing scatters the resources throughout the system to provide services close to the edge of the network. This chapter provides an overview of different segments associated with the fog computing paradigm for implementing efficient Internet of Things (IoT) applications. Section 1 provides an overview and motivation behind the provision of healthcare services using cloud and fog computing paradigms. Section 2 provides the literature and research work related to the deployment of healthcare applications using cloud and fog computing architectures. Section 3 provides the architectural design of a fog computing-based remote pain monitoring application. Section 4 provides the simulation parameters and architecture that are arranged for the evaluation of the proposed policy. Finally, Section 5 concludes and discusses the results of simulations obtained on different scales.

Keywords: e-healthcare, fog computing, cloud computing, remote pain monitoring, latency, network consumption

1. Introduction

Due to recent technical advances in the field of information and technology, the provision of online services in every area of life has become possible. The IoT technology links the devices in regular use by humans with the Internet and provides an interconnection between billions of devices throughout the globe. According to Ref. [1], the number of such devices is estimated to reach 12 billion by the year 2021, which will bring an enormous revolution in living aspects and social routines of human lives. The limited processing and storage capacity of IoT devices restricts them from implementing applications involving data of heterogeneous nature or performing tasks involving big data. So, most of the IoT applications are designed on cloud computing architecture that allows resourceful cloud servers to access the data sensed by the IoT devices for processing and storage [2]. This integration of the cloud computing paradigm and IoT technology has numerous benefits allowing the deployment of diverse types of applications with different requirements.

Integration of IoT technology in the healthcare industry is shifting toward the remote provision of health services to patients without the physical intervention of doctors. This will not only accelerate the healthcare process but also provide ease to the patients to get doctor prescriptions and diagnostics required by uploading their health-related data. Smartphones are a perfect example of IoT devices. Cloud computing offers massive computational resources for the fast processing of diverse and huge amounts of data coming from a large number of patients in healthcare applications [3]. However, latency and network load problems arise in cloud-based IoT healthcare applications when implemented on large scales due to a huge rise in data to be processed [4]. Therefore, it is not viable to implement latency-sensitive healthcare systems in the cloud computing paradigm.

Fog computing term was introduced by CISCO in 2012 [5]. The fog computing paradigm provides the solution to the challenges that evolved in the cloud computing paradigm by the provision of computational and storage resources in a distributed manner near the edge of the network to implement IoT applications. The fog paradigm introduces fog devices having limited version of cloud resources between the IoT devices and the cloud servers, which offers computational supports to edge devices to process heterogeneous types of data generated by IoT devices, which results in less delay and reduced network load. Hence, these formerly mentioned prominent features of the fog computing paradigm make it a better choice for the implementation of IoT healthcare applications.

This chapter briefly describes the beneficial aspects of adopting the fog computing paradigm for the design and implementation of healthcare applications. Initially, a literature review covering different healthcare applications designed on the cloud computing paradigm, their architecture, benefits, and challenges is presented. Later, the architecture of the fog computing paradigm to implement healthcare applications in a distributed manner is presented. Correspondingly, a detailed literature review of different applications designed using the fog computing paradigm is presented. Finally, the design of a remote pain monitoring application using the fog computing paradigm is presented with a comparative analysis between fog and cloud-based implementations to show the effectiveness of the fog computing paradigm.

Internet of Things (IoT) applications are drastically growing to facilitate mankind. Before the adaptation of the fog paradigm, mostly these applications are deployed on cloud-centric architectures. Due to the high demand for IoT applications, cloud computing faces numerous challenges, such as high delay, burdened network bandwidth, poor Internet connectivity, scalability, and high execution cost. To address these challenges, fog paradigm comes into play that extends the cloud resources close to the edge of the network by employing fog devices throughout the network. Fog devices have limited resources for the storage and processing of detected information. To provide real-time response to the end users, some applications are interested in providing computational services near the edge of the network but still, some of the applications are there that require big data analysis that needs to be processed at the cloud server. To implement efficient IoT infrastructure, there is a need of seamless and effective orchestration of resources. Fog devices work as smart gateways between cloud and end devices, providing fog and cloud connectivity. The main objective of this research is to address the critical issues involved in the deployment of IoT applications on cloud and fog computing paradigms. A solution is implemented in this research to improve the efficiency of the applications. The second aim of the research is to investigate the architectural performance of the fog computing paradigm from an application perspective and the design of policies to implement applications in a way to achieve optimal performance. Simulations are executed on multiple scales to evaluate the proposed design. The simulations results confirm the effectiveness of the proposed paradigm in achieving a reduction in delay, network utilization and processing cost at the cloud.

2. Related work

Several remote e-healthcare monitoring applications deployed on different computing paradigms are presented in this section. In Ref. [6], a mobile cloud computing paradigm is adopted to deploy applications to provide remote healthcare services. The authors discussed various schemes for the interconnection of different healthcare systems and proposed a design of an application used for fall detection of patients based on the cloud paradigm. The authors in Ref. [7] presented a design of an application that utilizes the cry of newborn babies as a pathological tool for the detection of pain. This remote pain detection application is designed on a cloud paradigm. The Support Vector Machine (SVM)-based neural networks are used for the classification of patterns and the proposed application provides remote access to the detected pain statistics by using the Thinkspeak IoT platform. Medical practitioners and medical service providers can access the detected pain by using mobile devices. The research in Ref. [8] presents a cloud paradigm-based application for remote pain monitoring of patients. In the proposed design, the cloud server acts as a link between the edge nodes and the web platform. The proposed design includes a wearable sensor mask as an edge node for the detection of different biopotential signals of patients, which are processed at the cloud server for the detection of pain intensity. Afterward, the detected pain information is transmitted to the web platform connected to the cloud server for providing remote access to the end users. Researchers adopt the same paradigm in Ref. [9] for the implementation of an application for remote monitoring of patients that are in a persistent vegetative state (PVS) by analyzing their real-time facial expressions.

For the provision of pervasive healthcare services to end users, the system deployed in Ref. [10] is based on the mobile cloud paradigm. High network consumption, latency, and reliability are the major limitations in the large-scale deployment of efficient e-healthcare applications on mobile computing paradigm for the provision of real-time medical services to the patients. To resolve these problems and to provide high QoS the researchers designed a layered healthcare architecture named as UbeHealth. For remote services and supervision related to healthcare, the first layer is based on medical practitioners and doctors. The second layer contains cloudlets that are used for the prediction of the upcoming network traffic volume which is used for adaptation of a specific data rate to maintain high QoS. The cloud server is placed at the third layer for the provision of high computational and storage resources.

For the provision of advanced healthcare services to the end users, the importance of the placement of gateway devices close to the network edge is enlightened by authors in Ref. [11]. The authors proposed a fog-based healthcare warning system that provides an early warning related to healthcare issues. The authors in Ref. [12] describe the major issues involved in the deployment of healthcare applications on cloud computing and mobile computing paradigms. The authors also proposed the fog computing paradigm for the execution of healthcare applications in a scattered manner to efficiently utilize available resources. In Ref. [13], a fog-based healthcare application monitors the patients using the sensor nodes and processes this information using fog computing resources. The cloud server resides on the top of the network to provide additional processing services. An application for the monitoring of ECG signals of patients is designed in Ref. [14] that utilizes the cloud and mobile platforms for the provision of healthcare services.

In Ref. [15], a cloud-based system that employs a social-technical design scheme to implement a healthcare application in the Nigerian healthcare system is presented. The proposed system is used to provide services to the residents of rural areas, which results in the reduction of cost and delay. The fog-based remote healthcare monitoring design is emerging as a solution to several existing healthcare issues in developing countries. The system presented in Ref. [16] is specially designed to provide services to patients suffering from chikungunya. The proposed system avoids an outbreak by enabling real-time virus detection and diagnosis arrangement. In their strategy, classification is accomplished on patients' data using a decision tree for the detection of viruses and the result is instantaneously communicated to the users through mobile. Furthermore, the virus outbreak state is monitored by performing chronological network analysis on the patient's data collected from the vicinity.

Integration of IoT, biosensors, and cloud computing paradigm enhances the implementation of e-healthcare applications that results in addressing the factors limiting the delivery of healthcare services to each patient, which includes the availability of expensive, sensitive medical equipment in each medical unit, shortage of medics and health workers, limitations in hospital information systems. Cloud computing enhanced the medical facilities provision on large scales by providing a remote interconnection between patients and doctors. Besides this interconnection, the cloud also offers continuous access to medical records whenever and from wherever required, further enhancing patient care. Cloud servers have plenty of resources to handle the huge and heterogeneous types of medical data sensed by healthcare IoT devices.

Several e-healthcare applications are designed on the cloud paradigm. An existing challenge in the healthcare and medical support systems is the delivery of medical services to the increasing number of elderly people. To overcome the challenges involved in this area, the authors in Ref. [17] proposed a Cloud-Based Smart Home Environment (CoSHE) for home healthcare, which uses Software-as-a-Service (SaaS) architecture with wearable sensors to collect different biopotentials of the patient to provide information remotely to doctors and caretakers. This application uses a private cloud facility that enables remote monitoring of patient records by healthcare professionals. The proposed system consumes high energy as it uses non-invasive sensors for the monitoring of the entire home.

In cloud-based healthcare applications, the IoT devices are equipped with different types of sensors that are used to sense different medical information related to patients, which are conveyed to cloud servers by IoT devices through the wireless communication link. The sensed data of patients are stored in cloud databases and are used for further analysis in diagnostic procedures. Based on the patient's condition, alert signals are conveyed to the doctors and related caregivers. Cloud-based healthcare systems provide initial diagnosis and some precautionary measures for better health.

The integration of IoT devices, biosensors, and cloud paradigm results in an efficient structure for the implementation of real-time healthcare applications to remotely facilitate elderly and disabled persons. For real-time monitoring of disabled and elderly patients, a cloud-based structure is presented by authors in Ref. [6] based on sensors to continuously detect ECG signals of patients. Cloud computing provides a huge amount of storage and computational resources to process the sensed data from many patients. The cloud server provides access to the stored medical data to several healthcare service providers. To achieve medical data privacy, ECG signals are watermarked and enhanced on the client side and are stored in databases before sending to the cloud for further processing. This process enables sharing of specific medical information with the only relevant and appropriate healthcare services.

Owing to the integration of IoT technology in the healthcare industry, this area is not just limited to Electronic Medical Records (EMRs) and Hospital Management Systems (HMS). Healthcare systems are becoming more digital and patient-centric by providing computer-aided surgical treatments and remote patient healthcare management. The research in Ref. [18] provides the challenges faced by the healthcare industry related to the adoption of digital data. Afterward, a system as an example based on the cloud computing paradigm is illustrated, offering healthcare as a service (HaaS). By adopting cloud-based healthcare applications, patients can connect to healthcare specialists to attain medical guidance on time. Cloud computing is a centralized approach that stores all the collected data at cloud servers located at remote locations, which seems to be challenging in preserving the privacy of the stored data. The aforementioned concern is one of the key motives behind the limited adaptation of such centralized systems. In Ref. [19] a fog-based framework for cloud healthcare applications is presented that uses intermediate fog nodes to pre-process the patient's data to maintain privacy and confidentiality of their health record. The proposed approach provides an accurate outcome with the facility of content privacy and security at the edge. Privacy concerns appear to be more significant in cloud-based healthcare systems where the sensitive and heterogeneous type of data generated from wearable biosensors needs to be processed and stored. The existing privacy preservation techniques available are not applicable due to their high processing and communication cost. To address this issue, a cloud-based user validation scheme for medical data is presented in Ref. [20] that performs mutual authentication for secure transmission between patient and wearable sensor nodes by secret session key allocation. To address the existing problems in the information exchange procedures in healthcare systems, a novel hybrid cloud system named MedShare is presented in Ref. [21]. Medical organizations operating on large scales maintain their cloud servers, and to share the medical records of patients with other organizations, they use peer-to-peer (P2P) mode following some defined policies. To preserve the privacy of the sensitive medical record and patient identity on cloud-based healthcare networks from impostors and to maintain security, anonymous authentication data exchange is vital among the different peer organizations.

On pairing-based cryptography, an anonymous on-the-fly secure data exchange protocol is proposed in Ref. [22] that permits cloud servers to vigorously create temporary identities to generate session keys for each session of information exchange. The proposed approach is beneficial against different cyber-attacks. To significantly reduce the processing time of medical queries in cloud-based healthcare services, the optimal selection of virtual machines (VMs) plays an important role. To achieve optimal VM selection, a chronic kidney disease diagnosis and the prediction model are presented that employs Parallel Particle Swarm Optimization (PPSO) with linear regression and a neural network. The prediction of the proposed model is 97.8% with a reduction in execution time [23]. The engagement of mobile devices for the facilitation of human lives through useful applications has almost achieved its ultimate level. The factors restricting the use of mobile devices are the limited amount of processing, storage, and battery. A mobile cloud computing model for big data e-healthcare services is presented in Ref. [24] that engages cloudlets. A huge amount of data is generated and needs to be processed to provide remote healthcare services. One of the best choices to handle this big data is cloud computing.

A detailed analysis of cloud computing techniques to handle the healthcare big data segment and future research dimensions in this area are discussed in Ref. [25]. In Ref. [26], a mobile cloud computing-based effective and intelligible framework for stroke detection is presented, which consists of two application elements, for example, mobile application and server application. For the classification of subtypes of strokes, an artificial neural network module is used, whereas a server module is used to save the information from the patients. Robust protection against untrusted clouds and unauthorized users is mandatory to secure sensitive healthcare data in cloud-based healthcare systems.

Currently, security mechanisms adopted in most of the cloud-based healthcare systems are based on cryptography, SOA, Secure Multi-party Computation (SMC), and Secret Share Schemes (SSS). The computational cost of image processing tasks performed to prevent unauthorized access to healthcare records is a significant problem in the implementation of such security techniques. To protect healthcare information from possible disclosure, machine learning-based security schemes using SVM and Fuzzy C-means Clustering (FCM) to classify image pixels are applied. Results of the evaluations performed utilizing the proposed technique using two datasets confirm that for data protection and simultaneous image segmentation use of SVMs is an efficient concept. ECG monitoring plays a vital role in diagnosing and monitoring heart conditions.

Almost all ECG monitoring systems deployed so far are based on mobile applications. A new monitoring method was proposed that uses wearable sensor nodes for ECG detection. The proposed system uses a cloud-based framework with Hypertext Transfer Protocol (HTTP) and MQTT protocols to provide visual and timely access to recorded ECG data [27]. A blockchain-based approach for secure and robust healthcare data transmission is presented that collects the sensed data of patients using wearable devices to store it in cloud storage. The blockchain concept is implemented on individual patient records to maintain the privacy that generates a distinct block as a chain. Experimental results reveal that the proposed model provides a reduction in average delay and execution time with an improved success rate as compared to conventional models [28].

Cloud computing is the base architecture to implement IoT-enabled applications. Cloud due to its centralized architectural approach offers high latency and restricts large-scale implementation. Fog computing offers solutions to these problems. The issues involved in interoperability and integration of cloud and fog architectures are explored in Ref. [29] to provide healthcare services. To provide cost-efficient healthcare services with low latency and reliability, several IoT-based healthcare frameworks are designed using different paradigms. The challenges to maintaining the quality of service in such systems are due to the heterogeneous nature of healthcare data.

A five-layered heterogeneous architecture to simultaneously handle mist, fog, and cloud-based networks to efficiently handle and route real-time healthcare data is proposed. The proposed framework ensures efficient resource allocations, high QoS, and reduction in latency by adopting software-defined networking and link adaptation-based load balancing [30]. A new public, private, and hybrid cloud-based conceptual computing model is presented that adopts multiple cloud services to resolve existing critical issues involved in the modeling of health management systems [31].

A cloud-based framework using a fuzzy rule-based neural classification algorithm for the diagnosis of diabetes is designed in Ref. [32]. The cloud paradigm offers a two-level hierarchical processing structure that is inefficient in reducing delay and energy utilization. A model is proposed in Ref. [33] that provides an energy-efficient cloud paradigm for deploying IoT applications using dynamic voltage and frequency scaling (DVFS) technology. The proposed model migrates and reuses virtual machines with round-robin scheduling.

In Ref. [34], a module placement for the fog-cloud paradigm is proposed that splits the resources of fog nodes into slots to which slotted versions of services are allocated on availability to perform energy-efficient execution of services. To increase the reliability, efficiency, and performance of the computing systems with efficient network bandwidth consumption, a data duplication idea is proposed in Ref. [35] that provides a copy of original data near the end nodes. The proposed concept reduces the burden on the network. A cognitive intelligent IoT smart healthcare framework, based on a cloud paradigm to provide cost-efficient and rapid healthcare services for monitoring patient state, is presented in [36].

In Ref. [37], a deep learning-based seizure detection of epileptic patients is proposed that consumes cloud resources for the execution of sensed information. Cloud computing architecture proves to be a cost-efficient solution to deliver flexible and enhanced quality of service in the healthcare industry. Deploying e-Healthcare applications on the cloud paradigm results in the transfer of sensitive health-related data of patients between several entities. Due to the application of modern cryptographic techniques, the communication channels between these entities are secure enough but the protection of data at the endpoints from malicious insider attacks is still a problematic task. To prevent false examination of patients due to data manipulation from malicious insiders, the study in Ref. [38] provides an insider attack detection process. The proposed approach uses a combination of watermarking and cryptographic techniques to provide transparency of patient data.

ECG feature extraction plays a pivotal role in detecting and diagnosing various cardiac diseases. In cloud-based healthcare systems, the detected ECG signals of patients are directly transmitted from biosensors to cloud servers for processing. In Ref. [39], the fog computing concept is adopted to enhance the performance of such health monitoring systems by providing distributed storage and processing resources at the edge nodes. In their proposed model, ECG features extraction performed *via* the lightweight wavelet transform method at fog devices, which results in achieving high bandwidth efficiency and reduced latency.

In Ref. [40], a fog paradigm-based health monitoring system that uses Gigabit Passive Optical Network (GPON) as an access scheme is presented. The designed approach places fog nodes at optimum locations, calculated using Mixed Integer Linear Programming (MILP) for energy-efficient implementation. The experimental results confirm that the proposed approach is energy-efficient as compared to the centralized cloud computing approach when used for healthcare applications with low and high data rates.

In smart cities concepts, the fog computing paradigm bridges sensor networks and smart homes. Fog nodes usually execute basic data processing and data translation tasks. In smart healthcare systems, fog nodes, the gateway to sensitive medical data, have high privacy and security threats. So, to deploy a secure and smart healthcare system, a cognitive fog model is designed [41] that is capable of taking decisions related to processes joining and relieving. The proposed model is also self-capable and self-aware to initiate new processes to provide security to running modules in the fog environment. In addition, the proposed model provides better accuracy, detection, and error rate as compared to other available algorithms.

iFogSim is the simulator used for the execution of various scenarios based on cloud and fog computing paradigms. Most of the researchers have used this simulator for the evaluation of their fog computing-based applications. The authors explain the steps and procedures involved in modeling and implementing fog computing-based applications in iFogSim [42]. A fog paradigm-based disaster management system is implemented in Ref. [43] and is compared with the cloud-based deployment using iFogSim. Authors in Ref. [43] used iFogSim to monitor the effects of the CPU speed of fog devices on energy utilization and latency of the system.

For optimum scheduling of tasks, a whale optimization-based scheme is compared with the available several heuristic algorithms in implementing healthcare applications using the iFogSim simulator [44]. An efficient car parking application based on the fog paradigm is simulated using the iFogSim toolkit and is compared with the cloud-based deployment to illustrate the beneficial aspects of adopting the fog paradigm [45]. The research in Ref. [46] categorized the iFogSim toolkit as the most effective simulator available for the execution of different applications on the fog computing paradigm. An energy-efficient module allocation approach based on a heuristic algorithm is presented and simulated using the iFogSim toolkit by the authors in [45].

3. Internet of thing-based remote pain monitoring application

Wearable sensors existing in the market by 2020 are about to be 237.1 million, with an estimated reach of the market segment associated with the medical industry being $117 billion by 2020 [47]. The data communicated by these large number of applications based on such a large number of sensors is estimated to be 507.5 zettabytes [48]. Generally, these applications are deployed using the cloud paradigm. The cloud paradigm offers resources in a centralized way to process the huge amount of volume sensed by a large number of sensor nodes. Due to the availability of large resources at cloud servers, the cloud paradigm is very viable for implementing healthcare applications [49].

The cloud paradigm offers all resources in a centralized fashion for the completion of different tasks. Gigantic and diverse type of information is sensed by the edge nodes, which is to be handled by the cloud server. Due to the centralized nature, this paradigm offers high latency and huge network consumption, which limits the deployment of healthcare applications on large scale. Healthcare applications dealing with the processing of ECG signals have strict QoS and latency requirements that are not fulfilled by the cloud-centric paradigm when deploying applications on large scales [38]. Therefore, the cloud paradigm is not viable for providing healthcare services with stringent QoS requirements.

Pain is a significant factor in detecting a patient's distress and ailment. The consequences of an investigation performed on diverse groups of patients favor the necessity of remote pain monitoring [50]. The key restrictions in the manual reporting method are non-compliance of patients to manual entry, delay in medication, and the inability of patients to express their conditions. The main factor that makes the self-reporting scheme impracticable is the delayed provision of diagnosis. Significant methods applied for the monitoring of pain comprise facial expression recognition using face video [51], physiological signal fusion [52], and facial EMG. However, various methods have been applied in designing systems for the remote detection of pain that incorporates cloud services and various pain detection schemes [53]. The core issue in the large-scale deployment of healthcare applications that needs to be resolved is the attainment of strict QoS requirements. Huge network consumption and high latency are the major limitations in the implementation of pain monitoring applications on the cloud paradigm.

In Ref. [8], an application based on a cloud paradigm for the detection of pain is designed using wearable sensor nodes. The designed application provides remote access to pain statistics through a web platform. The designed sensor nodes are used to detect the patients' biopotential signals, which are further processed by using the cloud resources. The useful pain information is transmitted to the web platform for the provision of remote access. This consistent involvement of cloud server introduces high latency in the provision of services, which is not suitable for e-healthcare applications. Hence, a remote pain monitoring application based on the fog paradigm is designed in this research to resolve these issues.

A summary of the main contributions of this research is defined below:

- A three-layer fog computing-based design of an application for the provision of remote monitoring of pain is presented that utilizes fog resources for providing real-time computational facilities to the end nodes.

- For evaluation of the proposed fog computing-based healthcare application as compared to the cloud-based deployment, several scenarios are executed on multiple scales. The targeted assessment metrics during all these simulations are delay, network utilization, and cost of execution at the cloud.

- Outcomes of the evaluations executed on various scales confirm the proposed design's efficacy in decreasing delay and network utilization compared to cloud-based implementations. The proposed approach also provides a reduction in the execution cost in the cloud.

3.1 Background

Cloud computing architecture based on resourceful cloud servers delivers effective handling of big data generated by different applications. This provision of a resourceful solution by cloud paradigm makes cloud architecture the most viable paradigm for implementing Internet-based applications demanding analysis and processing of big data. Due to the rise in the deployment of these types of applications, the main restrictions confronted by the researcher in the cloud-based deployment of applications are high delay, and inefficient network consumption [54]. Owing to these problems, deploying latency-sensitive healthcare applications on a cloud paradigm is not feasible.

Fog paradigm, by offering resources close to the network boundary, significantly reduces the network load and improves the quality of experience (QoE). This provision of resources close to the edge also decreases the latency in the delivery of services to the end user. The fog-based model presented in Ref. [55] attains a 41% reduction in power consumption by effectively offloading data between cloud and fog nodes. To achieve stringent QoS requirements of the applications, the fog paradigm distributes resources throughout the network for the provision of services adjacent to the sensor nodes [56].

The latency offered by cloud-based healthcare applications is proportional to the scale on which they are deployed [11], thus failing to attain real-time data provision

Facilities	Applications	Media	Delay requirements
Audio transmission	Audio conversation	Audio	< 150 milliseconds one-way
Video transmission	Video conferencing	Video	< 250 milliseconds one-way
Robotic facilities	Tele-ultrasonography	Control signals	< 300 milliseconds round-trip-time
Monitoring facilities	Remote pain monitoring	Biosignal	< 300 milliseconds for real-time ECG.

Table 1.
QoS requirements for time-sensitive healthcare services.

for latency-sensitive healthcare applications [57]. Latency requirements to maintain QoS in e-healthcare services are presented in **Table 1** [58]. Cisco introduced the idea of fog computing in January 2014 to resolve the high network utilization and delay problems caused by cloud-based implementations [24].

The fog paradigm distributes the resources in such a manner that reduces the computational load. The resource-constraint fog devices exist throughout the system [27, 59]. The main reason behind the adoption of the fog paradigm is the real-time provision of healthcare services to users [60].

Various applications built on distributed paradigms are proposed in different studies providing efficient utilization of resources and cost-efficient implementations. For seamless service provision to the end users, a multi-tier fog paradigm is proposed in Ref. [61]. A mobility-aware three-layer fog computing structure for optimal resource allocation is presented in Ref. [62]. The proposed model engages a Gini coefficient-based FCNs selection algorithm (GCFSA) to get the optimum results. To enhance security in fog-based *ad hoc* vehicular networks, the authors in Ref. [63] presented a design of a new authenticated key agreement protocol. To provide services like network virtualization and edge resource management to the end-users by different network service providers using a fog-cloud paradigm is proposed in Ref. [64].

Fog computing architecture reduces repeated cloud server participation for the execution of tasks, resulting in reduced network utilization and delay. Several types of research have shown a decrease in latency by adopting the fog paradigm as an alternative to cloud architecture to implement different applications [26, 43, 65]. Due to the distributed structure of the fog paradigm, improved scalability and mobility are offered. The reduction in network utilization is achieved by adopting the fog paradigm because fog nodes process the sensed information near the end users. A double-matching resource allocation scheme is proposed in Ref. [66] that achieves cost efficiency by effectively allocating the network resources. Similarly, an algorithm is presented in Ref. [67], which offers dynamic offloading and resource assignment to achieve a reduction in cost and latency.

Fog computing distributes limited resources in the form of fog devices throughout the network. The limited resources available at the fog devices are sufficient to perform various dynamic tasks assigned by the edge nodes [29]. In this chapter, a three-layer fog paradigm-based design is proposed and implemented for the deployment of an e-healthcare application that provides remote access to pain-related information of the patients. The prominent characteristics of fog computing architecture include reduced delay and efficient network utilization, which make this architecture the most suitable candidate for the implementation of latency-sensitive e-healthcare applications [68].

The proposed design integrates a fog computing paradigm and web platform to provide real-time access to pain-related information of the patients. Several signal processing techniques are executed utilizing fog resources to complete the pain detection process. The pre-processing opportunity offered by the fog nodes in between the cloud server and edge nodes correspondingly reduces the execution cost.

3.2 Proposed architecture

Figure 1 describes the three-layer fog paradigm proposed for the deployment of a remote pain monitoring application. The first layer is at the edge of the network, which is based on biopotential sensors connected to patients admitted to the hospitals. This layer exploits the sensors to detect and transmits the sEMG and ECG signals of the patients to the second layer for further processing. The second layer consists of resource-constraint fog devices that provide resources near the edge layer to process the sensed biopotential information. The last layer in the proposed architecture consists of a cloud server that provides a massive amount of storage and computational resources for the execution of sensed and preprocessed information forwarded by the connected fog nodes. The designed architecture also provides remote access to pain-related information of patients through a web platform. The proposed architecture minimizes the latency and network utilization in providing remote services to the end users. A brief introduction of each component involved in the proposed design is described in the following sections.

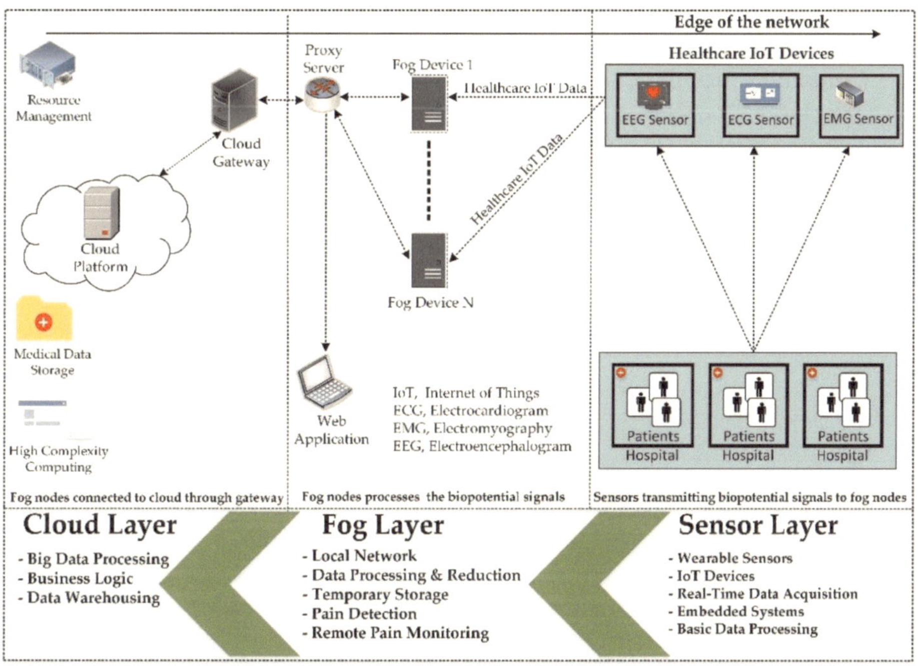

Figure 1.
Proposed fog-based remote e-healthcare application for pain monitoring.

3.2.1 The sensor layer

The sensor layer is responsible for detecting and transmitting biopotential signals from hospitals to the fog layer. For the fulfillment of this purpose, the sensor layer is comprised of wearable biosensors. The edge nodes contain battery-operated sensors and are equipped with passive electrodes to detect biopotential signals. The edge devices are responsible for the transmission of detected medical information to the fog nodes, which is why they are integrated with the Wi-Fi module. The designed sensor nodes for the detection of biopotential signals have a sampling rate satisfying the Nyquist criteria. The edge nodes transmit the detected biopotential signals of patients to the parent fog nodes for additional processing [69].

3.2.2 The fog layer

The fog layer exists in the middle of the proposed design. The fog computing layer is comprised of resource-constraint fog devices that are responsible for the provision of resources close to the edge of the network for providing real-time processing of pain-related sensed data detected at the edge layer. The fog layer performs primary processing on the detected biopotential signals for the recognition of pain in patients.

Interoperability is an important feature of fog computing that permits various fog devices to interconnect, allowing dealing with multiple types of edge devices. Multiple fog devices contribute some of their available resources to fulfill the assigned processing tasks [28]. The proposed design takes interoperability as an integral characteristic of fog computing which is why the delay factor in intercommunication between fog devices is not considered [45].

Specific indexes are used to distinguish between various patients, such as HS22 defines the second patient of hospital 2, as shown in **Figure 2**. To offer remote access for pain monitoring to doctors and users, the proposed design links a web platform with fog devices. The fog devices utilize limited available resources for the processing of the detected pain-related biopotential signals and transfer the results of the processed information to the web application. The cloud server is a resourceful entity used to permanently store pain-related statistics to maintain patient records. Before transferring pain-related information to a storage module located at a cloud server, this data is temporarily stored in a fog database using limited available storage. The proposed fog computing paradigm provides resources near the patients for providing real-time processing of the pain-related signals detected at the hospitals.

3.2.3 The cloud layer

This layer contains a cloud server accountable for providing storage and computational resources for processing tasks related to pain detection forwarded by the connected fog nodes. The cloud server being a resourceful device is used for maintaining the database related to pain-related medical records of patients. A proxy server provides a link between the fog devices and the cloud server. Fog nodes process patients' detected sEMG and ECG signals for detecting pain and forward the pain-

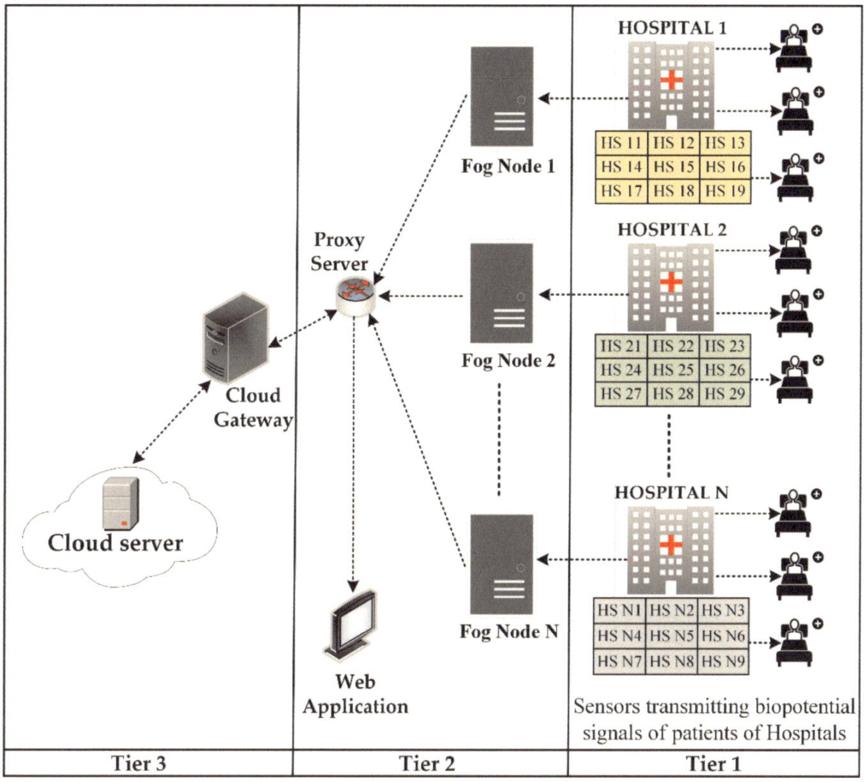

Figure 2.
The proposed design of e-healthcare application for multiple hospitals.

related information to the cloud server after periodic intervals. The cloud server is only used in the proposed scheme when the resources available at the fog nodes cannot complete the pain-related processing task.

3.2.4 Overview

The fog computing paradigm is deployed in the proposed scheme to implement a remote pain monitoring application that uses ECG and EMG sensors for the continuous detection of biopotential signals of patients residing in hospitals situated at distant sites. The designed application structure consists of Wi-Fi modules assigned to different network devices for providing an interconnection between different network nodes.

The proposed design contains a web platform to offer users and medical practitioners remote access to pain-related information. The designed approach places the edge nodes at the hospitals that continuously detect patients' pain-related signals and transmit this information to the fog node assigned to that hospital. For detecting pain based on the Facial Action Coding System [70], various facial muscles under the observation of the detectors are Frontalis, Corrugator, Orbicularis oculi, Levator Nose, Zygomaticus, NS Risorius, respectively. The pain-related signals detected by the edge nodes are processed using various signal processing and filtering techniques as defined in Ref. [8], by the fog devices utilizing limited local resources for identifying pain and its intensity. Afterward, the pain-related information is communicated to the web platform for remote visualization.

Each hospital in the proposed structure is equipped with multiple numbers of sensors to monitor patients. These sensor nodes are connected to fog nodes assigned to the hospitals. In the existing design, one fog device is assigned to each hospital to provide processing and storage facilities. The cloud server located at the top of the network structure periodically updates a medical database to keep a record of patients.

The resources available at the cloud server are enough to process the volume of biopotential signals generated by the connected fog nodes. However, this distant communication between sensor nodes and the cloud produces an additional delay and extra network utilization.

This increase in network consumption and latency restricts the practice of cloud paradigms for the implementation of such types of applications. The provision of a fog layer reduces network utilization and latency. This reduction in network consumption and latency is due to resource-constraint fog nodes providing computational services near the end users.

This pre-processing of detected information using fog resources also cuts the volume of information to be processed at the cloud server, resulting in saving execution costs at the cloud. Furthermore, the communication of pain-related statistics directly between fog devices and web applications eliminates the auxiliary involvement of cloud servers.

Figure 2 describes the structure in which multiple hospitals are to be monitored using multiple fog devices. The network consumption and delay rise with an increase in the number of hospitals to be monitored because of the simultaneous transmission of the amplified size of information to the cloud and web server by multiple fog devices.

Initially, all the sensors are initialized for the detection of biopotential signals of the patients. These detected signals are transmitted to the parent fog nodes. Fog devices consume available resources for the execution of various feature extraction techniques, pattern recognition algorithms, segmentation schemes and data reduction approaches to generate useful results related to pain-related information of patients [71–75]. This pain-related information extracted from the sensed information is communicated to the cloud and web platform to offer remote access.

3.3 Simulation setup and results

An average of three simulations per scenario is executed to assess the proposed design. In all the executed scenarios, the edge devices are increased to monitor the increasing number of patients. The end devices are directly connected to their parent fog nodes. The sensed signals by the sensors are instantly transmitted to the resourceful fog devices. The iFogSim toolkit is used for the simulations of multiple scenarios generated for the comparison of the proposed design with the cloud-based deployment. The parameters under observation during these scenarios are end-to-end delay, network utilization, and execution cost.

Algorithm A: Fog paradigm-based remote pain monitoring application with FCFS scheduling

Start iFogSim
Build fog broker.
Create application.
Create: Cloud Server, Proxy Server, Web application.
for $i = 0$ to $Hospitals_{max}$ **do**
  Create *Fog device*.
  for $i = 0$ to $i \leq Patients_{perhospital}$ **do**
    Create *Sensors*.
  end
end
Add modules (*RMS data stream module, Digital filtering module, Dimension reduction module, Pain detection module*).
Defining data dependencies by creating edges between the application modules:
RMS data stream module → *Digital filtering module* → *Dimension reduction module* → *Pain detection module*
Module mapping.
Tuple mapping.
Submit application.
Start Execution.
Call FCFS scheduling
for each VM_i **do**
  if $Module_{input} = Module_{VM_i}$ **then**
    Allocate PEs to VM_i
  end
  else
    Allocate $Module_{input}$ to VM_i
  end
end
Update energy utilization.
Stop Execution.
Simulation Result.

In the simulated scenarios, variables for the representation of hospitals and edge devices are created. In all the scenarios, four hospitals are simulated. One fog device is allocated to each hospital. In the first scenario, there are four sensors connected to each hospital for monitoring patients. The proxy server provides an interconnection between the cloud server and fog nodes. The sensors deployed in all the simulations are designed with a CPU length of 1200 million instructions. The sensing frequency of sensors used in simulations is 25 milliseconds. The number of sensors is increased in each new simulated scenario.

Algorithm A defines the steps involved in the creation and execution of different topologies for the evaluation of the proposed remote pain monitoring application on different scales. Network utilization and delay are the parameters observed during all the evaluations. The RMS data stream module is placed at the sensor nodes for the detection of biopotential signals of patients. The digital filtering and dimension reduction modules require more computational resources, so these modules are assigned to fog devices. Furthermore, for the visualization of pain-related information to the remote users the pain detection module is placed on the web server. The scheduling scheme employed in our simulations is the First Come First Serve (FCFS) scheduling strategy. The data dependency between different modules is shown in the algorithm. The tasks associated with any module are described in the form of tuples in the simulation environment. Tuples are transmitted between the modules for task assignment and are executed at modules.

For the assessment of the proposed design on multiple scales, the sensors associated with fog devices are increased in each subsequent simulation scenario. This increment of sensors gives rise to the volume of detected information to be processed at the fog node, which increases delay and network utilization. As a result, the resources available at the fog node are limited, and fog nodes have to perform all tasks within the limits of the available resources. The advantage of such distributed computing design is to reduce the processing burden on the cloud server and provide services near the edge of the network. The values of different network parameters adopted for the creation of different network devices in the simulation scenarios are defined in **Table 2**. The proposed design is compared with the traditional cloud-based deployment. One of the simulation scenarios created for fog-based deployments is shown in **Figure 3**.

3.3.1 Execution cost

In the scenarios, there are H number of smart hospitals ($H = \{h_1, h_2, h_3, \dots, h_H\}$) and the total volume of the sensed data of the system to be handled in a given time t is denoted by V_H^t is the sum of the individual volume of each hospital ($V_H^t = v_{h_1}^t + v_{h_2}^t + v_{h_3}^t, \dots, v_{h_H}^t$).

Parameter	Cloud	Proxy server	Web server	Fog node	Sensor node
RatePerMIPS	0.01	0.0	0.0	0.0	0.0
RAM (GB)	40	4	4	4	1
Idle power	16*83.25	83.43	83.43	83.43	82.44
Downlink bandwidth (GB)	10	10	10	10	—
CPU (BIPS)	44.8	2.8	2.8	2.8	0.5
Uplink bandwidth (GB)	0.1	10	10	10	1

Table 2.
Value of parameters associated with different network devices used in simulations [47].

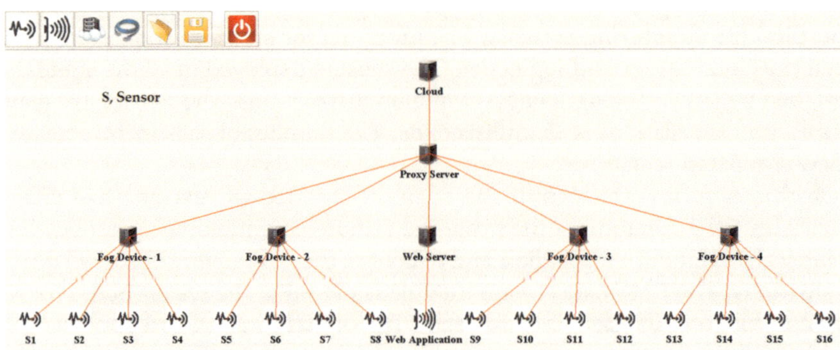

Figure 3.
One of the scenarios created in iFogSim for evaluating the proposed design.

The overall time consumed (T_s^t) in the processing of biopotential signals at any time t can be calculated by using Eq. (1), in which T_p^t denotes time spent at any interval t in the sensing and processing of signals of a patient.

$$T_s^t = T_p^t \times \sum_{i=1}^{H} v_{h_i}^t \tag{1}$$

Eq. (2) is used for the calculation of the overall time consumed (T_F) from detection of biopotential signals to the provision of pain-related information through the web platform.

$$T_F = T_s^t + T_{ef}^t + T_{fw}^t \tag{2}$$

Here, T_{ef}^t is the time spent in the transmission of detected information from edge nodes to fog devices and T_{fw}^t is the time spent to transmit pain evidence from fog device to web platform.

In cloud-based deployment, T_{ec} is the time spent in the transmission of detected information from edge nodes to cloud server and the time it takes to provide this pain-related information at web platform for visualization to end-users is T_{cw}. The overall latency (T_C) offered by the cloud-based deployment of remote pain applications is calculated using Eq. (3).

$$T_C = T_s^t + T_{ec}^t + T_{cw}^t \tag{3}$$

At any time t, network utilization for cloud $\left(U_c^t\right)$ and proposed fog-based design $\left(U_f^t\right)$ is calculated using Eqs. (3) and (4) in which δ is the length of data encapsulated in the tuple.

$$U_c^t = \delta \times \left(T_s^t + T_{ec}^t + T_{cw}^t\right) \tag{4}$$

$$U_f^t = \delta \times \left(T_s^t + T_{ef}^t + T_{fw}^t\right) \tag{5}$$

Fog nodes by utilizing the available resources process the sensed information. The tasks demanding additional resources than those available at the fog nodes are transferred to the cloud server. The proposed organization of network devices significantly reduces the load on the server resulting in the reduction of processing cost at the cloud server.

Eqs. (6) and (7) are derived from [76] to compute the cost of execution at cloud (E_c) and reduction in execution cost (Δ_{E_c}) respectively.

$$E_c = \xi_c + (S_{clock} \times L_{time} \times R_{MIPS} \times L_u \times T_{MIPS}) \tag{6}$$

$$\Delta_{E_c} = E_c^{cloud} \text{-} E_c^{fog} \tag{7}$$

Here, ξ_c is the execution cost, S_{clock} is the CloudSim clock, L_{time} is the last utilization update time, R_{MIPS} is the rate per MIPS, L_u is the last utilization, T_{MIPS} is the total MIPS of the host, E_c^{cloud} is the cost of execution for cloud scenario, and E_c^{fog} is the cost of execution for fog computing scenario.

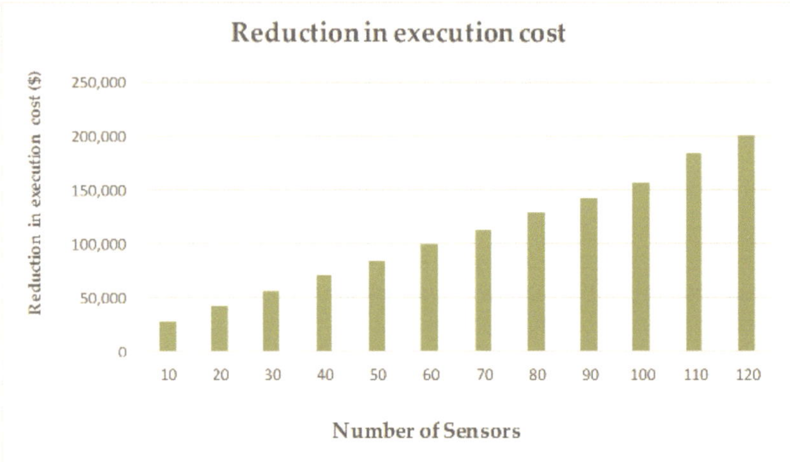

Figure 4.
Reduction in execution cost using the proposed approach.

The cloud architecture provides additional computational support to the fog paradigm by providing a resourceful cloud server. Fog computing delivers services close to the edge users. The fog node provides resources for the processing of the detected biopotential signals at the edge layer.

The processing cost at the cloud is based on the consumption of cloud resources for the execution of tasks in the cloud [76–78]. The decrease in the processing cost at the cloud can be attained by the induction of fog nodes in the system, as fog nodes process the detected data by using their resources, resulting in the reduction of information to be processed at the cloud server. **Figure 4** illustrates the reduction in execution cost by adopting the proposed model as compared to cloud implementation. The reason for this decrease in information to be processed in the cloud is the introduction of fog resources in the network.

3.3.2 Latency

Healthcare applications require real-time processing. The key factor limiting the large-scale deployment of such e-healthcare applications on the cloud paradigm is the high delay offered by cloud architecture. The fog computing paradigm distributes the resources reducing the repetitive access to cloud servers. This ensures the reduction of offered delays in the provision of processing services to edge users. In the proposed design, one fog node is assigned to each hospital that processes the sensed data at the hospital and transmits the suitable information to the web platform without incorporating a cloud server. This procedure reduces the overall latency offered in the provision of remote services to end users. iFogSim simulator is used to execute all designed scenarios. **Figure 5** presents the delay offered in the provision of pain-related remote access services by the cloud and fog-based deployments. The delay produced by the cloud-based deployment of the application significantly rises with an increase in the number of patients, while the proposed design offers reduced latency due to the provision of service near the hospitals.

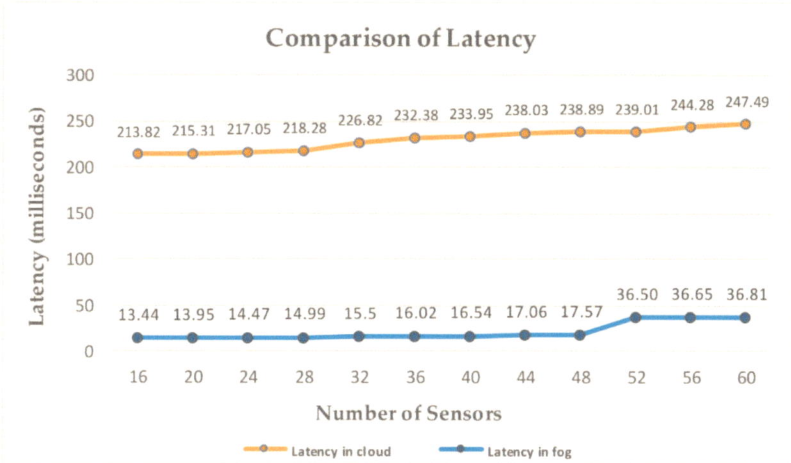

Figure 5.
Latency comparison between the proposed paradigm and the cloud paradigm.

To evaluate the proposed fog-based deployment, four fog nodes are installed to monitor four hospitals. In the initial scenario, each fog node is offered to process the data of four patients attached to it. Afterward, the number of patients per fog node increases in each succeeding scenario. The fog nodes have to process the information detected by the increasing number of patients. Therefore, a rise in the sensed volume results in an increased execution delay offered by the modules placed at fog nodes. This simultaneous rise in the sensed volume on each fog node results in a sudden rise in the latency of the system, as depicted in **Figure 5**, when the number of patients increases from 48 to 52. This abrupt rise in the delay is the effect of individual delays produced at each fog node which can be stabilized by the addition of more fog devices in the network.

3.3.3 Network consumption

In cloud-based deployment, the cloud server processes all the sensed volume of the patients. Thus, a rise in the number of patients to be monitored increases the volume of sensed data to be processed at the cloud server, resulting in higher network consumption. A reduction in network utilization is observed in the case of the proposed design due to the provision of resources near the patients through fog nodes. Furthermore, this reduction in network consumption is also because each fog device has to process the information of one specific hospital.

The achieved reduction in network consumption while deploying remote pain monitoring applications on the proposed design is depicted in **Figure 6**. In cloud-based deployment, all the connected patients' sensed data must be processed at the single cloud sever available. Thus, a simultaneous increase in the number of patients burdens the network due to a rise in the sensed load traffic toward the cloud server. Whereas, this abrupt increase of network load is not observed in the case of fog-based design because the fog devices have to process the sensed data of patients of only one hospital. In conclusion, the proposed design reduces latency and efficient network utilization compared to the cloud paradigm for the deployment of latency-sensitive e-healthcare applications.

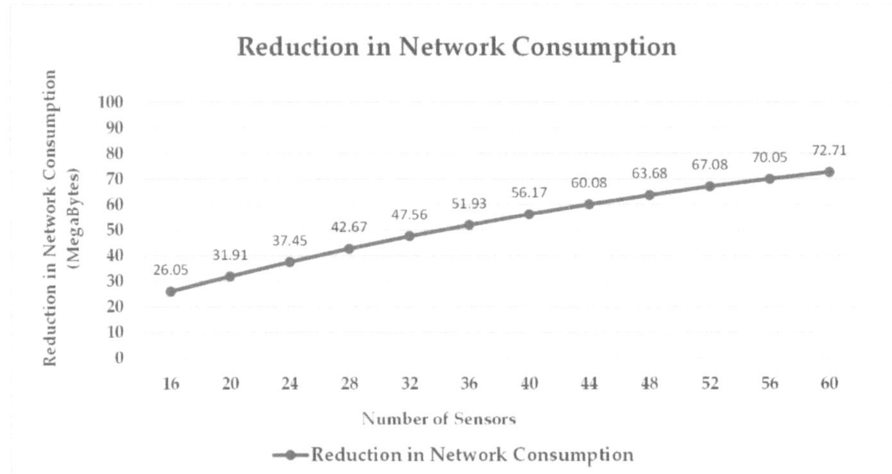

Figure 6.
Reduction in network utilization using the proposed fog paradigm.

4. Results and discussion

In this chapter, a design of remote pain monitoring applications using the fog computing paradigm is presented. To confirm the effectiveness of the proposed design as compared to cloud-based implementations several scenarios are implemented [55, 56, 79]. During all these assessments, the parameters under observation are execution cost, end-to-end delay, and network utilization. The reduction in the execution cost at the cloud is observed, as shown in **Figure 4** while deploying the application on the proposed paradigm. This reduction in processing cost at the cloud is due to the provision of fog resources throughout the system.

Figure 5 depicts the delay caused by both of the paradigms in implementing the application in all the simulated scenarios. The proposed design assigns one fog node to each hospital for the processing of the sensed data without incorporating a cloud server. This procedure reduces the overall latency offered in the provision of remote services to end-users. However, the latency provided by the cloud-based design significantly increases with an increase in the number of sensors, while the proposed design offers reduced latency due to the provision of service near the hospitals. **Figure 6** shows that very high network consumption is offered by the cloud paradigm for implementing remote pain monitoring applications. The reason behind this high network consumption in cloud-based deployment is the only availability of resources at cloud servers in a centralized manner.

4.1 Comparative analysis

The cloud computing paradigm offers resources in a centralized way. Real-time service provision is a major apprehension in the implementation of e-healthcare applications. Fog computing offers resources in a distributed manner through the deployment of fog nodes throughout the network. The fog resources are enough for the execution of processing tasks related to sensed medical signals. Hence, the fog paradigm is proved to be a more suitable candidate for the deployment of e-healthcare

References	Architecture	Monitoring	Delay	Processing cost	Network load
[80]	Cloud	Pain	Medium	High	High
[7]	Cloud	Pain	Medium	High	High
[81]	Cloud	Health	Medium	High	High
[9]	Cloud	Patient	Medium	High	High
[8]	Cloud	Pain	Medium	High	High
Proposed design	Fog	Pain	Minimum	Low	Low

Table 3.
Comparison between the proposed design and the existing systems.

applications. **Table 3** offers a brief comparison of the proposed fog-based design with the existing healthcare systems. The outcomes of the simulation carried out in this research validate that a decrease in network utilization and processing cost at the cloud is realized using the proposed approach.

5. Conclusions

For the provision of services to elderly patients, patients with disabilities, and patients residing in remote or rural localities, where frequent access to hospitals is not an easy task, the healthcare applications providing remote medical facilities are getting popular expeditiously. Mostly, the applications providing remote medical services are deployed using cloud architecture because the cloud paradigm provides plentiful resources for the execution and analysis of medical data involved in the procedure of such applications. Due to the reliance of human lives on such applications, these applications require real-time processing of medical information with minimum delay. Owing to centralized architecture, the cloud computing paradigm lacks the provision of real-time services to end users when such applications are deployed on large scale. On the contrary, the fog paradigm offers computational services adjacent to the network edge by distributing resource-constraint fog devices throughout the network. This chapter presents a remote pain monitoring system based on a fog computing paradigm that senses and processes the biopotential signals of remotely situated patients to detect pain. Furthermore, the designed application offers remote access to patient health-related information through a web platform for the rapid provision of medical facilitation to the patient. To evaluate the proposed fog computing-based design with the traditional cloud computing-based application, several scenarios are created and executed on multiple scales using the iFogSim toolkit. The outcomes of the simulations validate the effectiveness of the proposed design in the provision of services with minimized delay. Furthermore, the proposed design offers reduced execution costs at cloud and network load as compared to the cloud computing-based design.

Author details

Syed Rizwan Hassan[1*] and Muhammad Rashad[2]

1 Institute of Engineering and Fertilizer Research, Faisalabad, Pakistan

2 The University of Lahore, Lahore, Pakistan

*Address all correspondence to: syedrizwanhassan@gmail.com

References

[1] Awaisi KS, Hussain S, Ahmed M, Khan AA, Ahmed G. Leveraging IoT and fog computing in healthcare systems. IEEE Internet of Things Magazine. 2020; **3**(2):52-56

[2] Rao BP, Saluia P, Sharma N, Mittal A, Sharma SV. Cloud computing for internet of things & sensing based applications. In: 2012 Sixth International Conference on Sensing Technology (ICST). IEEE; 2012. pp. 374-380

[3] Elhoseny M, Abdelaziz A, Salama AS, Riad AM, Muhammad K, Sangaiah AK. A hybrid model of internet of things and cloud computing to manage big data in health services applications. Future Generation Computer Systems. 2018;**86**: 1383-1394

[4] Botta A, De Donato W, Persico V, Pescapé A. Integration of cloud computing and internet of things: A survey. Future Generation Computer Systems. 2016;**56**:684-700

[5] Dastjerdi AV, Gupta H, Calheiros RN, Ghosh SK, Buyya R. Fog computing: Principles, architectures, and applications. In: Internet of Things. Morgan Kaufmann; 2016. pp. 61-75

[6] Muheidat F, Tawalbeh LA, Tyrer H. Context-aware, accurate, and real time fall detection system for elderly people. In: 2018 IEEE 12th International Conference on Semantic Computing (ICSC). IEEE; 2018. pp. 329-333

[7] Tejaswini S, Sriraam N, Pradeep G. Cloud-based framework for pain scale assessment in NICU-a primitive study with infant cries. In: 2018 3rd International Conference on Circuits, Control, Communication and Computing (I4C). IEEE; 2018. pp. 1-4

[8] Yang G, Jiang M, Ouyang W, Ji G, Xie H, Rahmani AM, et al. IoT-based remote pain monitoring system: From device to cloud platform. IEEE Journal of Biomedical and Health Informatics. 2017;**22**(6):1711-1719

[9] Bharat, Kumar GJ. Internet of things (IoT) and cloud computing based persistent vegetative state patient monitoring system: A remote assessment and management. In: 2018 International Conference on Computational Techniques, Electronics and Mechanical Systems (CTEMS). IEEE; 2018. pp. 301-305

[10] Muhammed T, Mehmood R, Albeshri A, Katib I. UbeHealth: A personalized ubiquitous cloud and edge-enabled networked healthcare system for smart cities. IEEE Access. 2018;**6**: 32258-32285

[11] Rahmani AM, Gia TN, Negash B, Anzanpour A, Azimi I, Jiang M, et al. Exploiting smart e-health gateways at the edge of healthcare internet-of-things: A fog computing approach. Future Generation Computer Systems. 2018;**78**: 641-658

[12] Farahani B, Firouzi F, Chang V, Badaroglu M, Constant N, Mankodiya K. Towards fog-driven IoT eHealth: Promises and challenges of IoT in medicine and healthcare. Future Generation Computer Systems. 2018;**78**: 659-676

[13] Negash B, Gia TN, Anzanpour A, Azimi I, Jiang M, Westerlund T, et al. Leveraging fog computing for healthcare IoT. In: Fog Computing in the Internet of Things. Springer; 2018. pp. 145-169

[14] Gaigawali N, Chaskar U. Cloud based ECG monitoring and fibrillation

detection for healthcare system. In: 2018 Second International Conference on Intelligent Computing and Control Systems (ICICCS). IEEE; 2018. pp. 287-291

[15] Idoga PE, Toycan M, Nadiri H, Çelebi E. Factors affecting the successful adoption of e-health cloud based health system from healthcare consumers' perspective. IEEE Access. 2018;**6**: 71216-71228

[16] Sood SK, Mahajan I. A fog-based healthcare framework for chikungunya. IEEE Internet of Things Journal. 2017; **5**(2):794-801

[17] Pham M, Mengistu Y, Do HM, Sheng W. Cloud-based smart home environment (CoSHE) for home healthcare. In: 2016 IEEE International Conference on Automation Science and Engineering (CASE). IEEE; 2016. pp. 483-488

[18] John N, Shenoy S. Health cloud-healthcare as a service (HaaS). In: 2014 International Conference on Advances in Computing, Communications and Informatics (ICACCI). IEEE; 2014. pp. 1963-1966

[19] Elmisery AM, Rho S, Aborizka M. A new computing environment for collective privacy protection from constrained healthcare devices to IoT cloud services. Cluster Computing. 2019; **22**(1):1611-1638

[20] Srinivas J, Das AK, Kumar N, Rodrigues JJ. Cloud centric authentication for wearable healthcare monitoring system. IEEE Transactions on Dependable and Secure Computing. 2018;**17**(5):942-956

[21] Yang Y, Li X, Qamar N, Liu P, Ke W, Shen B, et al. Medshare: A novel hybrid cloud for medical resource sharing among autonomous healthcare providers. IEEE Access. 2018;**6**: 46949-46961

[22] Rahman SMM, Masud MM, Hossain MA, Alelaiwi A, Hassan MM, Alamri A. Privacy preserving secure data exchange in mobile P2P cloud healthcare environment. Peer-to-Peer Networking and Applications. 2016;**9**(5):894-909

[23] Abdelaziz A, Elhoseny M, Salama AS, Riad A. A machine learning model for improving healthcare services on cloud computing environment. Measurement. 2018;**119**:117-128

[24] Lo'ai AT, Mehmood R, Benkhlifa E, Song H. Mobile cloud computing model and big data analysis for healthcare applications. IEEE Access. 2016;**4**: 6171-6180

[25] Rajabion L, Shaltooki AA, Taghikhah M, Ghasemi A, Badfar A. Healthcare big data processing mechanisms: The role of cloud computing. International Journal of Information Management. 2019;**49**: 271-289

[26] Marwan M, Kartit A, Ouahmane H. Security enhancement in healthcare cloud using machine learning. Procedia Computer Science. 2018;**127**:388-397

[27] Yang Z, Zhou Q, Lei L, Zheng K, Xiang W. An IoT-cloud based wearable ECG monitoring system for smart healthcare. Journal of Medical Systems. 2016;**40**(12):1-11

[28] Mubarakali A. Healthcare services monitoring in cloud using secure and robust healthcare-based BLOCKCHAIN (SRHB) approach. Mobile Networks and Applications. 2020;**25**(4):1330-1337

[29] Mahmud R, Koch FL, Buyya R. Cloud-fog interoperability in

IoT-enabled healthcare solutions. In: Proceedings of the 19th International Conference on Distributed Computing and Networking. 2018. pp. 1-10

[30] Asif-Ur-Rahman M, Afsana F, Mahmud M, Kaiser MS, Ahmed MR, Kaiwartya O, et al. Toward a heterogeneous mist, fog, and cloud-based framework for the internet of healthcare things. IEEE Internet of Things Journal. 2018;**6**(3):4049-4062

[31] Doheir M, Basari ASH, Hussin B, Yaacob NM, Al-Shami SSA. The new conceptual cloud computing modelling for improving healthcare management in health organizations. International Journal of Advanced Science and Technology. 2019;**28**(1):351-362

[32] Kumar PM, Lokesh S, Varatharajan R, Babu GC, Parthasarathy P. Cloud and IoT based disease prediction and diagnosis system for healthcare using fuzzy neural classifier. Future Generation Computer Systems. 2018;**86**:527-534

[33] Mahmoud MM, Rodrigues JJ, Saleem K, Al-Muhtadi J, Kumar N, Korotaev V. Towards energy-aware fog-enabled cloud of things for healthcare. Computers & Electrical Engineering. 2018;**67**:58-69

[34] Mahmoud MM, Rodrigues JJ, Saleem K, Al-Muhtadi J, Kumar N, Korotaev VJC, et al. Towards energy-aware fog-enabled cloud of things for healthcare. 2018;**67**:58-69

[35] Verma S, Yadav AK, Motwani D, Raw R, Singh HK. An efficient data replication and load balancing technique for fog computing environment. In: 2016 3rd International Conference on Computing for Sustainable Global Development (INDIACom). IEEE; 2016. pp. 2888-2895

[36] Al-Khafajiy M, Otoum S, Baker T, Asim M, Maamar Z, Aloqaily M, et al. Intelligent control and security of fog resources in healthcare systems via a cognitive fog model. 2021;**21**(3):1-23

[37] Amin SU, Alsulaiman M, Muhammad G, Mekhtiche MA, Hossain MS. Deep learning for EEG motor imagery classification based on multi-layer CNNs feature fusion. Future Generation Computer Systems. 2019; **101**:542-554

[38] Garkoti G, Peddoju SK, Balasubramanian R. Detection of insider attacks in cloud based e-healthcare environment. In: 2014 International Conference on Information Technology. IEEE; 2014. pp. 195-200

[39] Gia TN, Jiang M, Rahmani A-M, Westerlund T, Liljeberg P, Tenhunen H. Fog computing in healthcare internet of things: A case study on ECG feature extraction. In: 2015 IEEE International Conference on Computer and Information Technology; Ubiquitous Computing and Communications; Dependable, Autonomic and Secure Computing; Pervasive Intelligence and Computing. IEEE; 2015. pp. 356-363

[40] Isa ISBM, El-Gorashi TE, Musa MO, Elmirghani JM. Energy efficient fog-based healthcare monitoring infrastructure. IEEE Access. 2020;**8**: 197828-197852

[41] Al-Khafajiy M, Otoum S, Baker T, Asim M, Maamar Z, Aloqaily M, et al. Intelligent control and security of fog resources in healthcare systems via a cognitive fog model. ACM Transactions on Internet Technology (TOIT). 2021; **21**(3):1-23

[42] Gupta H, Vahid Dastjerdi A, Ghosh SK, Buyya R. iFogSim: A toolkit for modeling and simulation of resource

management techniques in the internet of things, edge and fog computing environments. Software: Practice and Experience. 2017;**47**(9):1275-1296

[43] Qaddoura R, Al-Zoubi M, Faris H, Almomani I. A multi-layer classification approach for intrusion detection in iot networks based on deep learning. Sensors. 2021;**21**(9):2987

[44] Abdel-Basset M, El-Shahat D, Elhoseny M, Song H. Energy-aware metaheuristic algorithm for industrial-internet-of-things task scheduling problems in fog computing applications. IEEE Internet of Things Journal. 2020; **8**(16):12638-12649

[45] Fang J, Ma A. Iot application modules placement and dynamic task processing in edge-cloud computing. IEEE Internet of Things Journal. 2020; **8**(16):12771-12781

[46] Yousefpour A, Fung C, Nguyen T, Kadiyala K, Jalali F, Niakanlahiji A, et al. All one needs to know about fog computing and related edge computing paradigms: A complete survey. Journal of Systems Architecture. 2019;**98**: 289-330

[47] Shukla S, Hassan MF, Khan MK, Jung LT, Awang A. An analytical model to minimize the latency in healthcare internet-of-things in fog computing environment. PLoS One. 2019;**14**(11): e0224934

[48] Naha RK, Garg S, Georgakopoulos D, Jayaraman PP, Gao L, Xiang Y, et al. Fog computing: Survey of trends, architectures, requirements, and research directions. IEEE access. 2018;**6**:47980-48009

[49] Nandyala CS, Kim H-K. From cloud to fog and IoT-based real-time U-healthcare monitoring for smart homes and hospitals. International Journal of Smart Home. 2016;**10**(2):187-196

[50] Jonassaint CR, Shah N, Jonassaint J, De Castro L. Usability and feasibility of an mHealth intervention for monitoring and managing pain symptoms in sickle cell disease: The sickle cell disease Mobile application to record symptoms via technology (SMART). Hemoglobin. 2015;**39**(3):162-168

[51] Lucey P, Cohn JF, Matthews I, Lucey S, Sridharan S, Howlett J, et al. Automatically detecting pain in video through facial action units. IEEE Transactions on Systems, Man, and Cybernetics, Part B (Cybernetics). 2010; **41**(3):664-674

[52] Kächele M, Amirian M, Thiam P, Werner P, Walter S, Palm G, et al. Adaptive confidence learning for the personalization of pain intensity estimation systems. Evolving Systems. 2017;**8**(1):71-83

[53] Hossain MS, Muhammad G. Cloud-assisted speech and face recognition framework for health monitoring. Mobile Networks and Applications. 2015;**20**(3):391-399

[54] Moura J, Hutchison D. Review and analysis of networking challenges in cloud computing. Journal of Network and Computer Applications. 2016;**60**: 113-129

[55] Sarkar S, Misra S. Theoretical modelling of fog computing: A green computing paradigm to support IoT applications. Iet Networks. 2016;**5**(2): 23-29

[56] Alrawais A, Alhothaily A, Hu C, Cheng X. Fog computing for the internet of things: Security and privacy issues. IEEE Internet Computing. 2017;**21**(2): 34-42

[57] Lee G, Saad W, Bennis M. An online optimization framework for distributed fog network formation with minimal latency. IEEE Transactions on Wireless Communications. 2019;**18**(4): 2244-2258

[58] Gállego JR, Hernández-Solana Á, Canales M, Lafuente J, Valdovinos A, Fernández-Navajas J. Performance analysis of multiplexed medical data transmission for mobile emergency care over the UMTS channel. IEEE Transactions on Information Technology in Biomedicine. 2005;**9**(1):13-22

[59] Deng R, Lu R, Lai C, Luan TH, Liang H. Optimal workload allocation in fog-cloud computing toward balanced delay and power consumption. IEEE Internet of Things Journal. 2016;**3**(6): 1171-1181

[60] Thota C, Sundarasekar R, Manogaran G, Varatharajan R, Priyan M. Centralized fog computing security platform for IoT and cloud in healthcare system. In: Fog Computing: Breakthroughs in Research and Practice. IGI global; 2018. pp. 365-378

[61] Yang Y, Huang J, Zhang T, Weinman J. Fog and Fogonomics: Challenges and Practices of Fog Computing, Communication, Networking, Strategy, and Economics. John Wiley & Sons; 2020

[62] Wang D, Liu Z, Wang X, Lan Y. Mobility-aware task offloading and migration schemes in fog computing networks. IEEE Access. 2019;**7**: 43356-43368

[63] Ma M, He D, Wang H, Kumar N, Choo K-KR. An efficient and provably secure authenticated key agreement protocol for fog-based vehicular ad-hoc networks. IEEE Internet of Things Journal. 2019;**6**(5):8065-8075

[64] Kochetkov D, Vuković D, Sadekov N, Levkiv H. Smart cities and 5G networks: An emerging technological area? Journal of the Geographical Institute "Jovan Cvijić" SASA. 2019; **69**(3):289-295

[65] Zhang P, Zhou M, Fortino G. Security and trust issues in fog computing: A survey. Future Generation Computer Systems. 2018;**88**:16-27

[66] Jia B, Hu H, Zeng Y, Xu T, Yang Y. Double-matching resource allocation strategy in fog computing networks based on cost efficiency. Journal of Communications and Networks. 2018; **20**(3):237-246

[67] Gao X, Huang X, Bian S, Shao Z, Yang Y. PORA: Predictive offloading and resource allocation in dynamic fog computing systems. IEEE Internet of Things Journal. 2019;**7**(1):72-87

[68] Kumar V, Laghari AA, Karim S, Shakir M, Brohi AA. Comparison of fog computing & cloud computing. International Journal of Computer Mathematics. 2019;**1**:31-41

[69] Prada EJA. The internet of things (IoT) in pain assessment and management: An overview. Informatics in Medicine Unlocked. 2020;**18**:100298

[70] Ekman P, Friesen WV. Facial action coding system. Environmental Psychology & Nonverbal Behavior. 1978

[71] Van der Maaten L, Hinton G. Visualizing data using t-SNE. Journal of Machine Learning Research. 2008;**9**(11)

[72] Sadiq MT, Yu X, Yuan Z, Fan Z, Rehman AU, Li G, et al. Motor imagery EEG signals classification based on mode amplitude and frequency components using empirical wavelet transform. IEEE Access. 2019;**7**:127678-127692

[73] Nezam T, Boostani R, Abootalebi V, Rastegar K. A novel classification strategy to distinguish five levels of pain using the EEG signal features. IEEE Transactions on Affective Computing. 2018;**12**(1):131-140

[74] Afrasiabi S, Boostani R, Masnadi-Shirazi M-A. A physiological-inspired classification strategy to classify five levels of pain. In: 2019 26th National and 4th International Iranian Conference on Biomedical Engineering (ICBME). IEEE; 2019. pp. 106-111

[75] Ekman P, Friesen WV. Measuring facial movement. Environmental Psychology and Nonverbal Behavior. 1976;**1**(1):56-75

[76] Rahbari D, Nickray M. Scheduling of fog networks with optimized knapsack by symbiotic organisms search. In: 2017 21st Conference of Open Innovations Association (FRUCT). IEEE; 2017. pp. 278-283

[77] Martin JP, Kandasamy A, Chandrasekaran K. Mobility aware autonomic approach for the migration of application modules in fog computing environment. Journal of Ambient Intelligence and Humanized Computing. 2020;**11**(11):5259-5278

[78] Rahbari D, Nickray M. Low-latency and energy-efficient scheduling in fog-based IoT applications. Turkish Journal of Electrical Engineering & Computer Sciences. 2019;**27**(2):1406-1427

[79] Siam AI, Abou Elazm A, El-Bahnasawy NA, El Banby G, Abd El-Samie FE, Abd El-Samie F. Smart health monitoring system based on IoT and cloud computing. Menoufia Journal of Electronic Engineering Research. 2019;**28**(1):37-42

[80] Casti P, Mencattini A, Filippi J, D'Orazio M, Comes MC, Di Giuseppe D, et al. A personalized assessment platform for non-invasive monitoring of pain. In: 2020 IEEE International Symposium on Medical Measurements and Applications (MeMeA). IEEE; 2020. pp. 1-5

[81] Al-Khafajiy M, Baker T, Chalmers C, Asim M, Kolivand H, Fahim M, et al. Remote health monitoring of elderly through wearable sensors. Multimedia Tools and Applications. 2019;**78**(17): 24681-24706

Chapter 2

Perspective Chapter: A View – Cloud-Edge Computing Technology

C. Santhiya and S. Padmavathi

Abstract

In the computing era, the users of Internet grow tremendously. Each individual is using a number of devices that access data indefinitely. For any desired task, we will have three sorts of basic work in terms of storing, processing, and computation. In distributed world, many applications depending upon individual or enterprise rely on cloud computing. Edge computing has also evolved after cloud computing. Both the technologies have many common characteristics. The advantage of edge computing technology is service provisioning and it is done at the device level closer to the user rather than cloud. The application that needs faster response time or that holds sensitive data almost relied on edge technology for its computation.

Keywords: cloud, edge, latency, performance, cloud computing

1. Introduction

Cloud Edge technology is an innovative approach for managing and processing data in a distributed computing environment. It involves the integration of cloud computing with edge computing, which allows data to be processed and analyzed closer to the source of the data, reducing latency and improving response times.

At its core, cloud edge technology involves the deployment of edge devices or nodes that are connected to the cloud. These devices act as gateways that can process data in real time, and send only the relevant data to the cloud for further processing and analysis. This approach minimizes the amount of data that needs to be transmitted over the network, which in turn reduces network congestion and lowers the costs associated with data transmission.

The benefits of cloud edge technology are many. For one, it enables organizations to harness the power of cloud computing while still retaining the benefits of edge computing. This means that data can be processed and analyzed in real time, even when network connectivity is limited or unreliable.

Another benefit of cloud edge technology is its ability to support the deployment of new applications and services. By providing a distributed computing infrastructure, cloud edge technology enables organizations to deploy applications and services closer to their users, which improves performance and enhances the user experience.

Overall, cloud edge technology represents a significant advancement in the field of distributed computing. By combining the power of cloud computing with the benefits of edge computing, organizations can optimize their data processing and analysis capabilities, reduce latency, and enhance the overall user experience.

2. Background

Edge is the computing evolution after cloud computing but edge will not replace cloud in any means rather it will supplement cloud. On top level, always there will be cloud layer next to cloud layer bottom the edge layer will present, whenever applications is having data sensitive processing rather than cloud for faster processing. In research paper [1], all the basic scientific methods of cloud, edge, and fog computing have been discussed. Another research paper [2] compared this edge and cloud technology in performance parameters such as data filtering, processing, storage, and efficiency. Both the technological paradigms complement each other, n future industries such as manufacturing, mining, and transportation for detecting anomalies and sending alerts. In paper [3], comparison of fog nodes, edge nodes, and cloudlets is done on theoretical perspectives. The model reflects context awareness, access mechanisms, etc., and these have different set of characteristics that isolate them apart and it lacks standardization. The edge actually is acting as an interface, which connects all the edge devices to the cloud. Cloud will offer the services such as storing, processing, and analyzing the devices. By now in 2023 above 60% of the data is stored in network devices and managed in edge [4].

The major drawback cloud faces over edge is the amount of data processed per second, which is not passably supported by cloud. Next drawback is latency issues, and cloud also faces waste of resources as well. Also when data is piled and transferred to cloud it overloads the network so high bandwidth usage will occur. Edge computing [4] will not only helpful in minimizing data dependency over the app or service, and it will help in speeding up the process.

2.1 Why cloud computing?

Cloud computing offers many benefits that make it an attractive option for individuals and businesses alike. According to the research paper [5], there are some reasons why cloud computing is a popular choice:

Scalability: Cloud computing enables users to scale up or down their computing resources easily, depending on their needs. This means that users can adjust their computing resources as their requirements change, which can result in significant cost savings.

Cost-effectiveness: Cloud computing eliminates the need for organizations to invest in expensive hardware and software infrastructure. Instead, users pay for the computing resources they use on a pay-as-you-go basis, which can result in significant cost savings.

Accessibility: Cloud computing enables users to access their data and applications from anywhere with Internet connection. This means that users can work remotely, collaborate with others in real time, and access their data on any device.

Reliability: Cloud computing providers typically offer high levels of reliability and uptime, which ensures that users can access their data and applications when they need them.

Security: Cloud computing providers typically employ robust security measures to protect their users' data and applications from cyber threats. These measures often exceed what most organizations can implement on their own.

Agility: Cloud computing enables organizations to quickly deploy new applications and services, which can result in faster time-to-market and increased competitive advantage.

Cloud computing offers numerous benefits that make it an attractive option for individuals and organizations. By enabling scalability, cost-effectiveness, accessibility, reliability, security, and agility, cloud computing has become an essential component of modern computing infrastructure.

2.2 Types of cloud

There are three main types of cloud computing: public cloud, private cloud, and hybrid cloud. Here is a brief overview of each type.

Public Cloud: A public cloud is a cloud computing environment that is hosted by a third-party cloud service provider and made available to the public. These providers offer computing resources such as servers, storage, and applications to multiple customers who share these resources. Public clouds are accessible to anyone with Internet connection and are typically priced on a pay-as-you-go basis.

Private Cloud: A private cloud is a cloud computing environment that is dedicated to a single organization. These clouds are hosted either on-premises or by a third-party service provider and are typically used by large organizations that require a high degree of control over their computing resources. Private clouds offer greater control and security than public clouds but require significant upfront investment.

Hybrid Cloud: A hybrid cloud is a combination of public and private clouds that work together to provide a single computing environment. This approach allows organizations to leverage the benefits of both public and private clouds while addressing their specific needs for security, control, and scalability. In a hybrid cloud, organizations can use a public cloud for non-sensitive data and applications while using a private cloud for sensitive data and applications.

In addition to these three main types, there are also other types of clouds, such as community clouds and multi-clouds. Community clouds are clouds that are shared by multiple organizations with similar requirements, such as government agencies or healthcare organizations. Multi-clouds are environments that incorporate multiple cloud providers, enabling organizations to leverage the strengths of different providers for different applications or workloads.

Benefits of cloud computing:

- Lower IT infrastructure and computer costs for users
- Improved performance
- Fewer maintenance issues
- Instant software updates
- Improved compatibility between operating systems
- Performance and scalability

- Increased storage capacity
- Increase data safety

Drawbacks of cloud computing:

- Downtime
- Security and privacy
- Vulnerability to attack
- Limited control and flexibility
- Vendor lock-in
- Cost concerns

2.3 Edge computing

Edge computing is a distributed computing paradigm that involves processing and analyzing data at or near the source of the data, rather than sending it to a centralized data center or cloud for processing. The term "edge" refers to the edge of a network, where data is generated, collected, and analyzed in real-time.

The main goal of edge computing is to reduce the latency and bandwidth requirements associated with transmitting data to a centralized location for processing. By processing data at the edge of the network, organizations can improve their response times, reduce network congestion, and improve the overall performance of their applications.

Edge computing involves deploying edge devices, such as sensors, gateways, and other types of computing devices, at the edge of the network. These devices are responsible for collecting data, processing it in real time, and sending only the relevant data to the cloud for further analysis or storage.

Edge computing is particularly useful in scenarios where low latency and high reliability are critical, such as in industrial automation, autonomous vehicles, and healthcare. It also enables organizations to process and analyze data in environments where network connectivity is limited or unreliable, such as in remote locations or on mobile devices. It is an important development in the field of distributed computing, as it enables organizations to improve the performance, reliability, and scalability of their applications by processing data at the edge of the network.

2.4 Working of edge computing

EDGE computing involves processing and analyzing data at or near the source of the data, rather than sending it to a centralized data center or cloud for processing. The following are the basic steps involved in the working of edge computing.

Data collection: Edge devices, such as sensors, gateways, and other types of computing devices, are deployed at the edge of the network to collect data from various sources. These devices may also preprocess the data to reduce the amount of data that needs to be transmitted to the cloud for further analysis or storage.

Data processing: Edge devices process the collected data in real time using local computing resources. This enables organizations to perform analysis and make decisions quickly, without the delays associated with transmitting data to a centralized location for processing.

Data storage: Edge devices may also store data locally for quick access and offline processing. This helps to reduce the latency associated with transmitting data to the cloud for storage.

Data transmission: Edge devices transmit only relevant data to the cloud for further analysis or storage. This reduces the amount of data that needs to be transmitted over the network, reducing network congestion and improving overall performance.

Cloud-based analysis: The cloud receives the relevant data from edge devices and performs further analysis or storage. Cloud-based analytics can provide insights into patterns, trends, and anomalies that can help organizations make better decisions and optimize their operations.

IT enables organizations to process data at the edge of the network, reducing the latency and bandwidth requirements associated with transmitting data to a centralized location for processing. By processing data at the edge, organizations can improve their response times, reduce network congestion, and improve the overall performance of their applications.

2.5 Types of edge computing

There are four main types of edge computing, each with their own specific characteristics and use cases. These are as follows:

Local edge: Local edge computing is the simplest form of edge computing, and involves processing data at the edge of the network on a device or gateway that is directly connected to the data source. Local edge computing is used to minimize latency and ensure high availability for applications that require real-time processing.

Regional edge: Regional edge computing involves processing data at a regional data center or a group of data centers that are geographically close to the edge devices. Regional edge computing is used to support applications that require higher computational power or storage capacity than what is available on the local edge.

Distributed edge: Distributed edge computing involves processing data at multiple edge locations simultaneously. This approach is used to ensure high availability and redundancy for applications that require real-time processing and are critical to business operations.

Cloud edge: Cloud edge computing involves processing data at the edge of the network using a combination of cloud and edge resources. This approach is used to support applications that require scalability, high availability, and high computational power. Cloud edge computing can also enable edge devices to offload data processing and analysis to the cloud when needed.

Benefits of edge computing:

Edge computing offers several benefits to organizations, including the following:

Reduced latency: Edge computing reduces the time it takes for data to travel from the source to the processing location, resulting in lower latency and faster processing times. This is especially important for applications that require real-time processing and response times.

Improved reliability: Edge computing can improve the reliability of applications by reducing the impact of network outages or disruptions. By processing data at the edge of the network, applications can continue to function even if the network connection is lost.

Lower bandwidth requirements: Edge computing reduces the amount of data that needs to be transmitted to a centralized location for processing, resulting in lower bandwidth requirements and reduced network congestion.

Enhanced security: Edge computing can enhance security by processing sensitive data locally, reducing the risk of data breaches and unauthorized access. Additionally, edge devices can be configured to encrypt data at rest and in transit, further enhancing security.

Improved scalability: Edge computing [6] can improve the scalability of applications by distributing processing and storage resources across multiple edge devices. This enables organizations to handle increasing volumes of data and user requests without impacting performance.

Cost savings: Edge computing can result in cost savings by reducing the need for expensive data center infrastructure and network bandwidth. Additionally, edge computing can reduce the cost of data transfer and storage by processing and storing data locally.

Drawbacks of edge computing:

Edge computing offers several benefits, and it also has some drawbacks that organizations should be aware of. These include the following:

Limited processing power: Edge devices typically have limited processing power compared to cloud servers or data centers. This means that complex applications or processing tasks may not be able to be handled at the edge, and may need to be offloaded to the cloud.

Limited storage capacity: Edge devices also typically have limited storage capacity, which can be a constraint for applications that require large amounts of storage.

Increased complexity: Edge computing can increase the complexity of IT infrastructure, as it involves managing and coordinating a large number of edge devices and data sources. This can be challenging for organizations that do not have the necessary expertise or resources.

Security risks: Edge devices are often deployed in remote or unsecured locations, making them more vulnerable to cyber-attacks. Additionally, managing security across many edge devices can be challenging, and can require additional resources and expertise.

Integration challenges: Integrating edge computing into existing IT infrastructure can be challenging, especially if legacy systems are involved. This can result in additional costs and complexity.

Maintenance and upgrades: Edge devices require regular maintenance and upgrades to ensure that they are functioning properly and are up to date with security patches and software updates. This can be challenging in remote or hard-to-reach locations.

3. Examples and use cases

Edge computing is being used in a variety of industries and use cases. Some examples include the following:

Manufacturing: In manufacturing, edge computing is used to optimize production processes, monitor equipment performance, and reduce downtime. For example, edge devices can be used to collect sensor data from production lines in real time, analyze the data at the edge, and provide insights into operators and engineers to improve production efficiency.

Healthcare: In healthcare, edge computing is used to monitor patients in real time, analyze data from medical devices, and provide alerts to healthcare providers when necessary. For example, edge devices can be used to monitor vital signs of patients in real time and provide early warning alerts when a patient's condition is deteriorating.

Smart cities: In smart cities, edge computing is used to manage traffic, monitor air quality, and provide real-time public safety alerts. For example, in Ref. [7] edge devices can be used to collect data from traffic cameras, analyze the data at the edge, and provide real-time traffic updates to commuters.

Retail: In retail, edge computing is used to personalize customer experiences, optimize inventory management, and improve supply chain efficiency. For example, edge devices can be used to collect data from in-store sensors, analyze the data at the edge, and provide personalized recommendations to customers based on their shopping behavior.

Oil and gas: In the oil and gas industry, edge computing is used to monitor and optimize production processes, reduce downtime, and improve worker safety. For example, edge devices can be used to collect data from oil rigs in real time, analyze the data at the edge, and provide insights into operators and engineers to improve production efficiency and reduce downtime.

4. Cloud-Edge technology

Cloud-edge technology is the integration of cloud computing resources with edge computing devices. Edge computing is a distributed computing paradigm that brings computation and data storage closer to the location where it is needed, to improve response times and save bandwidth. Cloud computing, on the other hand, is the delivery of computing services—including servers, storage, databases, networking, software, analytics, and intelligence—over the Internet ("the cloud") to offer faster innovation, flexible resources, and economies of scale.

By combining the two technologies, organizations can take advantage of the scalability and flexibility of the cloud while also [2] enjoying the low latency and high performance of edge computing. This allows for real-time data processing and decision making, as well as the ability to offload data and processing to the cloud for storage, management, and advanced processing.

One of the main use cases of cloud-edge technology is in the Internet of Things (IoT) and Industry 4.0. IoT devices generate [8] large amounts of data that need to be processed and analyzed in real time. By using edge computing, this data can be processed locally, reducing the amount of data that needs to be sent to the cloud for processing. This can also reduce the cost of transmitting large amounts of data over long distances. In addition, edge devices can also make decisions based on the data they collect, without the need for a constant connection to the cloud.

Another use case of cloud-edge technology is in the field of autonomous vehicles. Autonomous vehicles generate huge amount of data from sensors that need to be processed in real time to make decisions. By using edge computing, the data can be processed locally, reducing the amount of data that needs to be sent to the cloud for processing. This can also reduce the cost of transmitting large amounts of data over long distances. Cloud-edge technology also plays a vital role in 5G networks, which helps to reduce the latency and increase the data rate for the end-users.

In conclusion, cloud-edge technology is an important trend in computing that allows organizations to take advantage of the scalability and flexibility of the cloud while also enjoying the low latency and high performance of edge computing. It has many use cases, including IoT, Industry 4.0, autonomous vehicles, and 5G networks.

5. Characteristics of cloud-Edge technology

The characteristics of cloud-edge technology can be summarized as follows:

1. **Distributed computing:** Cloud-edge technology is a distributed computing paradigm that brings computation and data storage closer to the location where it is needed, to improve response times and save bandwidth.

2. **Low Latency:** Edge computing can provide low latency as data does not need to be transmitted over long distances to a centralized location for processing.

3. **Real-time data processing:** Cloud-edge technology allows for real-time data processing and decision making, which is essential in some use cases such as IoT, Industry 4.0, autonomous vehicles, and 5G networks.

4. **Scalability:** Cloud computing offers scalability, as resources can be easily added or removed as needed. Edge computing, however, may have limitations in terms of scalability as resources are typically more constrained.

5. **Flexibility:** Cloud computing offers a high degree of flexibility as resources can be added or removed as needed. Edge computing, on the other hand, may have limitations in terms of flexibility as resources are typically more constrained.

6. **Security:** Edge computing devices are often located in remote or hard-to-reach locations, which can make them more vulnerable to security threats. Cloud computing, on the other hand, typically has more robust security measures in place to protect data.

7. **Cost:** Edge computing can be more cost-effective as it reduces the need for data transmission over long distances. However, the cost of deploying and maintaining edge devices can be higher than cloud computing.

8. **Integration:** Cloud-edge technology allows the integration of cloud resources for storage, management, and advanced processing, with edge devices for real-time data processing and decision making.

9. **Multi-cloud:** Cloud-edge technology can be used in a multi-cloud environment, where data can be processed on different cloud platforms depending on the use case.

10. **5G integration**: Cloud-edge technology plays a vital role in 5G networks, which helps to reduce the latency and increase the data rate for the end-users.

6. Why cloud-edge technology?

Overall, cloud-edge technology allows organizations to improve their operations and stay competitive by taking advantage of the scalability and flexibility of the cloud while also enjoying the low latency and high performance of edge computing.

6.1 Architectural concepts of cloud-edge technology

Cloud-edge technology refers to the integration of cloud computing and edge computing to create a hybrid computing environment. The main architectural concepts of cloud-edge technology include the following [9–19]:

1. ***Data processing:*** In a cloud-edge environment, data is processed both at the edge, near the source of the data, and in the cloud, allowing for real-time processing and analysis.

2. ***Distribution of resources:*** Cloud-edge technology allows for the distribution of resources such as storage, computation, and memory across the edge and the cloud. This enables efficient use of resources and reduces the need for large, centralized data centers.

3. ***Decentralization:*** Cloud-edge technology allows for a more decentralized computing environment, where data and applications can be distributed across a network of devices and locations.

4. ***Scalability:*** Cloud-edge technology allows for easy scaling of resources as needed, enabling efficient use of resources and cost savings.

5. ***Security:*** Cloud-edge technology can provide enhanced security by allowing sensitive data to be processed and stored at the edge, reducing the risk of data breaches.

6. ***Low Latency:*** Cloud-edge technology provides low-latency services by processing data on the edge devices, reducing the need for data transfer over the network.

6.2 Similarity of cloud-edge technology

A comparison of cloud and edge technology can be made based on several factors, including the following [9–19]:

Location of data processing: Edge computing involves processing data at or near the source of data collection, while cloud computing involves processing data in a centralized location such as a data center or the cloud.

Latency: Edge computing can provide lower latency as data does not need to be transmitted over long distances to a centralized location for processing. Cloud computing, on the other hand, may have higher latency due to the distance data needs to be transmitted.

Scalability: Cloud computing is known for its scalability, as resources can be easily added or removed as needed. Edge computing, however, may have limitations in terms of scalability as resources are typically more constrained.

Security: Edge computing devices are often located in remote or hard-to-reach locations, which can make them more vulnerable to security threats.

Cost: Edge computing can be more cost-effective as it reduces the need for data transmission over long distances. However, the cost of deploying and maintaining edge devices can be higher than cloud computing.

Flexibility: Cloud computing offers a high degree of flexibility as resources can be added or removed as needed. Edge computing, on the other hand, may have limitations in terms of flexibility as resources are typically more constrained.

By combining both cloud and edge technologies, organizations can take advantage of the scalability and flexibility of the cloud while also enjoying the low latency and high performance of edge computing. It also allows for real-time data processing and decision making, as well as the ability to offload data and processing to the cloud for storage, management, and advanced processing.

6.3 Dissimilarity of cloud-edge technology

The main difference between cloud and edge technology is the location of data processing and the way data is managed [9–19].

Cloud technology refers to the delivery of computing services—including servers, storage, databases, networking, software, analytics, and intelligence—over the Internet ("the cloud") to offer faster innovation, flexible resources, and economies of scale. Cloud computing is a centralized approach where data is stored and processed in data centers, which can be located anywhere in the world. It allows for scalability and flexibility as resources can be easily added or removed as needed.

Edge technology, on the other hand, is a distributed computing paradigm that brings computation and data storage closer to the location where it is needed, to improve response times and save bandwidth. Edge computing devices are located at the edge of the network, closer to the source of data collection. These devices process data locally, reducing the amount of data that needs to be sent to the cloud for processing. Edge computing can provide lower latency as data does not need to be transmitted over long distances to a centralized location for processing.

By combining both cloud and edge technologies, organizations can take advantage of the scalability and flexibility of the cloud while also enjoying the low latency and high performance of edge computing. It also allows for real-time data processing and decision making, as well as the ability to offload data and processing to the cloud for storage, management, and advanced processing.

6.4 Cloud-edge management

Cloud-Edge management refers to the processes and tools used to manage and maintain the hybrid cloud-edge computing environment. This includes managing the distribution and allocation of resources, monitoring performance, and ensuring security and compliance.

Some of the key elements of cloud-edge management include the following:

1. **Resource management:** Managing the distribution and allocation of resources such as storage, computation, and memory across the edge and the cloud. This includes monitoring resource utilization and ensuring that resources are used efficiently.

2. **Network management:** Managing the network infrastructure that connects the edge and the cloud. This includes monitoring network performance, troubleshooting issues, and ensuring secure communication between the edge and the cloud.

3. **Security management:** Ensuring the security of the cloud-edge environment by implementing security measures such as encryption, firewalls, and access controls. This also includes monitoring for potential security threats and responding to security incidents.

4. **Compliance management:** Ensuring that the cloud-edge environment is compliant with relevant regulations and industry standards. This includes implementing policies and procedures to meet compliance requirements and monitoring compliance status.

5. **Monitoring and analytics:** Monitoring the performance of the cloud-edge environment, including the edge devices, the cloud, and the network. This includes collecting and analyzing data to detect issues and identify opportunities for improvement.

6. **Automation:** Automating the management tasks and processes such as scaling, updates, and monitoring.

7. Cloud:-edge integration complexity

Cloud-edge integration can be complex due to a number of factors, such as:

1. **Data management:** Integrating data from the edge devices with data stored in the cloud can be complex, as the data may be in different formats and may need to be transformed or cleaned before it can be analyzed. Additionally, there may be issues with data privacy and security when transmitting data from the edge to the cloud.

2. **Network connectivity**: Ensuring reliable and secure communication between the edge and the cloud can be complex, as it requires a robust network infrastructure and may involve integrating different types of networks and protocols.

3. **Resource allocation:** Managing the distribution and allocation of resources between the edge and the cloud can be complex, as it requires balancing the needs of different edge devices and applications with the available resources in the cloud.

4. **Security:** Ensuring the security of the cloud-edge environment can be complex, as it requires implementing security measures at both the edge and the cloud, and monitoring for potential security threats.

5. **Compliance:** Ensuring compliance with relevant regulations and industry standards can be complex, as it requires implementing policies and procedures to meet compliance requirements and monitoring compliance status.

6. **Scalability:** The scalability of the cloud-edge environment can be complex as the number of edge devices and the amount of data that needs to be processed increases.

7. **Latency:** The latency of the cloud-edge environment can be complex as the processing of data at the edge devices improves the latency, but it can also increase the complexity of the environment.

8. **Management:** The management of the cloud-edge environment can be complex as it involves multiple layers and multiple teams, which need to work together seamlessly.

Integrating cloud and edge technology can be a complex task, requiring coordination and collaboration among multiple teams and technologies. However, with the right approach and tools, the benefits of cloud-edge integration can be well worth the effort.

8. Real world examples of cloud-edge technology

There are many real-world examples of cloud-edge technology being used in various industries. Some examples include the following:

Internet of Things (IoT): Cloud-edge technology is often used in IoT to process and analyze large amounts of data generated by IoT devices in real-time. For example, a smart city might use edge computing to process data from sensors in real time to adjust traffic lights and reduce congestion. The data can then be sent to the cloud for long-term storage and analysis.

Autonomous vehicles: Autonomous vehicles generate huge amounts of data from sensors that need to be processed in real time to make decisions. By using edge computing, the data can be processed locally, reducing the amount of data that needs to be sent to the cloud for processing. This can also reduce the cost of transmitting large amounts of data over long distances.

Industry 4.0: Cloud-edge technology is often used in Industry 4.0 to process and analyze large amounts of data generated by industrial equipment and machines in real time. For example, a factory might use edge computing to process data from sensors on machines in real time to improve efficiency and reduce downtime.

5G networks: Cloud-edge technology plays a vital role in 5G networks, which helps to reduce the latency and increase the data rate for the end-users.

Healthcare: Cloud-edge technology is also used in healthcare, for example, in telemedicine, remote patient monitoring, and in clinical research. Edge computing can be used to process data from medical devices in real time, while the cloud can be used to store and analyze the data.

Retail: Retail companies are using cloud-edge technology to support the use of Internet of Things (IoT) devices such as RFID tags and sensors to keep track of inventory and customer behavior in real time.

These are just a few examples of how cloud-edge technology is being used in various industries. As technology continues to evolve, it is likely that more and more companies will begin to adopt cloud-edge technology to improve their operations and stay competitive.

8.1 Market providers of cloud-edge technology

There are several major market providers of cloud-edge technology, including the following:

1. **Amazon Web Services (AWS):** AWS offers a range of services for cloud-edge computing, including AWS Greengrass for edge computing and AWS IoT for Internet of Things applications.

2. **Microsoft Azure:** Microsoft Azure offers Azure Edge Zones for low-latency edge computing and Azure IoT Edge for Internet of Things applications.

3. **Google Cloud:** Google Cloud offers Cloud IoT Edge for Internet of Things applications and Cloud Edge for edge computing.

4. **IBM:** IBM offers IBM Edge Application Manager for edge computing and IBM Watson IoT Platform for Internet of Things applications.

5. **Alibaba Cloud:** Alibaba Cloud offers Apsara Stack for edge computing and IoT Platform for Internet of Things applications.

6. **Huawei:** Huawei offers FusionSphere for edge computing and IoT Platform for Internet of Things applications.

7. **Cisco:** Cisco offers Cisco Edge Intelligence for edge computing and Cisco IoT for Internet of Things applications.

These providers offer a range of services for cloud-edge computing, including software, platforms, and infrastructure for edge computing and Internet of Things applications. They also offer services for data storage, data analytics, and machine learning, to name a few. These providers are well-established, and many have a wide range of customers and partners, which can be a good indication of their experience, scalability, and reliability.

These are just a few examples of cloud-edge technology providers, but as the market is constantly evolving there are many more providers that are emerging and offering similar services. It is important to choose a provider that meets your specific requirements and that has a track record of success in your industry.

9. Conclusion

Edge computing technology with its advance features associated with IoT, smart mobile connected devices, etc., are bringing processing closer to the end devices. This enables low latency, mobility, low bandwidth, mobility, QoS, etc. This technology will act as a thin line between cloud and device tiers. Edge computing differs with cloud technology in terms of distributed architecture and mobility. Even though edge is having advantages, there are still flaws in cloud computing model that remains as the lead of data that continues to increase. The technology of edge computing further needs improvement, which will help to draw a line between cloud and edge.

Author details

C. Santhiya[1*] and S. Padmavathi[2]

1 Department of Computer Science and Engineering, Thiagarajar College of Engineering, Madurai, India

2 Department of Information Technology, Thiagarajar College of Engineering, Madurai, India

*Address all correspondence to: csit@tce.edu

References

[1] Calo SB, Touna M, Verma DC, Cullen A. Edge computing architecture for applying AI to IoT. In: 2017 IEEE International Conference on Big Data (BigData). Boston, MA: IEEE; 2017. pp. 3012-3016. DOI: 10.1109/BigData.2017.8258272

[2] De Donno M, Tange K, Dragoni N. Foundations and evolution of modern computing paradigms: Cloud, IoT, edge, and fog. IEEE Access. 2019;7:150936-150948. DOI: 10.1109/ACCESS.2019.2947652

[3] Singh S. Optimize cloud computations using edge computing. In: 2017 International Conference on Big Data, IoT and Data Science (BID). Pune, India: IEEE; 2017. pp. 49-53. DOI: 10.1109/BID.2017.8336572

[4] Dolui K, Datta SK. Comparison of edge computing implementations: Fog computing, cloudlet and mobile edge computing. In: 2017 Global Internet of Things Summit (GIoTS). Geneva: IEEE; 2017. pp. 1-6. DOI: 10.1109/GIOTS.2017.8016213

[5] Gao J, Bai X, Tsai W-T, Uehara T. Testing as a service (TaaS) on clouds. In: IEEE 7th International Symposium on Service Oriented System Engineering (SOSE). San Francisco Bay, CA, United States; 2013. pp. 212-223

[6] Mell P, Grance T. Definition of cloud computing, Technical report, National Institute of Standard and Technology (NIST). July 2009

[7] Patel M, Naughton B, Chan C, Sprecher N, Abeta S, Neal, et al. Mobile-edge computing introductory technical white paper. White paper, mobile-edge computing (MEC) industry initiative. 2014

[8] Lin G, Fu D, Zhu J, Dasmalchi G. Cloud computing: IT as a service. IT Professional. 2009;**11**(2):10-13

[9] Plummer D, Bittman T, Austin T, Cearley D, Smith D. Cloud computing: Defining and describing an emerging phenomenon. Technical report, Gartner, 2008

[10] Available from: http://www.appcore.com/types-cloud-computing-private-public-hybridclouds

[11] NIST Cloud Computing Standards Roadmap Working Group NIST Cloud Computing Program Information Technology Laboratory. NIST Special Publication; 2011

[12] Armbrust M et al. A view of cloud computing. Communications of the ACM. 2010;**53**(4):50-58

[13] Kong LL. Study of cloud computing and virtualization technology In: Tinajin Vocational Institute, Tianjin, Applied Mechanics and Materials. Switzerland: Trans Tech Publications Ltd; 2014;**539**:407-411. DOI: 10.4028/www.scientific.net/AMM.539.407. ISSN: 1662-7482

[14] Chiang M, Zhang T. Fog and IoT: An overview of research opportunities. IEEE Internet of Things Journal. 2016;**3**(6):854-864

[15] Io Everything. Available from: http://www.cisco.com/c/dam/en_us/about/ac79/docs/innov/IoE_Economy.pdf. [Accessed 17 July 2017]

[16] Available from: https://www.forbes.com/sites/forbestechcouncil/2021/09/22/how-cloud-edge-technology-is-transforming-iot-and-industry-4-0/?sh=6d5c5c5f6b5f

[17] Available from: https://www.networkworld.com/article/3528187/the-rise-of-cloud-edge-computing.html

[18] Available from: https://www.techrepublic.com/article/edge-computing-vs-cloud-computing-whats-the-difference-and-why-does-it-matter/

[19] Available from: https://www.cio.com/article/3469113/cloud-edge-computing-explained-why-it-s-important-and-how-to-get-started.html

Chapter 3

Network Powered by Computing: Next Generation of Computational Infrastructure

Ruslan Smeliansky

Abstract

This paper is an extended version of my talk on the MoNeTec-2022. It gives a detailed presentation of the concept Network Powered by Computing (NPC). The main differences from the previously published one are that the functional architecture of the NPC is presented, the main problems on the way to its implementation are formulated, the mathematical statements of the problems of control and management of the resources in the NPC environment by methods of multi-agent optimization are given, the existence of a solution to these problems is justified, and the relationship between the problem of control in such an infrastructure and the Barabási-Albert model is shown. An example of the predicting execution time of services in the NPC environment is given.

Keywords: cloud computing, edge computing, software-defined network, network function virtualization, software defined wide area network, green computing, zero footprint

1. Introduction

MIT professors J.L. Hennessy and D.A. Patterson in their 2018 Turing Award lecture gave an excellent overview of the history of computer architecture and the lessons of this history in Ref. [1]. In the conclusion of this paper, they wrote: "The next decade will see a Cambrian explosion of novel computer architectures, meaning exciting times for computer architects in academia and in industry." This "explosion" brings great opportunities for computational infrastructure. To paraphrase the title of their paper, we can say that we are going through "A New Golden Age for Computational Infrastructure." The term computational infrastructure will be treated here as the architecture of computational infrastructure.[1] Organization of computations is one of the pillars of human civilization. Therefore, it is important to understand the main trends and prospects of its development, to understand what problems will need to be solved.

[1] This paper is extended version of my talk on the MoNeTec-2022 published in [2].

If we have a look at the history of the progress of computing infrastructure from the individual use of the first computers, the packaged organized computation on stand-alone computers to the client-server paradigm of computation based on high-speed data communication networks and large-scale (giant-like) data centers (DC), then the main lesson of this history is that the main drivers of this progress were the requirements of applications. Nowadays, the computational infrastructure paradigm is moving from "build your own" to the new one—"consume as a service" where a business does not need to buy and develop its own computational infrastructure, rent channels that connect it to the public network, hire expensive professionals for system and network administration, and so on. In the new paradigm, one can request and get the resources and services they need based on the model of "pay as you go." Also, computing paradigm based on the giant-like DC is being replaced by a new one—small cloud edges in [3]. Our applications became more and more real-time applications. So, the time for communication between user terminal and large scale DC where our ability to control communication delays became more and more critical for application operation. The increased restrictions on the interaction time between the application and the terminal device led to a contradiction with the concept of computing based on large-scale DC. Carbon footprint of such organized computation is a heavy burden on our ecology.

The necessity of this change has come from the requirements of new applications with their real-time interactivity, video streaming, and 5G communication. Over the past 10 years, cloud computing as the computing paradigm has completely changed the landscape of computational infrastructure; for example, see [4–7]. In the paper [3], I wrote: "It significantly contributed to the growth of both the number of data processing centers (DCs) and their size, the increase in throughput capacity of backbone channels [5], the increase in equipment density: virtualization of IT equipment in cloud architectures allowed to fit into one rack what previously required 10 racks improving and developing the capabilities of personal gadgets, various types and uses of sensors, the development of data transmission technologies such as OTN, 5G networks, network convergence, the emergence of SDN and NFV technologies gave impetus to the development of a large number of real-time applications (RT applications) in Ref. [8, 9]. Here are just some examples of such applications: smart city, smart home, healthcare (especially its areas such as surgery, telemedicine, emergency cardiology), interactive games, training, augmented reality, agriculture, infrastructure for scientific multidisciplinary research in [7], social communications, energy management systems (smart grid), wireless sensors embedded in a variety of robots, monitoring and control of transportation systems and facilities, assembly lines and production lines, gas and oil pipelines.

An important aspect of the computing infrastructure is power consumption. According to 451 Research, a technology research group within S&P Global Market Intelligence that provides a holistic view of innovation across the entire enterprise IT landscape, the computing power as well as the engineering equipment of all DC worldwide is estimated in 2022 about 200 GW in [10]. This means that in 2022 the energy consumption of all DC was 200 GWt $\times$ 24 hours $\times$ 365 days = 1 752 10^{12} Wt hours! Thus, the carbon footprint of the contribution of computational infrastructure was about 1.8 10^{15} Wt/year (53% of the US). This means that the organization of the computing infrastructure has a significant impact on the ecology of our environment.

2. Properties suite of modern applications

In my talk, I emphasized: "the main driving force of the development of infrastructure for computing, its operating environment, programming languages and tools have always been the needs of applications" [2]. The suet of these needs can be summarized as follows: distribution, self-sufficiency, real-time, elasticity, cross-platform, interaction and synchronization, and update-friendly. The definitions of these terms can be found in [2]. Nevertheless, for a better understanding of the further text, it is necessary to explain the term self-sufficiency, which is defined in [2] as: "application is no longer represented by code and source data only, it is accompanied by a description of the structure of the interconnection of the components (hereinafter application services) that make up the application, setting the required level of their productivity, explicitly formulated requirements for computing and network resources, data storage and access to data resources, intended timeframes for computing and data transmission in the form of a service level agreement (SLA), application launching procedures. This description is written in a special language, an example of which one can be the TOSCA language [6] (hereinafter such a description will be called Application Operation Specification—AOS)" [2].

3. Computational infrastructure requirements

Here, let me briefly list the requirements for the computational infrastructure described in [2]: behavior predictability, security, availability, reliability and fault tolerance, efficiency and fairness, virtualization, scalability, and serverless. The serverless was defined there [6] as follows: "[T]he infrastructure should automatically place application components in a way that allows them to interact according to the application stricture, and in a way that ensures that the SLA requirements of the application are met, while minimizing infrastructure resources utilization".

In order for NPC to be able to meet the requirement of efficiency and predictability and serve as the computational infrastructure for applications, in the above sense its behavior and functioning must meet the requirements such as:

- "predictability of time of execution of application components and their interaction time (data transfer) according to AOS;
- predictability of the characteristics of data transfer between application components along overlay channels;
- availability of a variety of virtualized network functions (VNF hereinafter) and other traffic engineering (TE) methods on Data Transmission Network (DTN) channels based on machine learning algorithms for distribution, balancing, shaping, filtering to control, and manage QoS of an overlay channel (further channel);
- reliable isolation of control plane and data plane in DTN from errors in network equipment, as well as isolation of different data flows, malicious influences in these planes" [2].

For predictability of the characteristics of data transfer between application components, it is necessary to:

- "set and guarantee variation ranges of end-to-end delay and jitter in DTN;
- guarantee the probability of packet loss in the DTN at the level corresponding to the SLA application;
- make the usability of the available bandwidth of DTN channels be maximal (mass overuse of resources is prohibited, such as flooding, broadcasting);
- exclude the unpredictable transmission delays caused by DTN, such as packet delays due to failure of order, retransmission, overload feedback, etc.;
- predict how much time will take the execution of certain application service on some computer installation to meet application SLA requirements" [2].

Techniques and methods for predicting the execution time of services and applications will be considered later.

4. NPC functional architecture

NPC functional architecture was presented in my talk [2]. Let me briefly repeat the main statements from there: "The computational infrastructure with properties above, we will call Network Powered by Computing (NPC)—it is a software-driven infrastructure, which is a tight software-driven integration of various computer installations with a high-speed DTN. Such an NPC is a fully manageable, programmable, virtualized infrastructure. In other words, the NPC becomes Computer!

The NPC organization should be based on the federative principle. Each federate has its own administration and possess an independent authority in whose jurisdiction there is a certain amount of computing, telecommunication, storage resources. Federate transfers part of these resources to the Federation authority, which forms and monitors a unified policy for their use.

Here is a summary of what a functional NPC architecture should look like. The core layers are the Application, Application Services, and Network Functions (ASNF) layer, the NPC Infrastructure Control (NPCIC) layer, NPC computational, networking, storage resources (NPCR) layer, and the E2E Orchestration, Administration, and Management (OAM) layer, responsible for organizing, administering and managing the NPC infrastructure.

The ASNF layer is responsible for application representation development: it's code and it's data, it's Application Operation Specification (AOS) representing application services (AS) and virtualized network functions (VNF) necessary for the operation of the application, specification of the data transmission network between application components. Specification of a network should include the topology for data transmission between application components, the requirements to the quality of service of the channels (QoS) that should include such characteristics as available bandwidth, admissible delay, admissible probability of packet loss, admissible jitter variation range. Based on this information and on SLA for the application as a whole ASNF calculates SLAs for each AS" [2].

NPCIC functionality provides scheduling and assignment of the application components to NPC resources in accordance with AOS and predicted time for computing, for data transfer, determination, collection, and aggregation of resources as necessary to comply with QoS resource requirements in accordance with the SLA of the application based on the current state of the resources, creating an overlay network according to AOS (topology, QoS channels, and security management). It is at this level that it is determined which VNFs will be required and where in the data transmission network.

The NPCR is responsible for a unified representation of the state of heterogeneous NPC resources, monitoring their current states, and predicting their states for the nearest future. The last functionality is the cornerstone to make NCP behavior be predictable.

The OAM layer orchestrates interactions of the application components in accordance with the AOS, collects resources consumption data for every application components, and manages the security and administration of NPC.

The basis for building NPC is formed by the technologies of software-defined networks (SDN) and network functions virtualization (NFV). Taking into account that the scaling range of network functions is wide and works in real time, the NPC will require low time complexity algorithms to optimize resource scheduling and resource allocation. And given the operation speed, as for data transmission networks and for computer installations, it becomes clear that only suboptimal solutions to the emerging optimization problems will be available based on Machine Learning (ML) methods. The functional architecture of the NPC described above is shown in **Figure 1** below.

Now, briefly consider the interaction components of NPC functional architecture. AOS can have two types of components: network functions (VNF) for managing data flows (traffic engineering) and application services for data processing and computational services (like modeling, simulation, etc.). Components of the first type (VNFs) are placed by DTN control plane on edge computing resources. Examples of VNF are NAT, Firewall, BRASS, balancers, shapers, and so on. Components of the second type —application services—are placed in a virtualized form (on virtual machines or

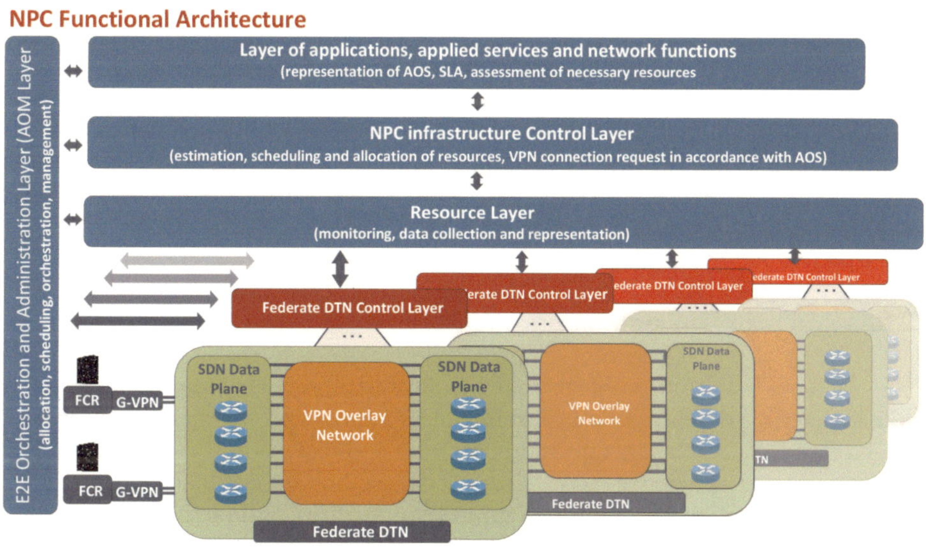

Figure 1.
Functional architecture of network powered by computing [2].

containers) or directly on computing resources (servers, edges, data centers (DC), and HPC installations) of federates (in **Figure 1** above, they are shown as FCR in the form of racks).

In [2], I emphasize that the application programmer is not required to foresee and explicitly insert the necessary VNFs or their chains into his application. VNFs can be automatically integrated into AOS of application by means of NPCIC, just as compilers or application libraries do: "plug in" the necessary functionality into the application code. NPCIC can do this based on the monitoring data of available channels QoS supplied by NPCR. Based on this data, NPCIC has also calculated the routs for the application with the given AOS.

As it can be seen in **Figure 1** that DTN of NPC may consist in the form of several local DTN of different federates. Each local DTN is SD-WAN overlay with control plane and data plane. In control plane of every local DTN, it is assumed that there are controllers with the set of network applications, channels QoS control and monitoring block, network security center with PKI management, and distributed ledger (DL) of overlay tunnels (chain of overlay channels).

When AOS application services interact through the DTN, the SDN controller of the overlay network "catches" the request for data transfer, accessing DL of the overlay network tunnels to find the proper tunnel. If there is no one there, then the SD-WAN controllers apply to the control center for application services in the NPCIC layer. If the DL does not have the required tunnel or its validity period has expired, then the SD-WAN controllers from the control plane apply to the NPCIC layer that, in cooperation with E2E OAM Orchestrator (end-to-end orchestrator), forms the data necessary for SD-WAN controllers to build the desired tunnel.

As mentioned in [2]:"NPC can run applications in three modes—pro-active, active, and mixed. In pro-active mode, application services are loaded in advance on the federate resources in passive state (in the form of code and data on external or internal memory). In this case, when running the application, it is only necessary to activate the required application services according to AOS on those computing resources that will ensure SLA compliance with the specific call to a specific application. It should be clear from the above that different references to the same application may have different SLAs. Same application but with different SLA is treated as different one.

The active mode involves loading the code and data of the necessary application/computing services in accordance with the AOS on the computing resources of the federates on demand in such a way as to ensure compliance with the SLA of the application. Mixed mode involves a combination of proactive and active modes, i.e. some of the application services and network functions are already pre-installed and are only being activated, the rest ones are loaded and activated upon request".

5. The main problem statements

In [2], there is a list of problems that NPC infrastructure should provide solutions to like the method of distribution (distributed vs. centralized) of computing resources between flows of computing/application services and request to them in a given NPC mode of operation (proactive, active, or mixed), method for optimal control of data flows in the interaction of computing/application services, and method for managing resource monitoring, prediction of the state of overlay network channels, selection of the optimal overlay network channel with the best QoS to meet the requirements of the SLA of the application, congestion control management, minimization of end-to-end delay, bandwidth monitoring, scheduling flows in queues and so on, scaling the NPC control plane and the data plane when changing the NPC scale, optimal channel routing of the overlay DTN, fair distribution of channel bandwidth, balancing data flow between computing/application services, and allocation of channel bandwidth on demand [8]. In the NPCR layer, it is necessary to choose the resource state scan frequency, data presentation format, and so on.

Here, the statements for the most important problems are considered:

1. Optimal distribution of the given set of application services on the NPC resources;

2. Distribution of a given set of services for proactive mode of operation of the NPC.

First of all, let us define the formal model of NPC.

Denote:

NPC as $\Gamma = (V, A)$, where

$V = CN \cup SN \cup P$, where

CN—set of NPC computational nodes,

SN—set of NPC VPN gateways,

P—set of Γ poles.

$A = \{(v_i, v_j) \mid v_i, v_j \in V\}$—multiple channels of overlay network.

$Q\ (l_{vi,vj}, \Delta t) \mid = (B, D, L, J)$ is the function defined on A, where.

Δt — interval of time;

$B = \left(\hat{b}, \overline{b}\right)$ – $\hat{b}, \overline{b}$ band width of $l_{vi,vj}$ in terms: $\hat{b}$—average and $\overline{b}$—maximum on Δt;

$D = \left(\underline{d}, \hat{d}, \overline{d}\right)$—delay on Δt in terms: $\underline{d}$– minimum, $\hat{d}$ —average, $\overline{d}$—maximum RTT;

L—percentage of lost packets;

$J = \hat{j}, \overline{j}$—jitter Δt in terms: $\hat{j}$—average, $\overline{j}$—maximum.

$CN = \{cn_i = <cr, m, h>\}$, where $cr, m, h \in N$—set of integers.

cr—number of cores (possible with characteristics);

m—amount of RAM;

h—storage size.

$P = \{p_i\}$, where p_i—source of requests/applications flows, which is characterized by the function of distributing the probability of requests/applications each with its SLA. Consider that the same request/application but with different SLAs are different requests/applications. The same p_i can be a source of requests for different applications. Each request is characterized by an application ID and a specific SLA—execution time plus result delivery time.

AS—set of application services, each characterized by the required computing resources, memory resources, and storage resources (cr, m, h).

VNF—set of virtual network functions with required resources (computing, memory, and storage)—$(cr, m,$ *and* $h)$ presented in AOS.

Here, for simplicity, we suppose that one application service/network function is always allocated per one cn_i and will consider an application as a chain of application services from *AS*. However, in general, it could be a directed acyclic graph (DAG). So, chain of application services (ASC) is $W = \{w_k = (s^k{}_1, \dots \dots, s^k{}_l)\}$, where $s^i{}_j \in AS \cup VNF$, $s^i{}_j = <cr, m, h>$.

Denote the function *ET:* $(AS \cup VNF) \times CN \rightarrow R$, where *R* – set of rational numbers. We will interpret *ET* as the estimation of execution time element from $AS \cup VNF$ on the certain $cn_i \in CN$. This function can be represented as a matrix, where columns correspond to elements from $AS \cup VNF$ and rows correspond to elements from *CN*; entries are execution times + data transfer time to the next s^i_j along the chosen channel. We will consider how to build this function in the next section.

In these terms, the problem of the optimal distribution of SFC on NPC can be formulated as follows:

Construct the mapping $F: W \rightarrow \Gamma$ for a given set *P* in such a way that

1. Meets the SLA requirements for all w_i from *W*;

2. Under the condition of minimizing the objective function, for example, in the following form:

$$F = min \sum_1^{|CN|} \left[\alpha \frac{\bar{c}_i}{c_i} + \beta \frac{\bar{h}_i}{h_i} + \gamma \left(\left(\frac{\bar{c}_i}{c_i} - \Theta \right)^2 + \left(\frac{\bar{h}_i}{h_i} - \Delta \right)^{2.} \right) \right] \qquad (1)$$

where

α, β, γ—constant values;

c_i, h_i—cn_i resources are used;

$\bar{c}_i, \bar{h}_i$—cn_i resources and queue length averaged over usage time;

Θ, Δ —the entire NPC resource usage averaged over time.

The α, β, γ values are the subject of adjustment of the application services allocation control. It is required to find the distribution of the AOS component $w_k \in W$ in such a way as to minimize the objective function *F* from Eq. (1), that is, in the table representing the *ET* function, one needs to add the application service ID in those positions that correspond to the appropriate resources. *F* from Eq. (1) gives us the set $\{cn_i\}_w$ of which it is necessary to select only those that are connected by channels that form a path in NPC corresponding to SLA (w_k).

The problem of distribution of application services over the resources of the NPC in proactive mode can be stated as: for given Γ, *AS*, *W*, and *P*, it is required to build a matrix *X* with dimension $|X| = |AS| \times |CN|$ where $x_{ij} = 1$; if s_i can be located on cn_j, it is subject to the following conditions:

1. The constraints of none cn_j and none of $(v_i, v_j) \in A$, incident to cn_j, from Γ are violated;

2. $\forall\, w_i \in W$, SLA applications always be met for any $p_j \in P$.

It is clear that for both problems, we have first of all proof for the existence of the solutions. Consider solving the problem of placing a chain of services in a NPC. It is divided into three subtasks:

1. Construct a set of all possible placements s^k_j for a given w_k on *cn* nodes from *CN*;

2. Select only those placements that meet the requirements of the SLA of the application and the limits on the resources of the *cn* nodes;

3. Among cn nodes selected at step 2, choose only those for which the NPC topology contains a route on which the selected cn nodes are ordered according to the order on w_k, that is, if s^k_j was assigned to cn_i and s^k_{j+1} to cn_r, then $(cn_i, cn_r) \in A$, which provides the necessary parameters for data transfer between cn_i, cn_r.

Since the length w_i, the number of computational nodes in CN, is limited, the problem certainly has a solution. You just need to go through a finite number of combinations. Let us estimate the space of possible solutions for some chain w from W. Let the length of any $w_k \in W$ not exceed N, where $N = |CN|$ and $|w_k| = k \leq N$. Then, the number of application service locations for w_k equals $\sum_{i=0}^{k+1} C_k^i = 2^k$. The number of possible placements of these 2^k substrings over NPC can be estimated by the following expression: $\sum_{i=0}^{k+1} C_N^i C_k^i$. This expression can be evaluated under the condition that the lengths $w_k \in W$ are uniformly distributed on [1, N], as follows:

$$\sum_{i=0}^{l+1} C_N^i C_l^i < \sum_{i=0}^{l+1} 2^l C_l^i = 2^l 2^N \approx 2^{\frac{3N}{2}}. \tag{2}$$

Even N≅100 gives us the estimation of this expression $2^{150} > 10^{100}$ (googol) options. This estimation must also be multiplied by $|W|$. The problem under consideration has a solution due to the finiteness of the number of options. If we recall that we are considering the simplest case, when the application is a chain of services, then it should be clear that the space of possible options in the case when the application is a directed acyclic graph (DAG) will be multiply increase: in this case, the estimation of (Eq. (2)) will need to be multiplied by the number of paths in this DAG. It is clear that classical mathematical optimization methods will not meet time restrictions to solve the problems. It is natural to consider the solution in the direction of splitting the solution space on domains and searching the solution in parallel in every domain based on ML technics.

The urgency to use ML methods is also argued by the following reasons. The NPC model described above is actually two random graphs. One is formed by data flows between the chain of application services that arise as a result of the action of poles from the set P. The vertices of this graph, let us call it an information flow graph (IFG)—application services, arcs—data flows between them. Both the first and second are of a stochastic nature and are determined by random processes initiated by poles. The second graph is the topology of the NPC network. This is also a random graph. Its dynamics are determined by the availability of resources of NPC, the failure dynamic of which is a set of random processes. The control in this model is the mapping of IFG graph to NPC graph. The optimality of control in this model is such a mapping of the IFG graph to the NPC graph, in which the lifetime of the information chain is minimal, subject to all restrictions on NPC resources.

Please pay attention that in the IFG graph, the number of the nodes is not fixed. It is a scale-free graph in terms of the Albert-Laslo Barabashi model from [11]. If NPC accepts the mobile edges, then NPC graph is also a scale-free graph. In this case, it seems that this model is very similar to the Barabási-Albert model described in [10]. Here and there, we have random scale-free graphs' interaction. However, the properties of such models in a computer world have never been investigated. The applicability and adequacy of such models in relation to computer networks require awareness and research.

The most appropriate mathematical technique for optimal control seems to be suitable for that is the multi-agent optimization (MA) technique. There are several approaches to MA optimization. **Centralized approach** assumes the presence of a control center and that agents are deployed one per node. Each agent forms local state-status of its node. The control center collects the status of each agent, makes a decision based on the optimization policy, and sends each agent a management impact. Another possible MA optimization approach induced by the NPC graph structure. The structure (topology) is divided into domains and agents that exchange information about their state only within the domain. The agents belong to the same domain called **neighboring** (interconnected) **agents**. In this case, each agent knows its local state and states of its neighbors. Information exchange is limited by neighboring agents only. Based on local and neighbor-based information, each agent decides on the optimal strategy. The way of topology dividing into domains has great importance when using the MA approach in control. Experiments with the usage of MA optimization for the routing have shown that by adjusting the domain size, it is possible to achieve the optimal combination of convergence and quality optimum solution of the routing problem.

The third option—**independent agents**. Each agent knows its local state. Each agent judges the control strategy and actions of other agents based on its experience. The agent implements control decisions in accordance with its local optimization strategy and based on its observations.

Thus, the choice of approach to MA optimization is another challenge for the problem under consideration. At the same time, it is important to bear in mind that:

a. there are no mathematical models that guarantee convergence to the optimal solution;

b. the constraint of the deviation from the optimal solution is not guaranteed.

6. Application services execution time prediction

6.1 Problem statement

The application services execution time prediction problem can be described in the following way. Let we know $ID(cn)$—ID for every computational node cn, for every w_k and every s^k_j it is known the set of cn computing installations identifiers (IDs), a set of variants of the s^k_j parameters (for more details see below), the amount of resources requested for known executions of the s^k_j with its parameter variants on certain cn node, and the execution time of this s^k_j with its input data variant and on some of $cn \in N$. Neither the source code of the program nor its binary code or the architecture of computer installations are unknown. We emphasize that only the s^k_j execution time is known on some cn nodes but not for each. Further, the application service will be treated simply as a program; for the sake of simplicity of terminology, we will use the term program and denote P_i. Because the set of s^k_j is limited ($|W|$ is finite, any $|w_k|$ is finite), there is a numeration that for every s^k_j defines the unique index i.

We will use the following notations for the problem statement:

1. P_i—unique program ID;

2. $\{P_1, P_2, \dots, P_N\} = \{P_i\}$—the set of *IDs* of programs under consideration;

3. $\{Arg^{(i)}{}_1, Arg^{(i)}{}_2, \dots, Arg^{(i)}{}_{Ai}\} = \{Arg^{(i)}{}_j\}_{j=1}{}^{Ai}$—the set where each $Arg^{(i)}{}_j$ is a set of the values of input parameters program P_i: amount of input data and program environment parameters (number of processes and number of threads). We will call this set as **arguments** of P_i.

4. $[(P_i, Arg^{(i)}{}_1), (P_i, Arg^{(i)}{}_2), (P_i, Arg^{(i)}{}_2) \dots, (P_i, Arg^{(i)}{}_{Ai}), (P_i, Arg^{(i)}{}_1)]$—a history of P_i;

5. cn_i—unique computational node ID;

6. $\{cn_1, cn_2, \dots, cn_N\} = \{cn_i\}_{i=1}{}^{N}$—a set of M unique IDs of computer installations;

By the notions above, the problem statement can be specified as following:

- **Given**

$\{P_i\}_{i=1}{}^{N}$—N program IDs;
$\{Arg^{(i)}{}_j\}_{j=1}{}^{Ai}$—the set of arguments P_i program;
$\{cn_i\}_{i=1}{}^{N}$—computational node IDs;
$V = \{[(P_i, Arg^{(i)}{}_j), cn_k]\}$, where $i = 1,M, j = 1,A_i, k = 1,N$ and $|V| = (\sum_{i=1}^{M} A_i) \bullet N$;
$T(v)$ where v is the partial defined function on V. The values of $T(v)$ is the execution time the program P_i with arguments $Arg^{(i)}{}_j$ on computational node cn_k.

- **Required**

Redefine the values of the function $T(v)$ at the undefined points of V.

The problem of estimating the execution time of a program on a computer is a classic problem that has been known since the 1960s. The problem still exists in many forms, for example, for worst-case execution time estimation and for different computer architectures [12–15]. Different ways for this problem were proposed as analytical [16] and statistical [17], based on program behavior analysis [18], time series prediction [19], and neural networks [20]. Execution time can be predicted from test runs [21]. All algorithms predicting program execution time mentioned above use the history of program executions. Their main drawback is that all of them are applicable only when the histories of program execution are known for the certain computer installation; that is, to predict the execution time on a certain computer installation, there is the need to know the whole history of the program executions on this computer installation.

As we will demonstrate below, to predict the program execution time on some computer nodes, just some running histories of this program on them are sufficient. There is no need to know each program run on each computational node. The accuracy of the prediction depends on the number of program running histories on computer installations from a certain set. To solve the execution time prediction problem, the following technique was used:

1. Let us represent the information about V set and function $T(v)$ as a matrix where each row corresponds to pair $(P_i, Arg^{(i)}{}_j)$ and each column to the computational node cn_k. The intersection of row and column is the execution

time of the corresponding program *Pi* with parameters $Arg^{(i)}{}_j$ on cn_k. We will denote such matrix as *PC*;

2. Form PC^* matrix (matrix closure) by the information about representative set of computer installations and the histories of execution of various programs on these computer installations. By this way, we will get everywhere defined function $T^*(v)$ *on* $V = \{[(P_i, Arg^{(i)}{}_j), cn_k]\}$, where $i = 1, M, j = 1, Ai, k = 1, N;$

3. Delete an arbitrary number of entries from PC^* to get partially defined $T\ (v)$ on the set *V*. Obtain thinned matrix—*PC* matrix.

4. Apply the developed prediction algorithm to redefine the values of the function $T\ (v)$ at uncertain points. This algorithm defines function $Or(v)$ in each point of the set *V*. $Or(v)$ coincides with the function $T\ (v)$ where it is defined and at other points, defines the predicted execution time.

5. Estimate the quality of the results of the developed prediction algorithm by the following metric:

$$PredictionError\left(P_i, Arg^{(i)}{}_j, C_k\right) = (|predict - target|/target) \tag{3}$$

where *predict* is predicted time if program P_i with parameters $Arg^{(i)}{}_j$ on cn_k, *target* is a true execution time of program P_i with the same parameters. *The total prediction error* is calculated as an average of the errors calculated using the Eq. (3) for all programs.

To form the *PC matrix*, the datasets from the website [22] dated 8 *June* 2021 (the datasets on this website are periodically updated) was used. These datasets contain the description of total amount of resources of numerous computer installations and the results of executions of programs with various input parameters. From this site, we took three datasets with execution results of programs as MPI as OpenMP on a wide range of computers. These programs cover numerous application areas [23].

Naturally, the question arises: why, when developing the method for estimating the execution time, MPI programs were taken? The fact is that this class of programs is used primarily on supercomputers. It is well known that the execution time of a supercomputer program is very dependent on its architecture. Therefore, if we manage to develop a time estimation method for this case, then for calculators used in traditional servers, it will certainly be no worse.

The brief description of the selected datasets are presented in **Table 1**.

The used data was uploaded on github in [24] along with the developed algorithm.

Name	Number of computer installations	Number of programs	Type
MPIL2007	180	12	MPI
MPIM2007	437	13	MPI
ACCEL OMP	30	15	OpenMP

Table 1.
Datasets of MPI and OpenMP programs executions on various computer installations from [22].

It has been recognized that the considered problem is very similar to the problems solved in recommender systems, in which matrix decomposition algorithms as in [25] are very widely used in various combinations. The proposed solutions were developed as a combination of several algorithms. They are run in parallel with the same PC matrix, each of which makes its own prediction. At the end, all predictions are averaged. The resulting value is considered the expected execution time of the program. This technique is called ensemble averaging in [26]. Three algorithms were chosen: ridge regression, Pearson correlation, and matrix decomposing.

1. Ridge regression: An unknown execution time of program P_i with parameters $Arg^{(i)}{}_j$ on computer installation cn_k is redefined by ridge regression in [27] based on known execution times of the program P_i with the same parameters on all other computer nodes;

2. Cliques: Firstly, group computer installations using the Pearson correlation coefficient. Secondly, redefine unknown execution time of program P_i with parameters $Arg^{(i)}{}_j$ on computer installation cn_k based on execution times of the group of computer nodes where cn_k belongs.

3. Matrix decomposition: Apply matrix decomposition in [28] of the *PC matrix* in order to fill in empty entries of the *PC matrix*;

4. It has to be noted that if the program was executed with different sets of input parameters, this program is represented by multiple rows in the *PC matrix*.

Ridge regression algorithm is used as is. It is only worth to mention that ridge regression is used to predict the value in empty entries in a row of *PC matrix*. If there is an empty value in a row of the *PC matrix*, this value is prediction using all known values. In fact, the problem of interpolation is solved. If the columns corresponding to the computer installations in the *PC matrix* are ordered by performance (this data can be taken from the description of the computer installations), then this type of regression can get quite well prediction. Ridge regression works well on dense matrices with a small number of empty entries in *PC matrix*.

Pearson correlation is proposed to estimate the proximity of the set of vectors of program execution times. Since the algorithm is used as is and no novelty was introduced into it is just recalled below. The columns of the *PC matrix* are considered as such sets in other words. The correlation between the columns cn_i and cn_j shows how close in performance different computational nodes running these programs are. If the Pearson correlation between these columns is close to 1, then cn_i and cn_j are close to each other from the point of view of performance on the given set of the program executions. In this case, the estimate of the program execution time for cnj can be obtained by multiplying by the constant of the time estimate on the cn_j node.

The procedure for distributing computing nodes into groups consists of the following steps:

1. Calculate Pearson correlation for each pair of columns of the *PC matrix* – $N^*(N\text{-}1)/2$ pairs, where N is the number of computational nodes;

2. Build the graph of cliques:

   a. Each vertex represents *cn*;

   b. An edge between the cn_i and cn_j exists if the Pearson correlation between the corresponding columns in the PC matrix is modulo greater than some threshold. The value of threshold is an algorithm parameter; this way brings us a graph where nodes are cn_i, and arcs are correlated pairs of computational nodes.

3. Find all groups such that any two vertices in the group are connected by an edge. To do this, we use the algorithms from [29, 30].

4. Each group contains computing nodes cn such that the program execution times on different nodes have a linear dependence, that is, one can be obtained from the other by multiplying by some coefficient. It should be borne in mind that the same calculator can be included in different groups.

5. The resulting cliques are groups of computational nodes.

To search for groups, a special algorithm was developed, presented in [24], whose complexity does not exceed H^3, the size of groups is less than $3H^{H/3}$. This algorithm was described with detail in [31].

However, if threshold for the value of Pearson correlation is close to 1, then further prediction algorithm described in [32] is pretty good even if some vertexes in the cliques would be missed.

If it is not possible to calculate Pearson correlation (e.g., the considered program *P* has not been run on any of the computer installations from clique) but corresponding row in *PC matrix* for *P* program is non-empty, then one needs to use ridge regression for the prediction. See step 4 above.

The error of prediction for the algorithm presented above can be estimated by Eq. (3).

Matrix decomposition: Because this stage in the proposed algorithms ensemble we consider as our main contribution to the considered problem, we will spend more space on it description. As mentioned above, the problem of programs execution time prediction is very similar to the problem solved in the recommender systems. In these systems, there are usually two types of objects, the relationships between which are measured. For example, such objects can be users and movies, users and books, users and goods, and so on. The relationship between them is often a measure to what extent the user prefers some movies, books, or goods. It is called goods rating. One can build a rating matrix where the rows (or columns) correspond to movies, books, or goods, and the columns (or rows) correspond to users. This matrix is often sparse, since there are a lot of users and objects, and users cannot physically rate all the objects. The problem that solve the recommender systems, is to determine the ratings of all users for all objects; in other words, the system has to fill in the empty entries in the rating matrix.

Let us consider the following analogy: users are computer installations, the goods are programs, and the ratings are execution times. Thus, the computer installations "rate" the programs, and the smaller rating (execution time), the better the computer installation meets the program.

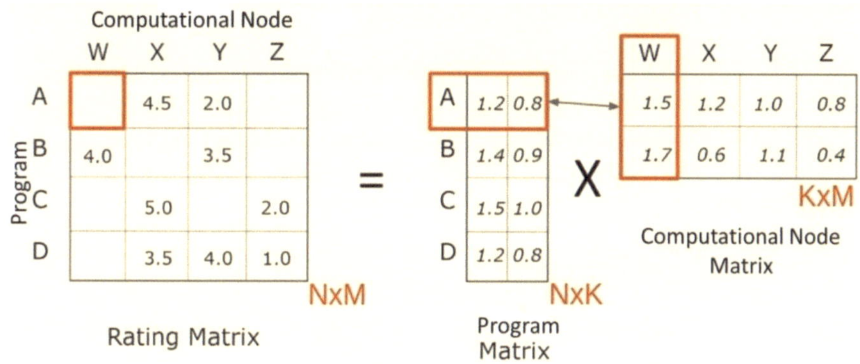

Figure 2.
Matrix decomposition.

The problem of filling empty entries in recommender systems is solved by matrix decomposition method in [23]. We propose to use this technique to solve the problem under consideration.

The application matrix decomposition techniques to some matrix result in two or more matrices, the product of which gives the approximation of the original one. For empty entries of the original matrix, that is, for unknown values, the product of the matrices gives values that estimate the unknown values.

PC matrix decomposition allows one to get a vector representation of programs and computational nodes, which have a remarkable property: the scalar product of the vector representation of the program and the vector representation of the nodes is the program execution time on the node. The vector representations of programs and computational nodes are called as embeddings of programs and computational nodes, respectively. Embedding techniques and methods of applying embeddings are very well-known in such areas as NLP in [33], topic modeling in [34], and recommender systems in [25].

Figure 2 demonstrates matrix decomposition. The rows are programs, and columns are computers that should be rated. The matrix entries are execution times corresponded to the pairs (program, computer). Some entry could be empty. K is a parameter of the decomposition and is a subject of tuning to get the admittable accuracy. The result of the decomposition procedure of rating matrix of size NxM is program matrix of size NxK and computer matrix of size KxM. The rows in program matrix are vectors represented execution times for the program on the corresponded computers. The columns are vector representations of the "computational power" the corresponded computer for the programs under consideration.

In our study, ALS algorithm [35] was selected.

As mentioned above, three algorithms were chosen: ridge regression, Pearson correlation, and matrix decomposition for the program execution time prediction. As it was said previously, the averaging ensemble in [26] of them to improve the accuracy of the predicted execution time was developed. These algorithms can be combined into an ensemble of algorithms to improve the accuracy of the prediction in [26].

6.2 Experimental study

Here, the results of experimental studies of the algorithms compassion are presented.

The purposes of the experiments are analysis of the quality of prediction results:

1. based on grouping computational nodes by the Pearson correlation;

2. based on ALS matrix decomposition algorithm. Selecting the parameter *K*—the number of components in the vector representation of programs and computer installations;

3. by the ensemble of algorithms.

4. the data for experimental study were used from the website *https://spec.org*. The quality of the proposed solution is estimated by the prediction error and prediction accuracy is calculated according to Eq. (3).

6.2.1 Analysis of the quality of prediction based on grouping computer installations by Pearson correlation

Dataset MPIM2007 with 13 programs and 437 computer installations from [22] was used for the experiments. The algorithm based on grouping computer installations by Pearson correlation is very sensitive to the presence of outliers in the data, as well as to what extent the *PC matrix* is low-density. In order to analyze the quality of prediction by this algorithm, three experiments were conducted. As a basic algorithm, the ridge regression algorithm was used. Each experiment was conducted according to the following methodology. In each row, only one value was removed, and then, the prediction was made based on the remaining values in this row of the matrix according to the algorithm above.

In the first experiment, the execution time is predicted by the ridge regression algorithm; as a result, the prediction error was 0.25 or 25%. In the second and third experiments, grouping algorithms based on Pearson correlation were used; threshold for correlation value was 0.97; the grouping resulted in 46 groups with two and more computer installations and 27 groups with only one computer installation. In the second experiment, execution time was predicted only for groups with size greater than or equal to 2; groups with size 1 were ignored. As a result, the prediction error was 0.068 or 6.8%. In the third experiment, execution time was predicted by Pearson correlation algorithm for groups with size greater than or equal to 2, but for groups with size 1, ridge regression algorithm was used. As a result, the prediction error was 0.115 or 11.5%. Thus, the accuracy of prediction on dense matrices is 88.5%.

6.2.2 Analysis of the quality of prediction based on ALS matrix decomposition algorithm

Dataset MPIM2007 with 13 programs and 437 computer installations from [22] was used for the experiments. Experiments were conducted according to the methodology described in Section 4. To study the quality of the predictions based on ALS matrix decomposition algorithm, 4 experiments were made with $K = 1, 2, 3, 4$. The results of the matrix decomposition were compared with each other, as well as with ridge regression algorithm that was chosen as the basic prediction algorithm. In **Figure 2**, *X*-axis is the percentage of empty entries in the *PC matrix* (which randomly was removed from it); *Y*-axis is the prediction error. Also, for comparison, the result of predictions by the Pearson correlation algorithm was added to **Figure 2**. According to the plots in **Figure 2**, the conclusion can be made that the ridge and cliques

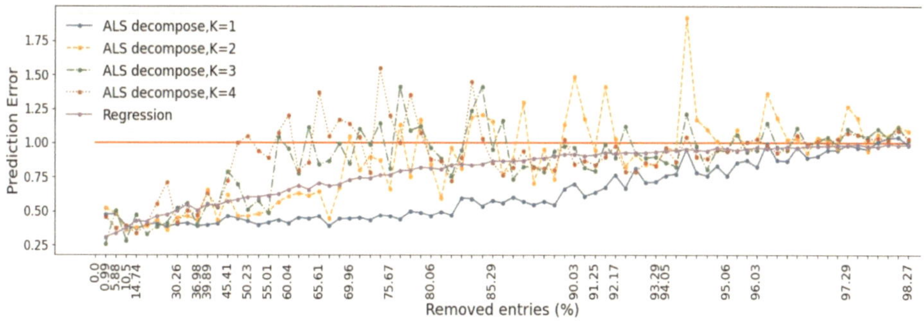

Figure 3.
Ridge regression and ALS matrix decomposition with K = 1, 2, 3, 4.

algorithms work well on dense matrices (up to 1% percentage of empty entries). The matrix decomposition technique with $K = 1$ gives the best results for sparse matrices in which the number of empty entries is more than 15%. Even if 80% of the entries are removed from the *PC matrix*, they can be predicted with an accuracy of 60%.

Thus, as a result of experiments, we can conclude that the matrix decomposition technique with $K = 1$ gives the best solutions when the percentage of empty entries in the *PC matrix* is more than **15%**.

An important advantage of using the matrix decomposition technique is the vector representations (embeddings) of programs, and computer installations in case K = 1 are the points in a space of dimension 1. So, the total ordering on the set of computer installations could be defined, and one can work with them as scalars. **Figure 3** shows the less embedding of computational node, the less execution time of the corresponded program.

6.2.3 Analysis of the prediction quality of an ensemble of algorithms

The ensemble averaging described by (Eq. (3)) was used. The prediction result was compared with the following algorithms: *ridge regression*, *Cliques*, and *ALS* with $K = 1$. All three datasets—MPIL2007, MPIM2007, and ACCEL OMP from [22] were used for the experiments. Experiments were conducted according to the methodology described in Section 4. As we can see in **Figure 3**, the best estimations give us the ALS algorithm when the matrix sparsity is at least 14%. According to **Figure 4**, the ensemble averaging is better when the matrix sparsity is over 14% up to 94%. One more testing of the proposed method was done of the dataset ACCEL OMP that covers 15 programs and 30 computers. The results of this experiment are shown in **Figure 5**.

7. Organization of NPC computing resources

As I presented in [2], the computing node (CN) could be as Edges in [36] as supercomputer or HPC installation. Existing data center construction approaches demand high quality of communication channels service, to ensure availability of service, and very high capital construction costs of a centralized data center. Significant problems of traditional DC are scaling and low level of resource utilization due to the lack of a centralized management system and orchestration system [37].

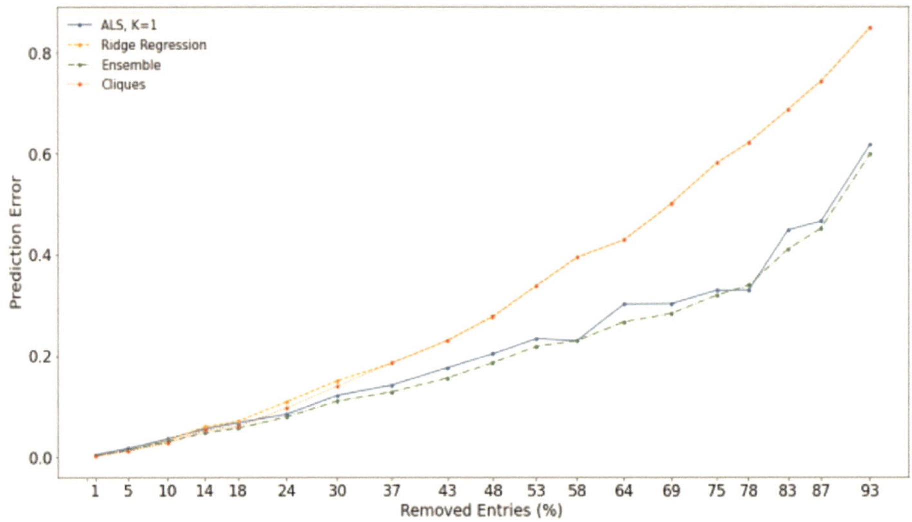

Figure 4.
Results of ridge, cliques, matrix decomposition, and an ensemble of algorithms on MPIM2007 (1–94%).

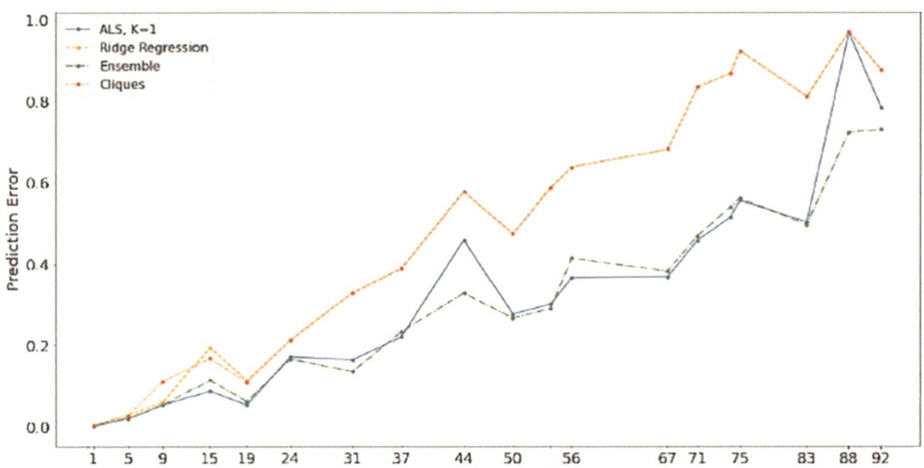

Figure 5.
Results of Ridge, Cliques, Matrix decomposition and an ensemble of algorithms on ACCEL OMP (1–92%).

The advantages of building a NPC based on edges over the traditional approach have been discussed in detail in [38] and characterized by: reduction of transport requirements by proximity of the service copy to the final consumer, reducing the cost of organizing a data center due to the absence of the need to build a centralized data center, efficient scaling through the use of a centralized cloud platform, increasing the efficiency of the network due to a centralized management and orchestration system, and the proximity of the service to the client. The problems of organizing the control plane and the data plane in edges are in many ways similar to those that were already listed above for the NPC Federate DTN control layer (see **Figure 1**). The main difference—the decision-making speed should be much higher.

Another important point is the following. Managing and optimizing power has been a long-standing challenge in computer systems, with many fundamental techniques, and has been increasingly receiving attention. Today, a wide range of applications such as IoT services, ML inference, data analytics, and scientific computing now use Functions as a Service (FaaS) offerings of cloud platforms such as Amazon Lambda, Azure and Google Functions, and so on. Widespread application deployment model has nowadays become serverless computing, where applications are partitioned into small, fine-grained "functions", whose execution is managed by the cloud platform as in [39]. However, the constant evolution of cloud abstractions and usage models poses new energy efficiency challenges.

Serverless features can provide unique opportunities to reduce cloud heat generation by reducing the level of concentration of computing power in a relatively small location and programming model. Many power-saving techniques, such as workload migration and on-demand scaling, that are difficult for regular VMs and containers, can be significantly easier to develop and optimize for serverless functions that can "run anywhere" [40]. In this way, FaaS can provide new power tools for cloud platforms to quickly and finely move applications to environmentally friendly locations, which will be especially useful for distributed cloud edges powered by renewable energy such as solar and wind, as in [41]. The FaaS programming model also allows power management at the functional level. A function can have multiple implementations that differ in power consumption and performance. This may allow the cloud provider to use the appropriate feature implementation based on power availability and application performance constraints. Finally, features are reused, enabling data-driven and machine learning methods such as transfer learning that can be used for general and practical energy management.

One possible approach to energy management is a computing infrastructure model based on the concept of a cloud data center network and cloud edges where computing can be scheduled based on energy consumption. In the FaaS model, functions are not tied to any specific servers or locations and can potentially "run anywhere" as long as the runtime platform has access to the function's code dependencies and the container/VM "image". By separating computing from its location, serverless computing allows us to run functions in the most power-efficient location. This location independence can be an extremely efficient technique for resilient computing but is often challenging for other workloads. Because renewable energy sources (such as solar and wind) can be fickle, the availability of servers powered by them is temporary [42].

AI routing in distributed edge clouds can offer different trade-offs between energy and carbon emissions depending on location, time, and availability of resources and hardware. Functions can be run on the edge to ensure low latency. The trade-off between power consumption and performance adds a new dimension to the discussion of future cloud architectures. While edge clouds may have performance and security/privacy benefits, their energy benefits require further analysis.

As you know, for maximum efficiency of program execution, a certain set of hardware and their configuration is required. Several attempts have already been made to implement the approach of dynamically adapting the architecture to the application, that is, see [32]. Currently, to meet this need, it is proposed to use the resource disaggregation approach in [27]. Its essence is as follows. Data centers have been using the monolithic server model for over 20 years, where each server has a motherboard that houses all types of hardware resources, typically including the processor, memory chips, storage devices, and network cards. Resource disaggregation involves dividing the server's hardware resources into standalone network-connected devices that applications can access remotely. Applications must be given virtualized and secure access to hardware resources, and data centers must support these applications with tools that ensure their good performance.

One of the possible approaches to manage energy consumption and carbon footprint is the computational infrastructure model based on the concept network of cloud DC and cloud edges, where computation can be organized by energy and carbon-based scheduling. In FaaS model, functions are not tied to any specific servers or locations and can potentially be "run anywhere", as long as the execution platform has access to the function's code dependencies and the container/VM "image". By decoupling computation from its location, serverless computing allows us to run functions at the most energy-suitable location. Thus, even though individual functions may not be energy efficient, they can be run in carbon-friendly locations to achieve better carbon efficiency. This location independence can be an extremely potent technique for sustainable computing, but is often challenging for other workloads. Since renewable energy (such as solar and wind) can be intermittent, the availability of servers powered by them is only transient [42].

AI routing in distributed edge clouds can offer different energy/carbon trade-offs depending on location, time, and resource and hardware availability. Functions can be run on the edge to provide low latency. The energy versus performance trade-off adds a new dimension to the discussion on future cloud architectures. While edge clouds may have performance and security/privacy advantages, their energy benefits need additional analysis.

In the history of computer architecture, there have been many attempts to make the architecture of computers dynamically adoptable to the structure of the algorithm of the program that it executes [32]. However, all of them were not very successful. Currently, a new direction is gaining momentum—resource disaggregation. This direction does not use the monolithic model of server that hosts all types of hardware resources like CPU cores, memory chips, storages, and NCIs. In resource disaggregation, server is split on individual devices connected by a high-speed network. The user can choose the architecture for the virtual machine and the configuration of individual devices to ensure the most efficient execution of his applications. Application has virtualized and reliable access to all devices. This approach to computer architecture requires a rethinking of the concept of the operating system. The traditional view of it has already become obsolete. But this is a topic for a separate post.

8. Conclusion

The Network Powered by Computing (NPC) concept of next generation computational infrastructure was presented. This concept based on the convergence of data communication networks with computing facilities like DC, edge, and HPC centers united by the functional architecture is presented in the article. The NPC concept is the incarnation of the slogan I got from Jhon Gadge from Sun Microsystems: "Network is a computer". Here, we considered the functional architecture of NPC, and the main problems on the way of its implementation are described. The presented concept allows to achieve deep automation in the management of resources of this infrastructure, load distribution, and energy consumption through the use of methods based on machine learning algorithms.

The issue of organizing the ASNF layer, which, together with the OAM and the NPCIC layers, is essentially new generation of the operating environment—an analogue of the traditional operating system. But this is an independent, large topic that requires a separate publication.

Acknowledgements

The author is grateful to Professor V. Korolev and Professor A. Borisov who read the manuscript and gave suggestions for its improvement and to Ph.D. student Andrey Chupakhin, who performed the entire cycle of experiments to evaluate the proposed method for predicting MPI program execution time.

Also, thanks to Marina Trukhova who helped a lot with shaping the text of this paper.

Conflict of interest

The author declares no conflict of interest.

Author details

Ruslan Smeliansky
Department of Computational Mathematics and Cybernetics, Moscow State University, Moscow, Russia

*Address all correspondence to: smel@cs.msu.su

References

[1] Hennessy JL, David A. Patterson. A new golden age for computer architecture. Communication of the ACM. 2019;**62**(2):48-60

[2] Smeliansky R. Network powered by computing. In: International Conference on Modern Network Technologies (MoNeTec). 2022. pp. 1-5. DOI: 10.1109/MoNeTec55448.2022.9960771

[3] Smeliansky R. Hierarchical edge computing. In: Proceedings of International Scientific and Technical Conference Modern Computer Network Technologies (MoNeTeC). 2018. pp. 1-11. DOI: 10.1109/MoNeTeC.2018.8572272

[4] Topology and Orchestration Specification for Cloud Applications [Internet]. Available from: http://docs.oasis-open.org/tosca/TOSCA/v1.0/os/TOSCA-v1.0-os.html [Accessed: December 10, 2022]

[5] Elasticity [Internet]. Available from: https://wa.aws.amazon.com/wellarchitected/2020-07-02T19-33-23/wat.concept.elasticity.en.html [Accessed: December 13, 2022]

[6] "What is Serverless Computing?" ITPro Today. December 13, 2021 [Retrieved: 23 March 23, 2022]

[7] Smeliansky R. MC2E: The environment for interdisciplinary research. Engineering Letters. 2021;**6**: 40-54

[8] Demonstration of the Bandwidth on Demand Application Based on the SDN Controller RunOS [Internet]. 2021. Available from: https://www.youtube.com/watch?v=TuzDDZT4NL4 [Accessed: December 11, 2022

[9] Total Datacenter Power [Internet] Available from: https://451research.com/total-data-management Accessed: 2022-12-12]

[10] Albert-László Barabási Network Science. Chapter 3 [Internet]. Available from: http://networksciencebook.com/chapter/3#degree-distribution

[11] Albert-László Barabási Network Science. The Barabási-Albert Model [Internet]. Available from: https://barabasi.com/f/622.pdf

[12] Random Forest Algorithm [Internet] [Online]. Available from: https://www.stat.berkeley.edu/breiman/RandomForests/cc home.htm [Accessed: April 4, 2022]

[13] Gonzalez MTA. Performance Prediction of Application Executed on GPUs Using a Simple Analytical Model and Machine Learning Techniques [Online]. 2018. Available from: http://doi.org/10.11606/t.45.2018.tde-06092018-213258 [Accessed: April 4, 2022]

[14] Snavely A, Carrington L, Wolter N, Labarta J, Badia R. A framework for performance modeling and prediction, SC '02. In: Proceedings of the 2002 ACM/IEEE Conference on Supercomputing. Baltimore, MD, USA; 2002. pp. 21-21. DOI: 10.1109/SC.2002.10004

[15] Nadeem F, Alghazzawi D, Mashat A, Fakeeh K, Almalaise A, Hagras H. Modeling and predicting execution time of scientific workflows in the grid using radial basis function neural network. Cluster Computing. 2017;**20**(3): 2805-2819. DOI: 10.1007/s10586-017-1018-x

[16] Yero EJH, Henriques MAA. Contention-sensitive static performance prediction for parallel distributed applications. Performance Evaluation. 2006;**63**(4):265-277

[17] Wu Q, Datla VV. On performance modeling and prediction in support of scientific workflow optimization. In: Proceedings of the 2011 IEEE World Congress on Services, SERVICES '11, IEEE Computer Society. 2011. pp. 161-168

[18] Li H, Groep D, Templon J, Wolters L. Predicting job start times on clusters. In: CCGRID '04 in Proceedings of the 2004 IEEE International Symposium on Cluster Computing and the Grid. 2004. pp. 301-308

[19] Liu X, Chen J, Liu K, Yang Y. Forecasting duration intervals of scientific workflow activities based on time-series patterns. In: Proceedings of the IEEE Fourth International Conference on eScience, eScience '08. 2008. pp. 23-30

[20] Lee BC, Brooks DM, de Supinski BR, Schulz M, Singh K, Mckee SA. Methods of inference and learning for performance modeling of parallel applications. In: Proceedings of the 12th ACM SIGPLAN Symposium on Principles and Practice of Parallel Programming, PPoPP '07. 2007. pp. 249-258

[21] Yang LT, Ma X, Mueller F. Cross-platform performance prediction of parallel applications using partial execution. In: Proceedings of the 2005 ACM/IEEE Conference on Supercomputing, SC '05, IEEE Computer Society. 2005. pp. 40-44

[22] Standard Performance Evaluation Corporation [Internet]. 2021, Available from: https://spec.org [Accessed: December 10, 2022]

[23] Benchmark Documentation [Internet]. Available from: https://spec.org/mpi2007/Docs/ [Accessed: December 13, 2022]

[24] MPI Program Execution Time Prediction Algorithms from the Article. IFIP Networking 2022 SLICES Workshop [Internet]. Available from: https://github.com/andxeg/ [Accessed: December 11, 2022]

[25] Ricci F, Rokach L, Shapira B, Kantor PB. Recommender System Hanbook [Internet] [Online]. Available from: https://link.springer.com/book/10.1007/978-0-387-85820-3 [Accessed: April 4, 2022]

[26] Dzˇeroski S, Panov P, Zˇ enko B. Machine learning, ensemble methods. In: Meyers R, editor. Encyclopedia of Complexity and Systems Science. New York: Springer; 2009

[27] Ridge Regression [Internet] [Online]. Available from: https://www.ncss.com/wp-content/themes/ncss/pdf/Procedures/NCSS/Ridge_Regression.pdf [Accessed: April 4, 2022]

[28] Cheng CM, Jin XQ. Matrix decomposition. In: Alhajj R, Rokne J, editors. Encyclopedia of Social Network Analysis and Mining. New York, NY: Springer; 2018

[29] Skiena SS. Clique and Independent Set and Clique. §6.2.3 and 8.5.1: The Algorithm Design Manual. New York: Springer-Verlag; 1997. p. 144 and pp. 312–314

[30] Johnston, H.C. Cliques of a graph-variations on the Bron-Kerbosch algorithm. International Journal of Computer and Information Sciences 5,

209-238 1976. Available from: https://doi.org/10.1007/BF00991836 [Accessed: December 10, 2022]

[31] Chupakhin A, Kolosov A, Smeliansky R, Antonenko V. New approach to MPI program execution time prediction. 10.48550/arXiv.2007.15338

[32] Smeliansky RL, Antonenko VA, Stepanov EP, Chupakhin AA, Kolosov AM. Chapter 1: On HPC and cloud environments integration. In: Performance Evaluation Models for Distributed Service Networks. Cham, Switzerland: Springer Nature Switzerland AG; 2020

[33] Li Y, Yang T. Word embedding for understanding natural language: A survey. In: Srinivasan S, editor. Guide to Big Data Applications. Studies in Big Data. Vol. 26. Cham: Springer; 2018

[34] Aggarwal CC. Matrix factorization and topic modeling. In: Machine Learning for Text. Cham: Springer; 2018

[35] Gabor Takacs and Domonkos Tikk. Alternating least squares for personalized ranking. In Proceedings of the Sixth ACM Conference on Recommender Systems (RecSys '12). Association for Computing Machinery. New York, NY, USA; 2012. pp. 83-90. Available from: https://doi.org/10.1145/2365952.2365972 [Accessed: December 11, 2022]

[36] Brun R, Urban L, Carminati F, Giani S, Maire M, McPherson A, Patrick G. 1993. GEANT: de tector description and simulation tool No. CERN-W-5013. CERN

[37] Masanet E, Shehabi A, Lei N, Smith S, Koomey J. Recalibrating global data center energy-use estimates. Science. 2020:**367**(6481):984-986

[38] Antonenko V, Petrov I, Smeliansky RL, Huang Z, Chen M, Cao D, et al. MC2E: Meta-cloud computing environment for HPC. In: Performance Evaluation Models for Distributed Service Networks. Cham, Switzerland: Springer Nature Switzerland AG; 2019

[39] Schleier-Smith J, Sreekanti V, Khandelwal A, Carreira J, Yadwadkar NJ, Popa RA, et al. What serverless computing is and should become: The next phase of cloud computing. Communications of the ACM. 2021;**64**:7684

[40] Prateek Sharma Indiana University Bloomington [Internet]. Challenges and Opportunities in Sustainable Serverless Computing. Available from: https://cgi.luddy.indiana.edu/~prateeks/papers/hotcarbon22.pdf [Accessed: December 10, 2022]

[41] Chien AA. Driving the cloud to true zero carbon. Communications of the ACM. Jan. 2021:**64**(2):5-5

[42] Singh R, Sharma P, Irwin D, Shenoy P, Ramakrishnan K. Here today, gone tomorrow: Exploiting transient servers in data centers. IEEE Internet Computing. 2014;**18**

Chapter 4

Perspective Chapter: Cloud Lock-in Parameters – Service Adoption and Migration

Justice Opara-Martins

Abstract

ICT has been lauded as being revolutionised by cloud computing, which relieves businesses of having to make significant capital investments in ICT while allowing them to connect to incredibly potent computing capabilities over the network. Organisations adopt cloud computing as a way to solve business problems, not technical problems. As such, organisations across Europe are eagerly embracing cloud computing in their operating environments. Understanding cloud lock-in parameters is essential for supporting inter-cloud cooperation and seamless information and data exchange. Achieving vendor-neutral cloud services is a fundamental requirement and a necessary strategy to be fulfilled in order to enable portability. This chapter highlights technical advancements that contribute to the interoperable migration of services in the heterogeneous cloud environment. A set of guidelines and good practices were also collected and discussed, thus providing strategies on how lock-in can be mitigated. Moreover, this chapter provides some recommendations for moving forward with cloud computing adoption. To make sure the migration and integration between on-premise and cloud happen with minimal disruption to business and results in maximum sustainable cost benefit, the chapter's contribution is also designed to provide new knowledge and greater depth to support organisations around the world to make informed decisions.

Keywords: vendor lock-in, security, ICT, cloud computing, parallel computing, IaC, Kubernetes, micro-services, terraform, Kotlin

1. Introduction

Cloud computing is a ubiquitous model for enabling network users' on-demand access to a shared pool of configurable computing resources that can be rapidly provisioned and released to the client without direct service provider interaction [1]. A cloud service provider is a party that makes cloud services available. Cloud computing technology is a new solution giving users the option to access software and information and communication technology (ICT) resources with the desired flexibility and modularity and at very competitive prices. In 2010, 80% of the US economy was driven by the service industry. But while there is more flexibility available in the cloud, there is a risk you can become dependent on the products and services from particular providers.

Cloud computing benefits the service industry the most and advances business computing with a new paradigm. As pointed out by Brynjolfsson et al. [2], the real strength of cloud computing is that it is a catalyst for more innovation. To assist corporations to adopt cloud computing services, Sahandi et al. [3] affirm that much research on cloud computing has concentrated on two broad areas: (i) business agility and (ii) catalysts for more innovation. The focus of this writing is to study both high-performance computing (HPC) for scientific computing and high-throughput computing (HTC) systems for business computing. Although many of the concepts do not appear to be new, the real innovation of cloud computing lies in the way it provides computing services to customers [3]. Further, this research examines clusters, massively parallel processors (MPP), grids, peer-to-peer (P2P) networks and internet clouds. These systems are distinguished by their platform architectures, operating system (OS) platforms, processing algorithms, communication protocols, security demands and service models applied. The study emphasises scalability, performance, availability, security, energy-efficiency, workload outsourcing, data centre protection, etc. The surge of interest when installing virtual machines (VMs) has widened the scope of system applications and upgraded computer performance and efficiency in recent years. An internet cloud of resources can be either a centralised or a distributed computing system. Cloud computing architecture relies on virtualisation techniques that create multiple virtual environments [3]. Parallel, distributed or both types of computing are used in the cloud. Clouds can be constructed using real or virtualised resources over sizeable, distributed or centralised data centres. A sort of utility computing or service computing, according to some authors [4, 5], is cloud computing. Cloud computing is used to equip virtual machines as central storage and processors to avoid ICT equipment costs in organisations or homes.

For example, using a cloud provider to manage your storage lifecycle might lead to lock-in, and it will reduce the work required to manage your service. Accepting some lock-in brings advantages that seem counter-intuitive, but one should balance this benefit of cloud lock-in against potential risks, so one can get the best value and reduce the burden of future legacy technology. By designing them as virtual resources over automated hardware, databases, user interfaces and application environments, clouds hope to power the next generation of data centres. In this way, the ambition to create better data centres through automated provisioning gives rise to clouds. ICT infrastructure is now shifting from locally managed software-enabled platforms and physical hardware to outsourced virtual infrastructure managed by cloud service providers [6]. But risks concerning security, privacy, financial aspects and the wider organisation are vital and require serious consideration before a cloud migration. In order to efficiently come to the correct decision about cloud migration with respect to business needs (as per lock-in avoidance), an organisation should be able to objectively consider the aggregated risks of cloud adoption. According to Khajeh-Hosseini et al. [7], it is emphasised that there is a need for guidelines and decision support tools for enterprises that are considering migrating their ICT systems to the cloud. The necessity of a comprehensive migration framework to support organisations through the migration decision cannot be overemphasised [8]. The process of cloud migration is therefore a complex undertaking, depending on many factors that contribute both for and against a decision to migrate.

Cloud technology has resulted in a variety of implementations and solutions where each vendor defines their own interfaces and approaches for similar products and services, which has resulted in heterogeneity application platform infrastructure (APIs) and libraries. These APIs complicate integration efforts for companies of all sizes and locations as they struggle to understand and then manage these unique application interfaces in an interoperable way, and integrate applications from cloud to cloud and cloud to on-premise systems [9]. The concept of cloud computing has evolved from cluster, grid and utility computing. Cluster and grid computing leverage the use of many computers in parallel to solve problems of any size. In order to offer a wide variety of services to end users, cloud computing makes use of dynamic resources. A big data centre or server farm serves as the infrastructure in the cloud computing high-throughput computing (HTC) paradigm. Through a linked device, users can share access to resources at any time and from any location thanks to the cloud model. According to Foster et al. [10], cloud computing leverages multitasking to achieve higher throughput by serving heterogeneous applications, large or small, simultaneously. From another perspective, the cloud computing environment assigns due importance to good governance and the integrity of systems and data. While research confirms the widespread adoption and usage of cloud computing services across enterprises, arguably it should be said primarily of cloud computing as a business phenomenon rather than a technological one [11]. Moreover, a corporation can benefit from cloud computing in two different ways: directly through lower expenses and indirectly by being able to concentrate more emphasis on key business tasks. Cloud computing is a promising endeavour with the potential to offer financial benefits to an organisation [12].

The rest of this chapter is structured as follows. Section 2 reviews the state of the art in the domain of cloud computing lock-in solutions. Through this review, a set of guidelines are extracted that a vendor-neutral cloud service should follow in order to mitigate lock-in risks. Section 3 introduces parameters and discusses its core dimensions. Section 4 confirms the set of guidelines to follow for a successful intra-cloud migration with low switching costs (customizability). Section 5 summarises good practices and guidelines for building a standardised infrastructure, portable data structures and interoperable platforms. Finally, Section 6 concludes this chapter by discussing the research findings and future work.

2. Related work

In the study by Opara-Martins [8], the author has shown that the complexity of vendor lock-in that exists in the cloud environment, with the complexity of service offerings, makes it imperative for businesses to use a clear and well-understood decision process to procure, migrate and/or discontinue cloud services. Some of the existing cloud solutions for public and private companies are vendor locked-in by design, and their existence is subject to limited interoperate with other cloud systems [13]. There are several works that highlight vendor lock-in as a concern for cloud adoption and migration. The goal of this research is to gain a comprehensive understanding of the type of solution and motivation driving widespread adoption of cloud computing across institutions, enterprises and government parastatals. The approach of cloud computing is practical due to the combination of security features and online services. Cloud computing continues to be one of the most vital and fast-growing models of ICT. Researchers and practitioners have been actively reporting solutions and motivation with this new technology. The use of a specific cloud service during an application design may affect its maintenance and forthcoming migration requirements. The effort required to migrate an application from one cloud environment to another varies depending on the particular cloud service that it consumes. Any organisation that is considering the adoption of cloud services must start by identifying the type of cloud service components it intends to take advantage of before starting plans for integration with existing enterprise networks. Therefore, enterprises' capability to ease switchability between cloud providers without any lock-in effect is important for its decision-making regarding service model adoption [14].

Prior to adopting cloud computing services, organisations must fully understand the impact they will have on existing business processes. The cloud service agreement is a documented agreement between the cloud service provider and cloud service customer that governs the covered services, while the cloud service level agreement is a part of the cloud service agreement that includes cloud service level objectives (i.e. commitment a cloud service provider makes for specific, quantitative characteristics of a cloud service. Where the value follows the interval scale or ratio scale) and cloud service qualitative objectives for the covered cloud service(s). Cloud service qualitative objective is the commitment a cloud service provider makes for a specific, qualitative characteristic of a cloud service, where the value follows the interval scale or ordinal scale. Therefore, a service level agreement (SLA) is a critical part of any service-oriented vendor contract. An SLA serves as an intermediary between the cloud service provider and a client organisation, while a cloud service broker is a service between cloud service customers and cloud service providers, in which the cloud service broker arbitrates, delivers and manages the cloud services from cloud service providers to cloud service customers. The SLA management is involved during the establishment of a cloud service agreement and manages cloud SLA by monitoring cloud services for cloud service level objective to verify the service level, by detecting failures to meet the terms of the cloud SLA through monitoring and by providing agreed remedies for failures to meet the terms of the cloud SLA. Cloud computing has the potential to transform a large part of the ICT industry, making software even more attractive as a service and shaping the way ICT hardware is designed and purchased. Cloud services exist under a shared security environment and both cloud service providers and users contribute to the overall security [15]. Thus, a less secure cloud service provider can lock-in users by providing the means for creating value within the security umbrella. Cloud computing presents an added level of risk because essential services are often outsourced to a third party, which makes it harder to maintain data security and privacy, support data and services availability and demonstrate compliance.

A cloud computing system typically consists of the following components: data, applications, platforms and infrastructure. Data are the machine-processable representation of information stored in computer storage. Applications are computer programs that carry out tasks associated with solving business issues. Platforms are computer programs that enable applications and carry out generic, non-business-related tasks. Physical resources for processing, storage and communication make up the infrastructure. A data model that specifies the data's structure and includes metadata that the application can use to interpret elements of the data is the application data. Therefore, unless an application is standalone, the effort is needed to integrate it into a system. The degree of interoperability of an application can be measured as its cost of integration. Hence, understanding the theoretical framework described in this study is an important first step in understanding the remainder of the cloud lock-in parameters. Overall, a detailed understanding of these areas is required in the research field in order to make the correct decisions concerning cloud migration.

The research approach used in this study is mixed methods. Opara-Martins [8] carried out a study on cloud vendor lock-in from 2012 to 2016. In the survey, technical experts from a wide range of organisations were asked about their use of cloud computing. The 114 business respondents, who represent organisations of various sizes in numerous industry verticals, include technical executives, managers and practitioners. Respondents are firms from a wide range of cloud-related industries, including both providers and consumers of cloud lock-in solutions. The survey also shows that as computing resources move from on-premise to the cloud environment, aspects like a contract (also referred to as commercial) lock-in are exacerbated to further complicate decision-making for/or against cloud adoption. Specifically, in this work [16], the author(s) discussed a number of technical and organisational factors that should be taken into account in order to assist businesses in enhancing their security posture, identifying and mitigating privacy-specific controls, and maintaining the flexibility to easily switch cloud providers (i.e., avoid lock-in), we will talk about a number of technical and organisational factors worth taking into consideration. This will increase ICT agility and business continuity. Their answers provide a comprehensive perspective on the state of the cloud today. The next section takes an unusual approach to further this study, whereas the subsections discuss the background and motivation for this study.

2.1 Background

Vendor lock-in is a topic of intense discussion in the ICT industry, and the general business community is now paying more attention to it. On the one hand, those who support open-source technology highlight the avoidance of vendor lock-in as a fundamental benefit. On the other hand, there are cloud service providers and suppliers of proprietary software who claim that vendor lock-in is nothing to worry about. Vendor lock-in has, according to some, always existed, and they are right. You will essentially be 'locked in' to the data centre operator, the hardware provider and, in the end, your engineer who operates and maintains it, even if you employ an engineer to create a specific solution internally. Any modification to such components will raise risks, extend project duration and raise costs. You might call this a lock-in. A growing problem is locating existing tools or adopting new ones that can lessen the effects of vendor lock-in. According to Satzger et al. [17], there are three types of solutions that have been suggested to mitigate vendor lock-in for the cloud, namely: (i) standards [18]; (ii) abstraction layers and adapters [19] and (iii) reducing accidental complexity, by adopting semantics and model-based solutions [20]. Based on these assertions, the chapter's contribution is also intended to provide new knowledge and greater depth to support organisations around the world in making informed decisions, ensuring that the migration and integration between on-premise and cloud happen with minimal disruption to business and results in maximum sustainable cost benefit.

2.2 Motivation

Fear of vendor lock-in is one of the main motivators for a multi-cloud strategy. When a consumer is 'locked in' to a single vendor for goods and services, it signifies that transferring to another vendor would be prohibitively expensive or disruptive to operations. Going all-in with a single vendor may enable you to streamline processes, increase your agility and maybe improve quality as single-vendor solutions are frequently better integrated. So, even while vendor lock-in has advantages in a perfect world, there is a serious potential for exorbitant expenditures. There are other issues as well, the technology you adore may be placed on hold or eliminated entirely when you are locked in since you are totally dependent on your vendor to drive innovation. This is particularly risky in our current 'as a service' world, when providers can decide to discontinue their product at any time, leaving you with few options and no time to transfer. Although utilising a single cloud provider plainly results in some dependence, you can migrate your data to any environment of your choice and only pay for the services you use. Therefore, your applications should be created or moved to be as flexible and loosely connected as possible to reduce the danger of vendor lock-in. The application components that communicate with cloud application components should be loosely coupled to them. Adopt a multi-cloud strategy as well. Consider putting the majority of your workloads in one cloud and the rest in another if your business requires the use of many vendors and the ensuing complexity is worth it. This will guarantee that you get some experience without suffering any negative effects. Additionally, if possible, employ automation to streamline processes and ensure consistency as later discussed in this chapter.

3. Systematic initial review

The author has carried out a systematic initial review (SIR) of the existing literature regarding cloud lock-in, not only in order to summarise the existing solutions and motivations concerning this area of specialty but also to identify and analyse the current state and the most important areas for cloud computing. The aim of the SIR is to identify and relate gaps in knowledge as it pertains to cloud lock-in with possible solutions for the advancement of this knowledge domain.

Understanding what lock-in parameters are in cloud computing will help organisations to make the shift towards the cloud since it leverages many technologies and it also inherits their heterogeneous features. As described in this chapter, storage, applications, data, virtualisation and networks are the largest lock-in areas in cloud computing. Providers, end users and developers should consider the lock-in areas to take good advantage of the cloud. It is also essential to analyse compatibility issues such as database schema semantics and data types of the database so that there are no inconsistencies between the database layer before and after cloud migration.

Requirements for open, interoperable standards for cloud management interfaces and protocols, data and data formats will develop as more businesses create cloud adoption strategies and execution plans. As a result, cloud service providers will be under pressure to base their offerings on open, interoperable standards in order to be given serious consideration by businesses. Cloud computing promises to make switching to a different provider quick and easy, but that is only possible if users are careful to avoid provider lock-in. The reason because standards influence choice and choice influences the market, standard-based cloud services are essential for the development and dissemination of this paradigm. Third-party suppliers will be allowed to create and provide value-added management capabilities in the form of separate cloud management solutions in the presence of standards-based cloud offers. Vendors who already have ICT management tools available on the market would leverage such products to manage cloud solutions and hybrid cloud deployment. Due to the heterogeneity of the runtime environments, there are extra compatibility concerns when creating hybrid clouds based on legacy hardware and virtual public infrastructure. The X86 machine mode is supported by hypervisors, which can be a technical hurdle to a seamless transfer from private to public contexts.

In cloud lock-in conditions, a big installed base of a client is kept within the virtual infrastructure of one vendor, who does not reveal the intervals of their system, preventing the customer from shifting their installed base to another provider without incurring a significant fee. The cloud service customer is a party that is in the business relationship for the purpose of using cloud services. Since most cloud offerings are proprietary, customers adopting the according services or adapting their respective applications to those environments are explicitly bound to the respective provider and other necessary parameters to support the migration. The amount of work a user is willing to put into transferring their skills to another environment, which typically involves reprogramming the corresponding programs limits their ability to move between providers. This makes the user dependent on both the provider's success and failure, as leaning too much on a single source might have major negative effects on service use [21]. In this respect, dependency, lock-in, privacy and security have been identified as a hurdle to cloud computing in companies and have been discussed in subsequent sections. The next subsection details the pragmatic approach used in this study.

3.1 Philosophical approach

Adopting cloud computing is a complex decision involving many factors [12]. Although cloud-based offers are proliferating on the web and there is competition among cloud computing services, the rules and standards governing cloud computing are insufficient to provide customers with conditions of use ensuring that they will not experience lock-in situations or dependency with regard to the cloud computing providers. In fact, a client or another provider cannot always use the data formats and application interfaces used by a cloud computing service. Similarly, users want to be able to recover their data whenever they wish, without distortion or loss. Also, when it comes to recovering disputed data, the laws in the region where the data are physically located may present difficulties (act). All of these factors highlight the need for rules and standards that enable the interoperability and reversibility of the cloud computing ecosystem. The long-term development of cloud computing depends on this. Here again, it is evident that circumstances change, however, and as they become complex the simplifications can fail. However, this does not automatically imply that all new economic models brought about by cloud computing, whether for cloud service providers or for cloud service users, systematically guarantee significant financial gains. Due to the complexity of the cloud computing model, as it has been presently proposed, various outcomes of the corresponding economic analyses regarding the costs and benefits associated with adopting a cloud computing model have been found. This chapter is based on the *CYNEFIN* (pronounced ku-nev-in) framework, which allows executives to see things from new viewpoints, assimilate complex concepts, and address real-world problems and opportunities. The framework divides the problems that leaders face into five contexts based on how cause and effect relationships differ: four of these simple, complicated, complex and chaotic-demand that leaders analyse circumstances and take necessary action. When it is difficult to determine which of the other four contexts is dominating, the fifth context disorder applies [22].

Executives can avoid problems that arise when their preferred management style causes them to make poor decisions by using the CYNEFIN framework to help them to identify the context in which they are operating. The author's focus in this chapter is on the fifth context since the disorder is not uncommon in the cloud computing business world and this writing concentrates particularly on that context. Moreover, leaders who understand that the world is often irrational and unpredictable will find the *CYNEFIN* framework particularly useful and disorder makes it difficult to recognise when one is in it. Effective leaders learn to shift their decision-making to match changing business environments.

Cloud environments provide a powerful and flexible computing option for many researchers. Now is the time for organisations and institutions to reassess, and in many cases, readjust their approaches to take full advantage of the agility, speed, scalability and availability of the cloud at a time when such capabilities are more important than ever. So when you look at cloud computing through an ethicist's eye, an economist's eye or with a policy dimension the impact of the decisions, we take now will have economic and societal impacts for generations to come [23]. In the following section, author will demystify the cloud paradigm with substantial evidence and undeniable facts.

4. What is in the 'Cloud'

The survey report conducted by Sahandi et al. [3] revealed that 25.1% of participants were not sure about the term cloud computing; therefore, this section fills in this gap by providing substantial evidence on what the 'cloud' literally means. This is important because the increase of cloud computing understanding is expected to accelerate cloud adoption by enterprises. Cloud separates application and information resources from the underlying infrastructure, and the mechanisms used to deliver them. Cloud computing, more specifically, refers to the use of a set of services, applications, information and infrastructure made up of pools of compute, network, information and storage resources that can be quickly orchestrated, provisioned, implemented and decommissioned, as well as scaled up or down, enabling on-demand utility-like (as in electricity) models of allocation and consumption. More discussion, from the standpoint of the introduction, is focused on how the cloud differs from and is similar to the current computing models, as well as how these similarities and differences affect organisational, operational and technological approaches to network and information security practices. The keys to understanding how cloud architecture affects lock-in parameters are a common, succinct vocabulary, along with a consistent taxonomy [24], of offerings, by which cloud services and architecture can be dissected, mapped to a method of compensating security and operational controls, risk assessment and management frameworks and ultimately to business process compliance standards. Cloud is usually the preferred option when organisations procure new ICT services, as reflected in the UK government's cloud first policy. Against this background, it is essential that new services are chosen and built in a way that reflects their security needs. The European Council (EC) has pushed cloud computing because it may make cutting-edge software and services affordable for SMEs and other customers, driving the digitalisation of society and the economy. The US National Institute for Standards and Technology's (NIST) most official explanation of the cloud model explains why cloud computing is often likened to a utility model, similar to electricity or gas distribution. However, the cloud model is also widely used by universities and research centres for scientific computing and by governments for online public services. As companies continue to pursue the cloud for data processing needs, cloud data centres are becoming the new enterprise data repository. CSA [25] report suggests that consumers' understanding of the cloud has matured and signals a technology landscape where consumers are actively considering cloud migration.

The cloud is a service from the user's point of view. However, the architecture for cloud service providers, integrators and channel partners who build or construct the cloud is made up of numerous cloud computing components. Hypervisors, cloud operating system components and other such cloud components are examples of, virtual desktop infrastructure platforms, cloud dedicated firewalls, etc. The most basic cloud computing is the operating system (OS). Through the utilisation of virtualisation technology, cloud OS virtualised hardware resources of physical servers and storage area network devices and supported software-defined networking. Cloud OS enhances the performance and security of cloud computing systems as well as the user experience of administrators and users. Cloud is a primary accelerator of innovation. As pointed out in ITU [26], understanding the emerging trend in ICT services known as cloud computing is a requirement for businesses to successfully utilise it and all of its advantages. Before implementing the cloud concept, it is frequently necessary to obtain specialised knowledge in the areas of data centre administration and commercial interactions.

Cloud simplifies rapid application development, allowing resources to scale on demand with flexible, consumption-based billing models. Migrating to the cloud also allows enterprises to implement turnkey solutions that use consistent processes and protocols while ensuring regulatory and business process compliance. Despite the benefits of the cloud, any change brings new risks. Ultimately, cloud services offer organisations and research institutes security protection beyond anything an individual agency could deliver in-house. Although the cloud may be secure in and of itself, it is still the organisation's job to ensure the security of applications developed and deployed to production in the cloud. Because there are many different types of code and application building blocks to secure while developing cloud-native applications, application security safeguards enterprise data. When working with cloud products and services, the remaining section of this chapter is aimed at providing businesses with recommendations on how to best achieve portability and interoperability. As cloud standards customer council [27] concurs that the lack of portability and interoperability between components of cloud solutions could mean that the potential business benefits of cloud computing are not met.

Cloud computing is one of the enablers of the European Commission Digital Strategy (ECDS) transformation [28]. The European Commission (EC) has promoted cloud computing towards companies and public administrations alike since the adoption of the first European cloud computing strategy in 2012. Cloud first with a secure hybrid multi-cloud service offering is the EC's vision for cloud computing. The cloud first approach implies that any development should preferably be cloud-native, and existing information systems would be reassessed for transformation, rewiring or replacement within the context of the modernisation plans foreseen by the ECDS, setting the opportunities arising in the business and application lifecycle. Cloud computing relies on the sharing of resources to achieve coherence and economies of scale, similar to a public utility. The international market for cloud services has led to the development of a new paradigm for transformational programming in which cloud-native information systems are constructed without reference to the underlying ICT infrastructure on top of a variety of cloud-based services. Code written at a much higher abstraction level results in a large reduction in the amount of code required to achieve the same functionality. This reduced code base enables faster rewrites to adapt to changes, boosts agility, lowers operational costs and requires less maintenance work. All of this enables companies to focus on business issues rather than ICT issues. Besides, the real value of cloud computing can only be unlocked by moving information systems to a cloud-native development pattern. ICT teams must start employing agile and cloud-native development practices such as DevSecOps and design systems according to modern data-centric architectures supporting the consumption of loosely-coupled micro-services. Cloud systems should be conceived in such a way that they can benefit from the advantages of cloud-based delivery models regardless of whether the data or processing capabilities are on-premise or in the public cloud.

Cloud services must be designed and operated according to security best practices. The designers of new information systems would only be able to use a limited number of services if they tied an organisation to a single cloud provider. In order to avoid being dependent on a single public cloud provider, the organisation should opt for a multi-cloud strategy. As a result, the cloud service consumer organisation will, in a vendor-neutral manner, obtain ICT services from the cloud provider that is best suited for the services required, depending on the use case. The secure and safe usage of cloud services is intrinsically linked to an appropriate data classification for all data assets of an information system. Moreover, one of the most relevant factors for the success of the cloud is the ability to enable a modern way of managing Big Data. Cloud-based data services and solutions to manage the high volume of data and data operations are key elements for shaping the organisation of tomorrow. The usage of vendor-specific advanced cloud services increases the risk of lock-in with one particular cloud supplier. Such a situation is not inevitable though, but the switchability of one cloud provider to another one should just be a refactoring cycle away. Information systems that are cloud-native are always designed and built with a certain cloud platform in mind. The information system may be created in ways that make it difficult for portability and reusability in order to get the most out of the chosen cloud platform. This may result in a situation known as vendor lock-in, in which data or information systems are dependent on a single provider and are immobile [29]. The council recognises that one of the crucial elements for guaranteeing the stability and security of the internal market is avoiding vendor lock-in and diversifying ICT suppliers. Emphasises the importance of advocating for and putting into practice suitable measures that support vendor diversity and competitiveness in a way that is technology-neutral, further supports including provisions relating to preventing vendor lock-in in EU legislation. Accepts the proposal for a Regulation on Harmonised Rules on Fair Access to and Use of Data (Data Act), which aims to improve the interoperability of data processing services and remove barriers to switching between providers of data processing services. The next subsection(s) will discuss the different cloud delivery mechanisms and service deployment models as well as emerging trends in these aspects.

4.1 Service models

The choice of service models is important because it will largely determine the types and effectiveness of security separation mechanisms that are available. However, this choice of service model will also affect the amount of responsibility that one has for securing your data and workloads within the service and how much responsibility the cloud provider will take on your behalf.

- Infrastructure as a Service (IaaS)—According to Sen [30], cloud infrastructure can be a real risk as each implementation choice affects future scalability, service level and flexibility of the services being built. It is fair to denote that 'future-proofing' should be the primary concern of every system architect. There are huge incentives for any vendor to increase lock-in through contractual, fiscal and technical constrictions. Interest in cloud infrastructure has been driven by a huge urge to break free of the existing enterprise vendor relationships for which the lock-in costs are higher than the value provided. Resist lock-in mechanisms in areas such as long-term contractual commitments and pre-paid arrangements distort decision-making, although technical lock-in remains one of the most difficult to avoid. Additionally, many suppliers encase exclusive APIs in distinct services so that future applications might adopt their style. These 'stick services' or 'loss leaders' give IT businesses strong incentives to choose the fastest route to value and incur some lock-in risk. This is a common type of technological debt, especially as new vendors introduce products that are more potent and distinctive in the same market or as better solutions emerge from OSS community. In addition, proprietary APIs invite strategic disruption from cloud providers in order to preserve customer lock-in.

- Platform as a Service (PaaS)—platform for cloud computing service provision (customer service management, billing, etc.). The consumer is given the ability to upload programs they have developed themselves or purchased using the provider's supported programming languages and tools into cloud infrastructure. The consumer has control over the installed programs and perhaps the parameters of the application hosting environment but does not manage or control the underlying cloud infrastructure, including the network, servers, operating systems or storage.

- Software as a Service (SaaS)—business applications, customer relations and support (CRM), human resource (HR), finance (ERP), online payments, electronic marketplace (for very small- and medium-sized enterprises). The consumer does not manage or control the underlying infrastructure including network, servers, operating systems, storage or even individual application capabilities, with the possible exception of limited user-specific application configuration.

- Process as a Service for Business—Business Process Outsourcing as a Service (BPaaS) is the provision of BPO services that are derived from the cloud and designed for multi-tenancy. When human process actors are needed, services are frequently mechanised, so there is not a labour pool that is extensively devoted to each client. Commercial terms with consumption—or subscription-based pricing schemes are used in a cloud-based service. Access to the BPaaS paradigm is made possible by web-based technology.

- Communication as a Services (CaaS): unified communications, e-mail, instant messaging, video and audio communication, collaborative services and data sharing (web conference).

- Network as a Service (NaaS)—managed Internet (assured speed, availability, etc.), paired with virtual private networks (VPNs) and cloud computing services, flexible and on-demand capacity.

- Serverless blurs the line between PaaS and SaaS. What sets serverless apart is that each government solves just one functional problem so multiple components must be combined to build an application.

- Containers such as Docker are widely used to deploy applications in the cloud. Services that run customers' containers tend to fit somewhere between the IaaS and PaaS (which varies depending on your choice of service). Containerisation is the emerging virtualization technology to support more elastic service frameworks due to its flexibility and small resource footprint.

4.2 Deployment models

When assessing the suitability of a given cloud service, you will need to decide on the service model and deployment you adopt. This is the essential first step towards determining whether the separation measures needed for your intended use are in place. For enterprises cloud computing provides access to agile, robust and scalable solutions. These could be in the form of SaaS products or IaaS products that allow enterprises to add or remove servers with ease as they are needed.

- Public cloud—To make the public cloud economically viable, cloud providers do not usually provide each customer with dedicated compute resources. Instead, resources such as compute power, networks, storage and identity management are shared between multiple clients. In this scenario, the separation implemented within each of those shared resources will affect the security of your deployed workloads and data. This makes it imperative you choose a cloud service provider whose separation techniques match your security needs.

- Private cloud—The cloud infrastructure is operated solely for a single organisation. It may be managed by an organisation or a third party and may exist on-premises or off-premises.

- Hybrid cloud: The cloud infrastructure is made up of two or more clouds (private, community or public), each of which is distinct from the others but which are connected by standardised or proprietary technology that enables the portability of data and applications (such as cloud bursting for load-balancing between clouds).

- Community cloud: The infrastructure is shared by a number of organisations, supporting a number of communities with similar issues (e.g. mission, security requirements, policy or compliance considerations). The organisations or a third party may administer it and may exist on-premises or off-premises.

- Edge Computing—Some public cloud providers offer the ability for users to deploy some of their services in their own data centre using hardware that is provided by them. This is known as edge computing and should be treated as a variant of the public cloud since its control plane (and sometimes its data plane) will be shared with the public cloud. You will need to have confidence that you can trust your physical data centre (and the network that you use to host the provided edge devices), as well as the cloud service that provided the device. Edge computing is usually deployed by organisations that require extremely low latency between client and service, to each data on sites where internet connectivity is unreliable, or to reduce internet bandwidth requirements by pre-processing raw data, prior to sending or derivation of the cloud.

- Multi-cloud—A multi-cloud strategy allows you to take advantage of more than one cloud service provider. Different cloud services may better meet the needs of different projects so it is common for an organisation to choose to use more than one platform to get the benefits of each.

Having read and understood to a certain degree the impact of cloud computing on businesses and institutions, the remainder sections of this chapter is meant to contribute to a further understanding of the overarching lock-in parameters.

5. Understanding cloud lock-in

In Refs. [14, 24], the author(s) have addressed several misconceptions regarding the cloud computing lock-in effect for the widespread adoption of cloud services. Organisations must approach the cloud with the understanding that they have to change providers in the future. It is advisable to do business continuity planning, to help to minimise the impact of a worst-case scenario. Various businesses will in the future suddenly find themselves with urgent needs to switch cloud providers for varying reasons. Companies seeking to adopt DevOps practices like continuous integration (CI) could face cloud lock-in due to the complexity of the required tools and effort needed to integrate them into their workflows. Even those companies that have already transitioned to DevOps could encounter lock-in, as the environments and tools are changing fast and constantly [31]. In the study by Opara-Martins [16], the author believes vendor lock-in appears when software companies become dependent on the tools they are using, not being able to substitute them when they need to is an issue that relates to the flexibility that is incompatible with DevOps. García-Grao and Carrera [32] concur that the DevOps paradigm is taking over software development systems, helping businesses increase efficiency, accelerate production and adapt quickly to market changes. A report by the UK Government (2019) states that there are generally two different types of lock-in. Many organisations have experience with commercial lock-in where long and inflexible contracts with providers can prevent organisations from changing their technology strategy when circumstances change. The opposite is true for public cloud services, where providers frequently use rolling, pay-as-you-go agreements. Although technically speaking you are free to discontinue utilising their services at any moment, in practice, this can be challenging and is referred to as technological lock-in. The lack of comparable services from other providers, technical architecture that depends on doing things a certain way, excessive integration with provider-specific services or products, and a lack of technical architecture expertise within the organisation are the main causes of this.

The popularity and use of cloud computing have largely been driven by the reported benefits on firm performance [33]. In this chapter, the author confirms that cloud adoption decisions [16] are complex and therefore require creativity, seeing as managers are advised to consider mindfulness as a criterion for job selection [34]. While several initiatives have been taken to prevent vendor lock-in risks [16], federated access control policies and identity management are too important features to design and implement inter-cloud security solutions [35]. In contrast to the aforementioned, Oulaaffart et al. [36] stipulate that the stakeholder may be reluctant to share information related to security with each other. This is to show that inter-cloud migration efforts have thus far been faced with several major solutions in terms of interoperability and security management.

In that context, moving resources across different cloud providers still frequently involves high prices, legal restrictions or even voluntary incompatibilities in technology, which promotes effective management of cloud resources [16]. But the integration of these resources and the development of cloud composite services depend heavily on the portability and interoperability qualities. The study by Opara-Martins [37] has been discussed by previous and recent researchers on the current state of the adoption process and associated effects of cloud computing by SMEs means they are very much interested because of the cost savings, flexibility and scalability of ICT that a cloud provides. SMEs have helped to take advantage of technology to facilitate and improve business [38]. Recently, cloud computing and application environments have evolved from monolithic to microservice architectures and platform support [39]. Cloud lock-in which is a user difficulty of switching from one vendor to another is regarded as one of the major motivations in the adoption of cloud by developers and SMEs [37]. Cloud computing offers good tools for organisations to conduct business efficiently.

Individuals and ICT organisations have begun to profit from cloud providers such as Amazon Web Services (AWS), Google cloud platform (GCP), Microsoft windows azure and others based on their demand for IaaS, PaaS and SaaS resources with pay-as-you-go pricing model. Cloud lock-in is now a well-known phenomenon [40, 41] in spite of its involvement with big automation companies. The proper deployment of novel methods can greatly reduce vendor lock-in. Although cloud provisioning has a dark side, it too often prioritises economic gain over the cost of long-lasting sustainability [42]. Moreover, vendor lock-in is economically unsustainable for cloud users because it makes it difficult for them to react if a provider does not deliver the promised service, reduces their bargaining power and even puts their company assets at risk in the event of data breach or cyberattack on the cloud provider's end [16]. To recall, the author reiterates here that cloud lock-in is characterised by a time-consuming procedure to migrate one application, data or service to another competitive cloud or establish communication among distinct cloud entities. Several solutions have been proposed to overcome lock-in situations, and middleware platforms are one of them [43]. The main solution identified in the composition of services for supporting the lifecycle of digital products is less dependency on services, infrastructure, platform, programming language or third-party services [16].

From the dimension of services computing, the cloud provides techniques for the construction, operation and management of large-scale internet service systems. It represents the frontier development direction of software engineering and distributed computing [44]. Due to the fact that cloud computing is built on many pre-existing technologies, hence to understand the complexities in cloud adoption, there are various factors such as knowledge management, technology interoperability, business operations, system integration, ICT infrastructure update, etc., that need to be considered during cloud computing adoption [45]. Likewise, there is a body of research that has general factors that influence the adoption of cloud-based services [46, 47], but these factors do not specifically address complexity dimensions [16]. Standards are a critical topic in the field of cloud computing [48] as they allow customers to compare among and evaluate cloud providers [49]. Proprietary technologies make cloud migration hard for end-users, and some providers note that standards to support interoperability between devices are needed [50]. As more applications make use of the cloud and more providers appear, vendor lock-in becomes an increasingly important factor.

The need for a common and interoperable standard is further augmented due to the appearance of Fog computing [51]. Lack of understanding of cloud technology and lack of confidence in cloud security are the major risks of applying cloud solutions [52]. The quest for supremacy among major players enhances their unwillingness to settle for a universal standard and thus upholding their incompatible cloud standards and design configurations [53]. One of the main hurdles in the cloud adoption of data-intensive applications is the absence of mature data management solutions that address vendor lock-in [54]. The risk of vendor lock-in can occur in any public-private collaboration, yet ICT products trigger particularly strong lock-in effects as a vendor can create a monopoly position by closing its technologies. Dependencies make the process of changing cloud providers or even the collaboration of processes between different providers a very difficult task. However, cloud service providers may also offer non-compatible solutions with proprietary interfaces, complicating the cloud landscape [16].

Cost of migration, integration, interoperability and customisation needs are attributed to a lack of skills in the effective implementation and management of a cloud solution. In Ref. [55], vendor lock-in is addressed by multi-cloud resource management (MCRM). To support the MCRM and exhibit a suitable automation level, different cloud modelling languages (CMLs) have been identified in many research projects and prototypes. The adoption of cloud computing and its implementation depend upon a variety of technical and non-technical factors. Cloud computing and the services that cloud providers offer are expanding much beyond simply the bare minimum of computation, storage and networking. These larger capabilities include edge caches, workflow managers, functions-as-a-service microservices, database services on demand and a variety of additional capabilities that are located higher up in the system stack. A group of remote users may also share these features from several suppliers. At the software-as-a-service level, this may likewise be done for any arbitrary, application-level services. When working with heterogeneous clouds, synchronisation of access, capabilities and resources is crucial. A multi-cloud strategy is possible when standard exchange mechanisms are accessible for services.

Interoperability and portability for data systems, and services are crucial factors facing consumers in cloud adoption. Consumers need confidence in moving their data and services across multiple cloud environments. A cloud system is a collection of network-accessible computing resources that customers (i.e. cloud consumers) can access over a network. The cloud system and its consumers employ the client-server model, which means that consumers (the clients) send messages over a network to server computers which then perform work-in response to the messages received. Cloud computing requires consumers to give up (to providers) two important capabilities: (1) control—the ability to decide with high confidence and what is allowed to access consumer data and programs and the ability to perform actions have been taken and that no additional actions were taken that would subvert the consumers intent. (2) Visibility—the ability to monitor, with high confidence, the status of a consumer's data programs and how consumer data and programs are being accessed by others. In order to guarantee proper security and privacy protection, new problems in cloud design, construction and operation must be overcome. The implementation of the required controls turns into a collaborative effort between suppliers and consumers.

The ownership of the computing resources within a cloud is determined by cloud business models. Cloud service offerings that rent traditional computing resources (such as VMs or disk storage, i.e. IaaS) are closely related to existing standards, and hence, some usage scenarios illustrating portability can be expressed using existing standard terminology. Portability relies on standardised interfaces and data formats, while cloud computing relies on both consensus and *de facto* standards such as TCP/

IP, XML, WSDL, IA-64, X509, PEM, DNS, SSL/TLS, SOAP, ReST. Moreover, most substantial applications are using the Internet today regardless of whether cloud computing is employed. Therefore, the reader should not assume that by avoiding a cloud a user automatically avoids risks associated with Internet outages. Cloud systems have been conceptualised through a combination of software/hardware components and virtualisation technologies. Managing various sorts of access to the service components is necessary for various service delivery models. These service delivery approaches may be seen as hierarchical. As a result, the same functional components in a higher service model can use the access control guidance of functional components in a lower-level service model.

Cloud systems offer application services, data, storage, data management, networking and computing resources management to consumers over a network. Access control (AC) dictates the subject (i.e. users and processes) can access objects based on defined AC policies to protect sensitive data and critical computing objects in the cloud systems. Cloud interoperability has emerged as a crucial business concern as business use cloud-based solutions at an increasing rate. ICT departments are aware of the need of being able to use cloud metadata to guarantee data protection and data portability, giving end users a safe way to remove their data from the cloud. This is especially useful in the event that you want to switch cloud service providers or if one of them goes out of business. ICT departments, therefore, anticipate providers to adhere to cloud data interoperation standards.

The academic literature pinpoints two issues as the two most important determining factors in this respect, with security ranking first, and vendor lock-in (specifically in PaaS and SaaS context) second. The current business methods of cloud service providers obstruct innovation and a free and open market, which has an effect on how data is used throughout the economy. Particularly, users are now prevented from migrating from one provider to another by porting their digital assets across due to contractual, financial and technical barriers. Over the past 10 years, this vendor lock-in has grown significantly more severe. It is made worse by the current trend, in which providers are increasingly offering a variety of cloud services within an integrated cloud ecosystem, preventing customers from switching providers. Such ecosystems frequently devolve into 'data-silos' that hinder the adoption of cutting-edge data-sharing tools and the market's open nature for data processing. Achieving data portability will depend on the standardisation of the import and export functionality of data and its adoption of "data acts" by the providers. The next subsection describes some obstacles encountered during service migration.

5.1 Cloud migration hurdles

Advances in cloud computing have in recent years resulted in a growing interest for migration towards the cloud environment [16]. The transition to cloud computing frequently involves unforeseen, additional expenditures. While these costs are manageable and do not jeopardise the benefits of adopting cloud, some activities may prove to be quite expensive, especially if they are not planned for in a timely manner. The frequent movement of data between the company and the cloud can also rack up costs, particularly in terms of bandwidth consumption where transfer times are lengthy. As things currently stand, lock-in is a perceived risk that there is more flexibility available in the cloud and users can become dependent on the products and services from a particular provider. In this case, switching from one technology or provider to another is difficult, time-consuming and disproportionately expensive. In the cloud, the benefits of lock-in frequently outweigh the drawbacks. Using a cloud provider, for instance, to handle your storage lifecycle may result in lock-in, but it will also need less work to manage your service. Consumers of cloud services should be able to unilaterally provision computing capabilities such as server time and network storage as needed without requiring human interaction with service providers. Unless we implement new technologies, we keep an eye on fundamental goals and values. We will not be able to fulfil our consumers' increasing expectations, and we will not be ready for even more significant changes that are sure to occur as we deal with constantly increasing data quantities and a proliferation of devices and sensors, says [56].

The fact that, when selecting cloud services, engineers must consider heterogeneous sets of criteria and complex dependencies between infrastructure services and software images which are complex. Cloud providers such as Amazon Web Services (AWS), Salesforce.com or Google App Engine (GAE) give users the option to deploy their application over a network of infinite resource pools with low capital investment and with very modest operating costs proportional to the actual use. A migration strategy defines migration procedure in means of order and data transfer [57]. The following five steps outline a migration of an organisations web application to a cloud infrastructure service (IaaS), whereas migration of a company's asset to a software application/applistructure or SaaS involves six holistic decision steps [16] and the steps of a migration to a Platform-as-a-Service (PaaS) offering would differ in several regards [58, 59]. PaaS migration is the process of moving from the use of one software operating and deployment environment to another environment. In order to develop (or adapt) software for cloud-based development and deployment, cloud-specific architecture and programming techniques need to be followed. Cloud migration can be categorised in terms of the cloud stack layers [60].

Cloud migration is a process of partially or completely deploying an organisation's digital assets, services, ICT resources or application to the cloud. The cloud migration process may involve retaining some ICT infrastructure onsite. However, the migration process involves the risk of accidentally exposing sensitive business-critical information. Thus, cloud migration requires careful analysis, planning and execution to ensure the cloud solutions' compatibility with organisational requirements, while maintaining the security and integrity of the organisation's ICT system. A cloud migration process involves many concept variants and several ways of instantiation. As with any software development project, migration projects should be planned carefully and have a good methodology to guarantee successful execution. There is a need for live migration of virtual machines (VMs) at IaaS because the current cloud provider ecosystem is heterogeneous and, hence, hinders the live migration of VMs [61]. In spite of the aforesaid, with the combination of different paradigms, live migration can be conducted between edge servers, physical hosts in the local area network (LAN) and data centre sites through the wide area network (WAN). In the next subsection, security is presented as a bottleneck for service adoption.

5.2 Security lock-in

Cloud environments challenge many fundamental assumptions about the application and data security. Cloud-based software applications require design rigour similar to applications residing in classic DMZ. With cloud computing, application dependencies can be highly dynamic, even to the point where each dependency represents a discrete third-party service provider. The cloud security environment embodies shared security and joint responsibility, which produces a form of lock-in with the cloud services providers [59]. However, this form of lock-in differs from using security and tamper-resistance to explicitly hinder users' ability to switch cloud service providers. This article's author has confirmed in the works of [16, 24] that such lock-in is anti-competitive and motivates consumers to adopt anti-lock-in solutions such hybrid clouds, cloud management providers or brokers, and routine manual data exports [17]. In this aspect, functional misalignment with business needs and technical limitations in areas including integration, security or extensibility are major inhibitors to data switchability from one vendor to another [14]. If cloud service providers and their customers are fully informed of human error as a major root cause of security risks encountered in the cloud, both parties can fully benefit from the advantages this model of computing offers [62].

Previously, various vendors have introduced different types of clouds with heterogeneous resources available in each, varying with respect to computation (CPU/GPU) memory and telecommunication network capabilities. Quite recently, cloud providers like IBM cloud have offered multi-cloud capabilities to improve interoperability and facilitate data or computation portability between clouds [63]. The cloud industry has recently moved into a hybrid of cloud-edge computing, but this creates a whole set of new risks regarding interoperability and APIs, managing heterogeneous capacities, workload offloading data integrity and privacy, storage decentralisation application restructuring [64]. In the process of digital transformation, organisations respond to changes in the surrounding environment by exploiting digital technologies [65]. However, combining new Internet of Things (IoT) solutions can be challenging and technology with legacy systems aiming to exploit heterogeneous data from these different sources [66, 67]. Interoperability plays a prominent role in multi-vendor ICT platforms where various systems need to interact efficiently making standardisation crucial for collaboration [68].

The cloud lock-in is less when applications are dynamically developed in an agnostic cloud platform environment such as Google App Engine (GAE) or Microsoft Windows Azure and it is removed with substantial cost to a different platform. Moreover, both PaaS and SaaS as platforms create network effects that enable the growth of users across both supply and demand sides. But at the SaaS layer, the hurdle of data integration requires a combination of technical and business processes used to combine data from disparate sources into heterogeneously meaningful, valuable and reusable information [69]. Respectively, service developers making use of cloud services can use SaaS providers and APIs as building blocks to develop composite services by integrating data and composing functionality provided by different SaaS resources [70]. Security, usability and vendor characteristics are the three main areas of lock-in risks in the cloud computing environment when adopting enterprise-class software like cloud ERP systems. Effectively integrating cloud ERP into existing cloud computing infrastructure will allow suppliers to determine organisations and business owners' expectations and implement appropriate tactics [71]. Orchestration of cloud services is important for companies and institutions that need to design complex cloud-native applications or to migrate their existing services to the cloud. Tools such as Chef, Ansible and Puppet provide infrastructure as code (IaC) language to automate the installation and configuration of cloud applications. Clarity about security tasks and responsibilities is a crucial consideration in the procurement process. In this regard, it should be stressed that the responsibility for security cannot be outsourced [72].

Adaptation of containerisation and serverless technologies is the most trending microservices research area for practitioners focused on cloud-related domains. Solutions that provide cloud computing with end-to-end security reduce vendor lock-in risks as it relates to stored data. The information must be protected in cloud storage and transmission to reduce this risk, so only the data provider and the final consumer can access or modify it [73]. Regarding stored data, cloud service providers integrate cryptographics mechanisms based on encryption protocols such as advanced encryption standard (AES) or Rivest-Shamir-Adleman (RSA). To a certain degree, cloud service providers practise security-induced lock-in when employing cryptography and tamper-resistance to limit the portability and interoperability of users' data and applications, says Satzger et al. [17]. This security-induced lock-in and users' anti-lock-in strategies intersect within the context of platform competition. Thus, cloud services providers, therefore, favour security-induced lock-in over price leadership. Continued advancement of computing and digital technologies is transforming markets, economics and society. Migration to the cloud is strongly affecting corporate ICT strategies.

The security benefits of moving to a cloud-based system are often overlooked. A good cloud service will mitigate some existing risks and bring new benefits as well. Cloud provider is the vendor and operator of the cloud services. Cloud services vary substantially in size, from an entire e-business suite to a single component within a software development ecosystem (such as a storage or cryptographic key management service). It is simple for the cloud service to use a text template (like IaC) that outlines the desired configuration and contacts the APIs to make the necessary modifications because cloud infrastructure is typically maintained through APIs. As a result, IaC enables you to track your configuration in text documents where changes can be examined, and analysis can be carried out automatically. The use of automated processes to enforce security or policy requirements is known as guardrails and is an emerging technique in the cloud. This could entail a stipulation that only a select group of authorised operating system images may be utilised for computing services, or that all bulk data storage encrypts data at rest. Cloud services have been designed with an array of security benefits for your organisation and it is worth taking the time to find out what is available (and how to apply it to your specific needs) in order to gain the most benefits. The more you take the time to understand the cloud services available, the bigger the benefits will be. When selecting a cloud service, make sure that it meets your needs and helps you to secure your data. The process of digital transformation involves adopting technologies that enhance operational and customer experiences. Evaluating cloud and business risk together provides a better understanding of its impact on enterprises' overall risk maturity, including adopting a shared fate partnership between cloud service provider and customers [74]. This chapter affirms that an organisation's best path to viable risk management involves ICT modernisation into the cloud or cloud-like on-premise infrastructure. The CSA [74] report further confirms that there is no consistency of data classification across the use of cloud platforms and services. Tripathi and Mishra [75] note that the cloud is becoming less of a risk to manage and more of a means to manage these risks and modernisation. The approach helps both businesses and providers to improve their cloud adoption. The next subsection presents DevSecOps as a philosophy to combat security lock-in issues in the cloud environment.

5.3 DevSecOps mitigates lock-in

A number of additional problems regarding the tools and services needed to develop and maintain running applications are brought on by cloud computing. These consist of program administration utilities, coupling to external services, development and testing tools, libraries and operating system dependencies, some of which may come from cloud providers. It takes a lot of work to design, integrate and deliver software in the modern software engineering process. Continuous integration (CI) is the process of automatically adding new code from several developers to the same version of the software while simultaneously checking it for bugs. When deploying new software to production using continuous delivery (CD), the frequency of the deployments differs from traditional software deployment being the frequency of deployment, which can happen multiple times every day. DevSecOps is a software engineering culture that guides, breaks down silos, and unify software development, security and operations. IaC evolved to solve a real-world problem referred to as environmental drift in the release pipeline. It is important to consider vendor lock-in versus product lock-in when selecting technology or IaC formats.

While the debate on cloud lock-in lies on the heavy reliance on the single cloud provider or perhaps the inability to use services of multiple vendors, closed proprietary software or systems purposely encourage technology lock-in, ensuring long-term customers and revenues while discouraging innovation. Abu-Libdeh et al. [76] strongly note that going all-in with a single cloud provider may allow organisations to simplify things and become more agile, potentially achieving better quality as single vendor solutions are often better integrated. Since no application is platform-specific containerisation can help isolate software from its environment, while DevOps helps to maximise code portability and makes it easier to deploy to different environments. However, applications built for the cloud have developed into a standardised architecture made up of many small, loosely linked parts known as micro-services (implemented as containers), supported by a program known as mesh that runs services. A container orchestration and resource management platform, such as Kubernetes, is home to both of these components and is referred to as a reference platform. Now, DevSecOps have been found to be a facilitating paradigm for these applications with primitives such as continuous integration, continuous delivery and continuous deployment (CI/CD) pipelines for providing continuous authority to operate (C-ATO) using risk-management tools and dashboard metrics [77]. DevSecOps puts security at the forefront of requirements to avoid the costly mistakes that come from treating security as an afterthought. Traditional security has been about exclusion and using the security policy to prevent people from disclosing secrets. DevSecOps is about inclusion and working as a team. Successful implementation of DevSecOps happens when the security team provides knowledge and tools and the DevOps team runs them. However, there is no reason for a security team to run tooling as a completely out-of-band management process. Before concluding that DevSecOps is a methodology or framework for agile application development, deployment and operations for cloud-native applications, DevOps uses a forward process with a delivery pipeline and a reverse process with a feedback loop that forms a recursive workflow. The role of automation in these activities is to improve this workflow *via* the following tools for automation (e.g. Ansible [78], and Terraform [79]), DevOps stack (e.g. Maven [80] and Jenkins [81]) and programming languages like Kotlin [82].

For example, maven is a software project management and comprehension tool. Based on the concept of a project object model (POM), maven can change a project's build, reporting and documentation from a central piece of information to sharing jars across several projects. In other words, it can be used for enabling and managing any Java-based project and one of the goals of maven is allowing transparent migration to new features as it has become the *de facto* build system for Java applications. When migrating an application to the cloud and selecting a cloud service provider, the cost weighs heavily on the mind of every ICT manager in the automation industry. As a result, using an open-source system such as Jenkins can integrate with any cloud provider. Selecting tools based on strengths rather than vendor merit will help to avoid using one cloud provider for everything (which often leads to a single point of failure). Designing a solution using well-known patterns decouples its functional characteristics from the underlying cloud implementation, making it easier to avoid lock-in or go multi-cloud. By adopting standardisation, automation, cross-platform programming languages and containerisation, organisations are flexible and adaptable. In the next subsection, SDN is presented as a means to surpass some of the incumbent networking challenges caused by technical lock-in parameters.

5.4 Software-defined networks

A more open standards-driven approach to networking is necessary for the cloud and digital transformation era as opposed to the proprietary network architectures and Application Specific Integrated Circuits (ASIC). Software-defined Networking (SDN), built on OpenFlow protocol, enables an organisation to virtualise their network, automate operations, enable efficient network configuration and integrate network functions across dozens of switches creating a unified network architecture [83], that is programmable and dynamically definable. SDN as an emerging paradigm is set to logically centralise the network control plane and automate the configuration of individual network elements. In cloud data centres, however, network and server resources are collocated and managed by a single administrative entity; still, disjoint control mechanisms are used for their respective management. While unified server-network resource management is ideal for such a converged ICT environment, machine virtualisation can have a negative effect on cloud systems, resulting in drastic changes in performance and cost that mostly relate to networking constraints rather than software limitations. For example, network congestion caused by consolidation itself, particularly at the core levels of data centre topologies, has a substantial impact on the infrastructure as a whole and becomes the primary bottleneck, impeding effective resource utilisation and, as a result, provider's income. SDN runs on the principle of centralising control-plane intelligence while maintaining the separation of the data plane in order to allow open user-controlled administration of the forwarding hardware of a network component. The switching fabric (data plane) is retained by the network hardware devices, while the controller receives the intelligence (switching and routing functionalities). Because the entire network is under centralised control, the administrator can configure the hardware right from the controller, which gives the network a high degree of flexibility. SDN is monitored and implemented using a variety of tools and languages. A developing platform called Onix has been the focus of some SDN attempts in order to instal SDN controllers as a distributed system for flexible network management. Veriflow, a network debugging tool has been introduced in other studies, is capable of finding the flaws in SDN application rules and preventing them from impairing network performance. With the help of additional initiatives, the routing architecture Routeflow was created. It is based on SDN concepts and allows for interaction between the performance of commercial hardware and adaptable open-source routing stacks. As a result, it makes it possible to switch from traditional IP deployments to SDN.

By separating the control plane and forwarding plane, SDN provides centralised topology discovery and networking management, which enables the capability of managing resource contentions in finer granularity [84]. This gives academics and industry more options in a variety of network virtualisation-related areas, including novel LAN and WAN networking protocols, optimised virtualised data planes, traffic and flow management, software function chaining *via* virtualised network functions, etc. As a result, OpenFlow and the OF-CONFIG management and configuration protocol are accepted as the *de facto* standard SDN communication and control protocols. With SDN, policies, configuration and network resource management can be implemented quickly, and a single control protocol may handle a variety of tasks such as access control, routing and traffic engineering. The majority of open-source SDN controllers (Ryu, POX, FloodLight, OpenDaylight) expose APIs to manage firewalls, configure network components and obtain traffic counters, among other things. Additionally, they have been widely employed for other network-related applications, including QoS management, participatory networking, new management interfaces and for complete network migration. Minimising vendor lock-in has become important due to the degree and pace of network transformation that is required to keep up with business modernisation, to reduce hardware manufacturer lock-in, the network must be made programmable, and control and other functionality must be abstracted using software-driven strategy. It is crucial for ICT experts to choose the appropriate network operating system when utilising such a strategy in order to maximise cost-effectiveness and prevent problems with system integration and network availability [85]. The right approach to avoiding vendor lock-in is to counteract it strategically from the outset, instead of relying on one vendor, focus on several different ones. Internal systems should be built with the goal that subcomponents may be replaced later. Where a technology or vendor may seem like a riskier choice in terms of vendor lock-in, an exit strategy should be defined, obtain cloud services from several rather than a single provider, avoid using proprietary solutions, APIs, and formats and reduce the cost to switch. The next subsection highlights the need for effective strategies to mitigate the concerns of vendor lock-in.

5.5 Strategies

Organisations are under pressure to find and implement new strategic ideas at an even faster pace to gain a competitive edge over rivals within the global market. Towards this goal, it is fair to highlight herein that the absence of standardisation may also bring disadvantages, when migration, integration or exchanges of resources are required [3]. Strategies can be understood by referencing cloud lock-in taxonomies [24], which illustrate various components from which a cloud environment can be composed. Combining components into a solution introduces boundaries between the various components of a cloud system such as operational boundaries and trust boundaries. During the course of ordinary business processing or as data and applications migrate to new providers or platforms, data and application processing commonly crosses boundaries. A crucial issue that can be solved by portability and interoperability is ensuring operational integrity across boundaries as processing demands migrate to the cloud. Moreover, it must be enunciated that customers must be aware that they might need to switch service providers due to unacceptably high contract renewal costs, service provider business operations ceasing, partial cloud service closures without migration plans, unacceptably low service quality and business disputes between cloud customers and providers, among other reasons. Again, as part of risk management and security assurance for any cloud initiative, portability and interoperability should be taken into account upfront. It is also the core strategy in the process of migrating towards cloud technologies, both within the public and private sectors. Companies will be responsible for evaluating their sourcing strategy to fully consider cloud computing solutions as viable. An example of policy measures to consider in this respect is presented in the next subsection.

5.6 Policy measures

According to Lewis [86], the cloud computing community typically uses the term interoperability interchangeably with portability. Herein, the author makes a clear distinction to specify that the former refers to the ability to easily move workloads and data from one cloud service provider to another or between private and public clouds. On the other hand, the latter states the ability to move a system from one platform to another. While these two separate terms are pertinent to the enlisted policy measures below, the author also draws the readers' attention to the role of open standards in the cloud with an emphasis on mitigating potential areas of lock-in effect across the cloud ecosystem (whether in domestic or international settings). Standards will be critical for the successful adoption and delivery of cloud computing, both within the public sector and more broadly. Standards encourage competition by making applications portable across providers, allowing federal governments (e.g. G-Cloud) to switch service providers in order to benefit from cost-saving measures or cutting-edge new product features. Furthermore, standards are essential to ensuring that cloud platforms are interoperable so that services offered by various providers can coexist, regardless of whether they use public, private, community or hybrid delivery models [87].

- Support proposals to stipulate minimum requirements regarding data portability and retention periods to support migration.

- Lay a stable governance foundation that will outlast single individuals or administrations so as to empower the government for action, minimise unnecessary bureaucracy and ensure accountability for results.

- The European Council (EC) should set rules that govern cross-border operations as well as not lacking harmonisation of the regulatory framework.

- Explore and support further options to create a single market for digital services.

- Support the implementation of the consumer right directive.

- Support the harmonisation of data protection rules through the establishment of a common regulation.

- Address cloud-specific aspects within the E-commerce directive.

- Ensure global harmonisation of cloud computing standards.

- Support software adaptation process that facilitates the development of cloud applications that are not coupled to any specific platform.

While data protection attracts much attention and debate in current literature, other contractual clauses between cloud service providers and the clients including choice of law, intellectual property (IP) issues, terms of service and acceptance use also impact the adoption of cloud computing and are discussed herein [11]. Therefore, gaining the benefits of this more elastic environment requires appropriate planning to avoid being 'locked' into a cloud solution that may not measure up to the goals for moving to the cloud in the first place. For additional and supplemental policy measures, please refer to the study by Opara-Martins et al. [13]. The next section concludes this research output and contribution by maintaining that this chapter should be rated high as it has linked academia and industry with cutting-edge research to create new knowledge and innovation that converts ideas into wealth creation, jobs and human progress. Thus, researchers lacking adequate knowledge, dexterity and self-transformation cannot be helpful to society nor will they be useful to themselves.

6. Conclusion and future work

Cloud computing, as a catalyst for innovation, will not just be more innovative than we imagine, but it will be more innovative than we can imagine. Essentially, cloud computing refers to ICT services that are now instantly, unconditionally and on-demand available to everyone, from data processing and storage to software applications. The cloud has already become a go-to resource for some businesses with proprietary lock-in, and the trends indicate that this model is set for major development provided certain standards and compliance policies (e.g. data act) are taken in a timely manner. The experience of enterprises to date points to cloud computing being used at different levels according to the institutions concerned. Indeed, many researchers, research institutes and federal government agencies have adopted this technology in Europe. In the UK, specific data privacy, jurisdiction, contractual clauses and security pose a threat in that regard.

In the interest of fostering the emergence of cloud computing technology, this chapter advocates actions such that when choosing cloud services most cloud users cannot find an appropriate cloud service matching their individual requirements when they are using a given cloud service for the first time. Research emphasis is laid on parameters important to guide users in cloud service selection to provide a guide in choosing the appropriate strategy to mitigate cloud lock-in, and the author presents a state-of-the-art review of existing works in interoperable, portable and standard cloud migration techniques. These parameters provide a set of common functionality to all cloud services built using the cloud platform. Where skills or training in regard to cloud computing is concerned, the author surveyed DevSecOps tools, technology stack, programming languages like Kotlin and technical considerations pertaining to SDN, Edge, multi-cloud and Guardrails in dealing with the cloud lock-in parameters. The ICT sector in Europe is characterised by the very rapid development of mobile cloud computing (MCC) telecommunication networks. At the same time, however, UK businesses are seeking business process management (BPM) solutions whereby they can catch up on the deployment of context-aware services.

Against this background, in today's business marketing the main types of cloud services are cloud hosting services, object storage services, cloud database services, cloud engine services, block storage services, cloud caching services, online application services, load balancing services and cloud distribution services. The evidence shows that the implementation of strategies relating to contracts, selection of vendors and developed awareness of commonalities and dependencies among cloud-based solutions has greatly reduced the risks of cloud lock-in. Cloud computing could go a long way to mitigate ICT lock-in risks through a market oligopoly provided the corresponding technology is implemented on solid standard bases that inspire confidence in interoperability, portability and integration. To this end, enterprise decision-makers and leaders are in agreement CYNEFIN framework adheres to international requirements in terms of disorder as it pertains to heterogeneity of cloud technology ecosystem. Similarly, the deployment of vendor-neutral services with ensured business continuity, rapid elasticity and secure data storage in line with international standards organisations (like NIST, ENISA, CSA, SNIA, The OpenGroup, TOGAF, OASIS) constitutes the strong pillar of cloud computing for Europe. In conclusion, the study presents technical and policy recommendations related to regulation, SLA, contracts on cloud computing, the implementation of open (sourced) APIs, standardisation and the cross-border data plan. The main objective of these policy measure(s) is to ensure a harmonious and sustainable development of cloud products and services in the UK.

In future work, the author identifies opportunities for cloud platforms to support more secure, interoperable, portable, automated and systematic authentication within and between cloud-hosted components. This research has been mainly focused on solutions to avoid vendor lock-in making it an active area of study for circa 2023 and beyond.

Author details

Justice Opara-Martins
Computing and Informatics Research Centre, Bournemouth University, Poole, United Kingdom

*Address all correspondence to: dr.martinsjustice@gmail.com

References

[1] Mell P, Grance T. The NIST Definition of Cloud Computing. Recommendations of the National Institute of Standards and Technology [Online], Special Publication 800-145. 2011. Available from: http://faculty.winthrop.edu/domanm/csci411/Handouts/NIST.pdf. [Accessed: September 1, 2022]

[2] Brynjolfsson E, Hofmann P, Jordan J. Cloud computing and electricity: Beyond the utility model. Communications of the ACM. 2010;**53**(5):32-34

[3] Sahandi R, Alkhalil A, Opara-Martins J. Cloud computing from SMEs perspective: A survey based investigation. Journal of Information Technology Management. 2013;**24**(1):1-12

[4] Gannon D. The Client Cloud: Changing the Paradigm for Scientific Research. Keynote Address, IEEE CloudCom. Indianapolis; 2010

[5] Buyya R, Broberg J, Goscinski A. Cloud Computing: Principles and Paradigms. Melbourne, Australia: Wiley; 2011

[6] Ismail UM, Islam S, Mouratidis H. Cloud security audit for migration and continuous monitoring. In: Proceedings—14th IEEE International Conference on Trust, Security and Privacy in Computing and Communications. TrustCom; 2015, 2015. pp. 1081-1087. DOI: 10.1109/Trustcom.2015.486

[7] Khajeh-Hosseini A et al. Decision support tools for cloud migration in the enterprise. In: Proceedings of the 2011 IEEE 4th International Conference on Cloud Computing, CLOUD 2011. Washington, USA: IEEE; 2011. pp. 541-548. DOI: 10.1109/CLOUD.2011.59

[8] Opara-Martins J. A decision framework to mitigate vendor lock-in risks in cloud (SaaS category) migration. Doctoral dissertation, Bournemouth University; 2017

[9] Opara-Martins J, Sahandi R, Tian F. Implications of integration and interoperability for enterprise cloud-based applications. In: International Conference on Cloud Computing. Cham: Springer; 2015. pp. 213-223

[10] Foster I, Zhao Y, Raicu J, Lu S. Cloud Computing and Grid Computing 360-Degree Compared, Grid Computing Environments Workshop. Texas, USA: IEEE; 2008

[11] Opara-Martins J, Sahandi R, Tian F. A business analysis of cloud computing: Data security and contract lock-in issues. In: 2015 10th International Conference on P2P, Parallel, Grid, Cloud and Internet Computing (3PGCIC). IEEE; 2015. pp. 665-670

[12] Opara-Martins J. Understanding Cloud Computing From An SME Perspective. White Paper. 2013. Available from: http://www.budigitalhub.com/sites/default/files/white_papers/Cloud%20Computing.pdf. [Accessed: October 1, 2013]

[13] Opara-Martins J, Sahandi R, Tian F. Critical review of vendor lock-in and its impact on adoption of cloud computing. In: International Conference on Information Society (i-Society 2014). IEEE; 2014. pp. 92-97

[14] Opara-Martins J, Sahandi M, Tian F. A holistic decision framework to avoid vendor lock-in for cloud saas migration. Computer and Information Science. 2017;**10**(3):29-53

[15] Clement N, Arce DG. Dynamics of Shared Security in the Cloud. 2022. Available from: https://ssrn.com/abstract=4281973 or http://dx.doi.org/10.2139/ssrn.4281973

[16] Opara-Martins J, Sahandi R, Tian F. Critical analysis of vendor lock-in and its impact on cloud computing migration: A business perspective. Journal of Cloud Computing. 2016;**5**(1):1-18

[17] Satzger B, Hummer W, Inzinger C, Leitner P, Dustdar S. Winds of change: From vendor lock-in to the meta cloud. IEEE Internet Computing. 2013;**17**(1):69-73

[18] Govindarajan A, Lakshmanan. In: Antonopoulos N, Gillam L, editors. Cloud Computing. Vol. 0. London: Springer London; 2010. pp. 77-89

[19] Petcu D. Portability and interoperability between clouds: Challenges and case study. In: Abramowicz W, Llorente IM, Surridge M, Zisman A, Vayssiere J, editors. Towards a Service-Based Internet. Vol. 6994 LNCS, 2011. Poznan, Poland: Springer Berlin Hiedelberg; 2011. pp. 62-74

[20] Gonidis F, Paraskakis I, Kourtesis D. Addressing the challenge of application portability in cloud platforms. In: Proceedings of the 7th South East European Doctoral Student Conference (DSC 2012). Thessaloniki, Greece: SERC; 2012. pp. 565-576

[21] Kumari P, Kaur P. A survey of fault tolerance in cloud computing. Journal of King Saud University-Computer and Information Sciences. 2021;**33**(10):1159-1176

[22] Snowden DJ, Boone ME. A leader's framework for decision making. Harvard Business Review. 2007;**85**(11):68

[23] Murphy B, Rocchi M. Ethics and cloud computing. In: Lynn T, Mooney JG, van der Werff L, Fox G, editors. Data Privacy and Trust in Cloud Computing. Palgrave Studies in Digital Business & Enabling Technologies. Cham: Palgrave Macmillan; 2021. DOI: 10.1007/978-3-030-54660-1_6

[24] Opara-Martins J. Taxonomy of cloud lock-in challenges. Mobile Computing-Technology and Applications. 2018. pp. 3-21

[25] Cloud Security Alliance (CSA). Cloud Security Alliance Offers Recommendations for Using Customer Controlled Key Store. 2022. Available from: https://cloudsecurityalliance.org/press-releases/2022/09/27/cloud-security-alliance-offers-recommendations-for-using-customer-controlled-key-store/. [Accessed: September 5, 2022]

[26] ITU. International Telecommunications Union Rec. Y.3536 (02/2022) Cloud Computing. 2022. Available from: https://www.itu.int/ITU-T/workprog/wp_search.aspx?sg=13&wp=2. [Accessed: September 5, 2022]

[27] Cloud Standards Customer Council (CSCC). Interoperability and Portability for Cloud Computing: A Guide Version 2.0 [Online]. 2017. Available from: https://www.omg.org/cloud/deliverables/CSCC-Interoperability-and-Portability-for-Cloud-Computing-A-Guide.pdf. [Accessed: September 10, 2022]

[28] European Council (EC). European Commission Digital Strategy. 2022. Available from: https://ec.europa.eu/info/publications/EC-Digital-Strategy_en [Accessed: September 20, 2022]

[29] European Council (EC). Council of the European Union. Council

Conclusions on ICT Supply Chain Security [Online]. 2022. Available from: https://data.consilium.europa.eu/doc/document/ST-13664-2022-INIT/en/pdf. [Accessed: September 29, 2022]

[30] Sen J. Security and Privacy Issues in Cloud Computing. 2013. Available from: https://arxiv.org/pdf/1303.4814.pdf. [Accessed: September 30, 2022]

[31] Shahin M. An Empirical Study of Architecting and Organising for DevOps (Doctoral Dissertation); 2018

[32] García-Grao G, Carrera Á. Extending the OSLC standard for ECA-based automation in DevOps environments. New York, USA: Cornell University; 2022. pp. 1-25. arXiv preprint arXiv:2211.08075. 2022

[33] Oredo J, Dennehy D. Exploring the role of Organisational mindfulness on cloud computing and firm performance: The case of Kenyan organizations. Information Systems Frontiers. 2022;**24**:1-22

[34] Lin L, Cheung A. Cloud economy and its relationship with China's economy—A capital market-based approach. Financial Innovation. 2022;**8**(1):1-22

[35] Santoro D, Zozin D, Pizzolli D, De Pellegrini F, Cretti S. Foggy: A platform for workload orchestration in a fog computing environment. In: 2017 IEEE International Conference on Cloud Computing Technology and Science (CloudCom). Hong Kong, China: IEEE; 2017. pp. 231-234

[36] Oulaaffart M, Badonnel R, Festor O. C3S-TTP: A Trusted Third Party for Configuration Security in TOSCA-Based Cloud Services; 2022

[37] Opara-Martins J. Creative technology research seminar. PPT [online]. 2014. Available from: https://slideplayer.com/slide/12537021/ [Accessed: October 1, 2022]

[38] Alshamaila Y, Papagiannidis S, Li F. Cloud computing adoption by SMEs in the north east of England: A multi-perspective framework. Journal of Enterprise Information Management. 2013;**26**:250-275

[39] Bainomugisha E, Mwotil A. Crane cloud: A resilient multi-cloud service abstraction layer for resource-constrained settings. Development Engineering. 2022:100102

[40] Mohbey KK, Kumar S. The impact of big data in predictive analytics towards technological development in cloud computing. International Journal of Engineering Systems Modelling and Simulation. 2022;**13**(1):61-75

[41] Finta G. Mitigating the Effects of Vendor Lock-in in Edge Cloud Environments with Open-Source Technologies. Espoo, Finland: Aalto University; 2022

[42] Cai Z, Yang G, Xu S, Zang C, Chen J, Hang P, et al. RBaaS: A robust Blockchain as a service paradigm in cloud-edge collaborative environment. IEEE Access. 2022;**10**:35437-35444

[43] Mane AS, Sonaje M, Tadge P. Data security in cloud computing using an improved attribute-based encryption. In: Data Intelligence and Cognitive Informatics. Singapore: Springer; 2022. pp. 261-272

[44] Agarwal P, Sharma DK, Varun VL, Venkatesh PR, Kanchibhotla C, Ventayen RJM, et al. A survey on the scope of cloud computing. Materials Today: Proceedings. 2022;**51**:861-864

[45] Morawiec P, Sołtysik-Piorunkiewicz A. Cloud computing, big data, and

Blockchain technology adoption in ERP implementation methodology. Sustainability. 2022;**14**(7):3714

[46] Won D, Hwang BG, Samion BM, N.K. Cloud computing adoption in the construction industry of Singapore: Drivers, challenges, and strategies. Journal of Management in Engineering. 2022;**38**(2):05021017

[47] Jayeola O, Sidek S, Abd Rahman A, Mahomed ASB, Hu J. Cloud computing adoption in small and medium enterprises (SMEs): A systematic literature review and directions for future research. International Journal of Business and Society. 2022;**23**(1):226-243

[48] Krishnaraj N, Bellam K, Sivakumar B, Daniel A. The future of cloud computing: Blockchain-based decentralised cloud/fog solutions–challenges, opportunities, and standards. Blockchain Security in Cloud Computing. 2022;**2**:207-226

[49] Vinoth S, Vemula HL, Haralayya B, Mamgain P, Hasan MF, Naved M. Application of cloud computing in banking and e-commerce and related security threats. Materials Today: Proceedings. 2022;**51**:2172-2175

[50] Ramalingam C, Mohan P. Addressing semantics standards for cloud portability and interoperability in multi cloud environments. Symmetry. 2021;**13**(2):317

[51] Ramchand K, Baruwal Chhetri M, Kowalczyk R. Enterprise adoption of cloud computing with application portfolio profiling and application portfolio assessment. Journal of Cloud Computing. 2021;**10**(1):1-8

[52] Shabbir M, Shabbir A, Iwendi C, Javed AR, Rizwan M, Herencsar N, et al. Enhancing security of health information using modular encryption standards in mobile cloud computing. IEEE Access. 2021;**9**:8820-8834

[53] Ahmad W, Rasool A, Javed AR, Baker T, Jalil Z. Cyber security in iot-based cloud computing: A comprehensive survey. Electronics. 2021;**11**(1):16

[54] Mukherjee S, Chittipaka V, Baral MM, Srivastava SC. Integrating the challenges of cloud computing in supply chain management. In: Recent Advances in Industrial Production. Singapore: Springer; 2022. pp. 355-363

[55] Munteanu VI, Şandru C, Petcu D. Multi-cloud resource management: Cloud service interfacing. Journal of Cloud Computing. London, England: SpringerOpen; 2014;**3**(3):1-23. DOI: 10.1186/2192-113X-3-3

[56] Zulifqar I, Anayat S, Kharal I. A review of data security challenges and their solutions in cloud computing. International Journal of Information Engineering & Electronic Business. 2021;**13**(3):30-38

[57] Schlögl E. The Perception of Customer Relationship Management by Customers Versus Managers as a Critical Success Factor (Doctoral Dissertation, SOE); 2021

[58] AlTwaijiry A. Cloud Computing Present Limitations and Future Trends. ScienceOpen Preprints; 2021

[59] Costa B, Barreto PS. A risk perception indicator to evaluate the migration of government legacy systems to the cloud. International Journal of Information Systems in the Service Sector (IJISSS). 2021;**13**(1):68-87

[60] El Ioini N, Barzegar HR, Pahl C. Trust management for service migration in multi-access edge computing environments. Computer Communications. 2022;**194**:167-179

[61] Mansour IEA, Bouchachia H, Cooper K. Exploring live cloud migration on amazon EC2. In: 2017 IEEE 5th International Conference on Future Internet of Things and Cloud (FiCloud). Prague, Czech Republic: IEEE; 2017, August. pp. 366-371

[62] Palwe R, Kulkarni G, Dongare A. A new approach to hybrid cloud. International Journal of Computer Science and Engineering Research and Development (IJCSERD). 2012;**2**(1):1-6

[63] Rafique A, Walraven S, Lagaisse B, Desair T, Joosen W. Towards portability and interoperability support in middleware for hybrid clouds. In: 2014 IEEE Conference on Computer Communications Workshops (INFOCOM WKSHPS). Toronto, Canada: IEEE; 2014. pp. 7-12

[64] Yussupov V, Breitenbücher U, Leymann F, Müller C. Facing the unplanned migration of serverless applications: A study on portability problems, solutions, and dead ends. In: Proceedings of the 12th IEEE/ACM International Conference on Utility and Cloud Computing. Stuttgart, Germany: ACM; 2019. pp. 273-283

[65] Liu Y, Ni Z, Karlsson M, Gong S. Methodology for digital transformation with internet of things and cloud computing: A practical guideline for innovation in small-and medium-sized enterprises. Sensors. 2021;**21**(16):5355

[66] Briscoe G, Marinos A. Digital ecosystems in the clouds: Towards community cloud computing. In: 2009 3rd IEEE International Conference on Digital Ecosystems and Technologies. New York, USA: IEEE; 2009. pp. 103-108

[67] Ferrer AJ. Inter-cloud research: Vision for 2020. Procedia Computer Science. 2016;**97**:140-143

[68] Mansour I, Sahandi R, Cooper K, Warman A. Interoperability in the heterogeneous cloud environment: A survey of recent user-centric approaches. In: Proceedings of the International Conference on Internet of Things and Cloud Computing. Cambridge, UK: ACM; 2016. pp. 1-7

[69] Kaur K, Sharma DS, Kahlon DKS. Interoperability and portability approaches in inter-connected clouds: A review. ACM Computing Surveys (CSUR). 2017;**50**(4):1-40

[70] Zhang Z, Wu C, Cheung DW. A survey on cloud interoperability: Taxonomies, standards, and practice. ACM SIGMETRICS Performance Evaluation Review. 2013;**40**(4):13-22

[71] Ullah S, Xuefeng Z. Cloud computing research challenges. New York, USA: Cornell University; 2013. pp. 1397-1401. arXiv preprint arXiv:1304.3203

[72] ENISA. Cloud Security Guide for SMEs [Online]. 2022. Available from: https://www.enisa.europa.eu/publications/cloud-security-guide-for-smes. [Accessed: October 25, 2022]

[73] Kratzke N. Lightweight virtualization cluster how to overcome cloud vendor lock-in. Journal of Computer and Communications. 2014;**2**(12):1

[74] CSA. Security Guidance for Cloud Computing [Online]. 2022. Available from: https://cloudsecurityalliance.org/research/guidance/. [Accessed: November 19, 2022]

[75] Tripathi A, Mishra A. Cloud computing security considerations. In: 2011 IEEE International Conference on Signal Processing, Communications and Computing (ICSPCC). Xi'an, China: IEEE; 2011. pp. 1-5

[76] Abu-Libdeh H, Princehouse L, Weatherspoon H. RACS: A case for cloud storage diversity. In: Proceedings of the 1st ACM Symposium on Cloud Computing. Indianapolis, USA: ACM; 2010. pp. 229-240

[77] Bohn RB, Messina J, Liu F, Tong J, Mao J. NIST cloud computing reference architecture. In: 2011 IEEE World Congress on Services. Gaithersburg, USA: IEEE; 2011. pp. 594-596

[78] Hochstein L, Moser R. Ansible: Up and Running: Automating Configuration Management and Deployment the Easy Way. Sebastopol, USA: O'Reilly Media, Inc.; 2017

[79] Brikman Y. Terraform: Up and Running. Sebastopol, USA: O'Reilly Media, Inc.; 2022

[80] Ebert C, Gallardo G, Hernantes J, Serrano N. DevOps. IEEE Software. 2016;**33**(3):94-100

[81] Riti P. Pro DevOps with Google Cloud Platform: With Docker, Jenkins, and Kubernetes. Westmeath, Ireland: Apress; 2018

[82] Iglesias JAM. Hands-on Microservices with Kotlin: Build Reactive and Cloud-Native Microservices with Kotlin Using Spring 5 and Spring Boot 2.0. Birmingham, UK: Packt Publishing Ltd.; 2018

[83] Bailey J, Stuart S. Faucet: Deploying SDN in the enterprise. Communications of the ACM. 2016;**60**(1):45-49

[84] Brief OS. OpenFlow-enabled SDN and network functions virtualization. Open Netw. Found. 2014;**17**:1-12

[85] Shackleford D. A Devsecops Playbook. Rockville, USA: SANS Institute; 2016

[86] Lewis GA. Role of standards in cloud-computing interoperability. In: 2013 46th Hawaii International Conference on System Sciences. Pittsburgh, USA: IEEE; 2013. pp. 1652-1661

[87] Kundra, V. Federal Cloud Computing Strategy. Washington, USA: White House; 2011

Chapter 5

Swarm Computing: The Emergence of a Collective Artificial Intelligence at the Edge of the Internet

Laisa Costa de Biase, Geovane Fedrecheski, Pablo Calcina-Ccori, Roseli Lopes and Marcelo Zuffo

Abstract

Billions of devices are interacting in a growing global network, currently designated as the Internet of Things (IoT). In this scenario, embedded computers with sensors and actuators are widespread in all sorts of smart things, transforming the way we live. The complexity produced by the enormous amount of devices expected in the future IoT leads to new challenges. Furthermore, current IoT architectures are highly cloud-centric and do not take advantage of all its potential. To overcome these issues, we propose Swarm computing as the emergence of a collective artificial intelligence out of a decentralized and organic network of cooperating devices. The major contribution of this article is to provide the reader with a comprehensive vision of the key aspects of the Swarm Computing paradigm. In addition, this article addresses technical solutions, related projects, and the Swarm Computing challenges that the research community is called to contribute with.

Keywords: swarm computing, internet of things, collective intelligence, distributed computing, ubiquitous computing, computer architecture

1. Introduction

In this chapter, we present the Swarm Computing paradigm. It is expected to be the evolution of the Internet of Things, the edge of edge computing, in which devices gain protagonism over cloud, leveraging a true open computing resource-sharing infrastructure.

The Internet of Things (IoT) is a global infrastructure that connects objects from the physical world and provides advanced services [1]. Computers with sensors and actuators are embedded in everyday objects, making them smart. In traditional deployments, these devices retrieve huge data that generates knowledge with big-data analysis. The global Internet of Things (IoT) market was valued at US$ 201 billion in 2022 and is projected to reach US$ 410 billion by 2026 [2]. IoT advances are positively impacting diverse areas such as home, manufacturing, medicine, and urban life.

Due to their growing computing power, embedded devices are gaining higher responsibilities that, in the first IoT generation, were exclusively performed in the cloud. This paradigm, called Edge Computing, breaks the centralized model and reduces the amount of data sent to the cloud for processing and the response time for critical applications. Furthermore, the edge computing paradigm increases the security and privacy of data by avoiding the need for transmission and the overall reduction of costs of the cloud infrastructure [3, 4]. Among the main challenges in edge computing is the programmability of the heterogeneous platforms running in the edge, with different computing capabilities, operating systems, and programming languages. The naming of the enormous number of available things is also an unsolved challenge due to the various network protocols available and the lack of standardization. Privacy and security are among the most important challenges in terms of authentication and authorization for the use of devices. Finally, a common model for data abstraction, a comprehensive service management system, and metrics for optimization are among other relevant challenges.

We compare this expected evolution of the IoT to the changes that happened on the Internet. First, the Web was a provider of static content. Then, with Web 2.0, it became participative and democratic; that is, common people assumed a leading role, publishing their content and even trading goods. Finally, Web 3.0 emerged, favoring the culture of sharing, in which individuals exchange resources for mutual benefit (trading an English class for a text review, for example). Similarly, we expect that with the increasing computing power, smart objects will play a major role in the future IoT, by increasing their participation in data processing and establishing cooperative relations. Cooperation will occur through the spontaneous and autonomous organization of devices to solve problems collaboratively, resulting in the emergence of collective artificial intelligence. We call this network of autonomous cooperating devices Swarm computing.

The Swarm is a bio-inspired framework of autonomous smart objects. In parallel with swarms of bees, with specialized bees contributing to a common goal; the Swarm is composed of specialized devices whose interaction solves a common problem. Swarm computing behaves like an organism and shows an organized behavior that results in an emergent collective intelligence. Analogously to specialized honeybees, and the Swarm consists of heterogeneous devices, which might range from high-power processing servers to low-power wearable devices.

Human participation in the Swarm network is also of crucial importance, since the Swarm is at the service of humans. It shall be able to identify and meet real-life needs. Being able to "extract" needs – either inferring from the context or through direct human-interaction. It is especially relevant since the Internet of Things of the future will be composed of thousands of devices per human, new interaction mechanisms avoiding individual configuration and direct control are demanded.

To illustrate an application of the Swarm in our daily lives, we present the following example. Penny, Alice's cat, goes every day for a walk through the neighborhood and is back by dinner time. Once she did not come back, and Alice was really worried. How could the Swarm be used to help Alice to find her cat? Alice could simply ask for Penny, and opportunistically, the Swarm would gather sensors to capture Alice's request. Any microphone could be used, from Alice's smartphone or from a baby monitor. This request could be done at a high semantic level, asking directly "Where is Penny?", and local or remote resources could be used to realize that Penny is a cat and which her attributes are (appearance, weight, etc.). Alice home-network devices could be used to help find Penny: surveillance cameras, a baby monitor, and motion sensors that are usually used to automatically turn the lights on. However, it is not enough if Penny is out of the house. This way, the Swarm allows for actively gathering resources from other networks, such as the surveillance cameras from the street. The images could be processed by a computer vision service available in the cloud. Each usage of a third-party resource has associated retribution in the Swarm economy that will allow other owners to have priority to their own requests. The Swarm could also be applicable in other scenarios where resource sharing is key, such as looking for a missing person or object, in agribusiness with drone sharing, and in smart buildings by enabling automatic sharing of processing nodes, projectors, displays, windows and doors automation systems, HVAC systems, sensors, and many other devices.

The contribution of this paper is to provide a comprehensive description of the key aspects of the Swarm vision, focusing on its principles and challenges. We also review prior work and present an application example. Additionally, we present our initial architecture and implementation.

This is relevant for providing a software infrastructure that allows an open and global network of devices that can collaborate sharing resources with each other. Current Internet of Things implementations are restricted to niches and proprietary networks. An example is the home-network standards, such as UPnP which connects devices in the household environments, connecting TVs, computers, and smartphones, among others. On the other hand, the Swarm paradigm aims to provide technologies and strategies to connect billions of heterogeneous devices in a flexible and scalable way.

2. Other initiatives

While the IoT term refers to a large network of connected devices, some of those ideas were anticipated with other names. Already in 1994, the term ubiquitous computing (UC) [5] was used to describe a vision where computing devices are widespread at all scales throughout everyday life. While vastly present in human activities, this computation is almost invisible and does not draw attention to itself. This paradigm is part of the IoT current vision, embedding intelligence in everyday objects.

In 2001, Autonomic Computing (AC) [6] was proposed as a solution to the capital challenge that complexity represented for the future of computing systems, whose management goes beyond human capabilities. The AC approach deals with complexity reproducing the human autonomic nervous system, consisting of self-configuration, self-optimization, self-healing, and self-protection. This need for self-managed systems gains renewed importance in the context of the increasing complexity of the IoT, although this previously proposed solution was too complex to deploy.

The Swarm was inspired by a work that made an analogy between biological and digital ecosystems, in 2007 [7]. It briefly mentions the term swarm to refer to a set of computing agents interacting and engaged in solving a common problem. Four aspects were highlighted for digital ecosystems: interaction and engagement, balance, domain clustered and loosely coupled individuals, and self-organization. In addition, semantic Web technologies were recommended for information exchange, attribute modeling, and integrity check.

The Social IoT approach [8] looks forward to advancing the current IoT vision presenting an alternative to the producer-consumer paradigm, by collaborating with other counterparts toward a common goal, as the Swarm does. This approach, however, proposes the implementation of social-like capabilities to the objects, enhancing trust between "friends" objects. The inter-object relationship is related to the human social network.

In the last decade, the cloud has emerged as the principal responsible for data storage and processing that is provided and consumed by personal computers and mobile devices. The IoT adds a communication layer between the physical and logical (cyber) world. Initially, in the IoT first generation, devices are used as data providers. In the second IoT generation, devices are empowered, distributing the processing. This new paradigm is exploited in the Fog Computing [9] and Edge Computing [3] approaches. These definitions use the general idea of performing processing closer to the devices. In Fog Computing, network equipment, and PCs execute part of the processing. In the Edge computing approach, devices do it by themselves. The Swarm vision is aligned with the Edge Computing paradigm, as it aims to make devices less dependent on the cloud and favors a more decentralized IoT.

The Swarm term, applied in the IoT context, was first mentioned by Jan Rabaey in 2008, as a sensory swarm, connecting trillions of sensing and actuating devices connected through a single abstraction platform at the edge of the cloud [10, 11]. Subsequent work led to a more concrete definition of the Swarm [12, 13], proposing an initial architecture. They also outlined a common framework for devices to communicate and share resources, called Swarm OS [14], that was later developed.

3. Major challenges

We identify five main challenges to achieve the Swarm realization: *communication and cooperation* among devices, *human-interaction* with the network, support for *resource-constrained devices*, *security,* and the inherent *network complexity*.

3.1 Communication

Communication is the first step to establishing cooperation among devices. The Swarm is a highly heterogeneous environment that does not pose restrictions to its participants, configuring an open system. Traditional standards enable communication in open systems, but they generate niches (e.g., digital home, industry, etc.), limiting system evolution. This flexibility issue comes from static documents that generate products in which it is necessary to run firmware updates to accommodate standards reviews. Open systems pose security risks as well. Since, in IoT, many participants are resource-constrained, traditional security solutions are not applicable. Furthermore, at the Edge of the Internet, there is a fragmentation of IP and non-IP protocols, IoT technologies such as 6LoWPAN, Bluetooth, LoRa, and Sigfox, which causes fundamental interoperability problems. In summary, this challenge is related to how to achieve an open system with flexibility, broad scope, and security. Also, how to perform interoperability among Swarm agents, considering their different computing capabilities and network protocols.

3.2 Cooperation

In the Swarm context, cooperation consists of sharing resources among participants to accomplish high-level tasks. The result of this cooperation will manifest as a collective intelligence that emerges from the Swarm. Aspects that have to be dealt with are the discovery of resources spread around the globe and the autonomous and spontaneous orchestration of the shared resources, that is, how to use and "embed" this resource inside the consumer's business logic in execution time (in opposition to programming time) without human intervention. This cooperation must be balanced, satisfying objectives from individuals as well as from the Swarm participants as a whole. In this context, new concepts arise, such as trust, virtual currency, billing, reputation, and a full virtual economic system. This phenomenon represents a perfect parallel to a growing trend in the current world economy called the sharing economy, which favors the sharing of physical resources over the acquisition of new ones. Examples are Uber and Airbnb. The resource sharing in the Swarm represents its digital equivalent. A consequence is consumption reduction and better global use of resources.

3.3 Resource-constrained devices

Resource-constrained devices are an essential segment of the current IoT participants, whose operation has a strong focus on energy saving and miniaturization. The energy consumption of these wireless technologies has a significant impact on battery life. The device consumes energy to collect data by sensing the environment and processing and communicating the data. Therefore, all system parts, including software and hardware parts, should be considered to optimize energy consumption. Wireless energy harvesting from environmental sources like solar power is one of the best ways to supply energy for many sensors from the hardware perspective. It is also essential to consider the way how the IoT devices communicate to improve the efficiency of existing power sources in the device considering the data rate of IoT terminals and distances. These specifications should be considered in a communication system to efficiently use power and spectrum. Energy-efficient devices are imperative to make the existent applications greener and more environmentally friendly. On the other hand, to achieve a decentralized swarm of devices, increasing computer activity is expected to be delegated to the edge of the network, allow more efficient use of resources, provide highly responsive services, and enforce a privacy policy. This conflict represents a significant challenge to implementing the Swarm network.

3.4 Human-interaction

Although the Swarm consists of a nonbiological network, human beings play a central role in the Swarm, as it assists humans to interact with the physical world and with other humans. The complexity of the Swarm, involving billions of devices, makes it unmanageable by a person. Thus, a significant challenge is to develop interfaces with high-level semantics and proactive behavior. An interface with high-level semantics abstracts the network's actual resources allowing humans to focus on the intended result instead of focusing on the resources management and, in the process, to make this goal to be achieved. Additionally, the Swarm has the potential to explore an opportunistic gathering of available interfaces exploring the diversity of devices capable of interacting with people. Proactive behavior emerges from past interactions, extracting policies automatically. For example, an agent can infer that, for a given person, comfort takes priority over power saving, which will leverage a policy where the air conditioning will work almost continuously. A person that prioritizes power saving will have a home where the temperature oscillation is more tolerated so the air conditioner will often be off. Additionally, known preferences may be shared among agents to support this proactivity. For example, personal ambient temperature preference may be shared with occupants in a room with an HVAC (Heating, Ventilation, and Air Conditioning) system to maximize comfort.

3.5 Security

A large number of devices collecting and sharing data will open questions about what kinds of data are being shared, who has the right to perform this sharing, and how this data can be protected. Since the devices composing the Swarm will communicate openly across different networks, they will be exposed to a diverse array of cyber threats. Therefore, guaranteeing the privacy and trustworthiness of data in transit will represent a significant challenge. This is aggravated by the fact that, while many devices in the IoT are resource-constrained, cryptographic algorithms, such as those based on asymmetric cryptography, require significant processing and memory resources. Furthermore, since the messages will likely traverse different kinds of networks, the protocols for message security must be able to cope with such a heterogeneous environment. While a possible solution lies in protecting messages at the application layer, the currently accepted protocol for Internet security (Transport Layer Security—TLS) works at the transport layer. Another important challenge concerning security is device identification. Network identifiers such as MAC and IP addresses are easily spoofed, and more secure approaches such as certificates and cloud accounts depend on centralized architectures [15]. This raises questions and challenges regarding the need for secure and decentralized identification solutions for IoT devices [16]. Finally, while Swarm devices are expected to collaborate, they must do so in a controlled manner to prevent security issues. What is needed is a high-level authorization mechanism that device owners can use to specify the collaboration rules. Challenges in this respect arise from the global scale and decentralized nature of Swarm computing.

3.6 Complexity

The Swarm has characteristics of a complex network: autonomy, connectivity, self-organization, emergent behavior, and co-evolution with an environment, and billions of autonomous and interconnected computing devices interact. Among a diversity of resources, there are sensors and actuators. Sensors make the system subject to uncertain and unpredictable events from the physical world, and actuators will impact the physical environment, creating a symbiotic ecosystem. The opportunistic organization of these devices will provide a robust self-organization structure that is perceived as intelligent since it is capable of evolving over time.

4. Swarm principles

The Swarm computing approach can be better understood by examining its two underlying principles: resource sharing and autonomy. These principles can be subdivided into more specific aspects that guide the Swarm evolution, as shown in **Figure 1**.

Autonomy confers devices to the ability to share resources without needing manual input from humans (self-organization). These automatic interactions are not programmed into the system beforehand but emerge naturally during execution time (spontaneity). As a result, the participants may encounter optimized paths and

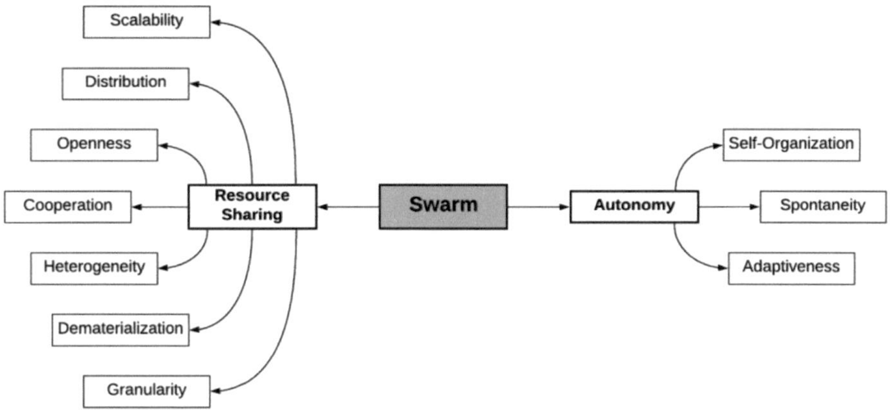

Figure 1.
The Swarm principles and their subsumed aspects.

risky interactions over time, from which they must learn to unexpected situations. Autonomy can be further subdivided into the following aspects:

- Self-organization: when a task or problem needs to be solved, the Swarm devices must be able to organize themselves to achieve the desired results. The devices should perform this behavior, that is, not requiring step-by-step commands from a human operator or a centralized entity.

- Spontaneity: Swarm devices should not necessarily only work in a predefined way. Rather, they should be able to infer changes in their context and react properly to new and unexpected situations.

- Adaptiveness: since each Swarm device can compute only a fragment of the global context, certain operations may be carried out in suboptimal ways, especially when confronted for the first time. Therefore it is important that devices can learn from previous experiences and adapt to perform better in future scenarios.

Resource sharing allows a set of entities (distribution) to provide and consume resources from each other for mutual benefit (cooperation). These entities may have different amounts (heterogeneity) of resources to share, use open and interoperable protocols (openness), and cooperate independently of their physical structure and location (dematerialized). Finally, resources can be composed at different levels (granular), and their scope may range from local to global (scalable). The following aspects are key to enabling resource sharing in the Swarm:

- Scalability: refers to the capacity to support a great number of participants, achieving billions, with global and local communication capability, comprising machine-to-machine and over-the-Internet interoperation;

- Distribution: the participant devices act without a central coordinator;

- Openness: the conditions to connect and interoperate with the Swarm are open, widely accessible, allowing for new products and services to be created by anyone. Despite, is that, security, and privacy risks, it makes systems more powerful (efficient, through sharing of resources), more resilient (by the use of redundant resources through dynamic reconfiguration), and more capable, enabling applications that have not been realized yet;

- Cooperation: allow a set of entities to provide and consume resources from each other, exploring synergies and generating economy;
- Heterogeneity: the Swarm participants are diverse, with different functions, complexity, processing and communication capabilities, operating systems, etc.;
- Dematerialization: participant resources are exposed and shared, making the physical boundaries to lose importance;
- Granularity: the cooperating services could be understood as a set of reusable components that can be organized to compose bigger ones, putting together a hierarchy of components.

The Swarm principles act as guidelines for the research and development of the Swarm computing paradigm and its applications. For example, imagine a set of cameras and smart doors that cooperate. When a person approaches the system, the cameras will tell the doors whether to open or not. Or in an emergency scenario, a car passing by accident can automatically share a danger alert with surrounding devices. Both examples work without human intervention (autonomy) and create value through cooperation (resource sharing). By combining these two principles in a cohesive model/platform/abstraction, the Swarm creates a new era for the Internet of Things.

5. Architecture

In this section, we propose our architecture for the realization of the Swarm Computing vision.

5.1 Processing balance

In the Swarm, devices are used not just for sensing and actuation, but also for hosting applications and business logic. This leads to architectural differences between the Swarm and other IoT solutions. Although the Swarm shares principles with the Edge Computing vision, many Edge Computing architectures still run applications on remote servers in the cloud, while edge devices are limited to preprocessing tasks.

Most IoT architectures are organized into three layers: perception/actuation, transport, and application. The perception/actuation layer is responsible for gathering information from the physical world and acting on it. The perception layer comprehends the devices with embedded electronics, particularly sensors and actuators. The transport layer connects devices to the cloud; it includes gateways and the network infrastructure (i.e., the Internet). The application layer includes IoT middleware and applications [17]. Other works split the application layer into three: Business Intelligence, Application, and Middleware [18]. These layered models evidence that despite the generic definitions of the IoT term, their architectures and solutions are centralized in servers in the cloud. In general, the application runs on a server in the cloud and devices become information providers.

Current Edge Computing efforts promote the participation of sensors and gateways in data processing and analysis [18]. The layered architecture in Edge Computing puts preprocessing between the layers of perception and transport. This preprocessing at the edge includes monitoring, storage, and security. While this approach aims to reduce the strong centralization of cloud computing, it still relies on the cloud and centralized applications.

The Swarm meets the goal of decentralization better, empowering devices in the autonomous composition of new services. In the Swarm, devices seek resources from other devices to cooperate and achieve complex goals. In addition, applications run on the devices themselves, thus creating a large and scalable network of distributed processing.

5.2 Distribution of resources

Cooperation in the Swarm is achieved through resource sharing. We use a microservices approach to expose device resources. Microservices are an evolution of traditional service-oriented architectures, to provide better scalability, performance, loose coupling, functional independence, reusability, resilience, and cost [19].

In the past decade, Service-Oriented Architecture (SOA) became a popular paradigm for integrating distributed services across organizations. SOA is a software design pattern based on the dynamic selection of services to other applications. The most serious drawback of SOA is its centralized integration, based on a service bus. Microservices move intelligence to the endpoints, eliminating this centralized integration. In addition, each service is either independent or broken into smaller independent services.

We propose two kinds of microservices in the Swarm: platform and application. The platform microservices consist of common microservices that the Swarm participants use to support the interaction among them. An example of a platform microservice is the discovery service, which helps to locate resources in the Swarm. In addition, swarm devices offer application microservices to share their resources, such as a service to read a temperature sensor.

While an application in the Swarm may run in isolation, the true potential of the Swarm lies in service composition. When a service uses other services, it creates a graph of resources. Devices that own those resources form groups of interacting participants in the Swarm.

5.3 Swarm OS

IoT frameworks usually provide a software module in the cloud, called Broker, that helps service consumers to access service providers. Our Swarm OS is a Broker enhancement. So the IoT Broker is a Swarm Broker or, finally, a Swarm OS.

MQTT [20] is a popular IoT framework based on the publish/subscribe protocol. The MQTT Broker is a central entity that manages data publications and subscriptions. The IoT Broker Generic Enabler is a component of the Fiware middleware [21] that interfaces with devices providing publish/subscribe managements and associations between device-level and things-level descriptions. The Fiware middleware resides in a server in the cloud.

The Swarm Broker is conceptually different. It is a software agent installed on each device, turning it into an "insect," that is, a member of the Swarm. The Swarm Broker is responsible for providing the platform microservices that provide service discovery; a distributed registry of services; access control to resources; protocol binding; policy management; service-level agreements; semantic mediation; and optimization.

As the Swarm is an open and heterogeneous environment, we propose a minimum Swarm Broker that includes a core set of the platform microservices to be installed on every device [22]. Advanced features are provided by more complex Brokers that run on more capable devices. Proxy servers can serve legacy or less capable devices that are unable to run the minimum Broker.

Device interaction in the Swarm happens in three phases: registration, cooperation initiation, and interaction support. In the Registration phase, services such as cameras, temperature sensors, and smart doors register themselves in a Swarm Broker, becoming available to be shared within the Swarm. The Cooperation Initiation phase starts when a Swarm participant demands a resource and is concluded by a service-level agreement establishment with the best available resource at the moment. Finally, the interaction support phase occurs when cooperation is already established and running. A direct link between the service consumer and the provider is established, while the Swarm Broker acts as a helper by providing contract maintenance, protocol adaptation, optimization, authentication, and access control.

The Registration phase consists of the check-in of a service provider to the Swarm. As each device has at least a minimum Broker inside, service providers will communicate with their own local Swarm Broker (i.e., in the same device), registering its resources. A service description is registered, containing all the necessary information to verify the resource's suitability and then access the service, such as the functional description, quality of service, and required retribution. Once the resource is registered, it is available to the Swarm for sharing. The registration is done in a local registry of the Broker and may be sent to another Broker that would act as a service directory. This strategy allows for an opportunistic registry that can be centralized, totally or partially distributed accordingly to the capabilities of the available Brokers at the moment.

Flexibility is achieved by using semantics in the service descriptions [23]. Semantics uses ontologies to define terms and their relationship, allowing to build standardized protocols for niches that can be expanded or interconnected by linking various ontologies together. For example, the services used in home networking, such as a television and a baby monitor, may connect to services from the city, such as a public surveillance camera pointing to the street. If a company association that deals with home network defines an ontology in which the service "camera" and "display" are defined; other association of companies that deals with smart cities may create an ontology with their own terms, such as "city_cameras," "semaphore," "surveillance_camera" and "biometrics_camera." If an application uses the television inside a house to display images from a street camera, the Swarm may automatically do this mapping linking both ontologies to finding the equivalences.

The Cooperation Initiation phase is started when a Swarm participant, a Service Consumer, searches for a given resource on its local Swarm Broker, that is, the Broker that is running in its same device. The local Swarm Broker that has received this request will then communicate with other Brokers in the Swarm to identify the best suitable resource and then negotiate the establishment of a service-level agreement.

The discovery has four stages. First, the Broker searches in its local registry. Second, the Broker sends a query to other Brokers that act as third-party registries.

Third, a bootstrap mechanism defines the address of the Brokers to forward the request. This mechanism is complemented by a history of past interactions and a heuristic search for Broker' addresses. Third, the request to locate the service is forwarded to the local network, using direct communication, such as multicast. The fourth mechanism uses a mediation service that expands the discovery request to equivalent services, based on a functionality taxonomy, instead of the exact matching of a keyword or hash code.

This discovery returns a set of services that meet the given functional requirements. The resulting set of services is evaluated from the quality of service point of view, verifying policies about access control, priorities, and retribution mechanisms. A contract is then established with the best service provider available, setting a service-level agreement. To achieve fairness, the Swarm supports a microeconomy model with credits exchange for sharing a resource (payments) and a reputation system. Finally, the Swarm Broker returns this contract and the service information to the participant that requested the service.

The discovery process returns directly the operation that the consumer will use to access the service, allowing direct communication between service consumer and provider; since the operation is not predefined and is discovered just as the provider, it is called as automatic execution.

Interaction Support occurs when cooperation is already established and running; thus, there is a direct link between service consumer and provider, and the Swarm Broker may provide some support services: contract maintenance, protocol adaptation, general optimization, authentication, and access control. Currently, just access control and CoAP-HTTP binding are supported. The Swarm Brokers store and process access control policies and rules, having the role of supporting decisions of their local service providers and participating in access control enforcement [22]. Proxies are platform services that are ideally transparent and bidirectional, creating a unified virtual network that merges distinct physical networks. This type of proxy intercepts messages and redirects responses to pass through them [23].

6. Implementation approach

So far, we have presented the Swarm challenges, principles, and architecture, which include the Swarm Broker as a key enabler. This section discusses the implementation aspects of the Swarm OS, including an overview of the technologies employed and the services it implements. As the Swarm is a heterogeneous platform, two versions of the Broker have been developed: a Minimum Broker and a Full Broker. We start by briefly describing the former and then proceed to give more details on the latter.

The minimum Swarm Broker implements only two essential services that enable the device to be discovered by other Swarm devices: Registry and Discovery. It was implemented using Lua programming language, targeting a node with an ESP8266 microcontroller. This implementation has only 2% of the size and uses 0.02% of memory compared to the full Swarm Broker implementation [24]. While this proof-of-concept can be enhanced, particularly by adding access control enforcement to protect its services, it showed that even highly restricted devices could participate in the Swarm network while relying on more powerful nodes for more complex services.

The full Swarm Broker is implemented using the Elixir programming language and has been tested on Linux laptops, servers, and single-board computers. As shown in **Figure 2**, it follows a protocol-agnostic architecture, in which the Broker Core module executes business logic, and is separated from protocol-specific modules, such as Broker HTTP and Multicast. A Broker HTTP Client is also present to help the Swarm Broker call other Swarm Brokers and services independently. As application services may also use the Swarm Broker Client, it is integrated within the Broker as an external library. Modules that implement alternative protocols also exist, such as the Swarm Broker CoAP [25] and its respective Client, as shown in faded colors in **Figure 2**.

The Swarm Broker implements the following platform services:

- **Registry:** responsible for keeping a record of available services in the Swarm. It receives a service description file serialized as JSON-LD via the Broker HTTP interface and saves it into memory. During registration, the Registry will verify whether there is a Semantic Registry Service available, to whom it will forward the service description as well. The Semantic Registry Service enhances the capabilities of the Swarm Broker by allowing service inference during the discovery process.

- **Discovery:** allow the search of services in the Swarm network. It receives a request containing a Query Description and responds with a list of matching services. The Query Description is a JSON-LD file containing parameters that specify the desired services. For example, a query may include "type: camera," to indicate that it is looking for camera services.

- **Distances:** stores the distance between a service and a Bluetooth beacon. It receives periodical updates from services capable of measuring their own distance against beacons. These distances can then be used to refine a Discovery query, for exmaple, search for services that are up to three meters from the TV.

- **Access control:** maintains and enforces access policies among services. It is divided into a Policy Decision Point (PDP), responsible for evaluating policies against requests, and a Policy Administration Point (PAP), responsible for managing policies.

- **Policy sharing:** allows policy sharing among services. The current implementation uses the Discovery service to discover other Swarm devices, and then pulls and pushes the access policies, according to the needs of a policy administrator.

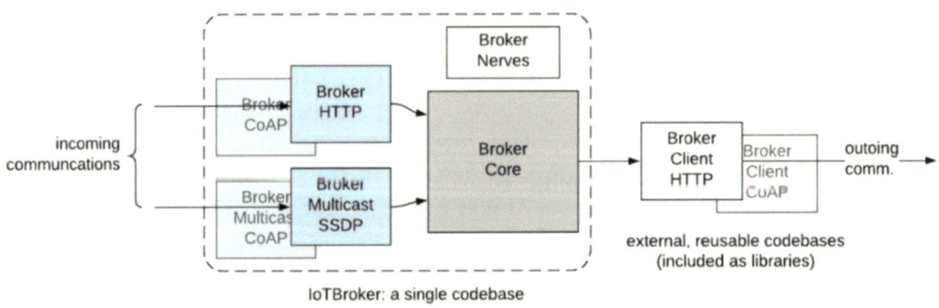

Figure 2.
Swarm Broker support for interaction.

- **Policy management**: provides a GUI for editing access policies. It first connects to the policy sharing services in order to obtain the policies from nearby devices, which are then shown in a Web interface. Next, a user edits and saves the new policies sent to the respective devices through the policy sharing service.

- **Contract:** allows a consumer to establish a service-level agreement with service providers, including the discovery and selection of suitable services, defining usage conditions, paying for it, and evaluating the service. It is one of the most complex Broker services, as it composes the Discovery, Access Control, and Reputation services and implements two blockchain clients. Creating a contract involves eight steps, depicted in **Figure 3**. The first step is to have a registered service provider (1) available to be contracted. Then, a service consumer tries to contract (2) a target service, by sending a query to its Broker, which will use the Discovery service (3) to find services within the Swarm network. After finding a list of services, the best service is selected (4), using price and reputation as the sorting criteria. Then, negotiation (5) takes place, which consists of having the consumer and the provider to accept the proposed contract. If all goes well, a (6) digital currency payment is made through a blockchain. After the payment is confirmed, establishing a service-level agreement (7) will be triggered, causing the service provider to create an access policy allowing the consumer to use its services. Finally, the two Brokers will evaluate each other

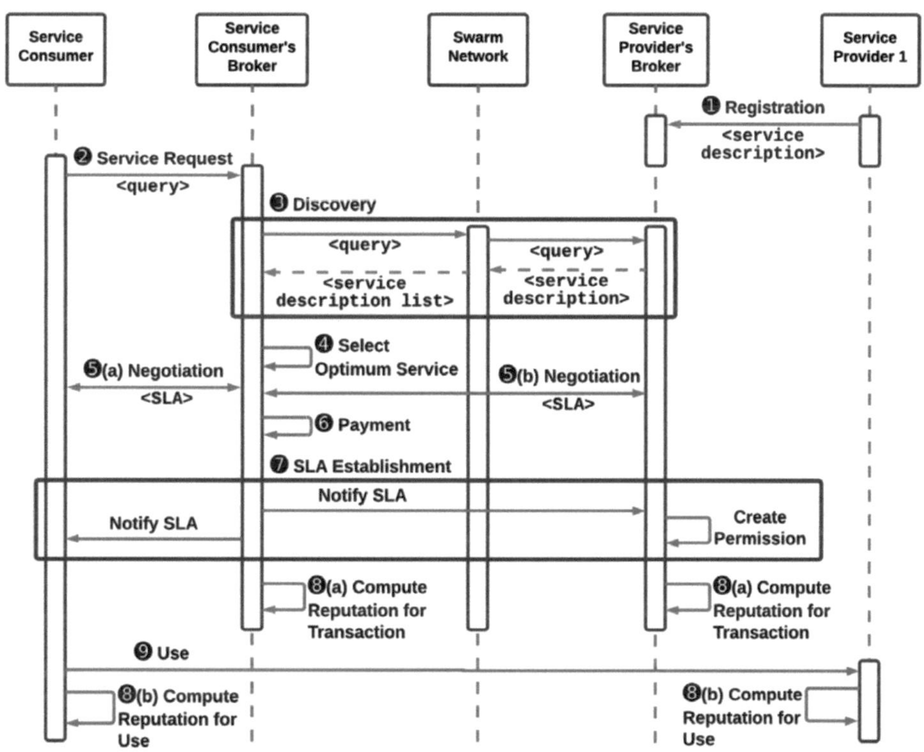

Figure 3.
Swarm broker codebase architecture.

Swarm broker stages	Services involved
Registration	Registry, policy sharing
Cooperation initiation	Discovery, contract, access control
Interaction support	Distances, access control, policy management, reputation

Table 1.
Swarm interaction stages and the main services involved.

and compute a reputation value (8a), the consumer will use the service provider (9) for a limited amount of time, and reputation for service usage will be computed (8b).

- **Reputation:** allows consumers and providers to rate each other. This service receives the reputation computed by service consumers and providers regarding a contract they have established and run. These reputations will be forwarded to a blockchain, which will act as a public ledger for the reputation of all Swarm services.

- **Semantic registry**: in addition to the basic functionality of the Registry module, the Semantic Registry stores the information of available services using a knowledge base that relies on an ontology and has a semantic representation of the services in the Swarm network. As in the Registry module, the Semantic Registry receives a service description based on the JSON-LD format, which natively includes semantic information about the services. Additionally, this module uses an inference engine to expand the original query and bring compatible services according to their semantic service description.

The described Broker services give support to application services, allowing them to be part of the Swarm. **Table 1** relates the three stages of Broker support, described in Section 5, to the services implemented in the Broker.

7. Proof-of-concept

To demonstrate the functionality of the Swarm Broker implementation, we have developed a use case applying the Swarm to a surveillance application, specifically the scenario described in the introduction of this article. To implement the scenario, we use the following services, also shown in **Figure 4**:

- **Personal assistant**: the system frontend, capable of natural language processing to identify commands and parameters. Additionally, the Swarm Assistant reunites information about the person who owns a device group. It might have information that the owner has a pet, a cat called Penny, and even have some pictures of it.

- **Object finder**: a service specialized in finding objects. It discovers and connects Camera Services to Identification Services.

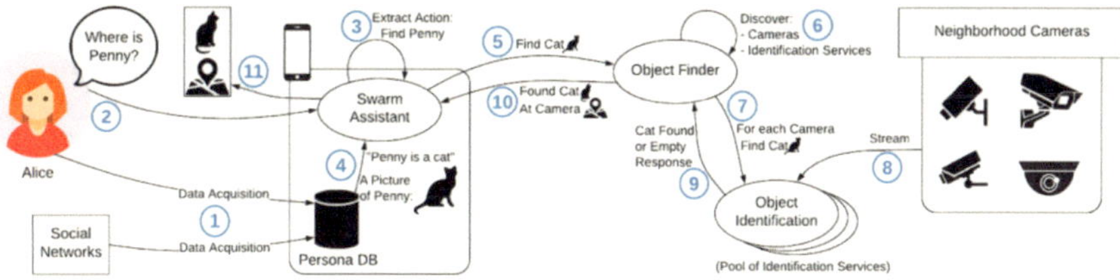

Figure 4.
Finding Penny implementation using the Swarm.

- **Camera service**: a service that makes camera frames available to allowed consumers.

- **Identification service**: an image processing service that takes two images as inputs, a picture of a cat and a camera frame, and returns whether the former appears in the latter.

It is important to highlight that, Since the Swarm uses a service-oriented approach, the physical location of devices is not important, except for limiting the scope of the interactions. In our implementation, each service is implemented in a different device to exercise the decentralization principle of the Swarm. Thus, each device has exactly one application service, and one Swarm Broker, that supports the service interactions. The communication flow of this example is described below:

1. **Data acquisition:** In this phase, the Persona Database is pre-populated. The "Persona" is a concept adopted by the Swarm to digitally represent human users. In our scenario, the Persona Database contains data about Alice, such as preferences, friends, and pets. This information may be manually inserted by Alice, or automatically extracted from her social networks, or a combination of both.

2. **Voice command:** issued by Alice, it is processed by the Swarm Assistant, an app that serves as an interface between users and the Swarm.

3. **Extract action:** using a Speech-to-Text service, the assistant obtains the action and other parameters from a voice command. In this case, the action ``Find" and the string "Penny," an unknown parameter, are extracted.

4. **Parameters qualification:** the assistant consults the Persona Database to get information about the extracted parameters. In this case, it learns that the object that it must Find is a Cat, obtains a picture of the cat, and also gets Alice's default preferences about the radius of object searches.

5. **Find cat:** the assistant uses the swarm network to discover an Object Finder, a service specialized in finding objects, and then asks the Object Finder to search for a cat, passing the cat's picture, and a radius relative to Alice's smartphone position, where the cat must be searched.

6. **Discover cameras and detection services:** based on Alice's preferences, the Object Finder will find the addresses of available cameras in her neighborhood and one or more Object Identification services.

7. **Identify cat:** for each of the discovered cameras, the Object Finder will call an Object Identification service, passing the address of the camera, the category of the object (i.e., cat), and a picture of the specific object that must be found. If there are less identification services than cameras, the requests will be enqueued and sent when an identification service becomes available.

8. **Stream:** each identification service will gather one camera's stream, and try to detect a cat. If successful, it will compare with the provided cat picture. Finally, if there is a match, the frame with the found cat will be returned, along with the position of the camera that captured the frame.

9. The frame and the location of the found cat are returned to Alice's Swarm Assistant. Now Alice knows where is Penny, her missing cat.

8. Discussion

As pointed out in the challenges section, communication and cooperation constitute the main challenges in the future of IoT. The importance of communication can be observed in two main areas: device-to-device and human-to-device. In the first case, we identify a research opportunity for autonomous intelligent agents to overcome the complexity of the resulting network. Regarding the second case, which involves human-to-device communication, we clearly see the need to deeply explore the understanding of human language, with emphasis on human commands. As the number of devices available to every person grows, a concise way to perform tasks involving several devices is more important. Recent advances in tools such as ChatGPT show the relevance of the convergence between the IoT and Natural Language Processing (NLP).

9. Conclusions

In this chapter, we have presented the Swarm computing vision, a decentralized and self-adaptive approach to overcome the limitations of cloud-centric architecture for the IoT. We presented the principles that have driven the conception of the Swarm and summarized the main challenges to achieving its realization: communication and cooperation of devices, the inclusion of resource-constrained devices, better interfaces for human-interaction, and the complex nature of the network. We also proposed an initial architecture, whose main component is the Broker, a communication mediator that aims to solve the interoperability of devices in the Swarm network. Besides, we listed a selection of technologies that enabled our implementation and described an application example that illustrates the potential of the Swarm network. Our advances in coping with the Swarm challenges can be summarized as follows. We developed four Broker implementations, using different programming languages: C, Lua, Java, and Elixir. We developed a minimum Broker implementation. We adopted open Web semantic technologies that facilitate device communication; we implemented a mechanism of semantic service discovery as a starting point for cooperation; and we implemented a CoAP-HTTP proxy that leverages transparent communication with resource-constrained devices with minimum impact. Additional effort is needed in all fronts of Swarm challenges to concretize the vision.

Acknowledgements

We could not have undertaken this journey without Dr. Jan Rabaey and inspiring work and talks. We would like to express our gratitude to CITI-USP.

This work was partially supported by LSI-Tec; FUNDEP-Rota2030, Stellantis and CEABS; MCTI and BNDES.

Author details

Laisa Costa de Biase*, Geovane Fedrecheski, Pablo Calcina-Ccori, Roseli Lopes and Marcelo Zuffo
Escola Politecnica of the University of Sao Paulo, Sao Paulo, Brazil

*Address all correspondence to: laisa.costa@usp.br

References

[1] International Telecommunication Union. Overview of the Internet of Things. Geneva, Switzerland: International Telecommunication Union; 2012

[2] IoT Analytics. Global IoT market size to grow 19% in 2023—IoT shows resilience despite economic downturn [Internet]. 2023. Available from: https://iot-analytics.com/iot-market-size/

[3] Shi W, Cao J, Zhang Q, Li Y, Xu L. Edge computing: Vision and challenges. IEEE Internet of Things Journal. 2016;**3**(5):637-646

[4] Shi W, Pallis G, Xu Z. Edge computing [Scanning the Issue]. Proceedings of the IEEE. 2019;**107**:1474-1781

[5] Weiser M. The computer for the 21st century. Scientific American. 1991;**265**(3):94-105

[6] Abeywickrama DB, Ovaska E. A survey of autonomic computing methods in digital service ecosystems. Service-Oriented Computing and Applications. 2017;**11**(1):1-31

[7] Boley H, Chang E. Digital ecosystems: Principles and semantics. In: 2007 Inaugural IEEE-IES Digital EcoSystems and Technologies Conference, Cairns, QLD, Australia, 2007. pp. 398-403

[8] Atzori L, Iera A, Morabito G. From "smart objects" to "social objects": The next evolutionary step of the internet of things. IEEE Communications Magazine. 2014;**52**(1):97-105

[9] Chiang M, Ha S, Risso F, Zhang T, Chih-Lin I. Clarifying fog computing and networking: 10 questions and answers. IEEE Communications Magazine. 2017;**55**(4):18-20

[10] Maliniak D. Visions Of The Future (Part 1): A Ubiquitous Cloud Of Computing. In Electronic Computer. Sept. 15, 2008. Available from: https://www.electronicdesign.com/markets/mobile/article/21778269/visions-of-the-future-part-1-a-ubiquitous-cloud-of-computing

[11] Lee EA, Hartmann B, Kubiatowicz J, Rosing TS, Wawrzynek J, Wessel D, et al. The swarm at the edge of the cloud. IEEE Design & Test. 2014;**31**(3):8-20

[12] Alippi C, Fantacci R, Marabissi D, Roveri M. A cloud to the ground: The new frontier of intelligent and autonomous networks of things. IEEE Communications Magazine. 2016;**54**(12):14-20

[13] Costa LC, Rabaey J, Wolisz A, Rosan M, Zuffo MK. Swarm os control plane: An architecture proposal for heterogeneous and organic networks. IEEE Transactions on Consumer Electronics. 2015;**61**(4):454-462

[14] Rabaey JM. The human intranet—Where Swarms and humans meet. IEEE Pervasive Computing. 2015;**14**(1):78-83

[15] Fedrecheski G, Rabaey JM, Costa LC, Ccori PCC, Pereira WT, Zuffo MK. Self-sovereign identity for IoT environments: A perspective. In: 2020 Global Internet of Things Summit (GIoTS). Dublin, Ireland. 2020. pp. 1-6

[16] Bartolomeu PC, Vieira E, Hosseini SM, Ferreira J. Self-sovereign identity: Use-cases, technologies, and challenges for industrial iot. In: 2019 24th IEEE International Conference on Emerging Technologies and Factory Automation (ETFA), Zaragoza, Spain. 2019. pp. 1173-1180

[17] Milić L, Jelenković L. A novel versatile architecture for internet of things. In: 2015 38th International Convention on Information and Communication Technology, Electronics and Microelectronics (MIPRO), Opatija, Croatia; 2015. pp. 1026-1031

[18] Sethi P, Sarangi SR. Internet of things: Architectures, protocols, and applications. Journal of Electrical and Computer Engineering. 2017;**2017**. Article ID 9324035, pages 25

[19] Salah T, Zemerly MJ, Yeun CY, Al-Qutayri M, Al-Hammadi Y. The evolution of distributed systems towards microservices architecture. In: 2016 11th International Conference for Internet Technology and Secured Transactions (ICITST); Barcelona, Spain. 2016. pp. 318-325

[20] Hunkeler U, Truong HL, Stanford-Clark A. MQTT-S—A publish/subscribe protocol for wireless sensor networks. In: 2008 3rd International Conference on Communication Systems Software and Middleware and Workshops (COMSWARE'08); Bangalore, India. 2008. pp. 791-798

[21] FIWARE Foundation. Fiware. The Internet. 2023. Available from: https://www.fiware.org/

[22] De Biase LC, Calcina-Ccori PC, Fedrecheski G, Duarte GM, Rangel PS, Zuffo MK. Swarm economy: A model for transactions in a distributed and organic iot platform. IEEE Internet of Things Journal. 2018;**6**(3):4561-4572

[23] Calcina-Ccori PC, De Biase LCC, Fedrecheski G, da Silva FSC, Zuffo MK. Enabling semantic discovery in the swarm. IEEE Transactions on Consumer Electronics. 2018;**65**(1):57-63

[24] De Biase LC, Ccori PC, Fedrecheski G, Navarro D, Lino RY, Zuffo MK. Swarm minimum broker: An approach to deal with the internet of things heterogeneity. In: 2018 Global Internet of Things Summit (GIoTS). Bilbao, Spain: IEEE; 2018. pp. 1-6

[25] Esquiagola J, Costa L, Calcina P, Zuffo M. Enabling CoAP into the swarm: A transparent interception CoAP-HTTP proxy for the internet of things. In: 2017 Global Internet of Things Summit (GIoTS). Geneva, Switzerland. 2017. pp. 1-6

Section 2

Edge Computing Applications

Chapter 6

Optimal Unmanned Aerial Vehicle Control and Designs for Load Balancing in Intelligent Wireless Communication Systems

Abhishek Mondal, Deepak Mishra, Ganesh Prasad and Ashraf Hossain

Abstract

Maintaining reliable wireless connectivity is essential for the continuing growth of mobile devices and their massive access to the Internet of Things (IoT). However, terrestrial cellular networks often fail to meet their required quality of service (QoS) demand because of the limited spectrum capacity. Although the deployment of more base stations (BSs) in a concerned area is costly and requires regular maintenance. Alternatively, unmanned aerial vehicles (UAVs) could be a potential solution due to their ability of on-demand coverage and the high likelihood of strong line-of-sight (LoS) communication links. Therefore, this chapter focuses on a UAV's deployment and movement design that supports existing BSs by reducing data traffic load and providing reliable wireless communication. Specifically, we design UAV's deployment and trajectory under an efficient resource allocation strategy, i.e., assigning devices' association indicators and transmitting power to maximize overall system's throughput and minimize the total energy consumption of all devices. For these implementations, we adopt reinforcement learning framework because it does not require all information about the system environment. The proposed methodology finds optimal policy using the Markov decision process, exploiting the previous environment interactions. Our proposed technique significantly improves the system's performance compared to the other benchmark schemes.

Keywords: unmanned aerial vehicle, reinforcement learning, energy efficiency, offloading, throughput

1. Introduction

With the proliferation of mobile electronic devices, such as smartphones, tablets, and more internet of things (IoT) gadgets, the need for high-speed wireless connectivity has been growing rapidly [1]. But, the existing cellular networks with limited spectrum, coverage, and energy capacity fail to satisfy users' quality of service (QoS) requirements. Hence, the next generation 5G technologies, such as device-to-device (D2D) communications, ultra-dense small cell networks, and millimeter wave (mmW) communications, are emerging as potential alternatives to deal with such issues [2, 3]. However, these modern 5G cellular networks face several challenges due to resource allocation, backhaul interferences, high reliance on the line of sight (LoS) link, and signal blockage. On the other hand, integration of unmanned aerial vehicles (UAVs) into the fifth-generation (5G) and sixth-generation (6G) cellular networks as aerial base stations would be a promising aspect to achieve several goals, namely ubiquitous accessibility, robust navigation, ease of monitoring and management, etc., because they can establish LoS dominant air to ground channel in a controllable manner [4]. Notably, cellular-connected UAV-assisted system gains significant performance improvement over the existing point-to-point UAV-ground communication in terms of coverage and throughput [5]. UAV also offload temporary high-traffic demands from terrestrial BSs during huge crowd events such as festivals, concerts, and stadium games [6]. Therefore, UAVs' utility in the cellular network is directly related to the highest number of serving users. Nevertheless, many challenges related to the utilization of UAVs need to be addressed, including their deployment strategy, trajectory optimization, and resource allocation under flight time limitations which affect instantaneous LoS probability and remarkably influence the system performance.

The relevant studies [7–10] optimized the trajectory and deployment of UAVs in different circumstances. However, most of them incorporate nonlinear algorithms that rely on average spatial throughput. Thus, computational complexity grows rapidly with the higher number of users and flight time. Moreover, practically without prior knowledge about the network state, it becomes very difficult for a UAV to find its path to accomplish a given real-time task. Alternatively, machine learning (ML) techniques [11–13] intelligently support UAVs and ground users in performing mission-oriented operations with low complexity when complete network information is not available. Particularly, reinforcement learning (RL), being a part of ML, can search for the optimal policy through trial and error while interacting with the environment [14]. Hence, this chapter investigates the optimal deployment, trajectory, and resource allocation of UAVs to meet the throughput requirements of the cellular network.

2. Background

The existing literature focuses on the deployment and movement of UAV relays for numerous applications. In [15], the authors estimated the optimal UAV relay position in a multi-rate communication system using theoretical and simulated analysis. The work in [16] investigated the mission planning of UAV relays to improve the connectivity of ground users. The authors of [17, 18] maximized the lower bound of the uplink transmission rate over the link between UAV relay and ground devices using dynamic heading adjusting approaches. For throughput maximization of the mobile relaying system, an iterative algorithm was developed [19, 20], which jointly optimized the relays' trajectory and transmitting power of the sources and UAVs by satisfying the practical constraints. In [21], the authors maximized the UAV relay network's throughput by optimizing transmit power, bandwidth, transmission rate, and relay deployment. However, in these works, a model-based centralized approach is used where all necessary system parameters are required. Additionally, the research gap still exists on enhancing network performance for source-destination device pair communication. To overcome these shortcomings, Indu et al. [22] minimized the energy consumption of UAV during its trajectory using genetic algorithm (GA). The authors in [6] proposed two meta-heuristic algorithms, such as GA and particle swarm optimization (PSO), to find the optimal UAV trajectory for satisfying users' minimum data rate requirements. They showed that PSO significantly improves the UAV's wireless coverage compared to GA. Although the meta-heuristic algorithms can deal with the complexity of UAV path planning, there are still some challenges in exchanging information between UAV and core network due to either unavailable constraints or obtaining their gradient analytically.

Another line of research studied the mobility management of UAVs for resource allocation and coverage optimization using RL techniques to deal with convergence issues. Kawamoto et al. [23] have presented a resource allocation algorithm of UAV using Q-learning techniques for allocating time slots and modulation schemes. The work in [24] presented a framework for the optimal UAV trajectory under a given data rate constraint, which relies on a state-action-reward-state-action (SARSA) algorithm. Hu et al. [25] proposed a real-time sensing and transmission protocol in UAV-aided cellular networks and designed optimal UAVs' trajectories under limited spectrum resources using RL based on a Q-learning algorithm. Furthermore, the authors of [26] transformed UAV trajectory optimization problem for maximizing cumulative collected sensors' data into a Markov decision process (MDP) and proposed two stochastic modeling RL algorithms, namely Q-learning and SARSA, to learn UAV's policy. They proved that SARSA outperforms Q-learning due to the adaptive system's state update rule. From the state-of-the-art, the coupled relationship among UAV trajectory, device association, and transmit power allocation of IoT devices for the enhancement of network lifetime has not been investigated during the data collection process of UAV-assisted IoT networks.

3. Channel characterization of UAV-operated communication system

This section proposes a multi-hop radio frequency and free space optical (RF-FSO) communication framework that analytically optimizes the UAV's altitude for performance enhancement of a relaying system. Here, we minimize the outage probability and symbol error rate based on independent and identically distributed statistical parameters i.e., pointing errors, atmospheric turbulence, and scintillation.

3.1 Channel model

Consider a multi-hop hybrid RF–FSO system as shown in **Figure 1**, where single antenna-equipped ground base stations realize periodic data exchange. Since there are significant obstacles in the LoS path, direct link cannot be established between them. Therefore, two UAVs are deployed at a certain altitude which are employed as relays between the source and destination. These UAVs operate as RF and optical link transceiver modules with single-directional apertures. Depending on various environmental conditions, three different channels categorize the source-to-destination link, i.e., Ground to UAV (G2U), UAV to UAV (U2U), and UAV to Ground (U2G) channels.

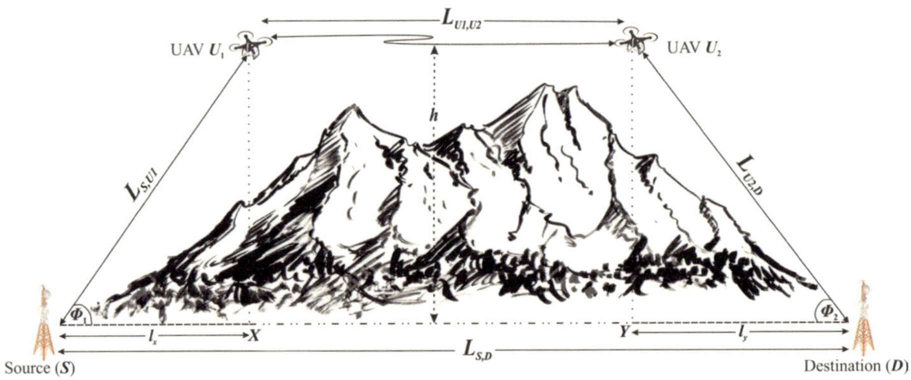

Figure 1.
UAV-assisted multihop hybrid RF–FSO system.

3.1.1 G2U channel model

As ground to UAV channel consists of RF signals, experiencing small-scale fading and large-scale path loss, the received symbol at UAV U_1 can be estimated as [27],

$$Y_{U_1} = \sqrt{P_{S,U_1}}\sqrt{a_{S,U_1}}h_{S,U_1}x_S + n_{U_1} \tag{1}$$

where, x_S is the transmitted symbol of power P_{S,U_1}, n_{U_1} represents the additive white Gaussian noise (AWGN) power of zero mean and variance N_0 at U_1, h_{S,U_1} defines the channel gain of S-U_1 link and $a_{S,U_1} = \kappa_{S,U_1}L_{S,U_1}^{-\epsilon_{S,U_1}}$ is path loss corresponding to link distance L_{S,U_1}, ϵ_{S,U_1} denotes the path loss exponent and κ_{S,U_1} is the environment-dependent constant. As multipath components govern the S-U_1 link, therefore $|h_{S,U_1}|^2 = \chi$ follows a non-central chi-square distribution, and its probability density function (PDF) is given by [28],

$$f_\chi(t) = \frac{(K_{S,U_1}+1)e^{-K_{S,U_1}}}{\overline{A_{S,U_1}}} exp\left\{\frac{-(K_{S,U_1}+1)t}{\overline{A_{S,U_1}}}\right\} \times I_0\left(2\sqrt{\frac{(K_{S,U_1}+1)K_{S,U_1}}{\overline{A_{S,U_1}}}t}\right) \tag{2}$$

where $\overline{A_{S,U_1}} = E\left\{|h_{S,U_1}|^2\right\} = 1$, is average fading power, $E\{.\}$ denotes expectation operator, $I_0(.)$ defines zero order modified Bessel function, $K_{S,U_1} = |m_{S,U_1}|^2/2\sigma^2$ is Rician factor, m_{S,U_1} is the amplitude of LoS component and σ^2 is average power of multipath components. The instantaneous signal-to-noise ratio (SNR) received at UAV U_1 is expressed as [29],

$$\Upsilon_{S,U_1} = \frac{P_{S,U_1}a_{S,U_1}}{N_0}X = \overline{\Upsilon}_{S,U_1}X \tag{3}$$

where, the average SNR is given as, $\overline{\Upsilon}_{S,U_1} = \frac{P_{S,U_1}a_{S,U_1}}{N_0}$

3.1.2 U2U channel model

UAV U_1 first receive the RF signal Y_{U_1}, then convert and encode it into the optical signal and then forward it to UAV U_2 over FSO link. The received signal at UAV U_2 can be obtained as [27]

$$Y_{U_2} = \eta_{U_1}\sqrt{P_{U_1,U_2}} h_{U_1,U_2} x_{U_1} + n_{U_2} \tag{4}$$

where η_{U_1} is electrical to optical conversion coefficient of UAV U_1, x_{U_1} indicates the converted and encoded optical symbol of power P_{U_1,U_2}, n_{U_2} denotes AWGN with zero mean and variance N_0 at UAV U_2, and $h_{U_1,U_2} = h_a h_p$ is optical channel coefficient depending on atmospheric turbulence-induced fading (h_a) and pointing errors (h_p). The instantaneous SNR received at UAV U_2, can be expressed as [27]

$$\Upsilon_{U_1,U_2} = \frac{\eta_{U_1}^2 P_{U_1,U_2} h_{U_1,U_2}^2}{N_0} \tag{5}$$

Since the optical link between UAV U_1 and U_2 experience several atmospheric turbulence and corresponding optical axis misalignment, the PDF of its instantaneous SNR follows the variation of atmospheric turbulence and pointing errors, which can be expressed as [30]

$$f_{\Upsilon_{U_1,U_2}}(\Upsilon) = \frac{\xi^2}{2\Upsilon\Gamma(\alpha)\Gamma(\beta)} G_{1,3}^{3,0}\left(\alpha\beta\sqrt{\frac{\Upsilon}{\overline{\Upsilon}_{U_1,U_2}}}\middle|_{\xi^2,\alpha,\beta}^{\xi^2+1}\right) \tag{6}$$

where Γ (.) is the Gamma function, α and β are scintillation parameters, ξ is the ratio between the equivalent beam radius and the misalignment displacement standard deviation at U_2, $G_{p,q}^{m,n}\left(x\middle|_{b_1,b_2,\dots,b_m,\dots,b_q}^{a_1,a_2,\dots,a_n,\dots,a_p}\right)$ is Meijer's G function and $\overline{\Upsilon}_{U_1,U_2} = P_{U_1,U_2}\eta_{U_1}^2 E\{h_{U_1,U_2}\}^2/N_0$ is average electrical SNR.

3.1.3 U2G channel model

After receiving the optical signal Y_{U_2}, UAV U_2 first decodes and converts it to RF signal and then forwards to the destination. Hence, the channel characterization is similar as the G2U channel model, and the received signal at the destination can be expressed as [27]

$$Y_D = \eta_{U_2}\sqrt{P_{U_2,D}}\sqrt{a_{U_2,D}} h_{U_2,D} x_{U_2} + n_D \tag{7}$$

where η_{U_2} is optical to electrical conversion coefficient of UAV U_2, x_{U_2} denotes the transmitted symbol of power $P_{U_2,D}$, n_D defines AWGN of zero mean and variance N_0, $h_{U_2,D}$ is channel coefficient and $a_{U_2,D}$ is path loss attenuation factor. Instantaneous SNR received at the destination is expressed as,

$$\Upsilon_{U_2,D} = \frac{\eta_{U_2}^2 P_{U_2,D} a_{U_2,D} |h_{U_2,D}|^2}{N_0} \tag{8}$$

where $\overline{\Upsilon}_{U_2,D} = \eta_{U_2}^2 P_{U_2,D} a_{U_2,D}/N_0$ is average SNR

3.2 Performance metrics of multihop RF: FSO system

3.2.1 Outage probability

It is defined as the probability that instantaneous SNR is less than the minimum required threshold level, Υ_{th}. For decode and forward relaying mode, the equivalent SNR at destination can be expressed as [27]

$$\Upsilon_{S,D} = min\left(\Upsilon_{S,U_1}, \Upsilon_{U_1,U_2}, \Upsilon_{U_2,D}\right) \tag{9}$$

Cumulative distribution function (CDF) of equivalent SNR is expressed by,

$$\begin{aligned} F_{\Upsilon_{S,D}}(\Upsilon) &= Pr(\Upsilon_{S,D} \leq \Upsilon) = Pr(min\left(\Upsilon_{S,U_1}, \Upsilon_{U_1,U_2}, \Upsilon_{U_2,D}\right) \leq \Upsilon) \\ &= 1 - \left\{1 - F_{\Upsilon_{S,U_1}}(\Upsilon)\right\}\left\{1 - F_{\Upsilon_{U_1,U_2}}(\Upsilon)\right\}\left\{1 - F_{\Upsilon_{U_2,D}}(\Upsilon)\right\} \end{aligned} \tag{10}$$

where $F_{\Upsilon_{S,U_1}}(\Upsilon)$, $F_{\Upsilon_{U_1,U_2}}(\Upsilon)$ and $F_{\Upsilon_{U_2,D}}(\Upsilon)$ are the CDF of Υ_{S,U_1}, Υ_{U_1,U_2} and $\Upsilon_{U_2,D}$ respectively. The outage probability of the overall system is obtained in terms of Q1 (., .) i.e., the first order Marcum Q function as [31]

$$\begin{aligned} P_{out} &= F_{\Upsilon_{S,D}}(\Upsilon_{th}) = Pr(\Upsilon_{S,D} \leq \Upsilon_{th}) \\ &= 1 - Q_1\left(\sqrt{2K_{S,U_1}}, \sqrt{2\Upsilon_{th} L_{S,U_1}^{\epsilon_{S,U_1}} (1 + K_{S,U_1})/\tilde{\Upsilon}_{S,U_1}}\right) \\ &\times Q_1\left(\sqrt{2K_{U_2,D}}, \sqrt{2\Upsilon_{th} L_{U_2,D}^{\epsilon_{U_2,D}} (1 + K_{U_2,D})/\tilde{\Upsilon}_{U_2,D}}\right) \\ &\times \left[1 - \frac{\xi^2}{\Gamma(\alpha)\Gamma(\beta)} G_{2,4}^{3,1}\left(\alpha\beta\sqrt{\frac{\Upsilon_{th}}{\overline{\Upsilon}_{U_1,U_2}}}\,\middle|\,\begin{matrix}1, \xi^2+1 \\ \xi^2, \alpha, \beta, 0\end{matrix}\right)\right] \end{aligned} \tag{11}$$

3.2.2 Symbol error rate

It is defined as the probability of false estimation of the received symbol, which can be expressed as [32]

$$P_{M,PSK}(e) = 1 - \sum_{k=1}^{M} P_k(\Upsilon_{S,U_1}) P_k(\Upsilon_{U_1,U_2}) P_k(\Upsilon_{U_2,D}) \tag{12}$$

$$P_k(\Upsilon_{s,d}) = \begin{cases} 1 - \dfrac{1}{\pi}\displaystyle\int_0^{\frac{(M-1)\pi}{M}} \mathcal{M}_{\Upsilon_{s,d}}\left(-\dfrac{sin^2\left(\frac{\pi}{M}\right)}{sin^2(\phi)}\right) d\phi, for\ k = 1 \\ \dfrac{1}{\pi}\displaystyle\int_0^{\frac{(M-1)\pi}{M}} \mathcal{M}_{\Upsilon_{s,d}}\left(-\dfrac{sin^2\left(\frac{\pi}{M}\right)}{sin^2(\phi)}\right) d\phi, for\ k = \dfrac{M}{2} + 1 \\ \left[\begin{matrix} \dfrac{1}{2\pi}\displaystyle\int_0^{\pi - a_k - 1} \mathcal{M}_{\Upsilon_{s,d}}\left(-\dfrac{sin^2(a_k - 1)}{sin^2(\phi)}\right) d\phi - \\ \dfrac{1}{2\pi}\displaystyle\int_0^{\pi - a_k} \mathcal{M}_{\Upsilon_{s,d}}\left(-\dfrac{sin^2(a_k)}{sin^2(\phi)}\right) d\phi \end{matrix}\right], \text{otherwise} \end{cases} \tag{13}$$

where, $a_k = (2k-1)\frac{\pi}{M}$. After substituting Eq. (6) in Eq. (13) and using [29], we can obtain the moment-generating function of instantaneous SNR corresponding FSO link as

$$\mathcal{M}_{\Upsilon_{U_1,U_2}}(s) = \frac{\xi^2 2^{\alpha+\beta-1}}{4\pi\Gamma(\alpha)\Gamma(\beta)} \times G_{3,6}^{6,1}\left(\frac{(\alpha\beta)^2}{16\overline{\Upsilon}_{U_1,U_2}s} \middle| \begin{matrix} 1, \frac{\xi^2+1}{2}, \frac{\xi^2+2}{2} \\ \frac{\xi^2}{2}, \frac{\xi^2+1}{2}, \frac{\alpha}{2}, \frac{\alpha+1}{2}, \frac{\beta}{2}, \frac{\beta+1}{2} \end{matrix} \right) \tag{14}$$

3.3 UAVs' optimal altitude

According to Eq. (11), outage probability is a function of UAV's altitude, distance from source to destination, and distance between the projection points of UAVs on the ground and end users. For these given parameters values, the optimal altitude is obtained as

$$\tilde{h} = l_y \tan(\tilde{\phi}_2) \tag{15}$$

where the optimal altitude must satisfy the following condition [33]

$$\tilde{h} = \arg \min_{h\epsilon[0,\infty]} P_{out}(h, l_x, l_y, L_{S,D}) \tag{16}$$

Finally, the optimal elevation angle at the receiver side $\tilde{\phi}_2$ is obtained by solving the equation,

$$[P_1.Q_1(v_2, w_2) + P_2.Q_1(v_1, w_1)].P_3 = 0 \tag{17}$$

where

$$P_1 = v_1 e^{-\frac{v_1^2+w_1^2}{2}} \left[I_1(v_1, w_1)\frac{K'_{S,U_1}(\phi_1)}{v_1} - I_0(v_1, w_1).\frac{w_1}{2}\left\{ \frac{K'_{S,U_1}(\phi_1)}{1+K_{S,U_1}(\phi_1)} + \epsilon'_{S,U_1}(\phi_1)\ln\left(\frac{l_x}{\cos\phi_1}\right) + \epsilon_{S,U_1}(\phi_1)\tan\phi_1 \right\}\right] \times \frac{l_x l_y}{l_x^2 cos^2\phi_2 + l_y^2 sin^2\phi_2} \tag{18}$$

$$P_2 = v_2 e^{-\frac{v_2^2+w_2^2}{2}} \left[I_1(v_2, w_2)\frac{K'_{U_2,D}(\phi_2)}{v_2} - I_0(v_2, w_2).\frac{w_2}{2}\left\{ \frac{K'_{U_2,D}(\phi_2)}{1+K_{U_2,D}(\phi_2)} + \epsilon'_{U_2,D}(\phi_2)\ln\left(\frac{l_y}{\cos\phi_2}\right) + \epsilon_{U_2,D}(\phi_2)\tan\phi_2 \right\}\right] \tag{19}$$

$$P_3 = 1 - \frac{\xi^2}{\Gamma(\alpha)\Gamma(\beta)} G_{2,4}^{3,1}\left(\alpha\beta\sqrt{\frac{\Upsilon_{th}}{\overline{\Upsilon}_{U_1,U_2}}} \middle| \begin{matrix} 1, \xi^2+1 \\ \xi^2, \alpha, \beta, 0 \end{matrix} \right) \tag{20}$$

3.4 Numerical results

In this section, we provide numerical insights of optimal UAVs' altitude and corresponding performance analysis and then cross-validate the proposed methodology using Monte-Carlo simulation. We assume that the system is operated under moderate and strong atmospheric turbulence conditions with a maximum free space optical distance 7 km, where the average SNR is set as $\overline{\Upsilon}_{S,U_1} = \overline{\Upsilon}_{U_1,U_2} = \overline{\Upsilon}_{U_2,D} = 75$ dB.

The variations of elevation angle corresponding to the optimal UAVs' altitude for the given distance between the projection points of UAVs on the ground and end users under moderate atmospheric turbulence conditions are depicted in **Figure 2**. According to this figure, the optimal elevation angles decrease with the increase in distance from the end-user location to the projection point of the UAVs on the ground because the variation of optimal elevation angle follows Eq. (15).

The variation of outage probability with respect to UAVs' altitude under moderate atmospheric turbulence conditions is statistically visualized in **Figure 3** when the SNR threshold is assumed as $\Upsilon_{th} = 0.4$. Since small-scale fading and signal path loss less

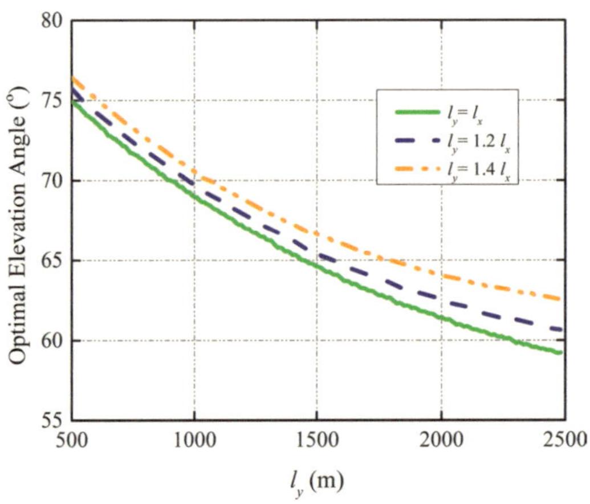

Figure 2.
Variation of optimal elevation angle while considering $\Upsilon_{th} = 0.1$.

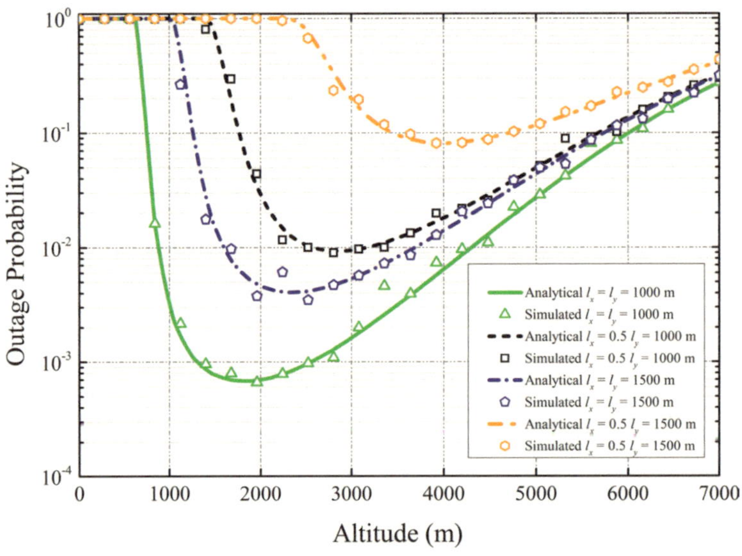

Figure 3.
Outage probability variation for different UAVs' altitude.

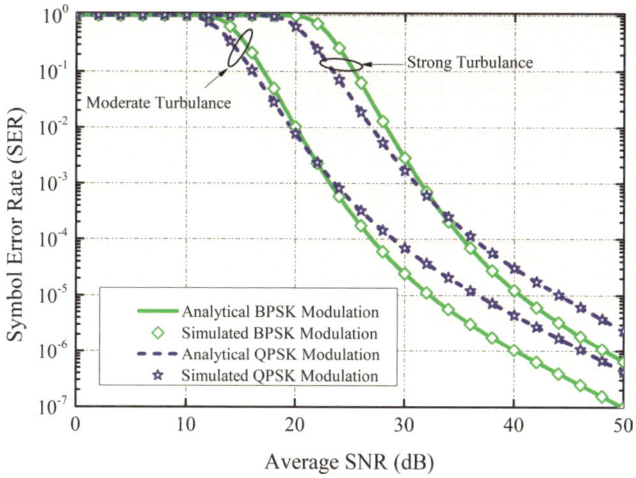

Figure 4.
Variation of symbol error rate for different modulation schemes.

affect the received SNR at the optimal altitude, minimum outage probability can be achieved at that altitude. On the other hand, outage probability increases if UAVs' altitude deviates from the optimal value.

Figure 4 shows the impact of various modulation schemes on symbol error rate when the distance between projection points of UAVs on the ground and end users is 2000 m under different atmospheric turbulence conditions. According to the result, it is observed that symbol error rate decreases with the average SNR value. Furtherore, binary phase shift keying (BPSK) outperforms the modulation scheme of quadrature phase shift keying (QPSK). Although higher modulation techniques offer more data rates and bandwidth efficiency, they are more complicated to implement, require a more stringent RF amplifier, and are less resilient to error. Therefore, BPSK offers more secure and errorless transmission than other modulation techniques.

4. Throughput maximization in UAVs-supported D2D network

This section proposes a UAVs-supported self-organized device-to-device (USSD2D) network containing multiple source-destination device pairs and multiple UAVs, where the objective is to find the optimal deployed location of UAVs to support reliable data transmission between source and destination device pairs. Here, we consider SNR-constrained maximization of the total instantaneous transmission rate of the USSD2D network by jointly optimizing device association, UAV's channel selection, and UAVs' deployed location at every time slot.

4.1 System model

Figure 5 depicts the UAVs-supported self-organized device-to-device (USSD2D) network where the stationary source and destination devices pairs are randomly deployed on the ground within the target area. The direct D2D pairs can establish LoS links due to good channel conditions and the short distance between them. On the other hand, UAV-assisted D2D pairs cannot establish direct links due to the presence

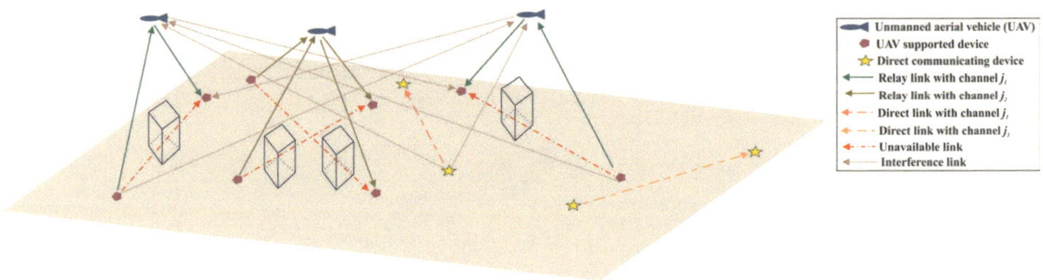

Figure 5.
UAVs-supported self-organized device-to-device network.

of significant obstacles in the signal propagation path and thereby utilize the deployed UAVs as relays.

4.1.1 Channel model

Consider M number of UAVs represented by $\mathcal{M} = \{1, 2, \ldots, M\}$ at a fixed altitude of H_u acting as relays for $\overline{K}$ number of direct D2D pairs and $\tilde{K}$ number of UAV-assisted D2D pairs. There are total J number of orthogonal channels represented by $\mathcal{J} = \{1, 2, \ldots, J\}$ in the USSD2D network, and each UAV selects a single orthogonal channel at a time. The set of source and destination devices of the direct D2D and UAV-assisted D2D pairs are represented as $\overline{\mathcal{K}}_S = \{1, 2, \ldots, \overline{K}\}$, $\overline{\mathcal{K}}_D = \{\overline{K}+1, \overline{K}+2, \ldots, 2\overline{K}\}$, $\tilde{\mathcal{K}}_S = \{1, 2, \ldots, \tilde{K}\}$ and $\tilde{\mathcal{K}}_D = \{\tilde{K}+1, \tilde{K}+2, \ldots, 2\tilde{K}\}$ respectively where kth device's location is $(x_k, y_k), \forall k \in \{\overline{\mathcal{K}}_S \cup \overline{\mathcal{K}}_D \cup \tilde{\mathcal{K}}_S \cup \tilde{\mathcal{K}}_D\}$. UAVs' flight period is discretized into T equally spaced time slots of duration δ each and mth UAV's location $U_m(t) = (x_m(t), y_m(t), H_u), \forall m \in \mathcal{M}, t \in \mathcal{T} = \{1, 2, \ldots, T\}$ is almost unchanged within each slot. Here, we assume that one source device can only associate with a single UAV at a time slot, but multiple devices can access a single UAV simultaneously. To avoid mutual interference from nearby devices, UAVs select the orthogonal channel, and data transmission follows amplify and forward relaying (AF) protocol [34]. The association indicator of the $\tilde{k} \in \{\tilde{\mathcal{K}}_S \cup \tilde{\mathcal{K}}_D\}$ device with UAV m at time slot t is defined as

$$\overline{I}_{\tilde{k},m}(t) = \begin{cases} 1, \text{if device} \tilde{k} \text{associates with UAV } m \\ \quad 0, \text{Otherwise} \end{cases} \tag{21}$$

Similarly, when UAV m selects an orthogonal channel j at tth time slot, the corresponding channel selection indicator is defined as

$$\tilde{I}_{m,j}(t) = \begin{cases} 1, \text{if UAV } m \text{ selects channel } j \\ \quad 0, \text{Otherwise} \end{cases} \tag{22}$$

The path loss between the device $\tilde{k}$ and UAV m can be expressed as [35]

$$L_{\tilde{k},m}(t) = \frac{\mu_{LoS} - \mu_{NLoS}}{1 + b_1 exp\left[-b_2\left(\frac{180}{\pi}\phi_{\tilde{k},m}(t) - b_1\right)\right]} + 20\log\left(\frac{4\pi f_c D_{\tilde{k},m}(t)}{c}\right) + \mu_{NLoS} \tag{23}$$

where c is the speed of light, f_c is the carrier frequency, μ_{LoS} and μ_{NLoS} are attenuation factors corresponding to the LoS and NLoS path, respectively, b_1 and b_2 are the constant. $\phi_{\tilde{k},m}(t) = \sin^{-1}\left(H_u/D_{\tilde{k},m}(t)\right)$ is the elevation angle between the device $\tilde{k}$ and UAV m, where the instantaneous distance between them is calculated as $D_{\tilde{k},m}(t) = \sqrt{\left(x_m(t) - x_{\tilde{k}}\right)^2 + \left(y_m(t) - y_{\tilde{k}}\right)^2 + H_u^2}$. The instantaneous channel gain between $\tilde{k}$th device and relay UAV m can be expressed as

$$G_{\tilde{k},m}(t) = 10^{-L_{\tilde{k},m}(t)/10} \tag{24}$$

4.1.2 Transmission model

The received SNR at UAV m from the source device $\tilde{k}$ over channel j can be expressed as [34]

$$\Gamma^j_{\tilde{k},m}(t) = \frac{P^{Tx}_{\tilde{k}} G_{\tilde{k},m}(t) \bar{I}_{\tilde{k},m}(t) \tilde{I}_{m,j}(t)}{N_0} \tag{25}$$

where $P^{Tx}_{\tilde{k}}$ is transmit power of $\tilde{k}$ device and N_0 is noise power. The expected SNR received by the destination device $\tilde{k} + \tilde{K} \in \tilde{\mathcal{K}}_D$ from UAV m over channel j can be expressed as

$$\hat{\Gamma}^j_{m,\tilde{k}+\tilde{K}}(t) = \frac{P^{Tx}_m G_{m,\tilde{k}+\tilde{K}}(t) \bar{I}_{\tilde{k}+\tilde{K},m}(t) \tilde{I}_{m,j}(t)}{N_0} \tag{26}$$

where P^{Tx}_m is transmit power of UAV m. The overall SNR at the destination device of the UAV-assisted D2D pair following AF relaying protocol can be expressed as [36]

$$\hat{\Gamma}^j_{\tilde{k},\tilde{k}+\tilde{K}}(t) = \left[\prod_{i=1}^{N}\left(1 + \frac{1}{\Gamma^j_i(t)}\right) - 1\right]^{-1} \tag{27}$$

where $\Gamma^j_i(t)$ is the instantaneous SNR of the ith hop over jth channel, and N is the total number of hops in the link. For direct D2D pair, we consider a conventional channel model where the instantaneous channel gain between the source device $\bar{k}$ and destination device $\bar{k} + \bar{K}$ can be expressed as

$$G_{\bar{k},\bar{k}+\bar{K}}(t) = \beta_0 D^{-\varrho}_{\bar{k},\bar{k}+\bar{K}}(t) \tag{28}$$

where $\beta_0 = \left(4\pi f_c/c\right)^2$ is free space path loss at a distance of 1 m, and ϱ is the path loss exponent. The expected instantaneous SNR received by the destination device $\bar{k} + \bar{K}$ from the source device $\bar{k}$ over channel j can be expressed as

$$\hat{\Gamma}^j_{\bar{k},\bar{k}+\bar{K}}(t) = \frac{P^{Tx}_{\bar{k}} G_{\bar{k},\bar{k}+\bar{K}}(t)}{N_0} \tag{29}$$

The instantaneous transmission rate achieved by the destination device $\overline{k} + \overline{K}$ can be expressed as

$$\overline{R}^{j}_{\overline{k},\overline{k}+\overline{K}}(t) = B\log_2\left[1 + \hat{\Gamma}^{j}_{\overline{k},\overline{k}+\overline{K}}(t)\right] \tag{30}$$

The total instantaneous transmission rate achieved by all direct D2D pairs can be calculated as

$$\overline{R}_{Sum}(t) = \sum_{j=1}^{J}\sum_{\overline{k}=1}^{\overline{K}} \overline{R}^{j}_{\overline{k},\overline{k}+\overline{K}}(t) \tag{31}$$

Similarly, $\tilde{k} + \tilde{K}$th device obtains the instantaneous transmission rate over channel j as

$$\tilde{R}^{j}_{\tilde{k},\tilde{k}+\tilde{K}}(t) = B\log_2\left[1 + \hat{\Gamma}^{j}_{\tilde{k},\tilde{k}+\tilde{K}}(t)\right] \tag{32}$$

The total instantaneous transmission rate of all UAV-assisted D2D pairs can be expressed as

$$\tilde{R}_{Sum}(t) = \sum_{j=1}^{J}\sum_{m=1}^{M}\sum_{\tilde{k}=1}^{\tilde{K}} \tilde{R}^{j}_{\tilde{k},\tilde{k}+\tilde{K}}(t) \tag{33}$$

The overall instantaneous transmission rate of the USSD2D network is formulated as

$$R_{Sum}(t) = \overline{R}_{Sum}(t) + \tilde{R}_{Sum}(t) \tag{34}$$

4.1.3 Problem formulation

From the practical scenario, it is observed that when UAVs fly toward a group of devices to obtain better channel conditions, the remaining devices of the network cannot receive adequate services from the UAV, and consequently, UAVs cannot allocate network resources fairly. Hence, we jointly optimize UAVs' location, device association, and channel selection indicators at every time slot to maximize the total instantaneous transmission rate of the USSD2D network while assuring that each device should achieve a minimum SNR of ς to maintain the required QoS. The corresponding optimization problem is formulated as

$$\text{P1}: \begin{matrix} \text{Maximize} \\ \left\{ \begin{matrix} (x_m(t), y_m(t)), \overline{I}_{k,m}(t), \tilde{I}_{m,j}(t) \\ \forall k \in \{\overline{\mathcal{K}}_S \cup \overline{\mathcal{K}}_D \cup \tilde{\mathcal{K}}_S \cup \tilde{\mathcal{K}}_D\}, m \in \mathcal{M}, j \in \mathcal{J} \end{matrix} \right\} \end{matrix} R_{Sum}(t) \tag{35}$$

Subject to the constraints

$$\text{C1}: \Gamma^{j}_{k,k+K}(t) > \varsigma, \forall k \in \{\overline{\mathcal{K}}_S \cup \overline{\mathcal{K}}_D \cup \tilde{\mathcal{K}}_S \cup \tilde{\mathcal{K}}_D\} \tag{36}$$

$$\text{C2}: \overline{I}_{k,m}(t), \overline{I}_{k+K,m}(t) = \{0,1\}, \tilde{I}_{m,j}(t) = \{0,1\}, \forall k \in \{\overline{\mathcal{K}}_S \cup \overline{\mathcal{K}}_D \cup \tilde{\mathcal{K}}_S \cup \tilde{\mathcal{K}}_D\}, m \in \mathcal{M}, j \in \mathcal{J} \tag{37}$$

$$\text{C3}: \sum_{m \in \mathcal{M}} \overline{I}_{k,m}(t) \leq 1, \sum_{m \in \mathcal{M}} \overline{I}_{k+K,m}(t) \leq 1, \forall k \in \{\overline{\mathcal{K}}_S \cup \overline{\mathcal{K}}_D \cup \tilde{\mathcal{K}}_S \cup \tilde{\mathcal{K}}_D\}, \tag{38}$$

$$\text{C4}: \sum_{j \in \mathcal{J}} \tilde{I}_{m,j}(t) \leq 1, \forall m \in \mathcal{M} \tag{39}$$

C1 indicates that a device should achieve a minimum SNR threshold to maintain the required QoS. C2 defines the instantaneous device association indicator and UAVs' channel selection indicator. C3 assures that each device can be associated with a single UAV at a time slot, and C4 implies UAVs' channel selection conditions at each time slot. The optimization variables $(x_m(t), y_m(t))$, $\overline{I}_{k,m}(t)$ and $\tilde{I}_{m,j}(t)$ are coupled and interactable, where the deflection of one variable impacts the optimization of other variables and the objective value. Hence, this optimization problem becomes complicated using standard optimization tools. In order to tackle this situation, we adopt an RL-based UAV deployment strategy to find their optimal position by estimating the required system parameters using real-time measurements and statistics of collected information.

4.2 RL-based solution methodology

UAVs acting as RL agents select the action depending on their current positions, which are only related to their previous states. Hence, the proposed framework follows Markovian properties composed of state, action, reward, state transition probability, and the flying time periods. In the next sub-section, we explain each of those elements elaborately.

4.2.1 State space

The state of the mth UAV at t-th time slot is the vector of two elements which represent its current position as $s_m(t) = (x_m(t), y_m(t)), \forall s_m(t) \in \mathcal{S}$. Here, $\mathcal{S}$ is the state space, whose elements are independent and identically distributed random variables arranged by combining all possible values across the time horizon.

4.2.2 Action space

UAV's action $a_m(t) \in \mathcal{A}$ in the current state is the change of its position, which is measured with respect to its immediate X and Y coordinates. Here, we consider a benchmark RL gridworld environment where UAVs have maximum of eight possible moving directions at each state, i.e., NORTH, NORTH-WEST, WEST, SOUTH-WEST, SOUTH, SOUTH-EAST, EAST, and NORTH-EAST. After selecting an action, the X and Y coordinate changes of UAV m at t-th time slot are represented as $\delta^m_x(t) \in \{-\vartheta(t)\delta, 0, \vartheta(t)\delta\}$ and $\delta^m_y(t) \in \{-\vartheta(t)\delta, 0, \vartheta(t)\delta\}$ respectively, $\forall a_m(t) = \{\delta^m_x(t), \delta^m_y(t)\} \in \mathcal{A}, t \in \mathcal{T}$, where $\vartheta(t)$ is the velocity of UAVs at time slot t and

$\mathcal{A}$ is the action set containing all possible actions. The obtained X and Y coordinate of UAV m for next time slot is measured as

$$x_m(t+1) = x_m(t) + \delta_x^m(t) \tag{40}$$

$$y_m(t+1) = y_m(t) + \delta_y^m(t) \tag{41}$$

4.2.3 Reward formulation

RL agents choose their actions in such a manner that maximizes long-term cumulative reward. Since our objective is to maximize the total instantaneous transmission rate of the USSD2D network, we need to find such locations of UAVs that impacts immediate objective value. Hence, we model the instantaneous reward function contributed by UAV m as

$$\mathcal{R}(s_m(t), a_m(t)) = \sum_{j=1}^{J}\sum_{\tilde{k}=1}^{\tilde{K}} \tilde{R}^j_{\tilde{k},m,\tilde{k}+\tilde{K}}(t) + \sum_{j=1}^{J}\sum_{\overline{k}=1}^{\overline{K}} \overline{R}^j_{\overline{k},\overline{k}+\overline{K}}(t), \forall m \in \mathcal{M} \tag{42}$$

4.2.4 State transition probability

It is the probability that UAV m changes its state from $s_m(t)$ to $s_m(t+1)$ after selecting an action $a_m(t)$, denoted as $P_{tr}\{s_m(t+1) \in \mathcal{S} | s_m(t), a_m(t)\}$. Let us consider the probability vectors of device association and UAVs' channel selection at time slot t as $P^{DA}_{\tilde{k}}(t) = \left[\tilde{P}_{\tilde{k},1}(t), \tilde{P}_{\tilde{k},2}(t), \dots, \tilde{P}_{\tilde{k},M}(t)\right], \forall \tilde{k} \in \{\tilde{\mathcal{K}}_S \cup \tilde{\mathcal{K}}_D\}$ and $P^{CS}_m(t) = \left[\overline{P}_{m,1}(t), \overline{P}_{m,2}(t), \dots, \overline{P}_{m,J}(t)\right], \forall m \in \mathcal{M}$ respectively where $\tilde{P}_{\tilde{k},m}(t)$ indicates the association probability of device $\tilde{k}$ with UAV m at time slot t and $\overline{P}_{m,j}(t)$ is the probability that UAV m selects channel j at time slot t. In each time slot, source and destination devices associated with a single UAV according to probability vectors $P^{UA}_{\tilde{k}}(t)$ and UAV selects a single orthogonal channel with a probability vector of $P^{CS}_m(t)$. The probabilities of device association and UAV's channel selections are updated for the next time slot as follows:

$$\tilde{P}_{\tilde{k},m}(t+1) = \begin{cases} \tilde{P}_{\tilde{k},m}(t) + w_1\tilde{r}_{\tilde{k},m}(t)\left(1 - \tilde{P}_{\tilde{k},m}(t)\right), m = U^{Max}_{\tilde{k}}(t) \\ \tilde{P}_{\tilde{k},m}(t) - w_1\tilde{r}_{\tilde{k},m}(t)\tilde{P}_{\tilde{k},m}(t), m \neq U^{Max}_{\tilde{k}}(t) \end{cases} \tag{43}$$

$$\overline{P}_{m,j}(t+1) = \begin{cases} \overline{P}_{m,j}(t) + w_2\overline{r}_{m,j}(t)\left(1 - \overline{P}_{m,j}(t)\right), j = C^{Max}_m(t) \\ \overline{P}_{m,j}(t) - w_2\overline{r}_{m,j}(t)\overline{P}_{m,j}(t), j \neq C^{Max}_m(t) \end{cases} \tag{44}$$

where w_1 and w_2 are the learning step sizes. $U^{Max}_{\tilde{k}}(t)$ is the current best UAV for device $\tilde{k}$ for a fixed selected channel and $C^{Max}_m(t)$ is the current best channel of UAV m for associated devices at that time slot respectively, which can be expressed as

$$U^{Max}_{\tilde{k}}(t) = \arg\max_{m \in \mathcal{M}} \tilde{R}_{\tilde{k},m,\tilde{k}+\tilde{K}}(t), \forall \tilde{k} \in \{\tilde{\mathcal{K}}_S \cup \tilde{\mathcal{K}}_D\} \tag{45}$$

$$C^{Max}_m(t) = \arg\max_{j \in \mathcal{J}} \tilde{R}_{m,j}(t), \forall m \in \mathcal{M} \tag{46}$$

where $\tilde{r}_{\tilde{k},m}(t)$ and $\overline{r}_{m,j}(t)$ are the normalized reward achieved by the source device $\tilde{k}$ and UAV m at time slot t respectively, which are defined as

$$\tilde{r}_{\tilde{k},m}(t) = \frac{\tilde{R}_{\tilde{k},m,\tilde{k}+\tilde{K}}(t)}{\max\limits_{m \in \mathcal{M}} \tilde{R}_{\tilde{k},m,\tilde{k}+\tilde{K}}(t)} \tag{47}$$

$$\overline{r}_{m,j}(t) = \frac{\tilde{R}_{m,j}(t)}{\max\limits_{j \in \mathcal{J}} \tilde{R}_{m,j}(t)} \tag{48}$$

From (43) and (44), it is observed that the update of selection probability vectors depends on the instantaneous transmission rate, which does not need any prior information. Thus, device association and UAVs' channel selection at each time slot is entirely model-free.

4.2.5 Updating the action value function

During the operation period, each UAV acts as an RL agent where UAV m takes an action $a_m(t)$ at current state $s_m(t)$. Then it generates an immediate reward $\mathcal{R}(s_m(t), a_m(t))$, and computes corresponding $Q(s_m(t), a_m(t))$ value. Finally, the current state $s_m(t)$ is updated to the next state $s_m(t+1)$ and UAV m selects the next action $a_m(t+1)$ using the same policy where the action-value function is updated as [37]

$$Q(s_m(t), a_m(t)) \leftarrow (1-\alpha)Q(s_m(t), a_m(t)) + \alpha[\mathcal{R}(s_m(t), a_m(t)) + \gamma\, Q(s_m(t+1), a_m(t+1))] \tag{49}$$

UAVs consider all the possible actions from the action space and select an action with a certain probability that provides maximum long-term reward. ϵ-greedy action selection policy is adopted under which the probability that UAV m takes action $a_m(t) \in \mathcal{A}$ corresponding to a state $s_m(t) \in \mathcal{S}$ at time slot t can be expressed as [37]

$$\pi_m^{\epsilon} = \begin{cases} \arg \max\limits_{a_m(t)=\{\delta_x^m(t),\, \delta_y^m(t)\}} Q(s_m(t), a_m(t)), \text{with probability } 1-\epsilon \\ \text{Random Selection, with probability } \epsilon \end{cases} \tag{50}$$

UAVs execute state-action pairs repeatedly to gain experience of interacting with the environment. These interaction results are recorded in Q-table and updated the learning policy in each episode until convergence. Algorithm 1 summarizes the optimal deployment strategy using the adaptive State-Action-Reward-State-Action (SARSA) technique.

4.3 Simulation results

In this sub-section, we validate the proposed analysis and provide various numerical insights on key system parameters to improve the system's performance. Later, we compare the obtained results corresponding to the proposed SARSA algorithm with the existing works [34], such as random selection with fixed optimal relay deployment (RS-FORD), an exhaustive search for relay assignment and channel allocation with fixed initial relay deployment (ES-FIRD), and alternative optimization for the

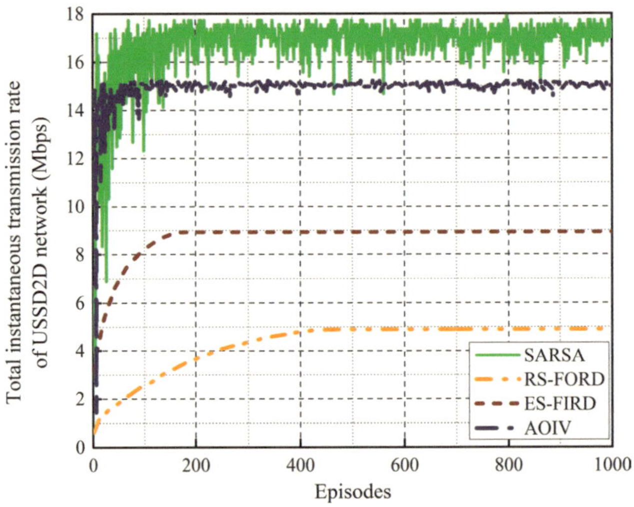

Figure 6.
The variation of the total transmission rate of the USSD2D network corresponding to each episode.

individual variable (AOIV). Here, we consider that direct D2D pair and UAV-assisted D2D pair devices are uniformly distributed in a 4 km×4 km square area where the primary simulation parameters are adopted from [38].

The iterative evolutions of the proposed and benchmark schemes are depicted in **Figure 6**, where the number of UAVs, UAV-assisted D2D pairs, direct D2D pairs, orthogonal channels, and transmit power are set as 5, 10, 2, 7, and 10 mW respectively. From this figure, it is clear that the proposed algorithm outperforms the benchmark scheme with respect to the converged value because it utilizes ϵ-greedy action policy to obtain the large search space by exploring the target region more efficiently. Furthermore, UAV acting as an RL agent learns to improve the cumulative reward, i.e., the total instantaneous transmission rate, from its past learning experiences. Hence, according to this figure, the SARSA algorithm enhances the overall transmission rate by 75.37%, 49.74%, and 11.01%, compared with RS-FORD, ES-FIRD, and AOIV schemes, respectively.

Algorithm 1: Optimal UAV deployment strategy using adaptive SARSA technique

Input: $N_0, B, \mu_{LoS}, \mu_{NLoS}, f_c, b_1, b_2, H_u, \vartheta_0, \overline{K}, \overline{\mathcal{K}}_S, \overline{\mathcal{K}}_D, \tilde{K}, \tilde{\mathcal{K}}_S, \tilde{\mathcal{K}}_D, P_k^{Tx}, M, \mathcal{M}, P_m^{Tx}, J, \mathcal{J},$
$w_1, w_2, \gamma, \alpha, \epsilon, \varsigma, \forall s_m(t) \in \mathcal{S}, a_m(t) \in \mathcal{A}, k \in \mathcal{K} = \{\overline{\mathcal{K}}_S \cup \overline{\mathcal{K}}_D \cup \tilde{\mathcal{K}}_S \cup \tilde{\mathcal{K}}_D\}, m \in \mathcal{M}$
Output: Instantaneous reward generated by all UAVs as $\mathcal{R}(t)$
Initialize $Q(s_m(t), a_m(t)) = 0, \forall s_m(t) \in \mathcal{S}, a_m(t) \in \mathcal{A}, m \in \mathcal{M}$
Set initial device association probability as $\tilde{P}_{\tilde{k},m}(1) = \frac{1}{M}, \forall \tilde{k} \in \{\tilde{\mathcal{K}}_S \cup \tilde{\mathcal{K}}_D\}, m \in \mathcal{M}$
Set initial channel selection probability of UAVs as $\overline{P}_{m,j}(1) = \frac{1}{J}, \forall m \in \mathcal{M}, j \in \mathcal{J}$
Initially deploy UAV m at the random position as $s_m(1) = (x_m(1), y_m(1), H_u), \forall m \in \mathcal{M}$
for $t = 1, 2, \ldots, T$ **do**
for $\tilde{k} = 1, 2, \ldots, \tilde{K}$ **do**
for $m = 1, 2, \ldots, M$ **do**
Obtain the association probability of device $\tilde{k}$ with UAV m as $\tilde{P}_{\tilde{k},m}(t)$
Calculate $\hat{\Gamma}^j_{\tilde{k},m}(t)$ and $\hat{\Gamma}^j_{m,\tilde{k}+\tilde{K}}(t)$ by (25) and (26), respectively, for a fixed assigned channel
if $\hat{\Gamma}^j_{\tilde{k},m}(t), \hat{\Gamma}^j_{m,\tilde{k}+\tilde{K}}(t) \geq \varsigma$ **then**

Calculate $\tilde{R}^{j}_{\tilde{k},\tilde{k}+\tilde{K}}(t)$ using (32) for a fixed assigned channel
else
$\tilde{R}^{j}_{\tilde{k},\tilde{k}+\tilde{K}}(t) = 0$
for $\tilde{k} = 1, 2, \dots, \tilde{K}$ **do**
for $m = 1, 2, \dots, M$ **do**
Set $\tilde{I}_{\tilde{k},m}(t) = 1$ when $m = \arg\max_{m \in \mathcal{M}} \tilde{P}_{\tilde{k},m}(t)$, otherwise $\tilde{I}_{\tilde{k},m}(t) = 0$
According to (43), update the association probability as $\tilde{P}_{\tilde{k},m}(t) \leftarrow \tilde{P}_{\tilde{k},m}(t+1)$
for $m = 1, 2, \dots, M$ **do**
for $j = 1, 2, \dots, J$ **do**
UAV m obtains the jth channel selection probability as $\overline{P}_{m,j}(t)$
Calculate $\hat{\Gamma}^{j}_{m}(t)$ according to (25) for the fixed associated devices
if $\hat{\Gamma}^{j}_{m}(t) \geq \varsigma$ **then**
$\tilde{R}^{j}_{m}(t) = \sum_{\tilde{k}=1}^{\tilde{K}} B \log_2\left[1 + \hat{\Gamma}^{j}_{\tilde{k},m}(t)\right]$
else
$\tilde{R}^{j}_{m}(t) = 0$
for $m = 1, 2, \dots, M$ **do**
for $j = 1, 2, \dots, J$ **do**
Set $\tilde{I}_{m,j}(t) = 1$ when $j = \arg\max_{j \in \mathcal{J}} \overline{P}_{m,j}(t)$, otherwise $\tilde{I}_{m,j}(t) = 0$
According to (44), update channel selection probability as
$\overline{P}_{m,j}(t) \leftarrow \overline{P}_{m,j}(t+1)$
for $m = 1, 2, \dots, M$ **do**
Choose the action values $a_m(t) = \left\{\delta^m_x(t), \delta^m_y(t)\right\}$ by (50)
Find next state as $s_m(t+1) = \left(x_m(t+1), y_m(t+1), H_u\right)$ by (40) and (41)
Calculate the immediate reward $\mathcal{R}(s_m(t), a_m(t))$ of UAV m by (42)
Choose the action $a_m(t+1) = \left\{\delta^m_x(t+1), \delta^m_y(t+1)\right\}$ by (50) and obtain $Q(s_m(t+1), a_m(t+1))$ value
Update $Q(s_m(t), a_m(t))$ value according to (49) and store it in Q-table
Update the state and action for the next time slot as $s_m(t) \leftarrow s_m(t+1)$ and $a_m(t) \leftarrow a_m(t+1)$ respectively
Calculate the instantaneous reward generated by all UAVs as $\mathcal{R}(t) = \sum_{m=1}^{M} \mathcal{R}(s_m(t), a_m(t))$

Figure 7a shows the variation of instantaneous transmission rate for different number of UAVs while the other3 network parameters are the same, as mentioned in **Figure 6**. It can be observed in this figure that the performance metric value increases with the number of UAVs because all UAVs utilize the available channels efficiently at their deployed location. But when the number of UAVs exceeds 7, the total instantaneous transmission rate does not increase significantly because all UAVs reuse the limited spectrum, which increases mutual interferences among UAVs and source-destination device pairs.

Figure 7b plots the objective value corresponding to the different number of available orthogonal channels. From this figure, we can say that the instantaneous transmission rate increases with the number of channels because all the communication nodes select individual channels according to the channel selection probability vectors. But when the number of channels exceeds 7, no such variation in objective value is found because this is a sufficient resource to avoid mutual interferences completely.

Figure 7c represents the network throughput variation for different UAV-assisted D2D pairs when their transmitting power is 10 mW. Since all the devices and UAVs share the fixed amount of orthogonal channels, the network's performance is

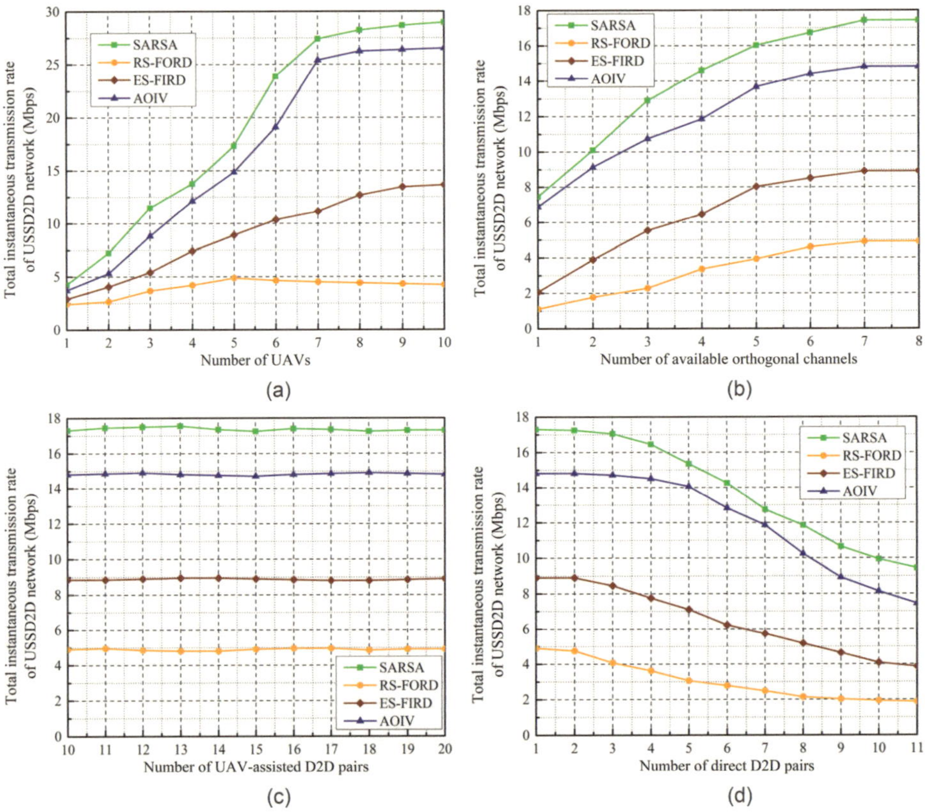

Figure 7.
Total overall network performance of the USSD2D network for different network parameters value. (a) Network throughput for different number of UAVs. (b) Network throughput for different number of channels. (c) Network throughput corresponding to the different number of UAV-assisted D2D pairs. (d) Network throughput corresponding to the different number of direct D2D pairs.

independent with respect to the number of UAV-assisted D2D pairs, and the performance metric value is almost constant for variation of the key system parameters.

The performance metric variations for different number of direct D2D pairs are illustrated in **Figure 7d** when their transmitting power is set as 10 mW. It is observed that the instantaneous transmission rate decreases with the number of direct D2D pairs because they utilize more orthogonal channels. As a result, mutual interference among UAV-assisted D2D pairs increases since they share limited network resources. Furthermore, our proposed scheme has the capabilities for adaptive action selection, which significantly outperforms the benchmark techniques. From **Figure 7**, we can say that the overall network throughput can be improved by 77.58%, 52.51%, and 12.14% compared to the RS-FORD, ES-FIRD, and AOIV schemes, respectively.

5. Minimization of devices' energy consumption in UAV-assisted IoT network

The devices at the cell edge consume high energy to achieve the required data rate when transmitting data to the nearest BS because of the large LoS distance between

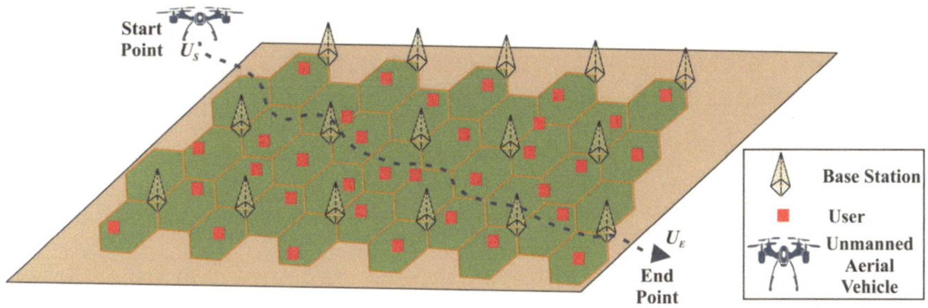

Figure 8.
Illustration of UAV-assisted IoT network.

BSs and those devices. Alternatively, a quad-rotor UAV-assisted IoT network could provide reliable communication compared to fixed terrestrial BSs. Therefore, in this section, we aim to find the optimal trajectory of UAV and the association of IoT devices that simultaneously support energy-efficient data collection.

5.1 System model

Figure 8 illustrates the UAV-assisted IoT network, in which M terrestrial BSs with fixed height of H_B and a single UAV collect data from K stationary uniformly distributed IoT devices. The UAV flies at a fixed altitude H_u with the constant speed of ϑ_u where its start and end locations are represented by $U_S = (x_s, y_s, H_u)$ and $U_E = (x_e, y_e, H_u)$ respectively. To track the UAV's location at each instance, we discretize its flight period into N equally spaced time slots, each of duration T_s, and assume that UAV's location at nth time slot $U[n] = (x[n], y[n], H_u), \forall n \in \mathcal{N} = \{1, 2, \ldots, N\}$ is constant. All devices transmit atleast $\mathcal{D}_{Min}$ bits data to the core network to maintain reliable QoS.

5.1.1 Data collection of core network

The transmission environment is categorized into two scenarios, i.e., ground to ground (G2G) and ground to air (G2A) channels. G2G channel establishes the links between BS and IoT devices, whereas G2A channel connects the IoT devices with the UAV platform. We generalize the wireless channel gain between each device and its destination (either UAV or BS) at each time slot as the combination of large-scale path loss and small-scale fading. The channel gain between each device and its destination can be modeled as [39]

$$h_k^i[n] = g_k^i[n]\sqrt{L_k^i[n]}, \forall k \in \mathcal{K} = \{1, 2, \ldots, K\} \tag{51}$$

where $i \in \{B \text{ or } U\}$ is the destination indicator in which B and U represent nearest BS and UAV, respectively, $L_k^i[n]$ is the large scale path loss, $g_k^i[n]$ is the small scale fading coefficient. The achievable instantaneous transmission rate of the kth IoT device can be formulated as [40]

$$R_k^i[n] = C_B \log_2\left[1 + \frac{|h_k^i[n]|^2 P_k^i[n]}{\eta_0}\right] \tag{52}$$

where C_B is channel bandwidth, $P_k^i[n]$ is transmitting power of the kth device, and η_0 is noise power. Instantaneous data transmitted by the kth device over G2G and G2A channel is measured as $\mathcal{D}_k^B[n] = R_k^B[n]T_s$ and $\mathcal{D}_k^U[n] = R_k^U[n]T_s$ respectively. The energy consumption of device k at nth time slot can be calculated as

$$E_k[n] = \left(I_k^U[n]P_k^U[n] + I_k^B[n]P_k^B[n]\right)T_s, \forall k \in \mathcal{K} \quad (53)$$

where $P_k^U[n]$ and $P_k^B[n]$ are the instantaneous transmit powers of kth device when connecting with UAV and BS, respectively and $I_k^U[n], I_k^B[n] \in \{0, 1\}$ are the binary device association indicators with UAV and BS respectively. The k th device transmits data to the core network during each time slot is measured as

$$\mathcal{D}_k[n] = I_k^U[n]\mathcal{D}_k^U[n] + I_k^B[n]\mathcal{D}_k^B[n], \forall k \in \mathcal{K}, n \in \mathcal{N} \quad (54)$$

5.1.2 Problem formulation

We aim for energy-efficient data collection that jointly exploit reliable data transmission, optimal instantaneous position of UAV and transmit power control. The fluctuation of channel gain causes unstable network performance, leading to quickly drain out devices' on-board battery energy. Thus, to minimize total energy consumption of all devices we jointly optimize UAV' trajectory, device association indicators and their transmit power allocation, while ensuring that each device should transmit a minimum data to the destination and UAV chooses a constant speed during its trajectory between the initial and final locations. Therefore the optimization problem is formulated as

$$\text{P1}: \underset{\left\{\substack{\{(x[n], y[n])\}, I_k^U[n], I_k^B[n], P_k^U[n], \text{ and } P_k^B[n] \\ \forall k \in \mathcal{K}, n \in \mathcal{N}}\right\}}{\text{Minimize}} \sum_{n=1}^{N}\sum_{k=1}^{K}\left[\left(I_k^u[n]P_k^u[n] + I_k^B[n]P_k^B[n]\right)T_s\right] \quad (55)$$

Subject to the constraints

$$\text{C1}: I_k^U[n]\mathcal{D}_k^U[n] + I_k^B[n]\mathcal{D}_k^B[n] \geq \mathcal{D}_{Min}, \forall k \in \mathcal{K}, n \in \mathcal{N} \quad (56)$$

$$\text{C2}: I_k^U[n] \in \{0, 1\}, I_k^B[n] \in \{0, 1\}, \forall k \in \mathcal{K}, n \in \mathcal{N} \quad (57)$$

$$\text{C3}: I_k^U[n] + I_k^B[n] \leq 1, \forall k \in \mathcal{K}, n \in \mathcal{N} \quad (58)$$

$$\text{C4}: \sum_{k=1}^{K} I_k^U[n] \leq K, \forall n \in \mathcal{N} \quad (59)$$

$$\text{C5}: U[1] = U_S, U[N] = U_E \quad (60)$$

Here, C1 ensures that each device transmits atleast $\mathcal{D}_{Min}$ bits data to either UAV or nearest BS at a time slot. C2 defines the device association indicators. C3 verifies that each device associates with either UAV or the nearest BS at each time slot. C4 implies that UAV can associate with maximum K number of devices instantaneously; and C5 guarantees that UAV starts its trajectory from an initial given position and ends to the final predefined location. The optimization problem contains multiple interactive and coupled variables, and they have a complex relationship by which changing one's value may impact to others. Furthermore, these discrete optimizing variables make the problem highly non-convex to find a limited time trajectory between the start and end points.

Hence, standard optimization methods face difficulties in obtaining exact solutions. In order to tackle this situation, we propose RL framework and adaptive decision-making policy to find UAV's successive locations, and device association along with their transmit power allocation. We adopt the SARSA algorithm to control the UAV, which acts as an RL-agent for taking the optimal action at each step to maximize its reward.

5.2 Reinforcement learning based on SARSA algorithm

As discussed earlier in Section 4.3, the RL framework follows MDP, where the current state only depends on the immediate past state, and the UAV acting as RL agent chooses an action according to the ϵ-greedy policy. Here, the generated reward depends on UAV's current state and taken action at each time slot. The expected trajectory is obtained more precisely when the reward generated by the UAV at the current time slot is beneficial for the long term. To reflect this property, we model the instantaneous reward for every time slot as UAV's instantaneous objective value, which is expressed as

$$\mathcal{R}(s[n], a[n]) = \left[\sum_{k=1}^{K} \left(I_k^U[n] P_k^U[n] + I_k^B[n] P_k^B[n]\right) T_s\right]^{-1} \tag{61}$$

Algorithm 2 summarizes the optimal trajectory learning procedure using the improved SARSA technique. In this framework, we first calculate UAV's current state, channel gain, and distances from all devices to UAV and the nearest BS at every time slot. Then, all devices select the destination (either UAV or nearest BS) by estimating the instantaneous device association indicator and the required transmit power while satisfying the data rate constraint value. This process is repeated at each step, and UAV obtains optimal policy at the final episode. Since the number of episodes is T and each episode goes through N time slots, the computation complexity depends on total steps TN, including state space and action space in RL. In our scenario, there are $L_1 L_2$ possible state locations and eight possible actions for each time slot. Therefore, the computational complexity of algorithm 1 is $\mathcal{O}(8TNL_1L_2)$, including the complexity of the action selection scheme in each step.

Algorithm 2: UAV trajectory learning process using SARSA

Input: $\gamma, \alpha, \hat{\epsilon}, \zeta, T, (x_s, y_s, H_u), (x_e, y_e, H_u), T_s, \beta_0, \vartheta_u, H_u, \mathcal{D}_{Min}, IoT_k, K, BS_m, M, N, e_{Max},$
$h_k^i[n], s[n], a[n], \forall s[n] \in \mathcal{S}, a[n] \in \mathcal{A}, k \in \mathcal{K}, m \in \mathcal{M}, n \in \mathcal{N}, i \in \{U \text{ or } B\}$
Output: Optimal policy π_h^*
1: Initialize $Q(s[n], a[n]) = 0, \forall s \in \mathcal{S}, a \in \mathcal{A},$ and $e[1] = e_{Max}$
2: **for** $t = 1, 2, \ldots, T$ **do**
3: Set the starting point as $s[1] = (x[1], y[1]) = (x_s, y_s)$
4: **for** $n = 1, 2, \ldots, N$ **do**
5: **if** $n \le N - 2$ and $\sqrt{(x_e - x_u[n])^2 + (y_e - y_u[n])^2} \le \vartheta_u (N - n) T_s$ **then**
6: Choose the action values $a[n] = \left\{\delta_x^u[n], \delta_y^u[n]\right\}$ by (50)
7: Find next state by (40) and (41) as $s[n+1] = (x[n+1], y[n+1])$
8: Calculate reward $\mathcal{R}(s[n], a[n])$ by (61)
9: Choose the next action $a[n+1] = \left\{\delta_x^u[n+1], \delta_y^u[n+1]\right\}$ by (50) and obtain $Q(s[n+1], a[n+1])$ value
10: Update $Q(s[n], a[n])$ value according to (49)
11: Update the respective state and action as $s[n] \leftarrow s[n+1]$ and $a[n] \leftarrow a[n+1]$

---

else if $n = N - 1$ and $\sqrt{(x_e - x_u[n])^2 + (y_e - y_u[n])^2} \le \vartheta_u T_s$ **then**
Obtain the next state as $s[n+1] = [x_e, y_e]$
Calculate reward $\mathcal{R}(s[n], a[n])$ by (61)
Choose the next action $a[n+1] = \left\{\delta_x^u[n+1], \delta_y^u[n+1]\right\}$ by (50) and obtain $Q(s[n+1], a[n+1])$ value
Update $Q(s[n], a[n])$ value according to (49)
Update the respective state and action as $s[n] \leftarrow s[n+1]$ and $a[n] \leftarrow a[n+1]$
else
Break
Find an optimal policy as $\pi_h^* = arg \max_{a[n]=\left\{\delta_x^u[n], \delta_y^u[n]\right\}} Q(s[n], a[n]), \forall s[n] \in \mathcal{S}, a[n] \in \mathcal{A}, n \in \mathcal{N}$

5.3 Simulation results

This sub-section presents the training outcomes corresponding to the proposed SARSA algorithm for optimal trajectory and subsequently evaluates the energy-efficient data collection. Here, we compare the effectiveness and superiority of the proposed design with the benchmark PSO technique [41], where 100 IoT devices are uniformly distributed within a square field of size 2000 × 2000 m. Moreover, we adopt the required simulation parameters from [40] and [24] to implement the proposed algorithm.

5.3.1 Convergence analysis

The agents' training evaluations using RL-based SARSA algorithm are illustrated in **Figure 9a**, when all IoT devices maintain the data rate constraint of 10 Mbps. In this figure, we have found that the convergence rate varies for flying time because UAV explores the target area more efficiently with the available time slots. As a result more devices associate with UAV and the convergence occurs before 10,000 episodes.

Figure 9b shows the episode-wise objective value evaluation using PSO algorithm. From this figure, it is visible that PSO takes more time to converge, and its final convergence value is less than the SARSA algorithm. This is because PSO updates particles' position and velocity according to the random inertial weight which causes less exact regulation of particles' moving directions and speed. Hence, its

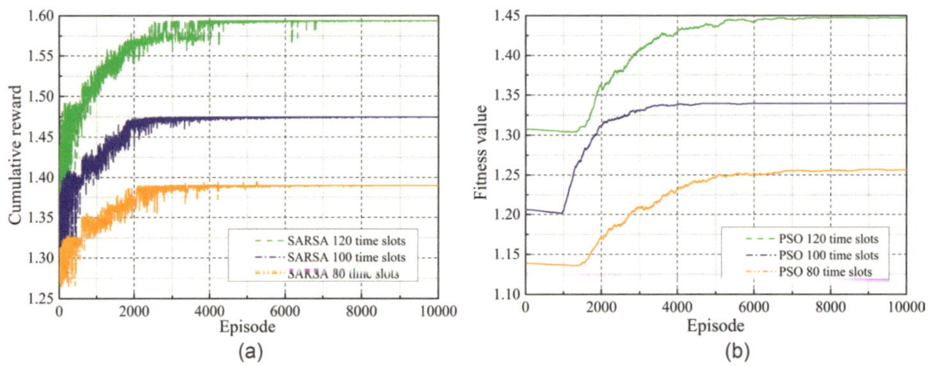

Figure 9.
Training results corresponding to the proposed and benchmark algorithms. (a) Cumulative reward generated by proposed SARSA. (b) Fitness value generated by benchmark PSO.

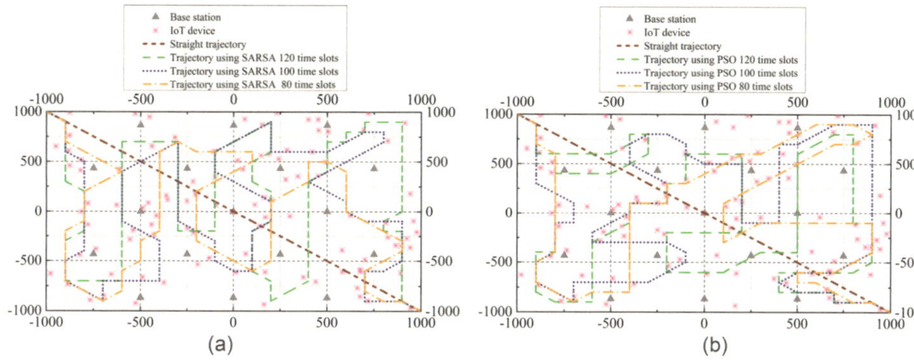

Figure 10.
Optimal trajectories corresponding to the proposed and benchmark algorithms. (a) Optimal UAV trajectory using SARSA. (b) Optimal UAV trajectory using PSO.

computational complexity increase due to the high dimensions of decision variables. Therefore, the proposed SARSA algorithm improves the cumulative reward by 10.26% with respect to the PSO.

5.3.2 Optimal trajectory

Using the same parameters mentioned in **Figure 9**, UAV finds its optimal trajectories with the help of SARSA and PSO algorithms, depicted in **Figure 10**. These figures indicate that UAV moves toward the devices, far away from the BS, and within the flight period, it reaches the final destination point. Since devices consume more energy while transmitting data to BS, UAV fly toward those devices to improve their channel conditions. as we mentioned earlier, device association with UAV increases with the flying time, more devices transmit their data to the UAV instead of BS, reducing their energy consumption.

5.3.3 Performance comparison of proposed SARSA with benchmark PSO

The variation of devices' average transmit power to achieve 10 Mbps data rate with the index value is demonstrated in **Figure 11a** where a device's index indicates its

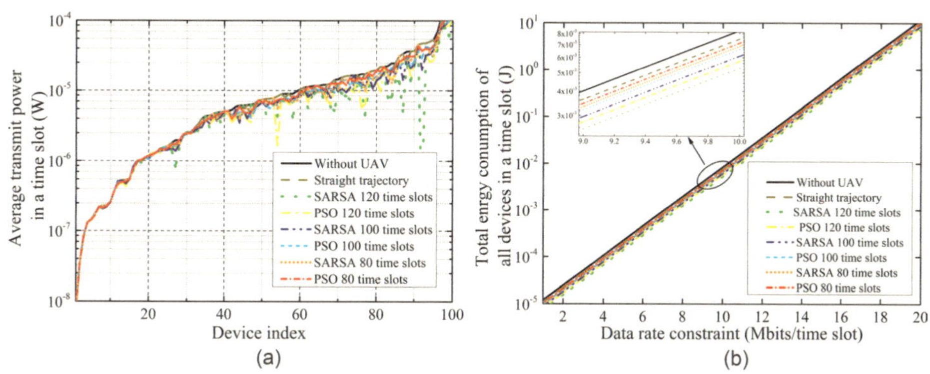

Figure 11.
Performance comparison of the proposed and benchmark algorithms. (a) Devices' transmit power corresponding to their index value. (b) Devices' energy consumption versus data rate constraint.

distance from the nearest BS. It is observed that, when there is no UAV support, average transmit power increases with the index value because, according to (52) devices far away from BS utilize more power to obtain the given data rate. But when UAV is employed, its optimal trajectory focuses the devices which are consuming more power and associates with them for data collection. Furthermore, since UAV's straight trajectory cannot improve all devices' channel conditions, the corresponding energy-efficient data collection would not be possible.

The total energy consumption of all devices for various data rate constraint values is illustrated in **Figure 11b**. It is clear that devices' energy consumption increases with data rate constraint because, according to (49), devices allocate more power to achieve the given rate constraint. Furthermore, from **Figure 11a**, UAV's optimal trajectory corresponding to the proposed SARSA algorithm reduces devices' transmit power with its available flying time as compared to PSO algorithm, because PSO achieves low convergence rate in an iterative process and could not identify the local optimal in high-dimension space. Hence, the proposed SARSA methodology significantly reduces the total energy consumption of all devices by 8.15%, 7.72%, and 5.67% for UAV's flying time of 80, 100, and 120 timeslots, respectively as compared to PSO.

6. Conclusion

This chapter proposes deployment and trajectory designs of UAVs for efficient resource allocation to achieve reliable wireless communication. The main features of this structure are three folded. In the first part, we optimize UAVs altitude to minimize outage probability and symbol error rate, considering pointing errors, atmospheric turbulence, and scintillation parameters where a hybrid RF-FSO channel governs the transmission environment. The second part finds the optimal deployed locations of UAVs to maximize the total instantaneous transmission rate of the devices in USSD2D network under SNR constraint. Finally, the last feature focuses on energy-efficient data collection where devices' total energy consumption is minimized by jointly optimizing their association with the nearest BS or UAV, their transmitting power, and UAV trajectory while satisfying a given data rate requirements. Numerical results validate the analysis and provide insights on the optimal UAV control design for various key system parameters. Our proposed methodology significantly improves system performance compared with the benchmark techniques. This work would be extended toward a multi UAVs-assisted energy-efficient data collection system considering the age of information aspect where the users follow a certain mobility model.

Author details

Abhishek Mondal[1*], Deepak Mishra[2], Ganesh Prasad[1] and Ashraf Hossain[1]

1 Department of Electronics and Communication Engineering, National Institute of Technology, Silchar, India

2 School of Electrical Engineering and Telecommunications, University of New South Wales, Sydney, Australia

*Address all correspondence to: abhishekmondal532@gmail.com

References

[1] Zanella A, Bui N, Castellani A, Vangelista L, Zorzi M. Internet of things for smart cities. IEEE Internet of Things Journal. 2014;**1**(1):22-32. DOI: 10.1109/JIOT.2014.2306328

[2] Samarakoon S, Bennis M, Saad W, Debbah M, Latva-Aho M. (2016, may). Ultra-dense small cell networks: Turning density into energy efficiency. IEEE Journal on Selected Areas in Communications. 2016;**34**(5):1267-1280. DOI: 10.1109/JSAC.2016.2545539

[3] Semiari O, Saad W, Bennis M, Dawy Z. Inter-operator resource management for millimeter wave multi-hop backhaul networks. IEEE Transactions on Wireless Communications. 2017;**16**(8):5258-5272. DOI: 10.1109/TWC.2017.2707410

[4] Mozaffari M, Saad W, Bennis M, Nam YH, Debbah M. A tutorial on UAVs for wireless networks: Applications challenges and open problems. IEEE Communications Surveys and Tutorials. 2019;**21**(3):2334-2360. DOI: 10.1109/COMST.2019.2902862

[5] Esrafilian O, Gangula R, Gesbert D. 3D map-based trajectory design in UAV-aided wireless localization systems. IEEE Internet of Things Journal. 2021;**8**(12):9894-9904. DOI: 10.1109/JIOT.2020.3021611

[6] Sawalmeh AH, Othman NS, Shakhatreh H, Khreishah A. Wireless coverage for mobile users in dynamic environments using UAV. IEEE Access. 2019;**7**:126376-126390. DOI: 10.1109/ACCESS.2019.2938272

[7] Lyu J, Zeng Y, Zhang R, Lim TJ. Placement optimization of UAV-mounted mobile base stations. IEEE Communications Letters. 2017;**21**(3):604-607. DOI: 10.1109/LCOMM.2016.2633248

[8] Wang Z, Duan L, Zhang R. Adaptive deployment for UAV-aided communication networks. IEEE Transactions on Wireless Communications. 2019;**18**(9):4531-4543. DOI: 10.1109/TWC.2019.2926279

[9] Alzenad M, El-Keyi A, Yanikomeroglu H. 3-D placement of an unmanned aerial vehicle base station for maximum coverage of users with different QoS requirements. IEEE Wireless Communications Letters. 2018;**7**(1):38-41. DOI: 10.1109/LWC.2017.2752161

[10] El-Hammouti H, Benjillali M, Shihada B, Alouini M. Learn-as-you-fly: A distributed algorithm for joint 3D placement and user association in multi-UAVs networks. IEEE Transactions on Wireless Communications. 2019;**18**(12):5831-5844. DOI: 10.1109/TWC.2019.2939315

[11] Zhang H, Hanzo L. Federated learning assisted multi-UAV networks. IEEE Transactions on Vehicular Technology. 2020;**69**(11):14104-14109. DOI: 10.1109/TVT.2020.3028011

[12] Liu X, Liu Y, Chen Y, Hanzo L. Trajectory design and power control for multi-UAV assisted wireless networks: A machine learning approach. IEEE Transactions on Vehicular Technology. 2019;**68**(8):7957-7969. DOI: 10.1109/TVT.2019.2920284

[13] Duong TQ, Nguyen LD, Tuan HD, Hanzo L. Learning-aided real-time performance optimization of cognitive UAV-assisted disaster communication. In: Proceeding IEEE Global

Communications Conference (GLOBECOM); 09–13 December 2019. Waikoloa, HI, USA: IEEE; 2020. pp. 1-6

[14] Liu X, Liu Y, Chen Y. Reinforcement learning in multiple UAV networks: Deployment and movement design. IEEE Transactions on Vehicular Technology. 2019;**68**(8):8036-8049. DOI: 10.1109/TVT.2019.2922849

[15] Larsen E, Landmark L, Kure O. Optimal UAV relay positions in multi-rate networks. In: Proceedings Wireless Days; 29–31 March 2017. Porto, Portugal: IEEE; 2017. pp. 8-14

[16] Han Z, Swindlehurst AL, Liu KJR. Optimization of MANET connectivity via smart deployment/movement of unmanned air vehicles. IEEE Transactions on Vehicular Technology. 2009;**58**(7):3533-3546. DOI: 10.1109/TVT.2009.2015953

[17] Jiang F, Swindlehurst AL. Dynamic UAV relay positioning for the ground-to-air uplink. In: Proceedings IEEE Globecom Workshop; 06–10 December 2010. Miami, FL, USA: IEEE; 2011. pp. 1766-1770

[18] Zhan P, Yu K, Swindlehurst AL. Wireless relay communications with unmanned aerial vehicles: Performance and optimization. IEEE Transactions on Aerospace and Electronic Systems. 2011;**47**(3):2068-2085. DOI: 10.1109/TAES.2011.5937283

[19] Zeng Y, Zhang R, Lim TJ. Throughput maximization for UAV-enabled mobile relaying systems. IEEE Transactions on Communications. 2016;**64**(12):4983-4996. DOI: 10.1109/TCOMM.2016.2611512

[20] Ono F, Ochiai H, Miura R. A wireless relay network based on unmanned aircraft system with rate optimization. IEEE Transactions on Wireless Communications. 2016;**15**(11):7699-7708. DOI: 10.1109/TWC.2016.2606388

[21] Fan R, Cui J, Jin S, Yang K. Optimal node placement and resource allocation for UAV relaying network. IEEE Communications Letters. 2018;**22**(4):808-811. DOI: 10.1109/LCOMM.2018.2800737

[22] Indu SRP, Choudhary HR, Dubey AK. Trajectory design for UAV-to-ground communication with energy optimization using genetic algorithm for agriculture application. IEEE Sensors Journal. 2021;**21**(16):17548-17555. DOI: 10.1109/JSEN.2020.3046463

[23] Kawamoto Y, Takagi H, Nishiyama H, Kato N. Efficient resource allocation utilizing Q-learning in multiple UA communications. IEEE Transaction on Network Science and Engineering. 2019;**6**(3):293-302. DOI: 10.1109/TNSE.2018.2842246

[24] Mondal A, Mishra D, Prasad G, Hossain A. Joint optimization framework for minimization of device energy consumption in transmission rate constrained UAV-assisted IoT network. IEEE Internet of Things Journal. 2021;**9**(12):9591-9607. DOI: 10.1109/JIOT.2021.3128883

[25] Hu J, Zhang H, Song L. Reinforcement learning for decentralized trajectory design in cellular UAV networks with the sense-and-send protocol. IEEE Internet of Things Journal. 2019;**6**(4):6177-6189. DOI: 10.1109/JIOT.2018.2876513

[26] Cui J, Ding Z, Deng Y, Nallanathan A, Hanzo L. Adaptive UAV trajectory optimization under the quality of service constraints: A model-free solution. IEEE Access. 2020;**8**:

112253-112265. DOI: 10.1109/ACCESS.2020.3001752

[27] Yang L, Yuan J, Liu X, Hasna MO. On the performance of LAP-based multiple-hop RF/FSO systems. IEEE Transactions on Aerospace and Electronic Systems. 2019;**55**(1):499-505. DOI: 10.1109/TAES.2018.2852399

[28] Azari MM, Rosas F, Chen KC, Pollin S. Ultra reliable UAV communication using altitude and cooperation diversity. IEEE Transactions on Communications. 2018;**66**(1):330-344. DOI: 10.1109/TCOMM.2017.2746105

[29] Puri P, Garg P, Aggarwal M. Outage and error rate analysis of network-coded coherent TWR-FSO systems. IEEE Photonics Technology Letters. 2014;**26**(18):1797-1800. DOI: 10.1109/LPT.2014.2333032

[30] Gappmair W. Further results on the capacity of free-space optical channels in turbulent atmosphere. IET Communications. 2011;**5**(9):1262-1267. DOI: 10.1049/iet-com.2010.0172

[31] Gil A, Segura J, Temme NM. Computation of the Marcum Q-function. ACM Transactions on Mathematical Software. 2013;**40**(3):280-295. DOI: 10.48550/arXiv.1311.0681

[32] Muller A, Speidel J. Exact symbol error probability of M-PSK for multihop transmission with regenerative relays. IEEE Communications Letters. 2007;**11**(12):952-954. DOI: 10.1109/LCOMM.2007.070820

[33] Mondal A, Hossain A. Channel characterization and performance analysis of UAV operated communication system with multihop RF–FSO link in dynamic environment. International Journal of Communication Systems. 2020;**33**(16):e4568. DOI: 10.1002/dac.4568

[34] Zhong X, Guo Y, Li N, Chen Y. Joint optimization of relay deployment, channel allocation, and relay assignment for UAVs-aided D2D networks. IEEE/ACM Transactions on Networking. 2020;**28**(2):804-817. DOI: 10.1109/TNET.2020.2970744

[35] Al-Hourani A, Kandeepan S, Lardner S. Optimal LAP altitude for maximum coverage. IEEE Wireless Communications Letters. 2014;**3**(6):569-572. DOI: 10.1109/LWC.2014.2342736

[36] Hasna MO, Alouini MS. Outage probability of multihop transmission over Nakagami fading channels. IEEE Communications Letters. 2003;**7**(5):216-218. DOI: 10.1109/LCOMM.2003.812178

[37] Mu X, Zhao X, Liang H. Power allocation based on reinforcement learning for MIMO system with energy harvesting. IEEE Transactions on Vehicular Technology. 2020;**69**(7):7622-7633. DOI: 10.1109/TVT.2020.2993275

[38] Mondal A, Hossain A. Maximization of instantaneous transmission rate in UAVs-supported self-organized device-to-device network. International Journal of Communication Systems. 2022;**35**(6):e5064. DOI: 10.1002/dac.5064

[39] You C, Zhang R. 3D trajectory optimization in Rician fading for UAV-enabled data harvesting. IEEE Transactions on Wireless Communications. 2019;**18**(6):3192-3207. DOI: 10.1109/TWC.2019.2911939

[40] Ho TM, Nguyen KK, Cheriet M. UAV control for wireless service provisioning in critical demand areas:

A deep reinforcement learning approach. IEEE Transactions on Vehicular Technology. 2021;**70**(7):7138-7152. DOI: 10.1109/TVT.2021.3088129

[41] Milner S, Davis C, Zhang H, Llorca J. Nature-inspired self-organization, control, and optimization in heterogeneous wireless networks. IEEE Transactions on Mobile Computing. 2012;**11**(7):1207-1222. DOI: 10.1109/TMC.2011.141

Chapter 7

IoT on an ESP32: Optimization Methods Regarding Battery Life and Write Speed to an SD-Card

Lukas M. Broell, Christian Hanshans and Dominik Kimmerle

Abstract

The ESP32 is a popular microcontroller for IoT use cases. For many IoT applications (e.g., environmental sensors or wearables), a continuous power supply is either not possible or too cumbersome, requiring battery operation. However, the ESP32 has a relatively high power consumption. This chapter focuses on battery life optimization methods for this family of microcontrollers. For scenarios where data logging is relevant, methods for increasing communication speed in relation to power consumption are examined in detail. Measurements of seven different commercially available development boards were evaluated in terms of sleep modes, reduced CPU frequencies, and serial communications with the goal of better power efficiency. Therefore, the common scenario of data logging was compared with the performance and power consumption when communicating with different SD cards and CPU frequencies via the SPI and SD bus. Our test results showed that peripheral components (such as voltage regulators) have a large impact on the power consumption of the ESP32 microcontrollers, especially in sleep mode. For data logging, higher clock rates combined with high-quality SD cards and using the SD bus in 4-bit mode resulted in the lowest battery discharge.

Keywords: ESP32, energy consumption, write speed, performance to energy, SD bus, SD-MMC, SDIO, CPU frequency, battery life, IoT, wearables

1. Introduction

For various research questions, comprehensive and objective data collection using appropriate sensor technology is essential. However, for some applications, there are no (affordable) devices available on the market or do not provide the needed data quality, form factor, or access to raw data. As a side effect, one might have special requirements regarding data privacy and protection. As a scientific institution in the biomedical field that has to deal with specific needs and research questions, financial restrictions, and sensitive data retrieved from the sensors, the above-mentioned aspects lead to many software and IoT-related hardware projects [1–4]. One of our medical projects intends to measure heart rate variability. The sensor has to exceed the precision of a clinical-grade ECG device, but at the same time has to be wireless, to be worn on the body, waterproof, heat resistant, and able to resist chemical disinfection [2].

The ECG-based measurement allows medical grade data quality for examining the activity or response of the autonomous nervous system, which is involved in many diseases such as chronic pain, addiction medicine, mental illnesses (e.g. depression) as well as in sports medicine and performance diagnostics. The device is used in several clinical trials and connected to an open-source IoT platform, that allows fleet management of many devices [1]. Another project that uses the same sensor deals with VR-based addiction diagnostics and treatment. In this use case, the main aspect is interoperability with the development environment and the flexibility of integrating further sensors. In both cases, it is particularly important that the battery life is as long as possible and that the raw data (ECG) is stored locally at the highest possible resolution, as correct wireless data transfer cannot always be ensured. There are many more applications in projects, where our custom build sensors came to use, for example, in environmental measurements (urban climate and fine dust measurements, spectro-radiometric measurements, or radiation sensors) or lab sensory, that is used as part of lab experiments or as a fundamental part of lab automation within microbial or cellular experiments [1].

Like us, many other research teams want to take data acquisition into their own hands and develop specially adapted instruments [5, 6]. It is also possible to describe exactly and transparently which algorithms were used to increase the reproducibility of the results. The widespread use and rapid development of easy-to-program microcontrollers such as the Raspberry Pi or microcontrollers based on the Arduino platform, as well as the many sensor modules, libraries and sample codes and projects available, make this easier, and once the basic system is developed, it is easy to add more sensors or adapt the system to different requirements. This allows data to be collected quickly under laboratory conditions. However, if the prototype is to be used in real-life scenarios or in field studies, additional obstacles need to be considered. Haghi et al. list the following points that should be considered when developing wearable IoT devices [7]:

- Easy and secure connectivity
- Low power consumption
- Wearability with small form factor
- Reduced risk of data loss through buffering

In order to limit the scope of this work, we will mainly focus on the aspects of reducing power consumption, as this is directly related to wearability and form factors. In addition, we will also look at data storage, as if large amounts of data are collected and need to be stored locally, this will also have a significant impact on battery life. The aim of this work is to list possible approaches for an optimal compromise between data write speed and energy efficiency in order to derive a best practice for custom development.

2. Background

This section provides background information for comparing different approaches to writing data to an SD card or improving the power efficiency of microcontrollers.

It also provides an initial comparison of commercially available microcontrollers in terms of functionality and power consumption.

2.1 Energy consumption of microcontrollers

To get a basic understanding of microcontroller power consumption, the following formula illustrates the factors that contribute to the microcontroller power consumption [8]:

$$P_d = fCU2 \tag{1}$$

P_d—Dnamic part of power consumption
f—CPU Clock-frequency
C—Total capacitance of the field-effect transistors (FETs) in the circuit
U—Operating voltage

This relation shows that power consumption can be reduced by lowering the CPU clock-frequency f, the capacitance C or by decreasing the operating voltage U [8]. Since the power consumption is proportional to the operating voltage U squared, it seems to be obvious to initially reduce it as much as possible. Historically, early microprocessors used to run on a 5 V supply voltage. Since then, the voltage has been continuously lowered for that reason. In contrast, the maximum clock frequency has increased over the years to achieve a higher computing performance. However, this has also led to increased power consumption. Nowadays the strategy is to max out the clock frequency capability of a microcontroller while running on a significantly lower clock frequency [8].

The total capacitance is the sum of the capacitances of the individual field-effect transistors (FETs). Due to miniaturization, the FETs' individual capacitances have become smaller, but the number of FETs per processor's core continues to grow. The total capacitance of a given system, therefore, can only be reduced by switching off individual parts of the proccssor [8].

2.2 General energy saving measures for microcontrollers

Microcontrollers are usually optimized for an energy-efficient operation with a number of mechanisms to minimize energy consumption available. An energy-efficient operation of the microcontroller is usually implemented without the need of an operating system, which means that the programmer has to give appropriate instructions in the application program. Most microcontrollers offer a flexible adjustment of the clock frequency as well as low-power or sleep modes. Depending on the architecture of the microcontroller, certain processor parts or peripheral components are clocked down, the operating voltage is lowered or even disconnected from the power supply. This results in the following rules for energy-efficient programming [5, 6]:

- Complete tasks via hardware instead of software
- Use interrupts and low power mode instead of pin or flag polling
- Use precalculated tables instead of on-demand calculations

- Avoid frequent calls of subroutines, use procedural programming if possible
- Use the fastest possible sampling-rate, transmission-rate, and highest possible clock frequency for executing tasks [9]

Before describing methods for implementing these rules, it is important to consider the SD card communication options in order to select a microcontroller that offers a good trade-off between power efficiency and write performance.

2.3 SD-card communication

An SD-Card (Secure Digital Memory Card) is a digital storage medium that works on the principle of flash storage. This section deals exclusively with standard SD-Cards with 9 pins. All information in this section is taken from the SD specifications of the SD-Card technical committee [10].

2.3.1 Communication systems

The host (microcontroller, card reader, laptop, smartphone, etc.) can access the SD-Card using either the Serial Peripheral Interface (SPI) or the proprietary SD bus protocol.

SD bus: Communication via the SD bus is based on command and data bit streams that are initiated by a start bit and terminated by a stop bit. Each message consists of a command, response, and data block tokens.

- 1-Bit SD bus: Data transfer via a single transmission channel.
- 4-Bit SD bus: Four transmission channels used for higher data transmission rates.

SPI bus: The SPI bus is a bus system consisting of three channels for serial synchronous data transmission. Microcontrollers mostly communicate with SD-Cards via the SPI bus. The SPI protocol does not allow all functions of SD-Cards, like energy saving functionality (e.g., low voltage). Additionally, the maximum transfer speed of the bus speed does not correspond to the maximum read/write speed of the used SD-Card.

2.3.2 Write speed

The maximum supported clock rate is decisive for the highest data transfer rate that can be achieved. Clock frequencies available for standard SD-Cards at the respective communication protocols are listed in **Table 1**.

Unfortunately, most microcontrollers only support the SPI bus for storing data on an SD card. However, the ESP32, which is widely used for IoT applications, supports both SPI and SD bus. For this reason, the features and power saving options of the ESP32 will now be examined in more detail.

2.4 ESP32: Energy options

Like many other microcontrollers, the ESP32 offers a wide range of power saving options. Its processor core is divided into different modules (radio module, main

Communication protocol	Supported clock rates	Max. write speed
SPI	½ of CPU Clock	1.6 MB/s
SD bus 1-bit mode	Default Speed (25 MHz) High Speed (50 MHz) UHS-I (208 MHz)	3.125 MB/s 6.25 MB/s 26 MB/s
SD bus 4-bit mode	Default Speed (25 MHz) High Speed (50 MHz) UHS-I (208 MHz)	12.5 MB/s 25 MB/s 104 MB/s

Table 1.
SD-card communication protocols and respective max write speeds [10].

Power Modi	Description			Current draw
Modem-sleep	CPU is active	240 MHz	Dual-core	30 mA ~ 68 mA
			Single-core	n.a.
		160 MHz	Dual-core	27 mA ~ 44 mA
			Single-core	27 mA ~ 34 mA
		80 MHz	Dual-core	20 mA ~ 31 mA
			Single-core	20 mA ~ 25 mA
Light-sleep	—			0.8 mA
Deep-sleep	ULP active			150 μA
	ULP sensor-monitored pattern			100 μA at 1% load
	RTC timer + RTC memory			10 μA
Hibernation	RTC timer only			5 μA
Power off	CHIP_PU is set to low level, CPU switched off			1 μA

Table 2.
Power mode and energy consumption of the ESP32 [11].

processor core, and memory, cryptographic hardware acceleration, ultra-low-power co-processor with real-time clock and recovery memory), which can be switched off individually to save energy. **Table 2** lists the different power options of the ESP32 with the power consumption in the corresponding mode, according to the manufacturer's specifications.

2.5 Comparison of ESP32 development modules

Not only the processor contributes to the total energy consumption of a microcontroller but also all the peripheral modules like voltage regulators, sensors or external flash memory do so as well. Therefore, different developer modules using the ESP32 should be considered with regard to the total energy consumption in the respective power modes. **Table 3** shows the results of the measurements at the different power options.

The differences in power consumption between the different developer boards are considerable, as shown in **Table 3**. As a possible reason for the distinct deviation in power consumption, the built-in voltage regulators come into consideration since the

cDeveloper Modules	Reference (mA)	Light-Sleep (mA)	Deep-Sleep (mA)	Hibernation (mA)
Adafruit HUZZAH32	47	8.43	6.81	6.80
ESP32—DevKitC	51	10	9	9
Ai-Thinker NodeMCU 32S	55	15.05	6.18	6.18
Sparkfun ESP32 Thing	41	5.67	4.43	4.43
FireBeetle ESP32	39	1.94	0.011	0.008
WiPy 3.0	192	—	0.015	—

Table 3.
Comparison of the energy consumption of different ESP32 developer modules [12].

measured energy consumption exceeds the specifications from the data sheet by far. Voltage regulators are known to contribute significantly to the overall consumption of the system due to their quiescent current, which is especially noticeable in sleep states [13]. The voltage regulator of the FireBeetle ESP32, for example, has a maximum voltage drop of 0.31 V at 600 mA and a quiescent current of 4 μA, while the voltage regulator of the Adafruit HUZZAH32 has a voltage drop of 0.4 V at 600 mA and a quiescent current of 80 μA.

Nevertheless, the ESP32 itself is rather an energy-consuming. In consequence, the ESP32 family expanded by some more energy-efficient versions with the ESP32-S2 being the most interesting one for IoT applications. It provides almost all the known functionalities but comes as a single-core processor for less power consumption. The comparison of the ESP32 to the ESP32-S2 and its power consumption is summarized in **Table 4**.

The ESP32-S2 is an excellent choice for a variety of IoT applications, but the lack of an SD bus is a limiting factor in achieving an optimal combination of SD card write speed and power efficiency.

Now that the various options for writing to the SD card have been presented, as well as general and specific methods for reducing microcontroller power consumption, the next step is to review related work to evaluate the current best practice for power optimization in combination with high-resolution data acquisition.

Power Mode	Description	ESP 32 nominal current	ESP32-S2 nominal current
Active	transmit 802.11b	240 mA	190 mA
	receive 802.11b	100 mA	68 mA
Modem-Sleep	240 MHz	30 mA ~ 68 mA	19 mA
	160 MHz	27 mA ~ 44 mA	16 mA
	80 MHz	20 mA ~ 31 mA	12 mA
Light-Sleep	—	0.8 mA	450 μA
Deep-Sleep	ULP active	150 μA	235 μA
	ULP sensor-monitored	100 μA at 1% load	22 μA at 1% load
	RTC timer + memory	10 μA	25 μA
Hibernation	RTC timer only	5 μA	20 μA

Table 4.
Comparison of power consumption between ESP32 and ESP32-S2 [11, 14].

3. Related work

One work that optimizes the energy consumption when writing data to an SD card was done by Bradley and Wright in which the energy consumption of the Arduino Atmega328P was determined at 5 V and 16 MHz and 3.3 V and 8 MHz [15]. In each case, the SD card communication was implemented via SPI. It was found that the lower clock rate resulted in a lower discharge. At 16 MHz the transmission time was 9–10 ms, while at 8 MHz, 15 ms was measured. Also, at 8 MHz, a slight delay in SD card response was observed. In deep sleep, the microSD card adapter used for SPI communication contributed significantly to the total power consumption. Without the SD card, 120 and 96 μA were measured, while 800 and 750 μA were measured with the SD card connected. To reduce power consumption, a BS170 power control N-channel MOSFET was used. This reduced the current consumption during deep sleep to 21.1 and 18.6 μA, respectively, which is a reduction factor of 40. However, this MOSFET also led to a reduction in the transmission speed for SD communication from 20 to 150 ms. Further work with higher clock speed and larger SRAM is announced [15]. This work demonstrated a good option to minimize power consumption when using SD cards but only if a low sampling or transmission rate is required.

Regarding optimizing the write speed to an SD card, we could not find any comparable work in the scientific literature, but a blog post has been written demonstrating the performance increase when using the SD bus on the ESP32 compared to the SPI and how this was achieved [16]. A difference of about 230% for write operations and about 400% for read operations was shown using the SD bus in 4-bit mode compared to SPI.

Similarly, only one paper was found that addressed the energy-efficient operation of an ESP32 [17]. This paper gives a best practice for using an ESP32 in an industrial wireless sensor network. The different operating modes of the ESP32, as mentioned above, are listed with a recommendation to switch between operation modes over time to perform tasks with the suitable operation mode. It is also noted that in active mode, energy efficiency can be further improved by adjusting the processor clock speed.

As shown in the introduction and related work, there has been scarce work addressing the requirements of microcontrollers for wearable IoT applications and optimizing communication to a local storage medium. This is certainly a niche area, but the steady growth, ease of access, and the resulting variety of use cases have shown that the evaluation of further optimization methods is nevertheless useful and relevant.

Therefore, in the following, possible approaches to optimize the speed of writing data to an SD card while taking power consumption into account will be investigated. In addition, possible methods for further reducing power consumption by making various adjustments to the ESP32's operating modes will be investigated and different microcontrollers will be compared.

4. Material and methods

This section lists all the microcontrollers used, the different operating states, power-saving measures, and SD communication methods, as well as the measurement methods and evaluation methods of each test.

4.1 Optimization of the SD-card communication speed

The ESP32 features an SD bus interface that allows communication to SD-Cards in 1-bit and 4-bit modes. Read and write speed was compared in both modes with the performance of the SPI bus. In addition, a SanDisk Extreme 32GB (Speedclass 10, UHS Speed Class 3, max. Transfer speed 160 MB/s) was compared with a SanDisk Ultra 32GB (Speedclass 10, UHS Speed Class 1, max. Transfer speed 98 MB/s) during the three different communication scenarios. The Arduino sample programs "SD_Test" [18] for SPI and "SDMMC_Test" [19] for 1-bit and 4-bit data transfer were used to control the SD-Card, transferring data and measuring the transfer time. The sample programs are included when installing the ESP32 board manager into the Arduino IDE. All codes were executed on a DFRobot FireBeetle ESP32. **Table 5** shows the GPIO-Pin connections of the setup, respectively.

4.2 Optimization of power consumption

For power consumption measurements, the developer boards were operated with a 3.7 V LiPo battery. The following subsections describe the individual energy-saving options and experimental setups in more detail, measured with a digital multimeter (Testboy 313).

4.2.1 Determination of the most energy-efficient SD communication method

In all above-listed communication methods, the same Arduino sample programs for SD-Card communication were used. The current was measured during read and write operations. Over the elapsed time, the actual discharge was calculated according to the following formula, where C is the discharge in coulombs, A is the measured current in ampere, and t is the elapsed time in seconds.

$$C = A * t \tag{2}$$

Name		Pin		FireBeetle Pins SD bus	FireBeetle Pins SPI
SD bus	SPI	SD	Micro-SD		
DAT1	—	8	8	D0/IO4	—
DAT0	DO	7	7	D9/IO2	MISO/IO19
VSS	VSS	6	6	GND	GND
CLK	SCLK	5	5	BCLK/IO14	CLK/IO18
VCC	VCC	4	4	V3.3	V3.3
VSS2	VSS2	3	—	GND	GND
CMD	DI	2	3	A4/IO15	MOSI/IO23
DAT3	CS	1	2	D7/IO13	D8/IO5
DAT2	—	9	1	MCLK/IO12	—

Table 5.
SD-card connection to a DFRobot FireBeetle ESP32 in SD and SPI bus.

4.2.2 Comparison of different developer boards

Three frequently used ESP32 developer modules, one ESP32-S2 module, and also non-ESP boards were compared (see **Table 6**). Developer boards without an integrated battery voltage regulator were operated via an external battery voltage regulator (Adafruit Micro-Lipo Charger) and the same LiPo battery.

For a comparison between the developer boards, the current consumption was measured during two different operating states:

- Normal mode + LED blink
- deep sleep

4.2.3 CPU clock frequency reduction

To evaluate the impact of reduced CPU clock frequency on power consumption, the system was put into different operating states (see **Table 7**).

Wi-Fi network scan and modem sleep were run on all three developer boards. The effects of different CPU clock frequencies on SD communication speed were run exclusively on the FireBeetle ESP32 as it has the lowest energy consumption among the ESP32 boards with little quiescent current (according to **Table 2**). Hence, it reflects the actual power consumption of the processor best, and the Adafruit Feather S2 has no built-in SD bus interface. The same "SDMMC_Test" sample program was used as before. For a more accurate current measurement on read and write

Development module	CPU	CPU-Clock (MHz)	Nominal current	Voltage regulator	Quiescent current
ESP32-DevKitC-32D	ESP 32	240	40 mA	AMS1117	5 mA
Adafruit HUZZAH32	ESP 32	240	40 mA	AP2112–3.3	80 μA
FireBeetle ESP32	ESP 32	240	40 mA	RT9080-33GJ5	4 μA
Adafruit Feather S2	ESP32-S2	240	19 mA	NCP167BMX3 0TBG	18 μA
Arduino Nano 33 BLE	Cortex M4F	64	6.4 mA	MP2322GQH-Z	5 μA
Feather M0 Bluefruit	Cortex M0+	48	5.0 mA	AP2112–3.3	80 μA
nRF52840 MDK	Cortex M4F	64	6.4 mA	n.a.	n.a

Table 6.
Development modules' specifications for energy efficiency comparison.

Operation state	Development modules	CPU-Clock rates (MHz)
Wi-Fi-Scan	HUZZAH32, FireBeetle ESP32, Feather S2	240, 160, 80
Modem sleep + LED blink	HUZZAH32, FireBeetle ESP32, Feather S2	240, 160, 80, 40, 20
Modem sleep + SD communication	FireBeetle ESP32	240, 160, 80, 60

Table 7.
Tested operating states and clock frequencies of different ESP32 boards for energy efficiency comparison.

operations, a data transfer of 8 MB was set instead of the default 1 MB. The Wi-Fi network scan was only performed up to a minimum clock frequency of 80 MHz as Wi-Fi connectivity is only guaranteed by the ESP32 up to this clock frequency [3].

5. Results

In this section, the results of the compared optimization methods for the communication speed to the SD-Card as well as for the energy efficiency of the ESP32 in different operating states are given.

5.1 SD-card communication speed

Figure 1 shows the comparison of transfer speed between SD bus in 1-bit and 4-bit mode as well as communication via SPI bus on a SanDisk Ultra 32 GB and a SanDisk Extreme 32 GB in milliseconds.

The SD bus is clearly superior to the SPI bus, but there is only a little difference between the 1-bit and 4-bit modes. In 4-bit mode, the write processes are about 10% and read processes are about 25% faster in comparison to the 1-bit mode. The differences in reading operations between SanDisk Ultra and SanDisk Extreme are neglectable, however, while writing, the SanDisk Extreme 32GB performed the task 20% faster.

5.2 Energy consumption

5.2.1 Comparison of SD communication methods

To further evaluate the best SD-Card communication method for mobile devices, the results of the current measurements during read and write operations are listed

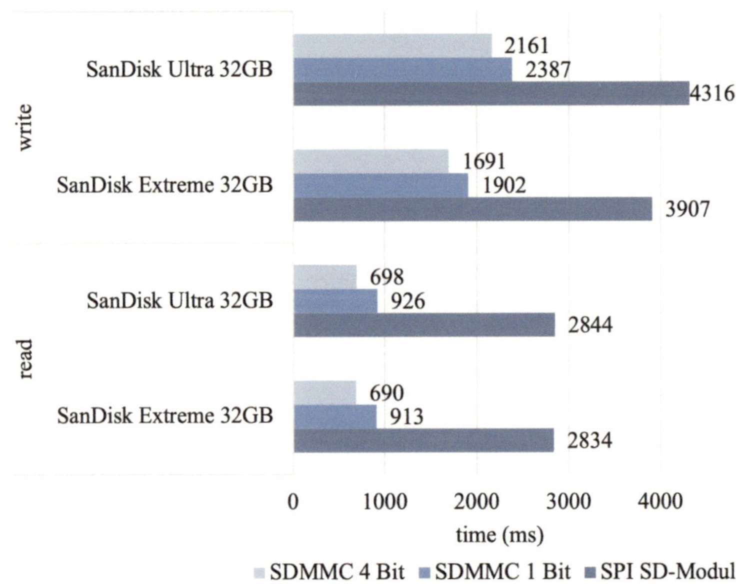

Figure 1.
Read and write speeds of different SD-cards in SD bus 1-bit mode, SD bus 4-bit mode, and SPI bus.

below. **Table 8** shows the durations and measured currents of the SPI bus with three different commercially available SD-Card modules as well as SD bus communication (1- and 4-Bit mode) using a wired SD-adapter.

No great difference was observed between the various SD-Card modules in the SPI bus mode, neither in read or write speed nor in current consumption. However, there is a considerable difference among both SD bus protocols: comparing SD bus to SPI during reading, the current consumption is increased by around 13% in 1-bit SD bus mode and by around 15% in 4-bit mode, however, while writing, the current draw is only increased by around 5% in 1-bit mode and by around 8% in 4-bit mode. Generally, reading processes showed a higher power consumption than slower writing processes.

To evaluate whether a faster write speed via the SD bus results in a less overall discharge of the battery (despite its higher current draw) each actual discharge was calculated and is shown in **Figure 2**.

As can be seen, the higher write speed causes less discharge of the battery despite a higher current flow during the operation. Therefore, the SD bus in the 4-bit mode has the lowest overall energy consumption in this scenario.

5.2.2 Comparison of various developer boards

The first comparison of the developer boards was carried out during a standard test program, the flashing of the built-in LED. **Figure 3** shows the current consumption of the various developer boards during this test program.

In this comparison, the ESP32 modules show the highest power consumption during the LED blink program, with the DFRobot FireBeetle ESP32 performing best among them. As expected, the newer single-core ESP32-S2 of the Adafruit Feather S2 shows a lower power consumption. The lowest power consumption is shown by the non-ESP32 boards, of which the Arduino Nano 33 BLE has the highest power consumption among the non-ESP32 boards. Even though having the same CPU as the Arduino, the nRF52840 MDK had the lowest power consumption. The Adafruit Feather M0 Bluefruit shows a slightly higher power consumption than the nRF52840 MDK despite the efficient ARM Cortex M0+ CPU. The comparison of the developer boards in deep sleep mode is shown in **Figure 4**.

SD-Card modules & communication methods	read		write	
	Current draw (mA)	Time (ms)	Current draw (mA)	Time (ms)
Standard SD-SPI	100	2851	86	3886
Adafruit µSD-Module	102	1738	89	2768
NoName SPI SD-Module	100	1736	86	2791
SD-Adapter SPI	103	1779	90	2766
SD bus 1-Bit mode	115	913	92	1902
SD bus 4-Bit mode	117	761	95	1744

Table 8.
Comparison of current consumption during read and write operations on the SD-card of different modules and communication methods.

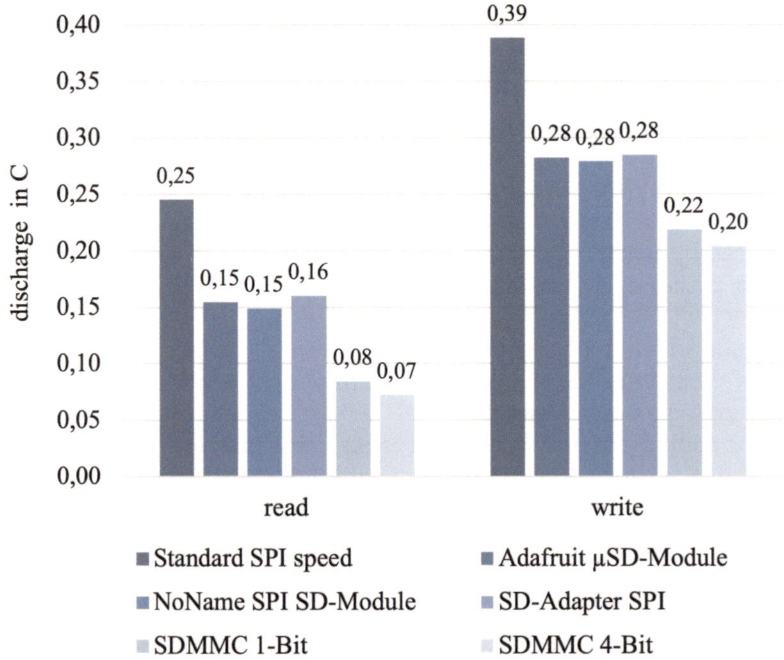

Figure 2.
Calculated battery discharge when reading and writing from and to an SD-card with different methods and modules.

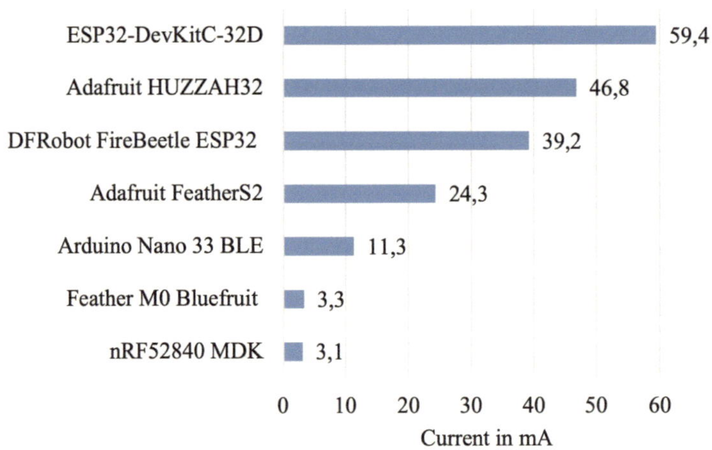

Figure 3.
Current measurement of different developer boards during a specific program sequence (LED blink).

The Adafruit HUZZAH32 (according to **Figure 4**) has the highest power consumption in the sleep state. This is consistent with **Table 2**. Correspondingly, the FireBeetle ESP32 shows a low power usage in the sleep state, only beaten by the Adafruit Feather S2, although the ESP32-S2 processor itself has a higher current requirement in deep sleep (see **Table 3**) and uses a less economical voltage regulator (see **Table 6**).

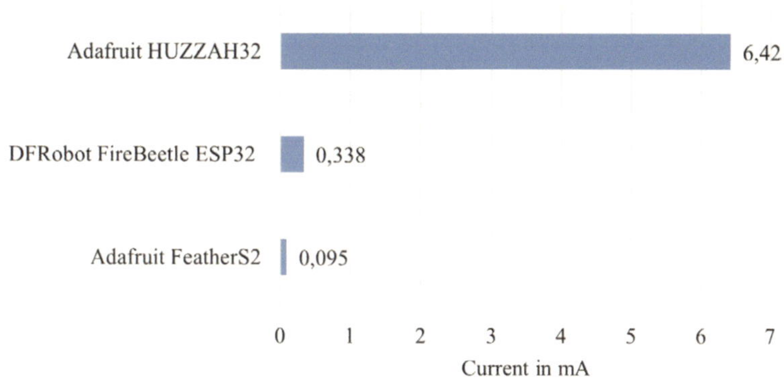

Figure 4.
Current measurement of different ESP32 developer boards in deep sleep. The ESP32 and ESP32-S2 boards were used due to their similar deep sleep functionality.

5.2.3 CPU clock frequency reduction

Since only the Adafruit Feather S2 among the non-ESP32 developer boards has Wi-Fi connectivity, for the comparison of current consumption at different CPU clock frequencies and operating states, it was compared with the two ESP32 boards. **Figure 5** visualizes the results of the current measurements. The Wi-Fi scan was performed up to a minimum clock frequency of 80 MHz, since the Wi-Fi module of the ESP32 is not supported at a lower clock frequency [3].

Figure 5 shows that the Adafruit HUZZAH32 consistently has the highest power consumption in different operating states and at reduced CPU clock frequencies, whereas the Adafruit FeatherS2 consistently shows the lowest power consumption in this comparison. It is noticeable that the DFRobot FireBeetle ESP32 only has a slightly higher power requirement than the FeatherS2 in Wi-Fi Scan and at a clock frequency

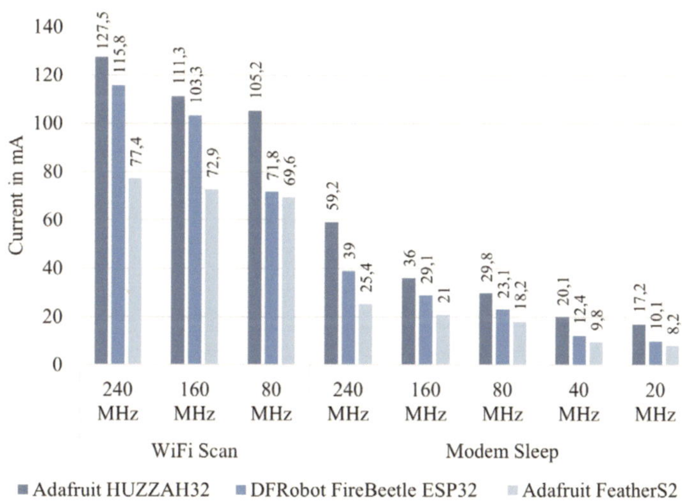

Figure 5.
Measurement of current at different CPU clock frequencies during Wi-Fi network scan and modem sleep of different ESP32 developer board.

CPU-Clock (MHz)		read			write		
		Time (ms)		Current (mA)	Time (ms)		Current (mA)
		M	SD		M	SD	
4-Bit	240	1221.3	16.95	120.3	3163.8	5.82	98.8
	160	1421.8	12.69	98.7	3622	3.74	78.5
	80	1842.5	20.27	80.7	4729	3.32	63.8
	60	1210.3	6.83	120.2	3330.3	276.9	99.9
1-Bit	240	2563.7	28.06	102.3	4376	4.08	92.8
	160	2762.8	12.65	86.2	4807.5	5.22	75.3

Table 9.
Comparison of current consumption and process duration during read and write operations at different CPU clock frequencies in 4-bit and 1-bit SD bus protocol.

of 80 MHz, as well as a constant approximation of current draw to the Feather S2 in modem sleep with reduced clock frequency.

To evaluate the functionality at reduced CPU clock frequencies in modem sleep, **Table 9** lists the performance when reading from and writing to the SD-Card at different clock frequencies as well as the simultaneously measured current flow. As with the Wi-Fi module, the ESP32 does not seem to support the SD bus protocol at clock frequencies lower than 80 MHz. 60 MHz could still be executed, but lower clock frequencies generated error messages and the data transfer was not executed.

Table 9 also shows that the current decreases with lower clock frequencies and a lower current requirement in 1-bit mode, the communication speed is also reduced in both manners. At 60 MHz in 4-bit mode, the measurement is comparable to 240 MHz, which indicates that the reduction of the clock frequency below 80 MHz leads to malfunctions. As before, the calculation of the actual battery discharge should provide information about which mode at which clock frequency means the lowest power

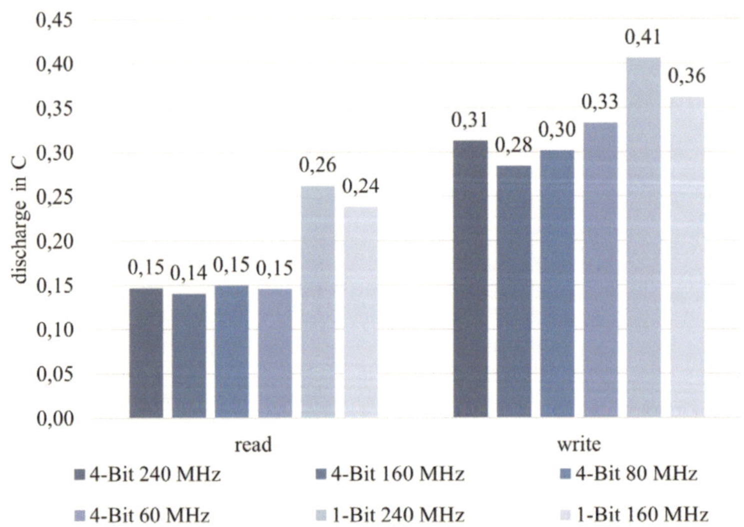

Figure 6.
Calculated actual battery discharge when reading and writing the SD-card at different CPU clock frequencies.

consumption and therefore longest battery lifetime. **Figure 6** shows the discharge calculated from **Table 9** during the read and write operations of the two modes at the different clock frequencies.

The direct comparison shows that despite the higher current requirement, the 4-bit mode causes less battery discharge than the 1-bit mode due to the faster communication speed. The comparison of the power consumption of the 4-bit mode at different clock frequencies shows only minor differences, of which the best efficiency was observed at a clock frequency of 160 MHz in 4-bit mode.

6. Discussion

In this section, the results presented above are discussed and possible reasons for controversial results are mentioned.

6.1 SD-card communication speed

As assumed, the SD bus showed higher data rates than SPI, but the difference was much smaller than expected. Data rates of only 1.45 MB/s in 4-bit mode while reading and 0.59 MB/s while writing were shown, even though the ESP32 supports the high frequency (50 MHz) 4-bit SD bus mode, which according to the datasheet should allow a transfer rate of up to 25 MB/s. Additionally, the 1-bit mode was not 4 times slower than the 4-bit mode. Only a 25% slower transfer rate for reading and 11% slower for writing data was measured. Lower transfer rates than those reported by the data sheets were also measured for the SPI bus, with 0.35 MB/s achieved while reading and 0.26 MB/s while writing, they are slightly less than a quarter of the nominal value of up to 1.6 MB/s. Possible causes for the deviations could be explained by inefficient register allocation of the libraries provided for the ESP32 SD bus interface, which is also shown by the fact that other colleagues could also not achieve higher transfer rates when using the ESP32 [16].

Nevertheless, **Figure 2** shows that the method with the highest transfer rate and thus a shorter transfer duration also causes the lowest battery discharge, which is why the SD-bus in 4-bit mode on the ESP32 is recommended even if its performance potential cannot be achieved. Likewise, the usage of a high-quality SD-Card is also recommended. The data can be transferred at three different CPU clock rates, whereby the differences in discharge turned out to be comparatively small, in this case, the rule faster data transfer equals lower discharge does not seem to apply. In our test, the clock rate of 160 MHz showed the lowest discharge.

6.2 Power consumption

Measuring the current with a multimeter while operating the microcontroller on a battery is not the most precise method, but sufficient for the extent of the differences between the respective compared developer boards and processes. In terms of energy consumption, it was basically found that the ESP32 has the highest energy consumption consistent with the data sheets, followed by the ESP32-S2, then the Cortex M0+ of the Adafruit Bluefruit M0, and with slightly less consumption of the nRF52840. Although the ESP32 has the highest power consumption, this processor also offers some advantages such as SD bus connectivity and high processor clock frequency for more computational performance and faster data rates, so further research was done with the ESP32.

Consistent with **Table 2**, in our series of measurements the FireBeetle ESP32 also showed the lowest quiescent current and power consumption in deep sleep among the ESP32 boards. However, the Adafruit Feather ESP32-S2 had an even lower power consumption, although the ESP32-S2 itself has a higher power consumption in deep sleep and a less efficient voltage regulator. The lower power consumption that we observed can be explained by the intelligent circuit layout: all peripheral modules are connected in a second circuit, which is switched off in deep sleep.

The reduction of the clock frequency showed a large effect up to a clock rate of 40 MHz. Below that, only a small reduction in energy consumption was detectable. At 20 MHz the ESP32 had a similar power consumption as the Arduino Nano 33 BLE at 64 MHz. But the Arduino Nano 33 BLE has several peripheral modules like the NINA Bluetooth module and a 9-axis IMU which is responsible for the higher power consumption compared to the nRF52840 MDK which uses the same CPU. Without the peripheral consumers, the Cortex M0+ as well as the nRF52840 showed a significantly lower power requirement than the throttled ESP32.

It could be demonstrated that the choice of a low-power developer board has a great impact on the overall power consumption of the system. If an economical module with low quiescent current is used, the power requirements can be throttled down to almost the level of the more economical microcontrollers such as the Adafruit Feather S2 or the Arduino Nano 33 BLE with still sufficient performance reserve. But if less performance is sufficient and small amounts of data have to be transferred, the Cortex M0+ or the nRF52840 are clearly recommended. As long as fast Wi-Fi data transfer and better performance are required but no fast data storage on SD-Cards is necessary, the ESP32-S2 would be the best choice.

7. Conclusion

In summary, the combination of high write speed and low power consumption is difficult to reconcile. It is recommended to write to the SD-Card as infrequently as possible and at 160 MHz using an ESP32 in SD bus 4-bit mode. In ordinary program cycles, the ESP32 should be operated in the state with the lowest power consumption. If a Wi-Fi connection is not necessary at any time or there is no stable Wi-Fi connection, the ESP32 should be operated in modem sleep mode and the clock rate should be reduced to the minimum necessary to function, although a reduction below 40 MHz has little effect. Tasks with high computational effort should be performed at the highest possible clock rate to reduce the duration of the increased power consumption. For our application, the FireBeetle ESP32 is best suited and is recommended for comparable applications. If similar computational performance but no high-speed data logging is required, we suggest using the ESP32-S2 instead. If less processing power is sufficient, either the ARM Cortex M0+ with an additional Wi-Fi module for Wi-Fi applications or the nRF52840 for Bluetooth Low Energy applications are the best choices.

Conflict of interest

The authors declare no conflict of interest.

Author details

Lukas M. Broell*, Christian Hanshans and Dominik Kimmerle
Department of Applied Sciences and Mechatronics, University of Applied Sciences Munich, Munich, Germany

*Address all correspondence to: lbroell@hm.edu

References

[1] Stadler S, Borrero ER, Zauner J, Hanshans C. Development and implementation of an OpenSource IoT platform, network and data warehouse for privacy-compliant applications in research and industry: A fast-growing, multi-user, hardware and cloud agnostic IoT data solution. Easy to deploy, privacy compliant, cost-effective, and OpenSource. Current Directions in Biomedical Engineering. 2021;7(2): 507-510

[2] Hanshans C, Broell LM, Plischke H, Offenbaecher M, Zauner J, Faust MMR, et al. Movement filtered heart rate variability (HRV) data from a chest-worn sensor. Current Directions in Biomedical Engineering. 2021;7(2):57-60

[3] Hanshans C, Maisch B, Zauner J, Faust MMR, Bröll LM, Karch S. Virtual therapeutics—Requirements to deliver value with virtual reality and biofeedback applications for alcohol addiction therapy. Current Directions in Biomedical Engineering. 2021;7(2):81-84

[4] Stadler S, Plischke H, Hanshans C. Development of bioimpedance sensors and measurement system for biomedical In-vitro applications: Versatile and cost-effective biosensing system for light-induced apoptosis and cell growth studies of epithelial and endothelial tissue. Current Directions in Biomedical Engineering. 2021;7(2):496-499

[5] Iribarren AP, Luján JP, Azócar G, Mazzorana B, Medina K, Durán G, et al. Arduino data loggers: A helping hand in physical geography. The Geographical Journal. p. 1-15. DOI: 10.1111/geoj.12480

[6] Kondaveeti HK, Kumaravelu NK, Vanambathina SD, Mathe SE, Vappangi S. A systematic literature review on prototyping with Arduino: Applications, challenges, advantages, and limitations. Computer Science Review. 2021;**40**:100364

[7] Haghi M, Thurow K, Stoll R. Wearable devices in medical internet of things: Scientific research and commercially available devices. Healthcare Informatics Research. 2017;**23**(1):4

[8] Wüst K. Energieeffizienz von Mikroprozessoren. In: Mikroprozessortechnik [Internet]. Wiesbaden: Vieweg+Teubner; 2011. pp. 237-248. DOI: 10.1007/978-3-8348-9881-4_12

[9] Al-Kofahi MM, Al-Shorman MY, Al-Kofahi OM. Toward energy efficient microcontrollers and internet-of-things systems. Computers and Electrical Engineering. 2019;**79**:106457

[10] SD Specifications Part 1 Physical Laywer Simplified Specification Version 8.00. Thechnical Comittee SD Card Association; 2020

[11] Espressif Systems. ESP32 Series Datasheet Version 3.8 [Internet]. 2021. Available from: https://www.espressif.com/sites/default/files/documentation/esp32_datasheet_en.pdf

[12] Christopher David. Guide to Reduce the ESP32 Power Consumption by 95% [Internet]. 2020. Available from: https://diyi0t.com/reduce-the-esp32-power-consumption/ [Accessed: July 11, 2022]

[13] Bui T. Why Low Quiescent Current Matters for Longer Battery Life [Internet]. maxim integrated; 2018. Available from: https://www.maximintegrated.com/content/dam/files/design/technical-documents/white-papers/why-low-quiescent-current-

matters-for-longer-battery-life.pdf [Accessed: January 7, 2023]

[14] Espressif Systems. ESP32-S2 Technical Reference Manual (Version 1.0) [Internet]. Espressif Systems; 2021. Available from: https:// www.espressif.com/sites/default/files/ documentation/esp32-s2_technical_ reference_manual_en.pdf

[15] Bradley LJ, Wright NG. Optimising SD saving events to maximise battery lifetime for Arduino™/Atmega328P data loggers. IEEE Access. 2020;**8**: 214832-214841

[16] A breakdown of my experience trying to talk to an SD card REALLY fast with the ESP32 using SDMMC [Internet]. r/esp32. 2019. Available from: www.reddit.com/r/esp32/comments/d 71es9/a_breakdown_of_my_experience_ trying_to_talk_to_an/ [Accessed: January 5, 2023]

[17] Gatial E, Balogh Z, Hluchy L. Concept of energy efficient ESP32 Chip for industrial wireless sensor network. In: 2020 IEEE 24th International Conference on Intelligent Engineering Systems (INES) [Internet]. Reykjavík, Iceland: IEEE; 2020. pp. 179-184. Available from: https://ieeexplore.ieee. org/document/9147189/ Accessed: February 18, 2023

[18] Arduino core for the ESP32, ESP32-S2, ESP32-S3 and ESP32-C3—Example Programm "SD_Test.ino" [Internet]. Espressif Systems; 2022. Available from: https://github.com/espressif/arduino-esp32/blob/3e65a5721ae17b578136db1c 55accb549a4d0204/libraries/SD/ examples/SD_Test/SD_Test.ino [Accessed: August 11, 2022]

[19] Arduino core for the ESP32, ESP32-S2, ESP32-S3 and ESP32-C3—Example Programm "SDMMC_Test.ino" [Internet]. Espressif Systems; 2022. Available from: https://github.com/espre ssif/arduino-esp32/blob/3e65a5721ae17b 578136db1c55accb549a4d0204/libraries/ SD_MMC/examples/SDMMC_Test/ SDMMC_Test.ino [Accessed: August 11, 2022]

Chapter 8

Perspective Chapter: 5G Enabling Technologies – Revolutionizing Transport, Environment, and Health

Kofi Sarpong Adu-Manu, Gabriel Amponsa Koranteng and Samuel Nii Adotei Brown

Abstract

The latest cellular technology, known as 5G, is anticipated to significantly improve the way systems in the physical and social environment (PSE) interact with technology. 5G technologies allow for the creation of a wide range of novel automation and applications. Recently, the Internet of Things (IoT), virtual and augmented reality (VAR), telemedicine, and autonomous vehicles have increased the growth of applications in the PSEs and can further benefit from 5G's fast data transfer speeds (ranging from 1 to 10 Gbps) and low latency. The introduction of 5G may cause a paradigm shift in the operations of some industries, offer new economic opportunities, and impact our daily lives and relationships with the PSE. In this chapter, we examine how 5G revolutionize transport, the environment, and health. The chapter focuses on recent technologies related to virtual and augmented reality, autonomous vehicles, telemedicine, and edge computing among others.

Keywords: 5G, Internet of things, virtual reality, augmented reality, wireless sensor networks (WSNs), autonomous vehicles, edge computing, environment

1. Introduction

Technological advances in communication have seen a new wave of the fifth generation (5G) networks. 5G networks are predicted to significantly impact areas of health, virtual and augmented reality, transportation, the environment, and edge computing. The healthcare sector is anticipated to be one of the biggest beneficiaries of 5G technology. Healthcare professionals will be able to offer telemedicine and virtual consultations to patients in remote locations with the advent of 5G networks. As a result, patients will not have to travel far to obtain medical attention. Advanced medical gadgets that need fast data transfer rates and low latency will also be able to be used thanks to 5G technology. Healthcare professionals will be able to diagnose and treat patients as a result [1]. Virtual and augmented reality is another area where 5G technology is anticipated to have a big influence. Users will be able to enjoy realistic, high-quality virtual and augmented reality experiences as a result of 5G networks. Virtual and augmented reality will make it possible for people to interact with virtual worlds in real-time, which will have a big influence on a lot of different businesses, like gaming, education, and entertainment. Edge computing, which will assist to lower latency and increasing the overall performance of virtual and augmented reality apps, will also be made possible by 5G technology [2]. 5G technology is also anticipated to have a big influence is transportation. The rollout of 5G networks will make it feasible to give drivers real-time traffic updates, which will lessen congestion and increase road safety. The usage of autonomous cars will also be made possible by 5G technology, which will have a big influence on the transportation sector. The ability of autonomous cars to interact with one another and the infrastructure will assist to improve traffic flow and lower accident rates [1]. 5G technology is anticipated to make a big difference in edge computing. 5G technology offers low latency and high data transfer rates to edge devices with the rollout of 5G networks. This will make it possible to employ cutting-edge edge computing applications, including real-time video analytics, which will have a big influence on a lot of different industries, including manufacturing, shipping, and retail. Local caching will also be possible thanks to 5G technology, which will lessen network traffic and enhance the performance of edge computing apps as a whole [3]. Although 5G technology may have advantages, there are worries about how it could affect people's health. According to research, electromagnetic radiation from 5G networks may cause cancer and reproductive issues, among other harmful health impacts [4]. The World Health Organization (WHO) has argued that there is no evidence to support a link between electromagnetic radiation exposure from 5G networks and adverse health effects in people [1]. Concerns about the possible effects of new technology on different facets of our life arise along with it. This chapter will look at the current studies on how 5G technology will affect things like edge computing, health, virtual and augmented reality, transportation, and the environment. We may better comprehend the opportunities and difficulties that lie ahead as we progress toward a more connected and technologically evolved society by looking at the possible advantages and hazards of 5G in each of these categories. This chapter offers a thorough assessment of the state of research on the effects of 5G on these important domains, as well as highlighting knowledge gaps and recommending topics for further investigation. Ultimately, this chapter will contribute to a more nuanced and knowledgeable conversation about the possible effects of 5G technology, and it will help direct academics, politicians, and the general public toward a more responsible and sustainable use of this formidable new technology.

The remaining parts of the chapter are divided into 10 sections. Section 2 discusses the methodology. In Section 3, recent related works in 5G technology are discussed. In Section 4, we present a discussion on wireless mobile technologies. Section 5 presents an overview of 5G technologies. Section 6 discusses 5G in virtual and augmented reality and Section 7 discusses 5G and transportation (autonomous vehicles). In Section 8, 5G in healthcare (telemedicine) is presented. Sections 9 and 10 present 5G and the environment and edge computing, respectively, and Section 11 concludes the chapter.

2. Methodology

The Prisma systematic review was used to conduct this research. At the identification stage of Prisma, a comprehensive literature review was conducted using various academic databases, including PubMed, Google Scholar, Scopus, Multidisciplinary Digital Publishing Institute (MDPI), ResearchGate, and Institute of Electrical and Electronics Engineers (IEEE). The search terms used included "5G," "health," "transportation," "augmented reality," "virtual reality," "environment," and "edge computing." The search was limited to articles published in English from the year 2017 to 2023. Initially, a total of 120 articles were collected from the various academic databases for this chapter. Upon careful study and review, only 85 of the obtained literature or articles were relevant to the research topic. The literature review was conducted in three stages. The very first stage was the identification of articles or papers that highlighted the general overview of 5G and its architecture. The second stage involved the identification of articles that focused on the potential benefits of 5G to the health sector. Such articles included articles on smart healthcare, remote surgery, and telemedicine. The third stage focused on the potential impact of 5G technology on transportation, augmented and virtual reality, the environment, and edge computing. During the first stage, articles that talked about evolution of cellular networks, and introduction to 5G and 5G architecture were included. Papers that had no direct connection to any of the above were discarded. In the second stage, articles were screened based on their relevance to the topic of health benefits associated with 5G technology. Articles that did not provide original research or data were excluded. In the third stage, articles were screened based on their relevance to the topics of transportation, augmented and virtual reality, the environment, and edge computing. Articles that discussed the potential benefits and drawbacks of 5G technology in these areas were included. Also, Articles that focused on the biological effects of electromagnetic radiation and the potential health risks associated with exposure to such radiation were included. Moreover, articles that discussed the harmful effects of 5G on the environment were also included. Articles that focused solely on the technical aspects of 5G technology or did not provide original research or data were excluded (see **Figure 1**).

Figure 1 illustrates a graphical representation of reviewed papers after going through the identification, screening, eligibility, and inclusion stages of Prisma. The selected articles were then read extensively and various knowledge and findings together with our contributions were synthesized together in this chapter.

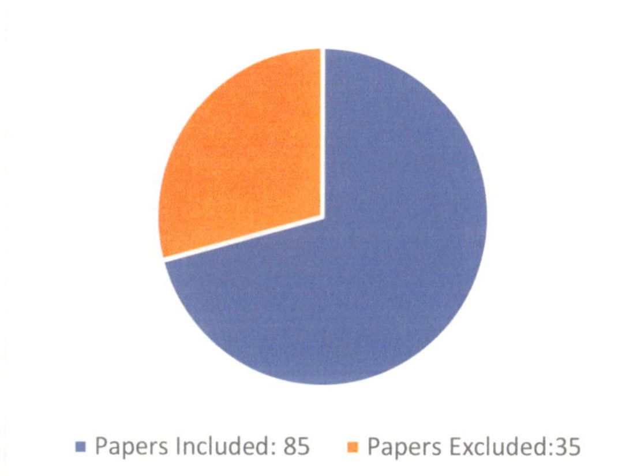

Figure 1.
Outcome of Prisma process.

3. Related works

This literature review aims to explore the existing research on the impact of 5G technology on health, virtual and augmented reality (VR/AR), transportation, environment, and edge computing. Tiwari and Sharma [5] present components, architecture, and applications of 5G-enabled Internet of Medical Things (IoMT). Butcher et al. [6] seek to ascertain if patient-reported Health-Related Quality of Life (HRQoL), together with or without other factors at baseline, predicts disability in people with kidney failure, aged 65 and older, after a year of follow-up. The aim of [7] is the development and clinical evaluation of a 5G usability test framework enabling preclinical diagnostics with mobile ultrasound using 5G network technology. Also, Nyberg et al. [8] present recent research from the European Union's expert groups, from a large collection of European and other international studies, and previous reviews of the effects of radiofrequency radiation (RFR) on humans and the environment. Balancing risks and rewards is the best strategy forward. Jain and Jain [9] researched the benefits, risks, and diligence of 5G technology for healthcare and its implications on human health. In their approach, the 5G network-connected technology project was split into two phases for proof-of-concept testing: the first phase initially focused on conducting examinations with portable ultrasound equipment at Hospital das Clnicas da Faculdade de Medicina da USP (HCFMUSP), and the second phase concentrated on conducting remote examinations with medical professionals in other states of Brazil who will be working in isolated regions in other states with little access to healthcare. Their outcome suggested that excellent healthcare will be accessible to everyone at all times with 5G technology.

The contribution of de Oliveira [10] is to evaluate the connectivity and capacity of the 5G private network for transmitting a large volume of data remotely with higher speed and lower latency. Lin [11] reviewed the benefits of 5G technologies, which are implemented in healthcare and wearable devices. Some benefits discussed include the use of 5G in patient health monitoring, continuous monitoring of chronic diseases, management of preventing infectious diseases, robotic surgery, and 5G with the future of wearables. A national sample of 5087 Spaniards [12] examines the prevalence of 10 specific misperceptions over five separate science and health domains (climate change, 5G technology, genetically modified foods, vaccines, and homeopathy). Sehrai et al. [13] present the design and analysis of an antenna array for the high gain performance of future mm-wave 5G communication systems. Currently, there is little research exploring how fellowship-trained sports medicine physicians (FTSMPs) address their mental health on a routine basis. Using the theory of secondary trauma stress to help navigate this study, the purpose of this expressive, all-purpose qualitative study is to improve the understanding of FTSMPs' perceptions of their mental health and the kinds of strategies used to manage these issues [14]. An alternate viewpoint to address the demands of the 5G Public Network and the hybrid deployment of 5GS and Wi-Fi on the campus network is provided by DecentRAN, also known as the Decentralized Radio Access Network [15]. Asif Khan et al. [16] presented a comprehensive survey of recent developments in MEC-enabled video streaming bringing unprecedented improvement to enable novel use cases. von Ende et al. [17] described the present and potential future applications of radiogenomics, augmented and virtual reality, and artificial intelligence in interventional radiology, along with the issues and constraints that need to be resolved before these applications can be fully integrated into standard clinical practice.

Hazarika and Rahmati [18] discussed the inclusion of 5G technology in allowing a low-latency environment for AR and VR applications, as well as a thorough examination and in-depth insight into different attractive options from the hardware and software viewpoints. Ali et al. [19] presented a state-of-the-art contribution to the characterization of the outdoor-to-indoor radio channel in the 3.5 GHz band, based on experimental data for commercial, deployed 5G networks, collected during a large-scale measurement campaign carried out in the city of Rome, Italy. In the case of fully grasping the principles of low-carbon tourism development and related policy protection, a suitable low-carbon tourism development model is found. Zhang [20] presented the evaluation of aggregate interference from 5G New Radio (NR) base stations located inside the victim satellites' footprints using Monte-Carlo analysis and calculation of signal-to-noise degradation and bit error rates of the fixed-satellite service (FSS) bent-pipe transponders for each scenario. Assimilating trailblazing technologies such as the Internet of Things (IoT), edge intelligence (EI), 5G, and blockchain into the autonomous vehicle (AV) architecture will unlock the potential of an efficient and sustainable transportation system. Jia et al. [21] propose the application of UAV Based on 5G communication technology, which overcomes the current bottleneck of UAV.

Pastukh et al. [22] provided a comprehensive review of the state-of-the-art literature on the impact and implementation of the aforementioned technologies into AV architectures, along with the challenges faced by each of them. Biswas and Wang [23] proposed a novel framework named Pyramid that unleashes the potential of edge artificial intelligence (AI) by facilitating homogeneous and heterogeneous hierarchical machine learning (ML) inferences. For the ubiquitous Internet of electric power, the application framework of 5G communication technology in over-voltage fault edge computing is proposed, the distribution grid fault identification and response model based on edge computing is built, and He et al. [24] imagine 5G communication application scenarios.

Gao et al. [25] presented a 5G edge computing framework for enabling remote production functions for live holographic Teleportation applications. Qian et al. [26] focused on edge computing, which is one of the cores of beyond 5G, to utilize the virtualization resources (see **Table 1** for a summary of some related works).

Unlike the previous works discussed earlier, Nakazato et al. [27] presented real data for more than one proposed robot working in parallel on-site, exploring hardware processing capabilities and the local Wi-Fi network characteristics. Zhou et al. [28] presented a Secure and lAtency-aware dIgital twin assisted resource scheduliNg algoriThm (SAINT). To provide a high-performance implementation of Module-LWE applications for the edge computing paradigm [29] proposed a domain-specific processor based on a matrix extension of RISC-V architecture. To assure secure and reliable communication in 5G edge computing and D2D-enabled IoMT systems, Yang et al. [30] presented an intelligent trust cloud management method. Mahenge et al. [31] considered task offloading on small cell network (SCN) structures unique to 5G. Jamshidi et al. [32] presented the design, fabrication, and evaluation of a super-efficient GSM triplexer for 5G-enabled IoT in sustainable smart grid edge computing and the metaverse.

4. Wireless mobile technologies

Since the dawn of time, communication has been a vital element in the lives of humans. Like the very food we eat, the air we breathe, and the shelter we seek, communication is now a basic necessity for human survival and development.

Contributions	References
Presenting components, architecture, and applications of 5G enabled Internet of Medical Things (IoMT)	[5]
Development and clinical evaluation of a 5G usability test framework enabling preclinical diagnostics with mobile ultrasound using 5G network technology	[7]
The benefits, risks, and diligence of 5G technology for healthcare and its implications on human health	[9]
Evaluating the connectivity and capacity of the 5G private network for transmitting a large volume of data remotely with higher speed and lower latency	[10]
Reviewing the benefits of 5G technologies, which are implemented in healthcare and wearable devices such as the use of 5G in patient health monitoring, continuous monitoring of chronic diseases, management of preventing infectious diseases, robotic surgery, and 5G with future wearables	[11]
Discussing the inclusion of 5G technology in allowing a low-latency environment for AR and VR applications	[18]
Presenting a 5G edge computing framework for enabling remote production functions for live holographic Teleportation applications	[25]
Focusing on edge computing, which is one of the cores of Beyond 5G, to utilize the virtualization resources	[26]

Table 1.
Summary of related works.

Communication occurs locally or remotely among connecting nodes. Remote communication has contributed enormously to globalization and the advancement of modern technologies. Since the advent of mobile phones in 1983 to facilitate remote communications, the world has already witnessed the full power of four different wireless mobile technologies approximately 10 years apart.

The first-generation (1G) technology was designed for voice communication in the late 1980s. The network speed of 1G was limited to 2.4 kbps. The 1990s witnessed second-generation (2G) technologies, which allowed audio and video files to be shared. 2G technologies had a network speed limitation of 64 kbps, which was not the best but was revolutionary. In the 2000s, the emergence of third-generation (3G) technologies took the network speed to 2 Mbps, which made browsing at high speed possible. Following 3G was the revolutionary Fourth-generation (4G) with a network speed of 100 Mbps, which was developed in 2011.

4G technologies brought about super-high-speed browsing, making digital streaming, online gaming, and downloading and uploading video calling, faster and more convenient. With the rapid increase of mobile phones, the demand to share files at an even faster rate with little to no delay is high. Despite the performance of 4G, there was a need for a flexible network with a shared infrastructure, hence fifth-generation (5G). With the new generation of mobile networking emerging, 5G will be a visionary innovation platform for the next 10 years and beyond due to its amazing speed of about 20Gbps. Most importantly, 5G will open up fresh opportunities and efficiencies that are not even imaginable with the networks in use presently [33]. **Table 2** presents a summary of the evaluation of cellular technologies from 1G to 5G technologies.

In comparison to 4G, 5G offers faster download and upload speeds, lower latency, with more dependable connections. The expected system latency for 5G is 2–5 ms.

DOI: http://dx.doi.org/10.5772/intechopen.111671

Generation	Access techniques	Data rate	Frequency bands	Applications	Key parameters	Transmission techniques	Error correction mechanism
5G	NOMA, FBMC	10–50 Gbps	1.8 GHz, 2.4 GHz, 30–300 GHz	Voice, data, video calling, ultra HD video, virtual reality applications	Ultra-low latency, ultra-high availability, ultra-speed, and ultra-reliability	Packet switching	LDPC
4G	LTEA, OFDMA, SCFDMA, WIMAX	100–200 Mbps	2.3 GHz, 2.5 GHz, 3.5 GHz	Voice, data, video calling, HD television, and online gaming	Faster broadband internet and lower latency	Packet switching	Turbo codes
3G	WCDMA, UMTS, CDMA	384 Kbps to 5 Mbps	800 MHz, 850 MHz, 900 MHz, 1800 MHz, 1900 MHz, 2100 MHz	Voice, data, and video calling	Broadband internet and smart phones	Circuit and packet switching	Turbo codes
2G	GSM, TDMA, CDMA	10 Kbps	800 MHz, 900 MHz, 1800 MHz, 1900 MHz	Voice and data	Digital	Circuit switching	N/A
1G	FDMA, AMPS	2.4 Kbps	800 MHz	Voice	Mobility	Circuit switching	N/A

Table 2.
Evaluation of technology generations from 1G to 5G.

The current long-term evolution (LTE) network has a round-trip delay of roughly 15 ms, compared to dedicated short-range communication (DSRC), which has a latency of about 10 ms. Some of the options that can help in providing this latency include device-to-device (D2D), software-defined networks (SDNs), and cloud radio access networks (C-RAN) [33].

5G is the newest and fastest generation of cellular technology. 5G technology is the replacement for 4G LTE technology. The Internet of Things (IoTs), linked cars, smart homes, virtual and augmented reality, and other innovative use cases that were not viable with 4G are all supported by 5G technology. Many facets of our everyday life, including entertainment, communication, healthcare, and transportation, are anticipated to change as a result of 5G technology [34].

5. Overview of 5G technology

5G technology is built to use a variety of frequencies, including low, middle, and high-band spectrum, to provide faster speeds and greater coverage. Low-band 5G is frequently used to improve existing 4G networks and provides greater coverage (see **Table 3** for a comparison of 4G and 5G's key features). Mid-band 5G, which strikes a balance between speed and coverage, is used to support most 5G services. Although its range is limited, high-band 5G, also known as millimeter-wave 5G, provides the fastest speeds. In addition to beamforming and massive MIMO (multiple-input multiple-output) technology, 5G technology combines multiple frequencies to improve signal quality and reduce interference. Beamforming utilizes canny receiving wires to think the remote transmission in a specific region, upgrading signal quality and bringing down obstruction. Numerous antennas are used in massive MIMO to increase data transport efficiency and increase network capacity.

5.1 5G architecture

To meet the ever-increasing demand for faster data rates, lower latency, and more dependable connectivity, the fifth generation (5G) of mobile communication networks was developed. This subsection gives an outline of the 5G design, its key parts, and the fundamental innovations that empower its high-level abilities. The 5G architecture can be divided into three main components: the radio access network (RAN), the core network (CN), and the user equipment (UE) as illustrated in **Figure 2** [36].

Feature	5G	4G
Speed	Fast, up to 20 Gbps	Fast, up to 1 Gbps
Latency	Low, 1 ms or less	High, 20 ms or more
Bandwidth	A high, wider range of frequencies	Limited, primarily below 6 GHz
Capacity	High, supports more devices	Limited, congestion in densely populated areas
Reliability	High, improved network architecture	Moderate, prone to network congestion

Table 3.
5G versus 4G key features.

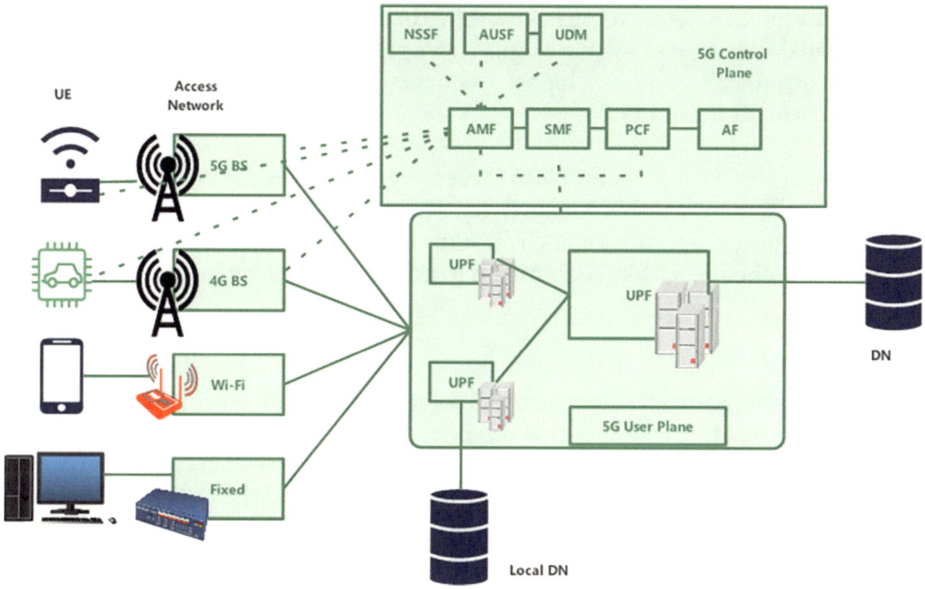

Figure 2.
5G architecture based on the control plane and user separation showing the UE, RAN, and CN [35].

The wireless communication between the UE and the CN is the responsibility of the RAN. Beamforming and massive multiple-input multiple-output (mMIMO) are two advanced technologies that have been incorporated into 5G's RAN [37]. The RAN can support higher data rates and more simultaneous connections thanks to beamforming and mMIMO, which also reduce latency. 5G's core network (CN) is in charge of data routing and connection management among various network components. Utilizing techniques of network slicing and virtualization, the 5G CN is designed to be more adaptable and scalable than previous generations [38]. It creates customized network configurations for various use cases. The smartphones, tablets, and IoT devices that are connected to the 5G network are referred to as the UE. To fully utilize the capabilities of the network, these devices must support the advanced features of 5G, such as new waveform designs and higher frequency bands [36].

5.2 Key technologies in 5G

Several key technologies enable the advanced capabilities of 5G networks. Some of these technologies include:

- Network Slicing: On a single physical infrastructure, multiple virtual networks can be created using network slicing, with each slice tailored to specific use cases [38]. Operators can optimize resources and provide individualized services to various user groups as a result of this.

- Massive MIMO: To boost capacity and spectral efficiency, Massive MIMO uses a lot of antennas at the base station [37]. Higher data rates and a greater number of simultaneous connections are made possible by this technology in 5G networks.

- Beamforming: Beamforming is a method that directs the radio signal in a particular direction to increase signal strength and decrease interference [37]. Beamforming also supports higher frequency bands and increases network capacity in 5G networks.

The goal of the 5G architecture is to meet the growing need for faster data rates, lower latency, and more stable connectivity. 5G networks have the potential to support a wide range of use cases and deliver improved performance by incorporating cutting-edge technologies like beamforming, massive MIMO, and network slicing.

5.3 Benefits of 5G

The fifth-generation (5G) wireless technology is a ground-breaking innovation in the telecommunications industry that offers numerous advantages over its predecessors. The benefits of 5G technology, such as increased data rates, decreased latency, increased network capacity, improved energy efficiency, and the facilitation of new applications and services [39]. The benefits of 5G include:

- Enhanced data rates: With peak data rates reaching 20 Gbps, 5G networks can deliver data speeds up to 100 times faster than 4G networks [40]. Users will be able to quickly download and stream high-quality content thanks to this increased speed [39].

- Reduced latency: The amount of time it takes for a signal to travel from the sender to the receiver is referred to as latency. When compared to 4G networks, which have a latency of approximately 50 ms, 5G networks have a significantly lower latency of as little as 1 ms [39]. In applications like gaming, virtual reality, and remote surgery [40], the reduction in latency makes it possible to communicate in real-time and enhances the user experience.

- Increased capacity of the network: 5G networks are essential for the expanding IoT ecosystem because they can simultaneously support a greater number of devices than 4G networks [39]. This increased capacity makes it possible to have better connectivity and less network congestion, making the network more reliable and effective [40].

- Improved energy efficiency: 5G technology is more environmentally friendly than previous generations because it uses advanced network architectures and techniques to save energy [39]. This improved energy productivity diminishes functional expenses for network suppliers as well as adds to worldwide maintainability endeavors [40].

- New applications and services: New applications and services that were not possible with previous wireless technology generations are made possible by 5G technology. Innovations in a variety of industries, including Industry 4.0, smart cities, telemedicine, and autonomous vehicles, are made possible by the convergence of high data rates, low latency, and increased network capacity [39].

5G technology offers numerous benefits, including enhanced data rates, reduced latency, increased network capacity, improved energy efficiency, and the facilitation of new applications and services. It also has the potential to transform the way we live, work, and communicate [40]. Because of these benefits, 5G will play a crucial role in the future of telecommunications and could have an impact on a variety of industries and aspects of daily life.

5.4 Challenges and limitations

- Implementing 5G technology comes with many drawbacks and difficulties that must be resolved. The use of millimeter wavelengths, which are smaller and do not travel as far as those used in 3G and 4G networks, is one of the primary limitations. As a result, 5G's coverage profile is smaller than that of previous generations. Carriers are deploying a larger array of antennas to provide sufficient coverage to overcome this limitation.

- The use of energy is another obstacle to 5G technology implementation. Due to the increased number of antennas required for coverage, 5G networks consume more energy than previous generations [41]. Businesses may face increased costs as a result, and additional infrastructure may be required to support the network.

- Implementing 5G technology poses another obstacle in the form of latency. Although 5G promises to have lower latency than previous generations, achieving this requires significant infrastructure and technology investments [42]. In addition, interference from other wireless signals can affect latency and slow down the network.

- 5G technology also presents a challenge in terms of spectral efficiency. Although 5G can transmit more information than earlier cellular networks, it needs a larger area to achieve higher spectral efficiency [42]. The need for higher spectral efficiency may require more infrastructure investment and reduce the amount of spectrum available for other uses.

Implementing 5G technology has several advantages in virtual and argument reality, transportation, healthcare, the environment, and edge computing. Some several drawbacks and difficulties must be resolved. These include difficulties with spectral efficiency, a small coverage area, high energy consumption, latency, and other issues. Tending to these difficulties will require a critical interest in foundation and innovation via transporters and organizations the same.

6. 5G in virtual and augmented reality

The way we interact with digital content has been transformed by transformative technologies like VR and AR. They enable users to interact with digital content in ways that were previously only possible in science fiction by providing immersive experiences that combine the real and virtual worlds. This chapter discusses the history, applications, and potential developments of virtual reality and augmented reality concerning 5G.

VR is a computer-created climate that recreates actual presence in genuine or envisioned universes, permitting clients to cooperate with the climate reasonably [43].

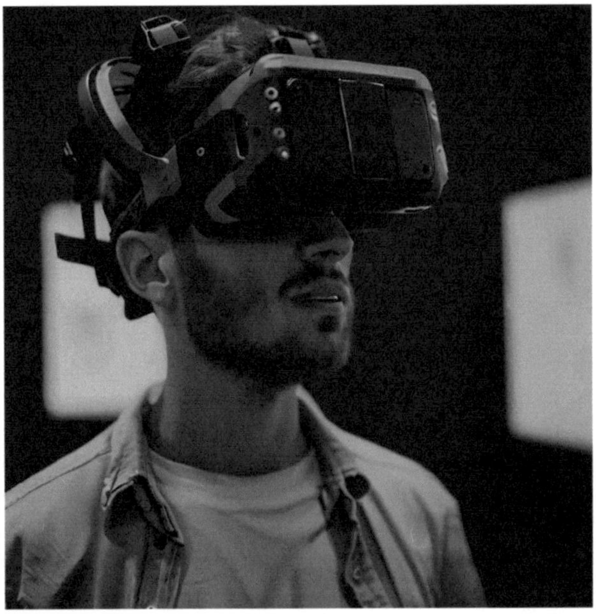

Figure 3.
A person in a head-mounted display (HMD).

Head-mounted displays (HMDs) as illustrated in **Figure 3** are used to create a VR experience which gives users a 360-degree view of the virtual environment. The system can adjust the view based on the user's head movements, giving the impression of presence.

AR enhances the user's perception of reality by overlaying digital content on their view of the real world. AR can be experienced with a variety of devices, including AR glasses (See **Figure 4**), smartphones, and tablets. This innovation can change how we access data and associate it with our general surroundings. Dissimilar to VR, AR does not supplant the client's current circumstance yet rather upgrades it with logically pertinent computerized content [44].

6.1 Brief history of VR and AR

The creation of the first head-mounted display (HMD), which Ivan Sutherland dubbed the "Sword of Damocles," in the 1960s is the beginning of the history of virtual reality and augmented reality. Since then, the market for consumer VR devices like the Oculus Rift, HTC Vive, and PlayStation VR has grown significantly. In a similar vein, advances in AR can be seen in the development of AR headsets like Microsoft's HoloLens and Magic Leap One and smartphone-based augmented reality experiences like Pokémon Go [45].

6.2 Applications of VR and AR

Various sectors, including manufacturing, education, healthcare, and entertainment, have utilized VR and AR. VR gaming and 360-degree videos have gained popularity in the entertainment industry, while AR has been used to enhance live events and create interactive experiences [46]. In education, VR and AR can provide immersive learning experiences that allow students to explore historical sites, visualize complex concepts, and practice skills in a secure setting [47]. VR is used for pain

Figure 4.
A lady in AR glasses.

management, rehabilitation, and surgical training, and AR is used to assist surgeons during procedures [48]. Healthcare has also benefited from these technologies. VR and AR have the potential to simplify procedures, enhance instruction, and support product design and prototyping in manufacturing [49].

As developments in software, hardware, and content creation continue, the future of VR and augmented reality holds a lot of promise. The development of new display technologies and input devices may further enhance immersion, and the integration of artificial intelligence and machine learning may result in experiences that are more realistic and personalized. The impact of these technologies on society and our interactions with the outside world will continue to expand as they become more affordable and accessible.

6.3 Benefits of 5G for VR and AR

The development of 5G technology has the potential to completely alter our relationship with the digital world. 5G is expected to significantly benefit AR and VR applications due to its extremely low latency, increased capacity, and high-speed connectivity.

- Providing an immersive and seamless experience is one of the primary advantages of 5G for AR and VR. Real-time interaction and instantaneous response in AR and VR applications are made possible by the extremely low latency of 5G, which can be as low as one millisecond [50]. Low latency is essential for applications like remote surgery, where a delay in response time could be detrimental [51]. In addition, the high-speed connectivity of 5G, with the potential to reach speeds of up to 20 Gbps makes it possible to stream content of high quality that uses a lot of data. 5G in AR and VR provides an experience that is both smooth and uninterrupted [50].

- 5G for augmented reality and virtual reality supports a large number of connected devices. 5G networks can accommodate the growing number of AR and VR devices because they can handle up to a million devices per square kilometer [51]. For large-scale deployments in smart cities, industrial applications, and entertainment venues, this increased capacity is necessary.

- Edge computing, made possible by 5G, enables data processing to occur closer to the data's source [51]. 5G technology makes it less necessary to send data between devices and data centers, which reduces latency and boosts AR and VR applications' performance. Edge registering likewise upgrades the protection and security of information by keeping it nearer to the client [51].

- New use cases and applications will also be made possible by combining 5G with AR and VR technologies. 5G-powered AR and VR can, for instance, provide users with immersive learning experiences that allow them to explore virtual environments and interact with digital content in real-time [52]. 5G can make telemedicine, remote patient monitoring, and VR-based therapies for mental health and rehabilitation possible in the healthcare industry [51].

Applications in AR and VR stand to gain significantly from 5G technology's ultra-low latency, high-speed connectivity, increased capacity, and edge computing. These advantages will make it possible to have an immersive and seamless experience, support a large number of connected devices, and open up new applications and use cases in a variety of industries.

7. 5G and transportation

New opportunities for innovation, efficiency, and safety are presented by 5G technology, which has had and will have a significant impact on the transportation industry. The development of new technologies, such as high-speed networks, decentralized storage systems, edge computing, and others, has made it possible to operate a car with little to no human involvement. The use of 5G means that the way cars connect and the infrastructure around cars could be completely altered by 5G. Vehicles that operate without the direct input of the driver are referred to as autonomous vehicles (AV). AVs do not require the driver to continuously monitor the road. AVs are also referred to as driverless automobiles or autonomous cars. With enhanced safety measures and enhanced energy efficiency, the AVs appear to be a promising technology with reduced environmental impact. Due to the impact of 5G, major automakers are adding more AVs to their fleets. For instance, Mercedes-Benz has implemented autonomous driving (AD) in its S-class automobile. Similarly, Tesla has already developed cutting-edge software and hardware to enable completely driverless driving (level 5 automated vehicle).

Figure 5 illustrates the levels of vehicle automation from conventional vehicles (CVs) to connected autonomous vehicles (CAVs) whereas **Figure 6** shows the levels of automation in autonomous vehicles. However, to enable fully autonomous driving and high-speed networks, fifth-generation (5G) or beyond 5G (B5G) technologies, is the key to a successful implementation of the levels of autonomy required by such vehicles [36]. The switch from conventional vehicles to fully autonomous vehicles is a slow but sure process that 5G will spearhead as illustrated in **Figure 6**.

	Features															Technologies			
	Data Transmission	Data Analysis	Safety	Energy Consumption	Comfort for Driver	Comfort for Passenger	Independent Decisions	Sensors	Computer Vision	Wireless Communication	Tracking	Environment Awareness	Resource Consumption	Process Optimization	Self- Protection	Co-operative Driving	Physical Layer Security	Cloud/Edge/Fog/Roof Computing	mmWave
Conventional Vehicles	N	N	L	H	L	M	N	N	N	N	N	N	H	N	N	NA	NA	NA	NA
Connected Vehicles	M	N	L	M	L	M	N	L	N	M	M	L	H	N	N	A	NA	A	NA
Advanced Connected Vehicles	M	L	M	L	L	M	N	L	L	M	M	M	H	N	N	A	NA	A	NA
Self-driving Vehicles	L	L	M	M	M	H	N	M	M	M	L	M	H	N	L	NA	NA	A	A
Autonomous Vehicles	M	M	H	L	H	H	M	H	H	M	M	M	M	M	M	A	A	A	A
Connected Autonomous Vehicles	H	H	H	L	H	H	H	H	H	H	H	H	L	M	H	A	A	A	A

L	Lower Level: This feature does not play a vital role and is not given importance while manufacturing.
M	Medium Level: This feature is taken into account while manufacturing but not wide coverage.
H	High Level: This feature plays a vital role and is given higher importance while manufacturing.
N	Not Available.
NA	Not Applicable.
A	Applicable.

Figure 5.
Conventional Vehicles to Connected Autonomous Vehicles (CV-CAV) [53].

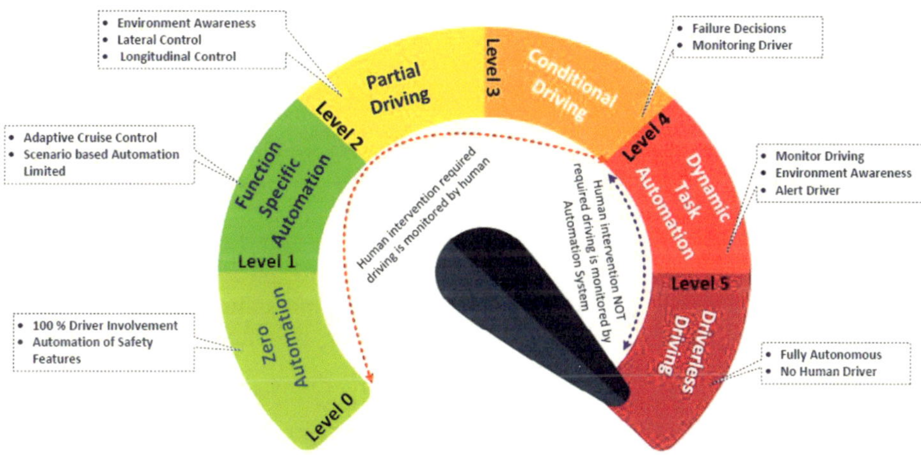

Figure 6.
Levels of automation in autonomous vehicles [53].

7.1 Evolution of autonomous vehicles

The idea of AVs has been around for decades. In recent years have seen significant technological advancements and the pursuit of more effective transportation systems accelerate their development [54]. The development of autonomous vehicles, from their infancy to the present, and the significant milestones achieved along the way will be briefly discussed in this subsection. AVs have been around since the 1920s when experiments with radio-controlled automobiles were carried out [55]. The first truly autonomous vehicle, the VaMoRs, was created in the 1980s by Ernst Dickmanns and his group at the Bundeswehr University Munich [56]. The VaMoRs paved the way for subsequent research in the field by utilizing cameras and computer algorithms to navigate and avoid obstacles.

The Autonomous Land Vehicle (ALV) program was started in the 1990s by the Defense Advanced Research Projects Agency (DARPA) of the US Department of

Defense. Its goal was to create vehicles that could operate independently in off-road environments. ALV program prompted the improvement of the NavLab series via Carnegie Mellon College, which exhibited the capability of independent driving in different circumstances. The DARPA Grand Challenge, a series of competitions in which teams were challenged to create autonomous vehicles capable of traversing desert terrains, spurred significant advancements in AV technology in the 2000s [57].

New algorithms and sensor technologies were developed as a result of these competitions, as were government, business, and academic partnerships. Google's self-driving car project, which is now known as Waymo, was the pioneer in the field of AV development in the 2010s [58]. In 2014, Tesla released its Autopilot feature, which enabled semi-autonomous highway driving [59]. In the interim, Uber and Lyft started investigating independent ride-hailing administrations, flagging the potential for AVs to upset conventional transportation frameworks [60]. Companies like Waymo, Cruise, and Argo AI are leading the charge in testing AVs in a variety of settings worldwide today [61]. Countries like Germany, China, and the United States have enacted policies and invested in infrastructure to support, regulate, and regulate the development and deployment of AVs [62]. The widespread use of AVs is anticipated to have a significant impact on transportation, urban planning, and society as a whole as the technology develops further [63].

7.2 Benefits of 5G for transportation

Increased safety, better efficiency, and new chances for innovation are some of the primary advantages of 5G for the transportation sector.

- Increased safety: Cars can interact with one another and the infrastructure around them with the help of 5G, which will improve traffic flow and reduce the likelihood of accidents. 5G-enabled automobiles, for instance, have the potential to make better decisions and steer clear of potential dangers thanks to real-time traffic and road condition updates.

- Improved efficiency: The transportation industry's productivity could rise as a result of 5G. 5G-enabled automobiles, for instance, may communicate with traffic control systems and with one another to enhance traffic flow and routing. This may result in less traffic and shorter travel times, which will reduce emissions and fuel consumption.

- More opportunities for creativity: Ultimately, 5G presents new opportunities for mechanical progression in the transportation area. For instance, 5G can enable previously impractical new services and applications by supporting emerging modes of mobility like connected drones and driverless cars.

7.3 Applications of 5G in transportation

There are several possible uses for 5G in the transportation sector, including:

- Vehicle connectivity: Real-time communication, improved efficiency, and increased safety can all be achieved through the use of 5G, which can connect cars to nearby infrastructure and one another as illustrated in **Figure** 7. For example, 5G can be used to make vehicle-to-vehicle (V2V) communication

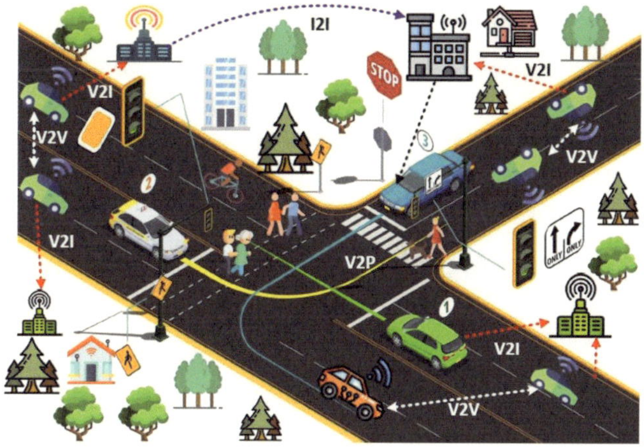

V2V – Vehicle to vehicle | I2I – Infrastructure to Infrastructure | V2I – Vehicle to Infrastructure | V2P – Vehicle to People

Figure 7.
Connected autonomous vehicles, infrastructure, environment, and communication [53].

easier. This lets cars share information in real-time about traffic conditions, potential road hazards, and other important information.

- Autonomous vehicles: Driverless vehicles can be built and used with the help of 5G, expanding mobility options and improving road safety. Due to its low latency and high speed, 5G can provide the real-time communication and data transfer that autonomous cars need to navigate their environment and make educated decisions.

- Intelligent transportation systems: 5G has the potential to facilitate the development of these systems, opening up new services and applications that improve traffic safety and efficiency. 5G could, for instance, support real-time traffic management and routing, which would improve traffic flow and reduce congestion.

- Drones: New transportation-related applications and services are now possible thanks to the use of 5G to connect drones to ground-based control systems and each other. 5G facilitates the use of connected drones for delivery, inspection, and surveillance.

8. 5G in healthcare

The introduction of 5G technology has the potential to have a significant impact on the healthcare industry because it presents new opportunities for innovation, efficiency, and improved patient outcomes. 5G has the potential to completely alter the way healthcare is provided and consumed because it can enable previously unimaginable new services and applications. Digital 5G technology has the potential to enhance healthcare services for patients and healthcare professionals at any time and from any location [64]. It can also contribute to more efficient medical research, diagnosis, and treatment. AI will support a variety of novel applications, including virtual and augmented reality [65, 66] and 5G technology will offer significantly faster data speeds. Deep learning technology has also been the subject of studies involving the application of technology to the secondary diagnosis of breast cancer [67]. However, in other fields, such as telerobotic surgery [68] and remote surgical procedures supported by the 5G network [69], significant progress has been made in recent years regarding its contribution.

8.1 Benefits of 5G for healthcare

Patient outcomes are better, efficiency is higher, and there are more prospects for innovation with the advent of 5G. One of the most significant advantages of 5G for the medical industry is the improvement of patient outcomes. With minimal latency, 5G can provide novel telemedicine and remote care models that enable physicians to diagnose and treat patients at a distance as illustrated in **Figure 8**. This may be very helpful to people who live in rural or isolated areas and may not have access to local healthcare facilities. Besides, 5G can give constant observing and following of patient information, empowering medical services professionals to go with better-taught choices and answer quickly to changes in a patient's condition. 5G in healthcare also provides proficiency gain and offers more opportunities for creativity among medical personnel.

- Proficiency gain: 5G can also boost the efficiency of the healthcare industry by making it easier for doctors and patients to communicate and send data in real-time. Medical professionals may be able to make decisions more quickly and thoroughly as a result of 5G's efficiency, which may reduce wait times and improve information flow. In addition, 5G can facilitate the automation of several procedures, decreasing the likelihood of human error and enhancing overall healthcare delivery efficiency.

- More opportunities for creativity: Last but not least, 5G opens up new opportunities for healthcare innovation. For instance, telemedicine platforms, remote

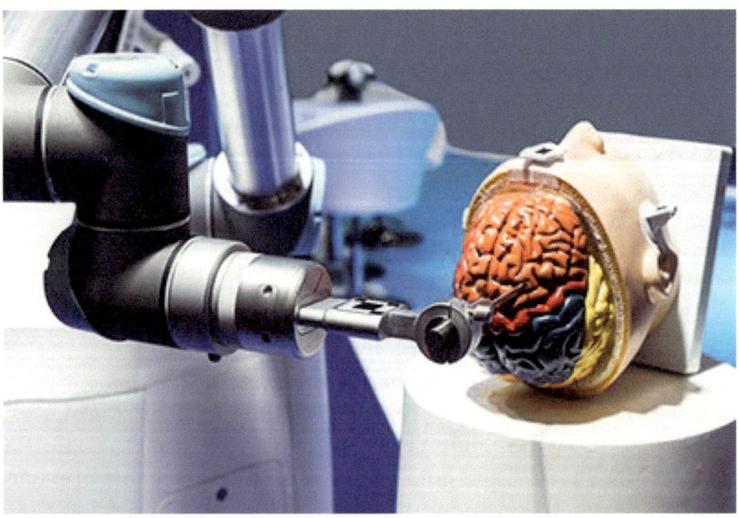

Figure 8.
5G-powered medical robot performs remote brain surgery [70].

patient monitoring systems, and wearable health monitors can all benefit from 5G's assistance in the creation and implementation of new medical technology and equipment. In addition, new services and apps like AR and VR in healthcare can be developed with 5G's assistance, opening up new opportunities for patient training, education, and treatment [71].

8.2 Applications of 5G in healthcare

There are many potential applications of 5G in healthcare, including:

- Telemedicine: With the backing of 5G, telemedicine services may be delivered, allowing medical professionals to diagnose and treat patients remotely. 5G can provide real-time video conferencing and data transmission with low latency and high-speed connectivity, allowing healthcare practitioners to make educated choices and react swiftly to changes in a patient's condition.

- Remote patient monitoring (RPM): RPM is possible with 5G, allowing healthcare professionals to gather and evaluate patient data in real-time. The adoption of wearable health monitors, for instance, can be supported by 5G, allowing patients to communicate data on their vital signs to their healthcare practitioners for immediate analysis and action [69].

- Virtual and augmented reality: 5G can facilitate the usage of VR and AR in healthcare, opening up new avenues for patient training, education, and treatment. For example, 5G can facilitate the use of VR simulations for surgical training, enabling healthcare personnel to perform complicated procedures in a safe, virtual environment.

- Medical equipment: 5G can help the creation and introduction of new medical devices, including telemedicine systems and wearable health monitoring. 5G can offer real-time data transfer and analysis with low latency and high-speed connection, allowing healthcare practitioners to make educated decisions and react swiftly to changes in a patient's condition. **Figure 9** presents a summary of the applications of 5G in healthcare.

9. 5G and the environment

The introduction of 5G technology has a significant impact on the environment. 5G has the potential to exacerbate environmental issues like rising energy consumption and technological waste.

9.1 Benefits of 5G for the environment

Given that the long-term effects of this new technology are unknown, the environmental impact of 5G is cause for concern. However, there may also be environmental advantages to 5G. The reduction of emissions and energy consumption is one of the most significant advantages. According to international standards, 5G should use much less power to operate than 4G, thereby transmitting more data while using less power. In 4G, for instance, 300 high-definition movies can only be downloaded with

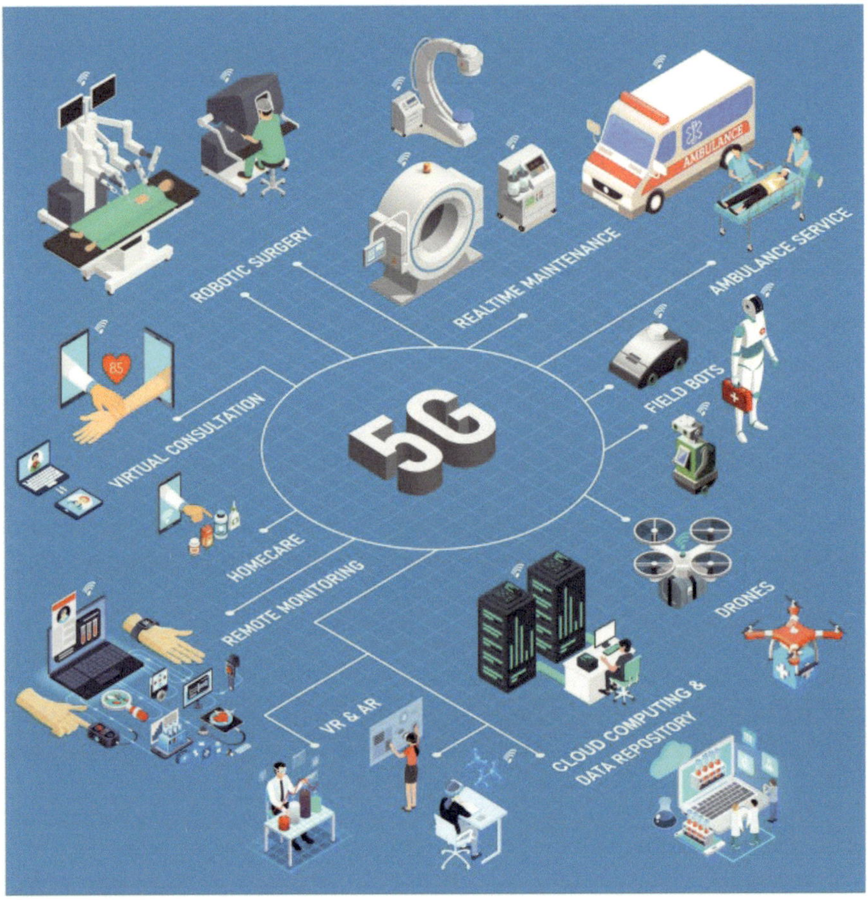

Figure 9.
5G technology revolutionizing healthcare [72].

one kWh of electricity; One kWh of 5G capacity can download 5000 HD movies. Data centers in 2020 were using 73 billion kWh of energy due to the increased efficiency of 5G technology [73].

5G is significantly more energy-efficient than previous generations of mobile networks, according to research conducted by the University of Zurich and Empa [74]. The study also concluded that applications like flexible working and smart grid technology that uses 5G have a lot of potentials to save energy and protect the environment [74]. Together with the increased use of environmentally friendly energy sources, real-time monitoring of the built environment has the potential to cut carbon emissions by 67.9 million metric tons [75]. This reduction will be made possible by energy grids, smart meters, and energy management systems that are enabled by 5G [75].

With IoT and 5G, we can fully comprehend the impact on the environment and respond accordingly [76]. Stakeholders will be able to forecast, optimize, and measure the impact of the environment using real-time data as 5G is implemented globally [76]. Once the right infrastructure is in place, 5G may also enable a new phase of the green revolution. Experts are hopeful that the increased speed of data sensors will result in a more efficient than ever real-time energy conservation system [76].

Although the long-term environmental effects of 5G are unknown, there may be advantages to using this new technology. Real-time monitoring of the built environment, as well as the facilitation of the green revolution, are some of the potential benefits of 5G. But it is critical to keep an eye on how 5G affects the environment and take steps to minimize any negative effects.

9.2 Challenges and limitations

Notwithstanding the advantages, there are several challenges and restrictions related to 5G and its effects on the environment. The challenges include but are not limited to:

- Increasing the amount of energy used: The extent to which 5G will impact energy consumption is a major issue. To support 5G, additional equipment and cell towers must be installed, which may raise energy costs and increase emissions of greenhouse gases. In addition, laptops and smartphones that are 5G-capable are anticipated to consume more energy than their 4G counterparts.

- Waste electronics: It is anticipated that 5G technology will increase the amount of electronic waste as older, 5G-enabled devices are replaced with newer ones. If electronic trash contains toxic substances that harm wildlife and the ecosystem, this could be bad for the environment.

- Human health and the environment: There are worries about 5G affecting human health and the environment. Although the scientific evidence is still murky, several studies have demonstrated that 5G radio frequency (RF) emissions may have negative effects on animal and human health, including decreased fertility, increased risk of cancer, and altered migratory patterns [4] Additionally, it is anticipated that the full rollout of the 5G infrastructure will have a significant impact on the environment due to the need for new cell towers and other equipment. This could lead to deforestation, habitat destruction, and other problems with the environment.

10. 5G and edge computing

Edge computing aims to move decision-making operations as close as possible to data by extending cloud computing services to the network's edge [77]. Edge computing is turning out to be progressively famous because of the developing interest in constant information handling and the need to diminish dormancy [78]. The architecture of edge computing consists of three layers: a cloud layer, an edge layer, and a device layer [78] as illustrated in **Figure 10**. Sensors, actuators, and other devices that gather data make up the device layer. Edge servers, gateways, and other data-processing devices make up the edge layer. Cloud servers, which store data and provide cloud services, make up the cloud layer [78].

10.1 Benefits of edge computing

There are several benefits to edge computing, including:

- Reduced latency: Edge computing can significantly shorten the time it takes for data to travel from the source to the processing unit by processing it locally,

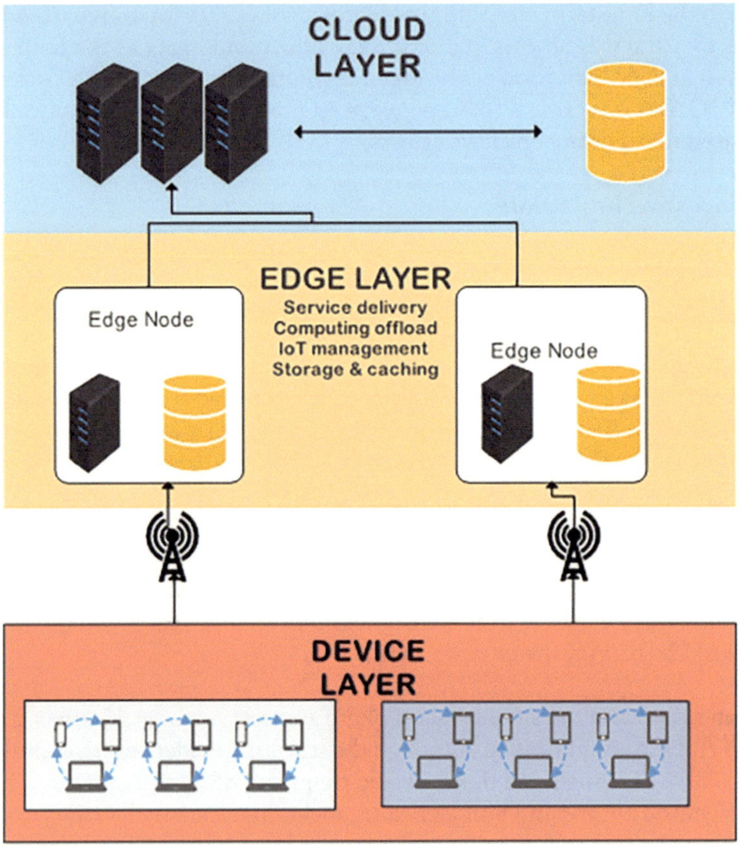

Figure 10.
Edge computing architecture.

resulting in faster response times [79]. This is especially important for applications like telemedicine, autonomous vehicles, and smart cities that require processing in real-time or near real-time [80].

- Bandwidth usage reduction: Sending a lot of data to a centralized cloud can use up a lot of network resources, which can cause congestion and increase costs [79]. By processing data locally, edge computing alleviates congestion and reduces the amount of data that must be transmitted over the network [81]. This can save a lot of monetary resources, especially in applications that collect a lot of data, like IoT devices and industrial automation [80].

- Improved data security and privacy: Organizations may ensure compliance with data protection regulations and reduce the risk of data breaches by storing sensitive data on the edge device [81]. Furthermore, by enabling localized encryption and decentralized authentication, edge computing can provide additional security layers [82].

- Adaptability: By dispersing computing resources across the network, edge computing can assist businesses in scaling their infrastructure more effectively as the number of connected devices and data volumes continue to rise [81]. Because a single-edge device's failure is less likely to have an impact on the entire network, this decentralized approach can also improve system resilience.

Edge computing offers advantages which include decreased latency, reduced bandwidth consumption, enhanced data privacy and security, and increased scalability. Edge computing is an appealing option for a wide range of applications, particularly those that involve large-scale data collection and real-time processing.

10.2 The benefits of 5G and edge computing

The combination of 5G and edge computing offers several key benefits, including:

- Low latency: The low latency of 5G connectivity enables real-time data processing and transfer. Edge computing significantly reduces latency by processing and storing data closer to the source rather than relying on centralized data centers. This combination of low-latency communication and local data processing is suitable for applications that require real-time data processing, such as driverless cars and virtual and augmented reality.

- Better connectivity: Numerous connected devices may be supported by 5G's improved connection. By processing and storing data closer to the source, edge computing may improve connection even further, reducing the need for centralized data centers and boosting productivity.

- Enhanced Privacy: Edge computing can improve privacy by reducing the need to send sensitive data to centralized data centers by processing and storing it locally. One of 5G's improved security features, network slicing, can further enhance privacy and security.

- Increased Adaptability: Edge computing may be easier to scale than centralized data centers because the number of devices can be increased as needed. Because it can handle the increasing number of connected devices, 5G is the best option for the Internet of Things.

11. Conclusion

Virtual and augmented reality (VR/AR), transportation, healthcare, the environment, and edge computing are just a few of the areas that have seen significant shifts since the introduction of 5G technology. The main effects of 5G on these industries are outlined in this concluding chapter, along with the potential benefits and challenges that lie ahead. 5G's ultra-low latency and high bandwidth capabilities have made it possible to create immersive and seamless VR/AR experiences [83]. Real-time applications like remote collaboration, gaming, and training have been made possible by these enhancements, paving the way for the widespread adoption of VR/AR technologies across various industries. Enhanced connectivity has fueled the growth of autonomous vehicles, smart traffic management systems, and vehicle-to-everything (V2X) communication, resulting in safer and more efficient transportation networks [84]. The transportation sector has also witnessed significant advancements as a result of 5G. The expansion of telemedicine, remote monitoring, and robotic surgery in the healthcare industry has been made easier by 5G, improving both access to medical services and the overall quality of care. In addition, the integration of 5G with IoT devices has sped up the creation of smart healthcare systems, resulting in better outcomes for patients and lower costs [85]. There are both benefits and drawbacks to the environment from 5G. Through increased efficiency across a variety of industries, 5G has the potential to, on the one hand, cut down on emissions and energy consumption. However, additional research is necessary due to concerns about the potential health risks posed by higher-frequency radio waves and the increased energy requirements for 5G infrastructure. Last but not least, real-time data processing and analytics at the network's edge have been made possible by 5G, which has revolutionized edge computing by lowering latency and increasing system efficiency. Innovative applications have emerged in a variety of fields, including smart cities, agriculture, and manufacturing [82]. 5G will have profound and far-reaching effects on VR/AR, transportation, healthcare, the environment, and edge computing. Stakeholders need to address the obstacles and take full advantage of this revolutionary technology as 5G networks continue to grow.

Author details

Kofi Sarpong Adu-Manu*, Gabriel Amponsa Koranteng and Samuel Nii Adotei Brown
Department of Computer Science, University of Ghana, Accra, Ghana

*Address all correspondence to: ksadu-manu@ug.edu.gh

References

[1] World Economic Forum. The impact of 5G: Creating new value across industries and society. Available from: https://www.weforum.org/whitepapers/the-impact-of-5g-creating-new-value-across-industries-and-society/ [Accessed: April 17, 2023]

[2] 5G and AR/VR. Transformative use cases with edge computing. Available from: https://stlpartners.com/articles/edge-computing/5g-edge-ar-vr-use-cases/ [Accessed: April 15, 2023]

[3] Huseien GF, Shah KW. A review on 5G technology for smart energy management and smart buildings in Singapore. Energy and AI. 2022;7:3, 6. DOI: 10.1016/j.egyai.2021.100116

[4] A. Tong, M. Hakimi Shamsudin, M. S. Haziq, M. S. Firdhaus, and N. J. Aliesa, Is 5G bad for health? Anti-face touching alarm cap with ultrasonic sensor view project IoT based e-waste monitoring system view project is 5g bad for health? [Online]. Available: https://www.researchgate.net/publication/358901180

[5] Tiwari S, Sharma N. Idea, architecture, and applications of 5G enabled IoMT systems for smart health care system. ECS Transactions. 2022;**107**(1):5499-5508. DOI: 10.1149/10701.5499ECST

[6] Butcher E, Walker R, Wyeth E, Samaranayaka A, Schollum J, Derrett S. Health-related quality of life and disability among older New Zealanders with kidney failure: A prospective study. Canadian Journal of Kidney Health and Disease. 2022;**9**. DOI: 10.1177/20543581221094712

[7] Berlet M et al. Emergency telemedicine mobile ultrasounds using a 5G-enabled application: Development and usability study. JMIR Formative Research. 2022;**6**(5). DOI: 10.2196/36824

[8] Nyberg NR, McCredden JE, Weller SG, Hardell L. The European Union prioritises economics over health in the rollout of radiofrequency technologies. Reviews on Environmental Health. 2022:1-13. DOI: 10.1515/REVEH-2022-0106

[9] Jain S, Jain PK. 5G technology for healthcare and its health effects: Wonders, dangers, and diligence. Journal of Family Medicine and Primary Care. 2022;**11**(11):6683. DOI: 10.4103/JFMPC.JFMPC_1426_22

[10] de Oliveira W et al. OpenCare5G: O-RAN in private network for digital health applications. Sensors (Basel). 2023;**23**(2). DOI: 10.3390/S23021047

[11] Lin JC. Incongruities in recently revised radiofrequency exposure guidelines and standards. Environmental Research. 2023;**222**. DOI: 10.1016/J.ENVRES.2023.115369

[12] Devi DH et al. 5G technology in healthcare and wearable devices: A review. Sensors. 2023;**23**(5):2519. DOI: 10.3390/S23052519

[13] Sehrai DA et al. Design of high gain base station antenna array for mm-wave cellular communication systems. Scientific Reports. 2023;**13**(1). DOI: 10.1038/S41598-023-31728-Z

[14] Stavitz J, Eckart A, Ghimire P. Exploring individual mental health issues: A qualitative study among fellowship-trained sports medicine physicians. International Journal of Environmental Research and Public Health. 2023;**20**(7): 5303. DOI: 10.3390/IJERPH20075303

[15] H. Xu et al., DecentRAN: Decentralized radio access network for 5.5G and beyond, 2023. Available: http://arxiv.org/abs/2303.17210

[16] Asif Khan M et al. A survey on mobile edge computing for video streaming: Opportunities and challenges

[17] von Ende E, Ryan S, Crain MA, Makary MS. Artificial intelligence, augmented reality, and virtual reality advances and applications in interventional radiology. Diagnostics. 2023;**13**(5):892. DOI: 10.3390/DIAGNOSTICS13050892

[18] Hazarika A, Rahmati M. Towards an evolved immersive experience: Exploring 5G- and beyond-enabled ultra-low-latency communications for augmented and virtual reality. Sensors. 2023;**23**(7):3682. DOI: 10.3390/S23073682

[19] Ali U et al. Data-driven analysis of outdoor-to-indoor propagation for 5G mid-band operational networks. Future Internet. 2022;**14**(8):239. DOI: 10.3390/FI14080239

[20] Zhang Q. Investigating the impact of transportation infrastructure and tourism on carbon dioxide emissions in China. Journal of Environmental and Public Health. 2022;**2022**. DOI: 10.1155/2022/8421756

[21] Jia T, Wei C, Tang J. Research on unmanned aerial vehicle application based on 5G communication technology. SPIE. 2022;**12171**:121710P. DOI: 10.1117/12.2631465

[22] Pastukh A, Tikhvinskiy V, Devyatkin E, Kostin A. Interference analysis of 5G NR base stations to fixed satellite service bent-pipe transponders in the 6425-7125 MHz frequency band. Sensors. 2023;**23**(1):172. DOI: 10.3390/S23010172

[23] Biswas A, Wang HC. Autonomous vehicles enabled by the integration of IoT, edge intelligence, 5G, and blockchain. Sensors. 2023;**23**(4):1963. DOI: 10.3390/S23041963

[24] He Q, Dong Z, Chen F, Deng S, Liang W, Yang Y. Pyramid: Enabling hierarchical neural networks with edge computing. WWW 2022 - Proceedings of the ACM Web Conference. 2022. pp. 1860-1870. DOI: 10.1145/3485447.3511990

[25] Gao Z, Shi G, Li J, Chen Z, Tian Y. 5G communication technology in over-voltage fault edge computing of distribution grid. SPIE. 2022;**12172**:121721Y. DOI: 10.1117/12.2634510

[26] Qian P, Huynh VSH, Wang N, Anmulwar S, Mi D, Tafazolli RR. Remote production for live holographic teleportation applications in 5G networks. IEEE Transactions on Broadcasting. 2022;**68**(2):451-463. DOI: 10.1109/TBC.2022.3161745

[27] Nakazato J et al. Proof-of-concept of distributed optimization of micro-services on edge computing for beyond 5G. IEEE Vehicular Technology Conference. 2022;**2022**. DOI: 10.1109/VTC2022-SPRING54318.2022.9860668

[28] Zhou Z et al. Secure and latency-aware digital twin assisted resource scheduling for 5G edge computing-empowered distribution grids. IEEE Transactions on Industrial Informatics. 2022;**18**(7):4933-4943. DOI: 10.1109/TII.2021.3137349

[29] Zhao Y, Xie R, Xin G, Han J. A high-performance domain-specific processor with matrix extension of RISC-V for module-LWE applications. IEEE Transactions on Circuits and Systems I: Regular Papers. 2022;**69**(7):2871-2884. DOI: 10.1109/TCSI.2022.3162593

[30] Yang L, Yu K, Yang SX, Chakraborty C, Lu Y, Guo T. An intelligent trust cloud management method for secure clustering in 5G enabled internet of medical things. IEEE Transactions on Industrial Informatics. 2022;**18**(12):8864-8875. DOI: 10.1109/TII.2021.3128954

[31] Mahenge MPJ, Li C, Sanga CA. Energy-efficient task offloading strategy in mobile edge computing for resource-intensive mobile applications. Digital Communications and Networks. 2022;**8**(6):1048-1058. DOI: 10.1016/J.DCAN.2022.04.001

[32] Jamshidi M(B), Yahya SI, Nouri L, Hashemi-Dezaki H, Rezaei A, Chaudhary MA. A super-efficient GSM triplexer for 5G-enabled IoT in sustainable smart grid edge computing and the metaverse. Sensors. 2023;**23**(7):3775. DOI: 10.3390/S23073775

[33] Mane S. 5G Communications & Networks. Basel, Switzerland: MDPI; 2022

[34] I. Elan Maulani and C. Amalia Johansyah, The development of 5G technology and its implications for the industry. Available: http://devotion.greenvest.co.id

[35] Leyva-Pupo I, Santoyo-González A, Cervelló-Pastor C. A framework for the joint placement of edge service infrastructure and user plane functions for 5G. Sensors (Switzerland). 2019;**19**(18). DOI: 10.3390/s19183975

[36] Zhang L, Yang W, Hao B, Yang Z, Zhao Q. Edge computing resource allocation method for mining 5G communication system. DOI: 10.1109/ACCESS.2022.0092316

[37] Ullah H, Gopalakrishnan Nair N, Moore A, Nugent C, Muschamp P, Cuevas M. 5G communication: An overview of vehicle-to-everything, drones, and healthcare use-cases. IEEE Access. 2019;**7**:37251-37268. DOI: 10.1109/ACCESS.2019.2905347

[38] Chen Q, Wang X, Lv Y. An overview of 5G network slicing architecture. AIP Conference Proceedings. American Institute of Physics Inc.; 2018. DOI: 0.1063/1.5038976

[39] Karunarathne GGKWMSIR, Kulawansa KADT, Firdhous MFM. Wireless communication technologies in internet of things: A critical evaluation. 2018. International Conference on Intelligent and Innovative Computing Applications, ICONIC 2018. 2019. DOI: 10.1109/ICONIC.2018.8601226

[40] BR, Recommendation ITU-R M.2083-0 IMT vision-framework and overall objectives of the future development of IMT for 2020 and beyond M series mobile, radiodetermination, amateur and related satellite services. [Online]. Available: http://www.itu.int/ITU-R/go/patents/en

[41] Taheribakhsh M, Jafari AH, Peiro MM, Kazemifard N. 5G implementation: Major issues and challenges. 25th International Computer Conference, Computer Society of Iran, CSICC 2020. Institute of Electrical and Electronics Engineers Inc.; 2020. DOI: 10.1109/CSICC49403.2020.9050110

[42] Sah MB, Bindle A, Gulati T. Issues and challenges in the implementation of 5G technology. Lecture Notes on Data Engineering and Communications Technologies. 2022;**75**:385-398. DOI: 10.1007/978-981-16-3728-5_29/COVER

[43] The VR Book. New York: Association for Computing Machinery

[44] Billinghurst M, Dünser A. Augmented reality in the classroom. Computer (Long

Beach Calif). 2012;**45**(7):56-63. DOI: 10.1109/MC.2012.111

[45] Carmigniani J, Furht B. Augmented reality: An overview. In: Furht B, editor. Handbook of Augmented Reality. New York: Springer; 2011. pp. 3-46. DOI: 10.1007/978-1-4614-0064-6_1

[46] Antonya C, Talaba D, Stavar A, Georgescu VC. Virtual reality in product design and robotics. 2011. Available: https://www.researchgate.net/publication/224255283

[47] Freina L, Ott M. A literature review on immersive virtual reality in education: State of the art and perspectives. 11th International Conference eLearning and Software for Education. Carol I National Defence University Publishing House; 2015. pp. 133- 141. DOI: 10.12753/2066-026x-15-020

[48] Gallagher AG, Ritter EM, Satava RM. Fundamental principles of validation, and reliability: Rigorous science for the assessment of surgical education and training. Surgical Endoscopy and Other Interventional Techniques. 2003;**17**(10):1525-1529. DOI: 10.1007/S00464-003-0035-4

[49] Li Y, Chen Y, Lu R, Ma D, Li Q. A novel marker system in augmented reality. Proceedings of 2nd International Conference on Computer Science and Network Technology. ICCSNT. 2012;**2012**:1413-1417. DOI: 10.1109/ICCSNT.2012.6526185

[50] ITU Towards 'IMT for 2020 and beyond.' Available from: https://www.itu.int/en/ITU-R/study-groups/rsg5/rwp5d/imt-2020/Pages/default.aspx [Accessed March 31, 2023]

[51] Orlosky J, Kiyokawa K, Takemura H. Virtual and augmented reality on the 5G highway. Journal of Information Processing. 2017;**25**:133-141. DOI: 10.2197/IPSJJIP.25.133

[52] Akcayir G, Demmans Epp C. Designing, deploying, and evaluating virtual and augmented reality in education:404

[53] Hakak S et al. Autonomous vehicles in 5G and beyond: A survey. Vehicular Communications. 2023;**39**. DOI: 10.1016/j.vehcom.2022.100551

[54] Anderson JM et al. Autonomous vehicle technology: A guide for policymakers

[55] A survey of autonomous vehicle technology and security. Available from: https://www.researchgate.net/publication/353417705_A_survey_of_Autonomous_Vehicle_Technology_and_Security [Accessed: March 31, 2023]

[56] Dickmanns ED. Dynamic vision for perception and control of motion. In: Dynamic Vision for Perception and Control of Motion. 2007. pp. 1-474. DOI: 10.1007/978-1-84628-638-4

[57] Buehler M, Iagnemma K, Singh S. The DARPA Urban Challenge. Vol. 562009. Berlin, Germany: Springer. DOI: 10.1007/978-3-642-03991-1

[58] How Google's self-driving car works. IEEE Spectrum. Available from: https://spectrum.ieee.org/how-google-self-driving-car-works [Accessed: March 31, 2023]

[59] Tesla's autopilot: Too much autonomy too soon, Available from: Google Search. https://www.google.com/search?q=Tesla%E2%80%99s+Autopilot%3A+Too+Much+Autonomy+Too+Soon%2C&oq=Tesla%E2%80%99s+Autopilot%3A+Too+Much+Autonomy+Too+Soon%2C&aqs=chrome..69i57.855j0j4&sourceid=chrome&ie=UTF-8 [Accessed: March 31, 2023]

[60] Uber, Lyft ... and now Waymo: The self-driving car service hits the road | On Point. Available from: https://www.wbur.org/onpoint/2018/12/10/waymo-self-driving-car-google-uber-lyft [Accessed: March 31, 2023]

[61] Anderson M. The road ahead for self-driving cars: The AV industry has had to reset expectations, as it shifts its focus to level 4 autonomy. IEEE Spectrum. 2020;**57**(5):8-9. DOI: 10.1109/MSPEC.2020.9078402

[62] Beroun and Vladimir. A global race for autonomous vehicles: views from the United States, Europe and Asia. 2017

[63] Fagnant DJ, Kockelman K. Preparing a nation for autonomous vehicles: Opportunities, barriers and policy recommendations. Transportation Research Part A: Policy and Practice. 2015;**77**:167-181. DOI: 10.1016/J.TRA.2015.04.003

[64] Angelucci A, Kuller D, Aliverti A. A home telemedicine system for continuous respiratory monitoring. IEEE Journal of Biomedical and Health Informatics. 2021;**25**(4):1247-1256. DOI: 10.1109/JBHI.2020.3012621

[65] Zhang Z, Wen F, Sun Z, Guo X, He T, Lee C. Artificial intelligence-enabled sensing technologies in the 5G/internet of things era: From virtual reality/augmented reality to the digital twin. Advanced Intelligent Systems. 2022;**4**(7):2100228. DOI: 10.1002/aisy.202100228

[66] Torres Vega M et al. Immersive interconnected virtual and augmented reality: A 5G and IoT perspective. Journal of Network and Systems Management. 2020;**28**(4):796-826. DOI: 10.1007/S10922-020-09545-W

[67] Yu K, Tan L, Lin L, Cheng X, Yi Z, Sato T. Deep-learning-empowered breast cancer auxiliary diagnosis for 5GB remote e-health. IEEE Wireless Communications. 2021;**28**(3):54-61. DOI: 10.1109/MWC.001.2000374

[68] Meshram DA, Patil DD. 5G enabled tactile internet for tele-robotic surgery. In: Procedia Computer Science. Amsterdam, Netherlands: Elsevier B.V.; 2020. pp. 2618-2625. DOI: 10.1016/j.procs.2020.04.284

[69] Lacy AM et al. 5G-assisted telementored surgery. The British Journal of Surgery. 2019;**106**(12):1576-1579. DOI: 10.1002/BJS.11364

[70] 5G-powered medical robot performs remote brain surgery. Available from: https://www.automate.org/blogs/5g-powered-medical-robot-performs-remote-brain-surgery [Accessed: March 31, 2023]

[71] Devi DH et al. 5G technology in healthcare and wearable devices: A review. Sensors. 2023;**23**(5). DOI: 10.3390/s23052519

[72] Dananjayan S, Raj GM. 5G in healthcare: How fast will be the transformation? Irish Journal of Medical Science. 2021;**190**(2):497-501. DOI: 10.1007/S11845-020-02329-W/METRICS

[73] Swisscom. What is the impact of 5G on the environment? Available from: https://www.swisscom.ch/en/about/news/2020/12/22-welche-rolle-spielt-5g-fuer-das-klima.html#ms-multipageStep-newsletter [Accessed: March 31, 2023]

[74] The coming 5G revolution: How will it affect the environment? Available from: https://news.climate.columbia.edu/2020/08/13/coming-5g-revolution-will-affect-environment/ [Accessed: March 31, 2023]

[75] The impact of 5G in climate change. Available from: https://www.nutanix.com/cxo/thought-leadership/the-impact-of-5g-in-climate-change [Accessed: March 31, 2023]

[76] 5G environmental benefits – VIAVI perspectives. Available from: https://blog.viavisolutions.com/2020/12/09/the-environmental-impact-of-5g/ [Accessed: March 31, 2023]

[77] Al-Dulaimy A, Sharma Y, Khan MG, Taheri J. Introduction to edge computing. In: Edge Computing. London: Institution of Engineering and Technology; 2020. pp. 3-25. DOI: 10.1049/PBPC033E_ch1

[78] Zoualfaghari MH, Beddus S, Taherizadeh S. Edge computing. In: Davies J, Fortuna C, editors. The Internet of Things. Wiley Telecom; 2020. pp. 21-35. DOI: 10.1002/9781119545293.CH3

[79] Mach P, Becvar Z. Mobile edge computing: A survey on architecture and computation offloading. 2017. DOI: 10.1109/COMST.2017.2682318

[80] Shi W, Cao J, Zhang Q, Li Y, Xu L. Edge computing: Vision and challenges. IEEE Internet of Things Journal. 2016;**3**(5):637-646. DOI: 10.1109/JIOT.2016.2579198

[81] Satyanarayanan M. The emergence of edge computing

[82] Roman R, Lopez J, Mambo M. Mobile edge computing, Fog et al.: A survey and analysis of security threats and challenges. Future Generation Computer Systems. 2018;**78**:680-698. DOI: 10.1016/J.FUTURE.2016.11.009

[83] Demestichas P et al. 5G on the horizon: Key challenges for the radio-access network. IEEE Vehicular Technology Magazine. 2013;**8**(3):47-53. DOI: 10.1109/MVT.2013.2269187

[84] Lu N, Cheng N, Zhang N, Shen X, Mark JW. Connected vehicles: Solutions and challenges. IEEE Internet of Things Journal. 2014;**1**(4):289-299. DOI: 10.1109/JIOT.2014.2327587

[85] Sabella D, Vaillant A, Kuure P, Rauschenbach U, Giust F. Mobile-edge computing architecture: The role of MEC in the internet of things. IEEE Consumer Electronics Magazine. 2016;**5**(4):84-91. DOI: 10.1109/MCE.2016.2590118

Chapter 9

Federated Learning Hyper-Parameter Tuning for Edge Computing

Xueying Zhang, Lei Fu, Huanle Zhang and Xin Liu

Abstract

Edge computing is widely recognized as a crucial technology for the upcoming generation of communication networks and has garnered significant interest from both industry and academia. Compared to other offloading models like cloud computing, it provides faster data processing capabilities, enhanced security measures, and lower costs by leveraging the proximity of the edge servers to the end devices. This helps mitigate the privacy concerns associated with data transfer in edge computing, by reducing the distance between the data source and the server. Raw data in typical edge computing scenarios still need to be sent to the edge server, leading to data leakage and privacy breaches. Federated Learning (FL) is a distributed model training paradigm that preserves end devices' data privacy. Therefore, it is crucial to incorporate FL into edge computing to protect data privacy. However, the high training overhead of FL makes it impractical for edge computing. In this study, we propose to facilitate the integration of FL and edge computing by optimizing FL hyper-parameters, which can significantly reduce FL's training overhead and make it more affordable for edge computing.

Keywords: edge computing, federated learning, hyper-parameter tuning, system overhead, internet of things

1. Introduction

As machine learning (ML) and hardware manufacturing technologies continue to advance, training and deploying ML models have become increasingly ubiquitous in our daily lives, from smart-home voice assistants to widely deployed camera surveillance systems. Edge computing is becoming more and more popular due to its advantages, such as fast data processing and analysis, security, and low cost [1]. By placing the edge servers near to the end device, which is the fundamental principle of edge computing, the border of an edge computing system is constrained and manageable.

However, even with the shorter distance between the end device and the edge server, typical edge computing systems still suffer from a significant data privacy issue, as user data is frequently transmitted from the end device to the edge server for training a centralized ML model.

Federated Learning (FL) [2] is a method of model training that is distributed and has been utilized in various applications, including mobile keyboard and speech recognition for mobile devices and IoT. It is naturally suited for edge computing since data is kept on the end devices. **Figure 1** illustrates the combination of FL and edge computing in training a distributed model. First, the model parameters are transferred from the edge server to the end device. After that, the end device trains the model locally and then transfers the model parameters from the end device to the edge server. At the end of this iteration, the edge server aggregates the received model parameters and updates the model parameters. The above procedure will be repeated until the entire training process converges or reaches a predetermined number of epochs.

Unfortunately, FL training incurs significant system overhead, making it difficult for edge computing systems equipped with FL to operate without appropriate acceleration or optimization. Therefore, we propose the integration of FL hyper-parameter tuning in edge computing to reduce the system overhead of FL training and make it more feasible. The FL tuning algorithm should focus on optimizing the four essential system overheads:

- *Computation Time (CompT)*. It measures the time spent by an FL system in model training. When confronted with application scenarios that need a rapid reaction to environmental changes (e.g., when dealing with security issues), the overall model training period must be short.

- *Transmission Time (TransT)*. It represents how long an FL system spends in model parameter transmission between clients and servers. For applications in poor network environments, the transfer of the model should be as fast as possible.

- *Computation Load (CompL)*. It is the number of Floating-Point Operation (FLOP) that an FL system consumes. For low-profile devices, s, a large

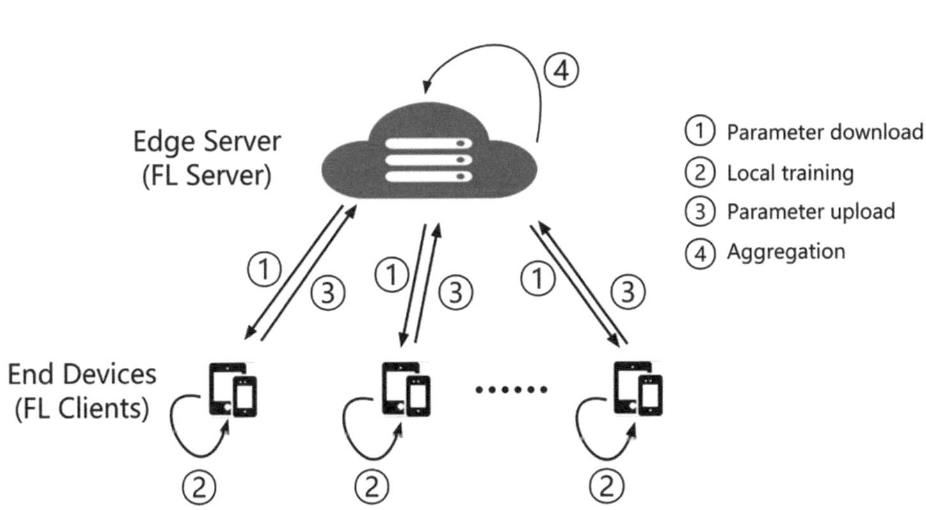

Figure 1.
An illustration of combining FL with edge computing. The model training process incorporates four steps: Model parameter download from the edge server to the end devices, local training on the end devices, model parameter upload from the end devices to the edge server, and model aggregation on the edge server.

computing load is beyond the reach of some low-profile devices (e.g., IoT nodes) with few computing resources.

- *Transmission Load (TransL)*. It is the total data size transmitted between the clients and the server. If the cost of data transfer is high (e.g., data transfer is expensive), the benefits of reducing the total amount of data transferred can be considerable.

Different application scenarios have distinct preferences for training parameters in terms of CompT, TransT, CompL, and TransL. For example, (1) detecting attacks and anomalies in computer networks, as shown in Ref. [3], requires quick adaptation to malicious traffic and is therefore time-sensitive (CompT and TransT); (2) smart home control systems for indoor environment automation [4], such as HVAC, have limited computation capabilities and therefore prioritize computation efficiency (CompT and CompL); (3) traffic monitoring systems for vehicles [5] rely on cellular communications and therefore emphasize communication efficiency (TransT and TransL); (4) precision agriculture based on IoT sensing [6] does not require urgent response but necessitates energy-efficient solutions, with emphasis on CompL and TransL; (5) healthcare systems, like fall detection for elderly individuals [7], require both quick response time and small energy consumption, and therefore prioritize all four training parameters (CompT, TransT, CompL, and TransL); and (6) human stampede detection/prevention systems, as discussed in [8], need efficient systems for time, computation, and communication.

In this chapter, we explore the problem of supporting FL in edge computing from the perspective of FL hyper-parameter tuning. FL hyper-parameters significantly affect the system overhead of FL training, and thus, optimizing FL hyper-parameters is greatly valuable for resource-constrained edge computing. We organize this chapter as follows. Section 2 provides related work on edge computing and FL hyper-parameter tuning. Section 3 explains the challenges of supporting FL in edge computing, and Section 4 presents some preliminary results. Last, Section 5 concludes this chapter.

2. Related work

In this section, we provide relate work with regard to edge computing and FL hyper-parameter tuning.

2.1 Edge computing

With the fast expansion of IoT, more smart devices are connected to the Internet, producing significant amounts of data. The device-generated data causes bandwidth and latency problems when it is sent to a centralized data center or the cloud. Due to this, typical cloud computing models experience problems such as bandwidth usage, slow reaction times, insufficient security, and poor privacy. Moreover, the growing amount of data also puts more strain on servers and drives up operating costs.

Edge computing solutions have evolved as a result of the fact that traditional cloud computing is no longer able to serve the diversified data processing demands of today's intelligent society. In simplest terms, edge computing is a network technology that analyzes data collected from an endpoint directly in a local device or network close to where the data is generated, without sending the data to a cloud-based data processing facility. Its core idea is to make computing closer to the source of the data [9].

Edge computing has several advantages. (1) **Low latency**: Since edge computing is closer to the data source, data storage and computational operations may be performed in the edge computing node, reducing the intermediate data transmission process. Therefore, service providers can process user requests in real time and allow users to experience low-latency services. (2) **Low bandwidth**: In edge computing, as the data to be processed do not need to be uploaded to a cloud computing centre, it does not need to use too much network bandwidth, therefore reducing the network bandwidth load and significantly reducing the energy consumption of intelligent devices at the edge of the network. (3) **Privacy**: Since the edge nodes are only responsible for tasks within their own scope and do not need to upload data to the cloud, network transmission concerns are avoided. Even if one of the edge nodes suffers a data breach as a result of a network attack, the other edge nodes will not be affected. Edge computing significantly secures data.

However, although edge computing protects user data privacy better than traditional cloud computing, it is inevitable that users will upload some or all of their personal information to edge servers, such as cloud data centers or edge data centers. These core infrastructures may be managed by the same third-party suppliers, such as mobile network operators, that may not be trusted. Data is exposed to data security issues such as data leakage and data loss during transmission. Also, personal private data may be used illegally by application providers. Thus, the security of outsourcing data is still a fundamental problem of edge computing data security [10].

2.2 FL hyper-parameter tuning

The area of Hyper-Parameter Optimization (HPO) has received a lot of attention [11]. The hyper-parameters of machine learning models are optimized using a variety of classical HPO techniques, such as Bayesian Optimization (BO) [12], successive halving [13], and hyperband [14]. These cannot, however, be directly applied to FL due to FL's unique hyper-parameters and different training paradigms. For example, FL has specific client-side and server-side aggregation methods that need to be optimized, and the data remains on end devices rather than being centralized on a server.

Work	Description	Single trial	System
FTS [15]	Optimize client models	✗	✗
Zhiyuan et al. [16]	PSO-based optimization	✗	✗
DP-FTS-DE [17]	Trade-off privacy and utility	✓	✗
Auto-FedRL [18]	Improve model accuracy	✓	✗
[19]	Improve training robustness	✓	✗
FedEx [20]	NAS based framework	✗	✗
FLoRA [21]	NAS-based framework	✓	✗
FedTune [22]	A simple framework	✓	✓

Table 1.
Related work on FL hyper-parameter optimization. We tag if (1) the work can run in an online and single trail manner and (2) the work targets system overheads of FL training.

Designing HPO algorithms for FL is an emerging area of research. In the past studies, several methods have touched the filed of FL HPO. **Table 1** provides an overview of various notable methods, indicating whether they can operate in a single-trial and online manner, and whether they address system overhead concerns in FL training.

For instance, BO has been combined with FL to strengthen client privacy [17] and enhance various client models [15]; Zhiyuan et al. utilized particle swarm optimization (PSO) to expedite the exploration process of FL hyper-parameters [16]. However, this approach lacked support for single-trial and system overhead. Multiple methods utilize reinforcement learning to fine-tune FL hyper-parameters [18, 19], but this leads to additional intricacy and reduced versatility. FedEx is a comprehensive framework that utilizes weight-sharing neural architecture search (NAS) techniques to optimize the round-to-accuracy of FL. This approach enhances the baseline by a few percentage points [20]. FLoRA chooses global hyper-parameters by identifying the ones that exhibit high performance in local clients [21]. Although a benchmark suite for optimizing federated hyper-parameters has been created [23], its efficacy has not been evaluated yet. FedTune suggests a basic framework for tuning FL hyper-parameters based on the specific requirements of an application [22]. There are two reasons why the current approaches are not applicable to the problem of federated learning in edge computing. Firstly, the measures such as CompT (in seconds), TransL (in seconds), CompL (in FLOPs), and TransL (in bytes) are not directly comparable, and incorporating various system factors in optimizing HPO is challenging. Secondly, hyper-parameter tuning must occur simultaneously with FL training, and there is no possibility of revisiting the model as the training continues until the final model accuracy is reached. Otherwise, this would lead to a substantial rise in the system's overhead.

3. Challenges of supporting FL in edge computing

In edge computing, a multitude of end devices with varying hardware and data are connected through an edge server, resulting in heterogeneous end devices. This heterogeneity in both system and data poses several challenges when integrating federated learning with edge computing.

3.1 System heterogeneity

The end devices typically possess a range of distinct hardware, which can vary in their capabilities regarding computation, communication, energy, and other factors.

- *Computation Capability*. Due to the increasing demand for gaming and AI applications, many end devices are now equipped with AI accelerators, such as GPU, NPU, or CUDA cores. Nevertheless, tests on popular end devices reveal that their running times for AI models can vary by a factor of tens or more [24]. This difference in time is even more pronounced when the AI models cannot fit into the memory of the AI accelerators, or if the AI model operators are not compatible with the end devices [25].

- *Communication Capability*. In federated learning, the speed of transmission plays a crucial role since it involves multiple rounds of model parameter transmission between the end devices and the edge server. However, since end devices can be equipped with different transmission standards (LTE vs. WiFi), be situated in varying locations (indoor vs. outdoor), and encounter different wireless channel conditions (congested vs. clear), their transmission speeds can differ greatly. By analyzing hundreds of end devices in a real-world FL deployment [26], it has been observed that there is a substantial order-of-magnitude difference in the network bandwidth [27].

- *Other Factors*. Apart from computation and communication capabilities, the availability and capability of end devices are influenced by many other factors. For instance, when the battery of an end device is low, its computation and communication capabilities are reduced to conserve power. Furthermore, end devices running heavy applications in the background can substantially limit the available computing resources.

3.2 Statistical heterogeneity

End devices in edge computing possess distinct characteristics in terms of their data properties, including massively distributed data, unbalanced data, and non-Independent and Identically Distributed (IID) data [2].

- *Massively Distributed Data*: The number of end devices in edge computing is typically much larger than the average number of data points per end device. For instance, in the Google keyboard query suggestion project [26], there are millions of smartphones involved, but an individual user typically generates only dozens of queries per day.

- *Unbalanced Data*: The local data size on end devices varies significantly due to different usage patterns. For instance, the Reddit comment dataset [28] demonstrates that 70% of users contribute to the first quarter of the normalized number of comments, whereas 10% of users generate three times more comments than the average user [27].

- *Non-IID Data*: The data on each end device is not a representative sample of the overall distribution of data, as it does not follow the Independent and Identically Distributed (IID) property. This non-IID property is commonly found in real-world scenarios [29], and it significantly impacts the training of FL models due to the presence of attribute and label skew [30].

- Traditionally, edge computing research has concentrated on examining a limited number of end devices and a basic edge server. Nonetheless, in order to facilitate Federated Learning, a comprehensive understanding of numerous end devices and their interdependent effects on the overall machine learning training process is necessary. Consequently, developing an edge computing system that is compatible with FL is more difficult than creating a cross-device FL system.

4. FL hyper-parameter tuning for edge computing

At present, there is no *de facto* method for incorporating FL into edge computing. We propose the use of automated tuning of FL hyper-parameters as a means to decrease the system overhead associated with FL training. The possibilities of adjusting FL hyper-parameters to minimize the system overhead of FL training are becoming more apparent. In this section, we use our preliminary work, called FedTune [22], to clarify the potential value of FL hyper-parameter tuning for edge computing. FedTune takes into account the application's prioritization for CompT, TransT, CompL, and TransL, which are represented by α, β, γ, and δ, respectively. We have $\alpha + \beta + \gamma + \delta = 1$. For instance, if we take $\alpha = 0.6$, $\beta = 0.2$, $\gamma = 0.1$, and $\delta = 0.1$, it means that the application gives the highest priority to CompT, some importance to TransT, and least importance to CompL and TransL. For two sets of FL hyper-parameters S_1 and S_2, FedTune defines the comparison function $I(S_1, S_2)$ as

$$I(S_1, S_2) = \alpha \times \frac{t_2 - t_1}{t_1} + \beta \times \frac{q_2 - q_1}{q_1} + \gamma \times \frac{z_2 - z_1}{z_1} + \delta \times \frac{v_2 - v_1}{v_1} \tag{1}$$

where t_1 and t_2 are CompT for S_1 and S_2 when achieving the same model accuracy. Similarly, q_1 and q_2 denote TransT, z_1 and z_2 represent CompL, and v_1 and v_2 indicate TransL for S_1 and S_2, respectively. If $I(S_1, S_2) < 0$, then S_2 is better than S_1. A set of hyper-parameters is better than another set if the weighted improvement of some training aspects (e.g., CompT and CompL) is higher than the weighted degradation, if any, of the remaining training aspects (e.g., TransT and TransL). The weights assigned to each aspect are determined by the application's training preferences on CompT, TransT, CompL, and TransL.

FedTune utilizes an iterative algorithm to update the hyper-parameters for the next round (refer to [22] for more details). This process is triggered only when the model accuracy has improved by a minimum amount of ε. After normalizing the current overheads, FedTune computes the comparison function between the previous hyper-parameters S_{prv} and the current hyper-parameters S_{cur}. It then updates the hyper-parameters and resumes the training process. Due to its lightweight nature, FedTune has a minimal computational burden on a standard edge computing system.

The results obtained by FedTune are promising. The performance of FedTune for various datasets when FedAvg is employed is illustrated in **Table 2**. For the speech-to-command dataset and EMNIST dataset, the learning rate is set to 0.01, while for the Cifar-100 dataset, it is set to 0.1, all with a momentum of 0.9. The standard deviation is presented in parentheses. The results demonstrate that FedTune consistently enhances the overall performance for all three datasets. Specifically, by averaging 15 combinations of training preferences, FedTune reduces the system overhead of the speech-to-command dataset by 22.48% compared to the baseline. We have observed that FedTune is more beneficial for FL training when the convergence of the training process takes more training rounds. The performance of FedTune with various aggregation methods is presented in **Table 3** for the ResNet-10 model using the speech-to-command dataset. A learning rate of 0.1, β_1 of 0, and τ of 1e-3 were used for FedAdagrad. As shown, FedTune can improve the performance of the system when using different aggregation methods. Specifically, when using FedAdagrad, FedTune reduces the system overhead by 26.75%.

Dataset	Speech-command	EMNIST	Cifar-100
Data Feature	Voice	Handwriting	Image
ML Model	ResNet-10	2-layer MLP	ResNet-10
Performance	**+22.48%** (17.97%)	+8.48% (5.51%)	+9.33% (5.47%)

Table 2.
Performance of FedTune for diverse datasets when FedAvg aggregation method is applied.

Aggregator	FedAvg	FedNova	FedAdagrad
Performance	+22.48% (17.97%)	+23.53% (6.64%)	+**26.75%** (6.10%)

Table 3.
Performance of FedTune for diverse aggregation algorithms. Speech-to-command dataset and ResNet-10 are used in this experiment.

5. Conclusion

Artificial intelligence is becoming increasingly important for enhancing people's quality of life and boosting productivity. Artificial intelligence is becoming increasingly important for enhancing people's quality of life and boosting productivity. The integration of edge computing with Federated Learning (FL) can help to tackle the data privacy issue. However, federated learning involves a significant amount of training overhead, which can be a challenge for resource-limited end devices. We propose a solution to reduce the system overhead of FL and make it more affordable to edge computing by automatically adjusting FL hyper-parameters. Our preliminary work has demonstrated promising results, with up to 26% reduction in system overhead. This suggests that FL hyper-parameter tuning is an effective approach for edge computing. However, further research is needed to fully support FL in edge computing, and more applications are required to drive the growth of the edge computing ecosystem.

Acknowledgements

The work was partially supported by NSF through grants USDA/NIFA 2020-67021-32855, IIS-1838207, CNS 1901218, OIA-2134901. It was also partially supported by the Jiangsu Funding Program for Excellent Postdoctoral Talent (No. 2022ZB804).

Author details

Xueying Zhang[1], Lei Fu[2], Huanle Zhang[1*] and Xin Liu[3]

1 Shandong University, Qiangdao, China

2 Bank of Jiangsu and Fudan University, Shanghai, China

3 University of California, Davis, USA

*Address all correspondence to: dtczhang@sdu.edu.cn

References

[1] Cao K, Liu Y, Meng G, Sun Q. An overview on edge computing research. IEEE Access. 2020;**8**:85714-85728

[2] Brendan McMahan H, Moore DRE, Hampson S, Arcas BA. Communication-efficient learning of deep networks from decentralized data. In: International Conference on Artificial Intelligence and Statistics (AISTATS). New York, USA: PMLR; 2017. pp. 1-10

[3] Haji SH, Ameen SY. Attack and anomaly detection in IoT networks using machine learning techniques: A review. Asian Journal of Research in Computer Science (AJRCOS). 2021;**9**(2):30-46

[4] Mekuria DN, Sernani P, Falcionelli N, Dragoni AF. Smart home reasoning systems: A systematic literature review. Journal of Ambient Intelligence and Humanized Computing. 2021;**12**: 4485-4502

[5] Won M. Intelligent traffic monitoring Systems for Vehicle Classification: A survey. IEEE Access. 2020;**8**: 73340-73358

[6] Sharma A, Jain A, Gupta P, Chowdary V. Machine learning applications for precision agriculture: A comprehensive review. IEEE Access. 2020;**9**:4843-4873

[7] Hassan MM, Gumaei A, Aloi G, Fortino G, Zhou M. A smartphone-enabled fall detection framework for elderly people in connected home healthcare. IEEE Access. 2019;**33**:58-63

[8] Maria Moitinho de Almeida and Johan von Schreeb. A smartphone-enabled fall detection framework for elderly people in connected home healthcare. Prehospital and Disaster Medicine. 2018; **34**:82-88

[9] Satyanarayanan M. The emergence of edge computing. Computer. 2017;**50**(1): 30-39

[10] Zhang J, Chen B, Zhao Y, Cheng X, Feng H. Data security and privacy-preserving in edge computing paradigm: Survey and open issues. IEEE Access. 2018;**6**:18209-18237

[11] Yang L, Shami A. On Hyperparameter optimization of machine learning algorithms: Theory and practice. Neurocomputing. 2020; **415**:295-316

[12] Snoek J, Larochelle H, Adams RP. Practical Bayesian optimization of machine learning algorithms. In: International Conference on Neural Information Processing Systems (NIPS). Red Hook, NY, USA: Curran Associates Inc.; 2012

[13] Karnin Z, Koren T, Somekh O. Almost optimal exploration in multi-armed bandits. In: International Conference on Machine Learning (ICML). New York, USA: PMLR; 2013. pp. 1238-1246

[14] Li L, Jamieson K, DeSalvo G, Rostamizadeh A, Talwalkar A. Hyperband: A novel bandit-based approach to Hyperparameter optimization. Journal of Machine Learning Research (JMLR). 2017;**18**:1-52

[15] Dai Z, Low BKH, Jaillet P. Federated bayesian optimization via Thompson sampling. In: Conference on Neural Information Processing Systems (NeurIPS). Red Hook, NY, USA: Curran Associates, Inc.; 2020

[16] Li Z, Li H, Zhang M. Hyper-parameter tuning of federated learning based on particle swarm optimization.

In: IEEE International Conference on Cloud Computing and Intelligent Systems (CCIS). Xi'an, China: IEEE; 2021

[17] Dai Z, Low BKH, Jaillet P. Differentially private federated bayesian optimization with distributed exploration. In: Conference on Neural Information Processing Systems (NeurIPS). Red Hook, NY, USA: Curran Associates, Inc.; 2021

[18] Guo P, Dong Y, Hatamizadeh A, Xu A, Xu Z, Li W, et al. Auto-FedRL: Federated Hyperparameter Optimization for Multi-Institutional Medical Image Segmentation. Cham: Springer; 2022. pp. 1-18

[19] Mostafa H. Robust federated learning through representation matching and adaptive Hyperparameters. arXiv. 2019;**1**:1-11

[20] Khodak M, Renbo T, Li T, Li L, Balcan M-F, Smith V, et al. Federated hyperparameter tuning: Challenges, baselines, and connections to weight-sharing. In: Conference on Neural Information Processing Systems (NeurIPS). Red Hook, NY, USA: Curran Associates, Inc.; 2021

[21] Zhou Y, Ram P, Salonidis T, Baracaldo N, Samulowitz H, Ludwig H. FLoRA: Single-shot hyper-parameter optimization for federated learning. arXiv. 2021;**1**:1-11

[22] Zhang H, Zhang M, Liu X, Mohapatra P, DeLucia M. Fedtune: Automatic tuning of federated learning hyper-paramcters from system perspective. In: IEEE Military Communications Conference (MILCOM). Rockville, MD, USA: IEEE; 2022

[23] Zhen WANG, Kuang W, Zhang C, Ding B, Li Y. FedHPO-B: A benchmark suite for federated Hyperparameter optimization. arXiv. 2022;**1**:1-27

[24] Ignatov A, Timofte R, Kulik A, Yang S, Wang K, Baum F, et al. Ai benchmark: All about deep learning on smartphones in 2019. In: IEEE/CVF International Conference on Computer Vision Workshop (ICCVW). Seoul, Korea (South): IEEE; 2019

[25] Zhang H, Han B, Mohapatra P. Toward mobile 3d vision. In: IEEE International Conference on Computer Communications and Networks (ICCCN). Honolulu, HI, USA: IEEE; 2020

[26] Yang T, Andrew G, Eichner H, Sun H, Li W, Kong N, et al. Applied federated learning: Improving google keyboard query suggestions. arXiv. 2018; **1**:1-9

[27] Lai F, Zhu X, Madhyastha HV, Chowdhury M. Oort: Efficient federated learning via guided participant selection. In: USENIX Symposium on Operating Systems Design and Implementation (OSDI). USA: USENIX Association; 2021

[28] Reddit comment dataset. Available from: https://files.pushshift.io/reddit/comments/ [Accessed: October 2022]

[29] He C, Li S, So J, Zeng X, Zhang M, Wang H, et al. Fedml: A research library and benchmark for federated machine learning. In: Conference on Neural Information Processing Systems (NeurIPS). Red Hook, NY, USA: Curran Associates, Inc.; 2020

[30] Zhu H, Jinjin X, Liu S, Jin Y. Federated learning on non-iid data: A survey. Neurocomputing. 2021;**465**: 371-390

Chapter 10

Perspective Chapter: Edge Computing in Digital Epidemiology and Global Health

Robert L. Drury

Abstract

Edge computation (EC) will be explored from the viewpoint of complex systems. An evolutionary and ecological context will be described in detail, including the subjects of epigenetics, self-domestication, attachment theory, scientific cosmology, deep learning, and other artificial intelligence issues and the role of wireless data acquisition analysis and feedback. A technical exemplar will be described and examples of potential integration with various systems such as public health and epidemiology, clinical medicine, operations, and fitness will be proposed. Also, various system vulnerabilities and failures will be discussed and policy implications in the global and clinical health and wellness domains will be identified.

Keywords: edge computation (EC), transdemic, digital epidemiology, internet of healthy things, global health, hardware/software/networked systems, wearable devices, heart rate variability (HRV), complex adaptive systems, i4P health, deep learning, consilience, digital twinning, psychological science, regenerative medicine

1. Introduction

As with any rapidly developing technology, Edge Computation (EC) seems to offer significant benefits to humans and society but also will likely have unanticipated consequences, some of which may harm or immiserate humans and even affect environmental functionality. Within this context, this chapter will attempt to define and describe EC from a variety of perspectives including germane theoretical frameworks and issues, methodological principles, and operational/technological applications. The major substantive issues covered will include defining EC, EC and global health, epidemiological aspects of EC, EC from an ecological perspective, EC and modern evolutionary neurobiology, EC and artificial intelligence, integrated sensor/software/hardware/network development, heart rate variability(HRV), and advanced technology for psychobiological assessment and intervention, including nanomaterials, implantable technology, and bioelectric power generation. The chapter will conclude with an identification of high-impact, high-risk applications and policy directions to address such applications.

2. Toward a definition of EC

The most immediate context for the emergence of edge computation is more general computation and the information sciences. Far from the roots of the abacus, the human "computers" in use during the Babbage age, and the Bletchley mechanical computers of Turing's time, the exponential growth of electronic information processing has been dramatic from the initial solitary transistor to more than 42 million transistors in current integrated circuits, following the prophetic Moore's Law. This has, of course, required an equally significant development of network systems designed by electronic engineers to take advantage of this increase in potential computing power. In the 1950s, electronic engineers began using a fuzzy circular icon in their otherwise very specific circuit design schematics to indicate an important but not specified part of the system, which came to be called the "cloud." This term has been applied as a metaphor in current usage and actually refers to the plethora of data centers using many sophisticated information processing schemes and interconnected by extensive arrays of communication links, including cable and wireless transmission modes. This has been a great opportunity for proprietary interests to market "cloud services," while many individual and corporate users have only a vague and metaphorical awareness of the real physical constituents of the "cloud," which otherwise may seem amorphous and impenetrable.

In truth, the cloud is a market-segmented information processing arrangement that uses the same general technology as more local computation but with a much-enlarged scope and scale. Like its less complex origins in "personal computing," the cloud of course is subject to issues of available computing power and efficient system design. In an effort to establish a specific boundary condition in information processing, the term "edge computing" has enjoyed a similar metaphorical usage functioning as the use of any type of computer program that delivers low latency nearer to requests. Of course, an air-gapped laptop carries out this function without the benefit of network availability. MIT's MTL Seminar, in 2015, defined edge computing broadly as all computing outside the cloud happening at the edge of the network, and more specifically in applications where real-time processing of data is required. In their definition, cloud computing operates on big data while edge computing operates on "instant data," which is real-time data generated by sensors or users. This, of course, begs the question, where is the edge of the cloud? According to The State of the Edge report, edge computing concentrates on servers "in proximity to the last mile network." Alex Reznik, Chair of the ETSI MEC ISG standards committee, loosely defines the term as "anything that is not a traditional data center could be the 'edge' to somebody."

For our purposes, edge computation will be the use of electronic data acquisition, processing, analysis, and actionable feedback with little and intermittent assistance from larger data processing resources. This definition demetaphorizes the use of "cloud" to indicate the use of literally nonlocal system intervention, although contact with larger systems is also a potential use of EC. Later in this chapter, a number of examples of integrated data acquisition, algorithmic analysis, and feedback systems will be described, most of which do not need "cloud services" to function.

The current scale and scope of global overall computing are massive with almost 200 zettabytes predicted by 2025, less than two years hence. With the rapid growth of IoT and particularly the internet of healthy things (IoHT), limitations of centralized data center nodes will become increasingly cumbersome and even prohibitive. The growing use of personal devices including smartphones and wearable devices, as well as smart objects and secure network gateways, will catalyze more autonomous EC. Such development will require a high degree of effective privacy, security and personal data retention, and ownership practices and privileges.

3. Theoretical and conceptual issues

The radical theoretical framework adopted here is complex systems theory as explicated by Wilson [1], Wilson [2], and Capra and Luisi [3]. Examining any system from this perspective includes identifying a delimited set of agents acting within operating rules and consistent with well-studied ecological principles, which constitute a scientific cosmology and resultant worldview. The importance of viewing any system as nested and situated within a larger context is essential and forces identification of boundary conditions, such as "cloud" versus "edge" as well as operative rules followed by system agents. This aids in the clarification of interface requirements such as rules of engagement for any edge computation process. It seems likely that EC will follow the common finding of fractal self-similarity, which can aid in stable and efficient system design. Systems should be designed and maintained with sensitivity to emergent and self-organizing phenomena, as well as the frequent finding of sensitivity to initial conditions (the "butterfly flapping its wings in Rio may cause a deluge in Boston" issue) which may greatly affect output variables.

The significant role of evolutionary processes known as the completed Darwinian revolution includes not only genetic technologies such as CRISPR-CAS 9 but the role of epigenetics, attachment theory, and self-domestication, known popularly as "survival of the friendliest." The importance and real necessity of acquiring large-scale longitudinal psychobiosocial data sets make EC ideally situated to better understand and manage these important processes since the pace of sociocultural and psychological evolution is orders of magnitude faster than classical genetic natural selection. This broadened understanding of the evolutionary process to include group selection and epigenetic modulation of methylation processes has massive implications for a variety of uses including computation-based interventions. Aside from Wilson's revered biophilia, appreciation of both ecological and evolutionary processes needs to include ecocognosy, the term meaning the acute observation of and learning from nature. Many invaluable lessons and facts have been drawn from acute observation of nature outside the built environment. Similarly, many important scientific discoveries have occurred after "accidental" events observed by perspicacious scientists that have been integrated into canonical science. A related principle is a biomimicry, which is the imitation of natural processes. This approach operationalizes the important Hippocratic Oath, second only to "Primum Non Nocere," which is to "follow the healing path of nature." A timely example of this may be the functional abilities of the octopus, which has not one "central nervous system," but a distributed distal system with each arm possessing an autonomous nervous system capable of many adaptive tasks that are only occasionally surveilled and supervised by the nervous plexus located in the octopus' head. It is perhaps only a slight exaggeration to say the octopus has nine brains, with each tentacle included "at the edge."

Another discipline that plays a central role in the systematic approach advocated here is epidemiology and its related health profession, global public health. The primary concern of epidemiology is the study of morbidity and mortality in specific populations, and the knowledge developed is invaluable in both disease prevention and management of disease manifestation progressing from outbreaks to epidemics to pandemics and transdemics (multiple interacting pandemics). A critical point is that epidemiology does not focus on physiological disease pathology alone but includes the psychosocial realm of dysfunctions as well, so biomedical problems such as obesity are appropriate for study, as is the occurrence of gun violence and traffic fatalities. The study of life expectancy and excessive mortality are also highly relevant areas of inquiry. As the Lancet Commission on lessons learned from the COVID-19 pandemic has noted, the development and widespread adoption of sensitive sentinel surveillance systems make effective use of epidemiological data on outbreaks usable to the global public health community. The chronic underfunding and low prioritization of both epidemiological research and public health planning and preparation may well turn out to represent existential threats, as it is common knowledge within the scientifically literate that future pandemics are certain to arise, and experience with COVID-19 demonstrates that as mutation leads to variants of concern, the next pandemic may have both greater virulence and transmissibility, requiring novel approaches to containment of outbreaks and disease management. It is of some comfort that historically, public health has shown major benefits from use of nonmedical interventions (NMI) such as improved sanitation, nutrition, air quality management, and self-management behaviors such as masking, distancing, and avoidance of crowds. Almost equally distressing is the ease with which reasonable conservative scientific pronouncements have been distorted into misinformation by politically conservative and reactionary interests, as exemplified by a recent Cochrane review of mask-wearing. The conclusions were that the studies reviewed had high risk of bias, which hampers drawing firm conclusions regarding the efficacy of mask-wearing. This was miscast by the less scientifically literate but politically astute to conclude that mask-wearing was ineffective at controlling aerosolized infectious agents. Further, a politically expedient tendency to declare "the pandemic is over" overrides scientific public health practices at great risk to society and tends to delegitimize and discredit scientific knowledge. This has led to attacks on prominent scientists and health professionals. As the technology of data acquisition, analysis, and data-based intervention continues to mature, digital epidemiology will become increasingly valuable, especially regarding wireless sensors, deep learning algorithmic analysis, and last-mile EC, which provided that the distortions caused by misinformation and disinformation are identified and discredited.

Related to these developments, science itself has recently suffered damage by failure to replicate key findings and the withdrawal of peer-reviewed studies. The epidemic of drug-related morbidity and mortality, especially related to opioids like fentanyl, has been poorly understood and framed by the scientifically illiterate as needing a renewed "war on drugs" aimed either at limiting supply, either illicit or professionally prescribed and commercially marketed, or criminalization and punishment of users. This approach has repeatedly failed since it does not address the demand side of the issue, and efforts at mandated "treatment" have shown equivocal results at best. Health literacy is often neglected and research has shown that the more negative attitudes toward science and medicine are not justified. Recent attention to terms and concepts such as polycrisis, traveler surveillance, food wastage, aridification, gender food gap, climate-inspired resilience, poverty, and zero-dose children by the World Economic Forum has been poorly understood or misunderstood. For example, zero-dose children, those that have received none of the generally recommended childhood vaccinations are commended by some ill-informed parents. Another troubling development facilitated by the prominence of social media, powered by internet availability is stochastic violence and terrorism, whereby provocative public pronouncements increase the level of perceived fear, threat, and danger and lead to incidents of aggression, while the instigators claim innocence, in that they "never directly" advocated the aggressive act. Such pronouncements have been issued even at the highest level of government responsibility—the President of the US.

The polyvagal theory proposed by Porges [4] and the neurovisceral integration model described by Thayer [5] highlight the role of the autonomic nervous system in mediating and modulating a wide variety of health-related systems including the central nervous system, cardiovascular system, the respiratory system, the digestive system, and the immune system as well as the sensory and motor components that embody these systems. They both focus particularly on heart rate variability as a key biomarker of health and various disease states. The great number of pathological states and functional indicators have been reviewed by Laborde et al. [6] and Drury et al. [7] and various metrics of HRV are described as well, including time-domain, frequency-domain, and nonlinear analyses [8]. A key conceptual component of these theories is the social engagement system, which is the basis for all attachment phenomena and sociality. The neurological CNS substrates for this system have been identified to include the orbitofrontal cortex, the fusiform gyrus, and the cingulate cortex. This system appears to be very similar to the default mode network, which is active when a person is not focused on external events. Together with the central executive network, they are perhaps the brain's dominant control networks, crucially involved in social competence and interactional skill. Since HRV is based on easily obtainable heart rate interbeat intervals, it is an ideal candidate for wireless sensor longitudinal data acquisition and local algorithmic data processing, given the considerable power of current smart devices. This will be discussed in detail in Section 5.

4. Information science including artificial intelligence (AI)

While innovations and advancements in electronically mediated information processing have led to countless valuable applications, it has been said that there has only been one breakthrough since the term artificial intelligence was introduced by John MccCarthy in 1955: the startling arrival of deep learning. In particular, the victory of an AI-mediated deep learning program over human players of the complex board game Go in 2016 produced a shocked reaction globally. This has been deemed a "Sputnik moment" regarding its impact since this technological achievement threatens the putative superiority of humans, and technophobes fear a singularity where the aggregate of computers, robots, and nanoparticles overpower, enslave, or even eliminate humanity. Technophiles, on the other hand, foresee a future of plenitude and security with humans only engaged in work that they deem worthy and non-repetitive, boring, or dangerous. A more moderate position recognizes both the achievements in information science and the often over-hyped promises of some investigators in the algorithmic artificial intelligence field. A very promising approach advocated by Topol [9] is deep medicine, which allocates routine tasks that deep learning excels at, while focusing the provider on the more difficult and nuanced process variables such as empathic engagement. The practice of digital twinning also shows promise for efficient use of both edge and cloud resources. Notorious and highly visible debacles, such as IBM's Watson effort at cancer intervention with MD Anderson Cancer Center are cautionary but illustrate the importance of scientific persistence and diligence in discriminating science from public relations. Indeed, this is only one illustration of the need to bolster the scientific literacy and transparency of current practice for both journalists, "media influencers," and the general public. One of the most important critiques of AI is the anthropocentric and narcissistic identification of human intelligence as the paragon and peak of all possible types of intelligence. The search for artificial general intelligence (AGI) needs to be informed by the reality that there are many forms of intelligence that are not premised on human problem-solving ability and that human intelligence is frequently very flawed and biased. Of course, the recent emergence of both focused and active disinformation campaigns targeting not only COVID-19 issues but science in general, and issues of journal retractions and non-replicability of findings have damaged the healthy formation and dissemination of public health information, weakening the essential role of public health advocacy. A very substantive critique of AI is that if it succeeds in replacing many repetitive, boring, or dangerous jobs, there will be many displaced workers who may become part of an "unnecessary class" similar to the role of many of our elderly population. Anticipating such conflicts, there have been calls for an AI code of ethics and regulation of professionals, which extend the excellent but mainly ignored Asimov's three laws of robots. To add to the anxiety and uncertainty of the general public, much AI research and development has been initiated by the military, often with minimal transparency and justified weakly by claims of national security and document classification. Recent developments have shown the dysfunctional nature and negative outcomes associated with overclassification of documents, often based on political expediency not national security.

5. Heart rate variability (HRV) and networked wireless sensor parameters and applications

As discussed in section three, HRV is an outstanding candidate for remote patient monitoring since increasingly unobtrusive, noninvasive, and efficient wireless sensor systems have been developed. Briefly, HRV is derived from the interbeat interval, which is defined as the period between successive R waves in the ECG signal and can be reliably and noninvasively obtained by photoplethysmography (PPG), which is included in many fitness training belts and smartwatches, as well as recently developed rings which capture interbeat data as well as three-axis accelerometer, temperature, and blood oxygen saturation data in longitudinal time series form. Further, this data can be transferred to a smartphone application that can store, analyze, and display those data to derive various HRV metrics, the most common being the root mean square of successive RR interval differences (RMSSD). Grounded in the theoretical and conceptual issues noted in section three, particularly polyvagal and neurovisceral integration theory, we have proposed deployment of the canary system, a geocoded networked wireless sensor system [10], based on existing proof-of-concept research [11] using the RMSSD HRV metric, which has been shown the ability to detect the onset of COVID-19 up to 9 days before the development of symptoms in symptomatic individuals and laboratory signs such as positive PCR results in both symptomatic and asymptomatic subjects [12]. Notably, Hirten et al. used a gradient-boosting machine-learning algorithm to detect circadian HRV variation in making the most accurate predictions. This targeted technology in response to the massive costs in mortality, morbidity, and socio-economic costs engendered by the COVID-19 pandemic, which is still producing variants of concern that may have both high transmissibility and virulence. Notably, the US DARPA has identified the important role of implantable aptamer-based biosensors to track ongoing health status of military personnel, especially in mission-sensitive settings, and has funded such development. As is typical, massive spending on military applications is rationalized as a national security priority, while the huge social and economic costs of the poorly managed COVID-19 pandemic are not identified as significant national and global security issues. In fact, concern regarding epidemics, pandemics, and transdemics is usually forgotten soon after the disturbance is deemed "over" by national governments, and funding and planning are cut or discontinued completely.

The role of the Canary System has been described above in application to the COVID-19 pandemic for several reasons. Most importantly, it is based on a rapidly scalable commercial technology of sensor devices and smartphones. Thus, its role in the detection of outbreak prevalence and spread is critical, with medical laboratory testing both expensive, time-consuming, and frequently inaccessible, while less expensive antigen tests are less reliable and subject to uneven application and reporting. The system is also well suited to the important but often neglected sentinel surveillance, which can massively improve response to outbreaks that otherwise can go undetected for weeks or months and, in fact, may facilitate original identification of new variants of concern. A recent Lancet Planetary Health recommendation [13] notes the urgency to identify "salient symptoms which need documentation of early routine evaluation of data validity, sentinel site designs and data collection methods to enable rapid implementation and analysis." Such sentinel site designs are applicable not only to high-risk populations but specific individuals.

An example of use by individuals or small operational groups is in military settings where infectious disease is not the only risk. The Canary System can also track mobility and operational behavioral status, which can be categorized in the typical simplified military jargon of green—"good to go" or fully functional; yellow—impaired capability; and red—nonfunctional or deceased. As explored by Thayer [5] and many others, HRV is not only a health biomarker but also an indicator of positive and adaptive psychosocial functioning. HRV has been used in tracking executive CNS function and in improving stress management and resilience enhancement [14]. When combined with longitudinal temperature, blood oxygen saturation, and activity level, HRV could also constitute a routine vital sign monitoring system useful in clinical medicine for both prevention activities and evaluation of clinical status of existing patients.

6. Conclusion

While the Canary System as currently conceptualized is premised on a wearable sensor system, the rapid development of microelectronics and materials science makes other enhancements feasible. Recently, an innovative use of the popular Raspberry Pi technology for ongoing EEG monitoring was described [15] and a wearable device has been shown to be able to accomplish single-neuron CNS recording [16]. The role of mosaic RBD nanoparticles in assessment and intervention in SARS CoV-2 virology has also been explored [17]. The use of wireless data transfer and battery charging has already been accomplished and will further the development of the Canary System. Developments in molecular biology may make it possible for implanted devices to be powered by internal body chemistry, as well. A related area of significant development We have described the positive uses of wireless networked devices here, which we advocate as a dynamic element of iP4 healthcare, which is an integrative approach to health that is personalized, preventive, prescriptive, and participatory [18]. A related highly significant development is the use of genetic and epigenetic interventions in regenerative medicine, which may allow regrowing of damaged or dysfunctional organs such as teeth using native DNA [19].

It is also important, however, to be vigilant regarding misuses of such approaches. In particular, the maintenance of stringent personal data privacy and confidentiality is an issue that has been identified in other applications but would be acute in this type of application. EC must assure that local data is as secure as other settings such as "the cloud." Also, concern with data ownership is salient, since HIPAA provides for health data accessibility but not strict ownership. In the era of increasing data monopolization and commodification by huge commercial ventures intent on profiting from ownership of the data of individuals, it would be pathological for individuals to lose their own biomedical data to commercial interests such as proprietary concerns, healthcare systems, or professional providers. Only with such protections can the potential of such applications flourish. It is also essential to recognize the crucial role played by scientific psychology since all efforts to implement sound scientific and technological innovations and quality improvements are premised on skillful use of the principles of behavior underlying human nature.

Author details

Robert L. Drury
Department of Psychiatry/Institute for Discovery, School of Medicine and Public Health, University of Wisconsin, Madison, United States of America

*Address all correspondence to: rl.drury@gmail.com

References

[1] Wilson EO. Consilience. New York: Vintage; 1999

[2] Wilson DB. This View of Life: Completing the Darwinian Revolution. New York: Pantheon; 2019

[3] Capra F, Luisi P. The Systems View of Life. Delhi: Cambridge; 2014

[4] Porges S. The Polyvagal Theory. New York: Norton; 2011

[5] Smith R, Thayer J, Khalsa S, Lane R. "The Hierarchical basis of neurovisceral integration". Neuroscience and Biobehavioral Reviews. 2017;**75**:274-296. DOI: 10.1016/j/neurobiorev.2017.02.003

[6] Laborde S, Mosley E, Bellenger C, Thayer J. 2030: Innovative applications of heart rate variability. Frontiers of Neuroscience. 2022;**2022**:16. DOI: 10.3389/fnins.2022.937086

[7] Drury R, Porges S, Thayer J, Ginsberg J. Heart rate variability, health and well-being: A systems perspective. Frontiers in Public Health. 2019;**2019**:7. DOI: 10.3389/fpubh.2019.00323

[8] Shaffer F, Ginsberg J. Overview of Heart rate variability Metrics and norms. Frontiers in Public Health. 2017;**2017**:258

[9] Topol E. Deep Medicine. New York: Basic Books; 2019

[10] Drury R. Geolocated wireless heart rate variability sentinel surveillance in immunological assessment, intervention and research concerning COVID-19 and other pandemic threats. Medical Research Archives. 2022;**10**(9). DOI: 10.18103/mra.v1019.3021

[11] Jarczok M, Koenig J, Whittling A, Fischer J, Thayet J. First evaluation of an index of low vagally mediated heart rate variability as a marker of health risks in human adults: Proof of concept. Journal of Clinical Medicine. 2019;**8**:E1940. DOI: 10.3390/jcm8111940

[12] Hirten R, Tomalin L, Fayad Z. Evaluation of a machine learning approach utilizing wearable data for prediction of SARS-CoV-2 infection in healthcare workers. JAMIA Open. 2022;**5**(2):ooac041. DOI: 10.1093/jamiaopen/00ac041

[13] Sachs J, Karim S, Aknin L, et al. The lancet commission on lessons learned for the future from the COVID-19 pandemic. Lancet Planetary Health. 2022;**400**(10359):1224-1280. DOI: 10.1016/s0140-6736(22)01

[14] Spira J, Drury R. Resilience Enhancement (Chapter) in Encyclopedia of Trauma. Figley ed. New York: SAGE; 2012

[15] Rakhmatulin I. Raspberry Pi to brain interface. Open source board for converting RaspberryPi to Brain computer interface. GPL-3.0 license. 2023

[16] Topalovic U. A wearable platform for closed-loop stimulation and recording of single-neuron and local field potential activity in free moving humans. Nature Neuroscience. 2023;**2023**:517-527. DOI: 10.1038/s41593023-01260-4

[17] Lee D, Kim H, Jeong H, et al. Mosaic RBD nanoparticles induce intergenus cross-reactive antibodies and protect against SARS-CoV-2 challenge. PNAS. 2022;**120**(4):e2208425120. DOI: 10.1073/pnas.22084251

[18] Drury R, Jarczok M, Owens A, Thayer J. Wireless heart rate variability

in assessing community COVID-19. Frontiers of Neuroscience (Autonomic Neuroscience). 2021;**2021**:8. DOI: 10.3389/fnins.2021.5

[19] Hanson-Drury S, Thao T. To, Liu Q, Vo AT, Kim M, Watling M, et al. Genome Announc. 2017. Draft genome sequence of *Tannerella forsythia*. Clinical Isolate. 2017;**5**(12):e00024-e00017. DOI: 10.1128/genomeA.00024-17

Chapter 11

Perspective Chapter: Edge-Cloud Collaboration for Industrial IoT – An Online Approach

You Shi, Yuye Yang, Changyan Yi, Bing Chen and Jun Cai

Abstract

In this chapter, we take the Industrial Internet of Things (IIoT) as the background for studying the energy-saving resource management framework to control the cloud center (CC), edge server (ES), and terminal equipment in a closed loop. In this framework, industrial sensors collect data and transmit it to the ES for aggregation. These data form computing tasks for data analysis. Our goal is to minimize the energy consumption of the whole system while ensuring satisfied data processing accuracy and service delay of all IIoT tasks. We formulate the ES preprocessing mode selection, sensor sampling rate adaptation, and edge cloud computing and communication resource allocation as a joint optimization problem. Due to the random arrival of data and time-varying channel conditions, we introduce an online dynamic algorithm with low complexity, which efficiently solves the problem.

Keywords: edge-cloud collaboration, industrial IoT, preprocessing method selection, sampling rate adaption, computing and communication resource allocation

1. Introduction

Due to the rapid development of 5G and Industry 4.0, IIoT-sensing devices, such as smart manufacturing, smart plants, and smart industrial services, have generated a abundant of data. For traditional cloud computing, it is considerably challenging to process such massive data efficiently. Fortunately, the edge computing can significantly reduce the cloud computing's computing load, and thus has been proposed as supplementary paradigm recently [1]. In industrial area, the edge server (ES) close to the data source can be enabled to process some computing tasks, so as to provide more effective data processing services and lead to less communication overhead.

Although some researchers have proposed edge cloud collaboration to increase the industrial systems' operational and energy efficiencies, there are still some inherent while unaddressed limitations. Particularly, computing and communication resources of the edge-cloud collaboration are relatively limited [2]. Hence, if closed-loop optimization is not considered in the management of cloud, ES, and terminal devices, edge cloud collaboration cannot fully make use of its advantages. Some relevant researchers have studied the resource allocation problem of IIoT's edge cloud collaboration [3, 4], including delay awareness, price-based service scheduling [2, 3], and energy-aware resource allocation [4, 5].

However, data collection and data analysis have some special requirements which will be affected by the complex industrial environment, which has been ignored by most studies: (*i*) In IIoT system, industrial equipment needs high-precision adjustment. Any small error may cause industrial equipment to make wrong behavior and cause serious troubles. [5]. Therefore, ensuring the accuracy of data processing in IIoT service is very important. This motivates the investigation and optimization of edge cloud management variables such as processing mode and sampling rate. (*ii*) There are commonly a variety of industrial noises in practical applications, such as electromagnetic noise [6]. Because of these, we cannot analyze the data collected by the sensor directly [7]. Hence, enabling data preprocessing at ESs is necessary (for example, data cleaning [7] and data denoising [6]) before conveying data to the cloud. This necessitates a balance of optimal resource allocations between the cloud and ESs. (*iii*) Since the IIoT system environment is always complex and there are random data arrival and time-varying channels, we are required to carefully manage the computing and communication resources with the guarantee of a long-term performance. Otherwise, the system will soon run out of limited CPU resources and network capacity [8]. As a result, the system efficiency will be seriously affected.

However, solving the aforementioned issues to achieve the closed-loop management is very challenging: (*i*) It is intuitive that the processing accuracy is increasing with the sampling rate. However, increasing the rate is equivalent to the increase of the computing load, and thus will also increase transmission delay and computing energy consumption, leading to the degradation of the system performance [5]. This implies that sampling rate must be carefully chosen for balancing different performance indicators. (*ii*) In practical applications, different preprocessing methods have different computing resource requirements and corresponding processing performance. In addition, data's edge preprocessing will bring extra computing delay and energy consumption. It is difficult to optimize service delay, processing accuracy, and power consumption with mutual trade-offs. (*iii*) In response to the random data's arrival and the time-varying channel, we need to jointly optimize and dynamically adjust the selection of preprocessing methods, sampling rate, and resource allocation. However, it is hard if not impossible to obtain random information of dynamic network in time, which is a necessary condition for long-term optimization of system performance. This will obviously lead to incomplete decision information of IIoT system. Lyapunov optimization method is often used to solve such problems. However, in IIoT applications, decision variables (such as preprocessing method and sampling rate) are often integers, and constraints like processing accuracy and service delay are sometimes nonlinear. This makes the problem much more complex than traditional ones.

2. Chapter contributions and organization

In this book chapter, we study an IIoT energy resource management framework. This framework is constructed on the basis of edge cloud collaboration, and aims to conduct a closed-loop management on the cloud center (CC), ESs, and terminal devices. To be more specific, in this chapter, we consider to optimize the selection of ESs' preprocessing mode, terminal devices' sampling rates, edge cloud computing and communication resource allocation for jointly to minimize the system's energy consumption. Meanwhile, we ensure service delay and accuracy of data processing in the long term. In addition, considering the random arrival of data and time-varying channel conditions, we introduce a dynamic online algorithm with a low complexity to solve this problem.

In particular, based on the network state of the current time slot, we decompose the long-term optimization problem into a sequence of deterministic instantaneous subproblems. After that, we define a continuous probability model and take into account the future influences, and by such we use the Markov approximation algorithm to solve these subproblems to near optimal. Finally, we theoretically analyze the system performance in terms of its asymptotic upper bound.

This chapter's main contributions are listed as follows.

- For controlling the IIoT edge cloud collaboration system in a closed-loop manner, we formulate a joint optimization with computing and communication resource allocation of CC, preprocessing method selection of ESs, and sampling rate adaptation of end terminals to minimize the energy consumption of the whole system while ensuring that all applications' service delay requirements and data processing accuracy demands can be met.

- Based on Markov approximation and Lyapunov optimization, we introduce a novel online joint optimization algorithm with a polynomial time complexity.

- Theoretical analysis and simulation results evaluate the proposed algorithm's asymptotic optimality and show its advantage with the comparison of counterparts.

This chapter's rest contents are listed below. Section 3 models the IIoT edge-cloud collaboration's system. Section 4 formulates the corresponding joint online optimization problem for the closed-loop resource management. Section 5 introduces a novel algorithm with a low complexity based on the Markov approximation and Lyapunov optimization. Section 6 analyzes theoretical performance. Section 7 demonstrates the simulation outcomes and Section 8 concludes the chapter.

3. System model

An IIoT system with a remotely located CC and multiple distributed on-site ESs is considered, as shown in **Figure 1**. Each ES connects multiple IIoT sensors for a known purpose (e.g., mechanical bearings' vibration monitoring) and is used to control devices (e.g., management of its data sampling rates), preprocessing the gathered original data, and further analyzing by offloading them to CC. Denote the ESs's set as $\mathcal{I} = \{1, 2, \dots, N\}$, where $|\mathcal{I}| = N$. Denote S_i as the set of ES i's associated devices. For example, we consider mechanical bearing vibration monitoring task [5], the vibration sensors sample the conditions of operation in the coverage area managed by ES i with specific sampling rate. After that, ES i collects vibration signals, then selects an appropriate mode[1] to preprocessing it. Afterwards, to conduct the computation-intensive data analysis, preprocessed data will be offloaded by ES i to CC. Clearly, this collaboration between edge clouds needs to be sustained by a good closed-loop management with three task decisions: (*i*) sampling rate adaptation of sensors, (*ii*) pre-processing mode selection for ESs, and (*iii*) computational and communication resources' allocation.

[1] Here, the preprocessing modes potentially denote different data cleaning or denoising methods [9].

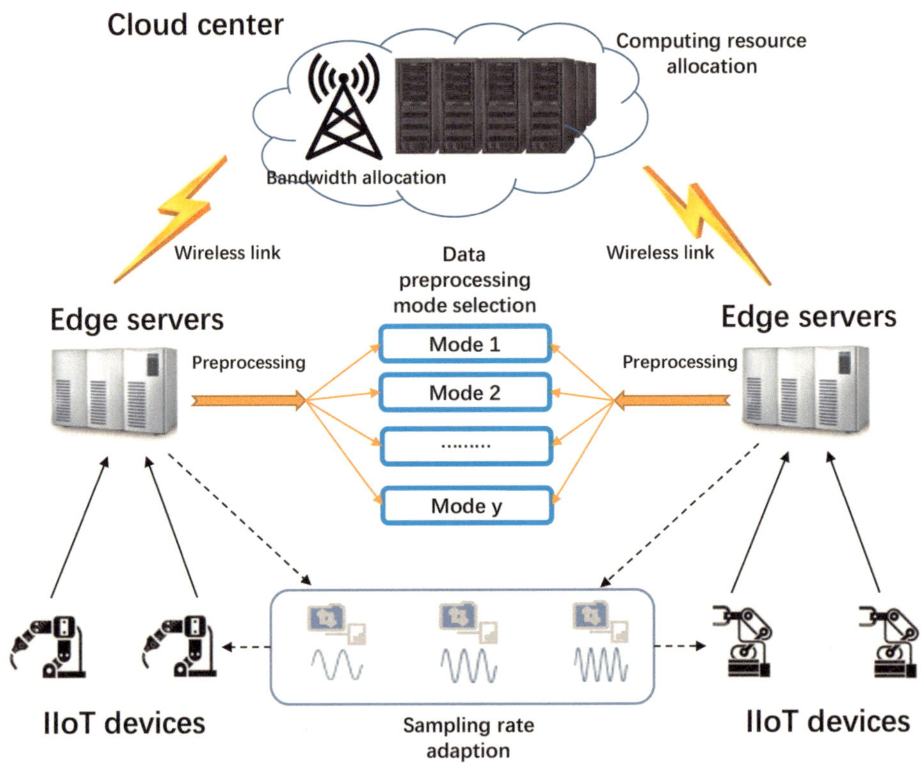

Figure 1.
An example of edge preprocessing enabled IIoT.

In addition, we investigate a time-slotted operation framework in order to portray the intrinsic IIoT systems' time-varying dynamics. Denote τ as time index, and $\tau \in \mathcal{T} = \{1, 2, \dots, T\}$. We show in **Table 1** all the important symbols appeared in this chapter for easy reference.

3.1 Communication model

IIoT devices' sampling rates can be adjusted according to the purpose of different applications. Define $\mathcal{K} = \{\varphi_1, \varphi_2, \dots, \varphi_K\}$ as the candidate sampling rate set, where φ_K (measured by Hz) indicates original sampling rate, K as the maximum sampling rate level. Calculate any level k's sampling rate as $\varphi_k = k\varphi_K/K$, where $1 \le k \le K$. In addition, v_K is defined as the original data size generated in each time slot with maximum sampling rate φ_K. θ indicates the time slot duration. We define $x_{i,k}^{\tau} = 1$, which denotes that in time slot τ, ES i chooses k-th sampling rate of all its affiliated devices. Else, $x_{i,k}^{\tau} = 0$. Denote $\lambda_{i,n}^{\tau}$ (measured by every second's data number) as device n's data arrival rate under ES i's control. Knowing all devices' sampling rate, the task size generated in time slot τ ES i is formulated by combining collected data from every its affiliated devices in current time slot, which is expressed as

$$d_i(\tau) = \sum\nolimits_{n \in S_i} \sum_{k=1}^{K} x_{i,k}^{\tau} \lambda_{i,n}^{\tau} \theta v_K k / K. \tag{1}$$

Symbol	Definition
$\lambda_{i,n}^{\tau}$	Device n's data arrival rate in slot τ
$h_{i,c}^{\tau}$	Channel gain between ES i and CC in slot τ
$x_{i,k}^{\tau}$	ES i's sampling rate vector in slot τ
$d_i(\tau)$	Task size received by ES i in slot τ
$b_i(\tau)$	Preprocessed task size in slot τ
W	Bandwidth level
p_i^{ES}	ES i's transmit power
$\alpha_i(\tau)$	ES i's bandwidth allocation
$c_i(\tau)$	Cloud resource allocation
$E_i(\tau)$	ES i's service energy in slot τ
$A_i(\tau)$	Accuracy of ES i's task in slot τ
A_i^{th}	Long-term accuracy requirement
H_i^{th}	Long-term delay requirement
V	Lyapunov parameter

Table 1.
List of important notations.

Then, ES i will preprocess this task. As data denoising application for preprocessing [10] usually reduces the computational task size, we particularly focus on it here. Assuming that m_y denotes maximum transforming rate in size of the computational task using the preprocessing mode $y \in \mathcal{Y}$, then after preprocessing, ES i's task size in time slot τ is represented as

$$b_i(\tau) = d_i(\tau)\left[\sum\nolimits_{y \in \mathcal{Y}} I_{i,y}^{\tau} m_y\right]. \tag{2}$$

All tasks' input bits should further transmit to CC for learning and analysis. The wireless channel between CC and ESs remains constant within each time slot and varies between time slots following independent identical distribution [11]. Based on the Shannon formula, CC and ES i's transmission rate is

$$r_i(\tau) = \begin{cases} \alpha_i(\tau) W \log_2\left(1 + \dfrac{p_i^{ES} h_{i,c}^{\tau}}{\alpha_i(\tau) W N_0}\right), & \alpha_i(\tau) > 0 \\ 0, & \alpha_i(\tau) = 0 \end{cases} \tag{3}$$

where W and N_0 denote communication bandwidth and channel noise power spectral density, respectively. p_i^{ES} is the predefined transmission power of ES i. From ES i to CC, channel gain is defined as $h_{i,c}^{\tau}$. It includes the effects of small-scale fading, path loss, and shadowing [12]. Significantly, $h_{i,c}^{\tau}$ is an environmental state uncontrollably where positive constant h_{max} has an upper bound [13]. Denote $\alpha_i(\tau)$ as ES i's bandwidth allocation ratio over time slot τ. It should satisfy conditions listed below: $0 \le \alpha_i(\tau) \le 1$, and $\sum_{i=1}^{N} \alpha_i(\tau) \le 1$. The similar definitions appear in [2, 13].

Computational task's transmission delay after preprocessing from ES i to CC is calculated as

$$F_i^{tra}(\tau) = b_i(\tau)/r_i(\tau), \tag{4}$$

and the corresponding transmission energy consumption is

$$e_i^{tra}(\tau) = p_i^{ES} F_i^{tra}(\tau). \tag{5}$$

3.2 Computation model

3.2.1 Edge preprocessing model

ES can provide several optional modes of data preprocessing. Denote y as a feasible algorithm of data denoising in a complete set $\mathcal{Y}$, and the corresponding CPU computation speed (cycles/s) for each data denoising algorithm is denoted by $f_y, \forall y \in \mathcal{Y}$.

Denote $I_{i,y}^{\tau} \in \{0, 1\}$ as ES i's selection index of preprocessing mode at time slot τ. $I_{i,y}^{\tau} = 1$ represents ES i has selected preprocessing algorithm $y \in \mathcal{Y}$. Otherwise, $I_{i,y}^{\tau} = 0$. It is obvious that we have $\sum_{y \in \mathcal{Y}} I_{i,y}^{\tau} = 1$. It is important to note that the computational delay for selecting mode y for data preprocessing of ES i at time slot τ can be indicated as

$$T_i^y(\tau) = d_i(\tau)\beta_i/f_y, \tag{6}$$

where β_i denotes CPU cycles' number that are needed to compute one bit in ES i. Thus $d_i(\tau)\beta_i$ is computational resource which is required by preprocessing step. After that, ES i's preprocessing computational delay in slot τ is indicated as

$$F_i^{pre}(\tau) = \sum_{y \in \mathcal{Y}} I_{i,y}^{\tau} T_i^y(\tau). \tag{7}$$

Therefore, ES i's CPU computation speed (in cycles/s) is described as $f_i(\tau) = \sum_{y \in \mathcal{Y}} I_{i,y}^{\tau} f_y$. Hence, ES i's preprocessing energy consumption in time slot τ can be characterized as

$$e_i^{pre}(\tau) = z_i^{ES} f_i^3(\tau) F_i^{pre}(\tau), \tag{8}$$

where z_i^{ES} is ES i's effective switching capacitance, which is dependent on its chip architecture [14].

3.2.2 Cloud computing model

Tasks received by CC are collected from multiple ESs and each ES's allocated cloud resources. Let $c_i(\tau)$ be cloud resources' allocated proportion for ES i. The proportion should satisfy conditions list below: $0 \le c_i(\tau) \le 1$, and $\sum_{i=1}^{N} c_i(\tau) \le 1$. After that, CC's computation delay in processing ES i's computation tasks should be indicated as

$$F_i^c(\tau) = b_i(\tau)\varepsilon_c/(c_i(\tau) f_c), \tag{9}$$

where f_c and ε_c respectively denote CC's CPU computation speed and CPU cycles number required to compute one bit in CC. In addition, CC's energy consumption for processing ES i's computational task is represented as

$$e_i^c(\tau) = z_c\left(c_i(\tau)f_c\right)^3 F_i^c(\tau), \tag{10}$$

where z_c is effective switched capacitance of CC [14].

3.3 Accuracy model for IIoT data analysis

Tasks' processing accuracy relies on two factors, ESs' data preprocessing method and IIoT devices' data sampling rate. We hypothesize that $g(\varphi_k), \forall\varphi_k \in \mathcal{K}$ is the association between sampling rate and accuracy, and $g_y(y), \forall y \in \mathcal{Y}$ is the association between preprocessing mode and accuracy. Moreover, learning models deployed in cloud center may have computational errors, resulting in reduced processing accuracy, which is denoted by $h_c \leq 1$ [5].

Because of sampling rate control, cloud process and preprocessing method control are independent with each other [2]. Task processing's accuracy for ES i is

$$A_i(\tau) = g\left(\sum\nolimits_{k=1}^{K} x_{i,k}^{\tau}\varphi_k\right) \cdot \left[\sum\nolimits_{y\in\mathcal{Y}} I_{i,y}^{\tau} g_y(y)\right] h_c. \tag{11}$$

It is important that we can modify the model flexibly in practice to another form depending on various demands. The analysis framework remains valid. In addition, data-based experiments allow to obtain accuracy values regarding sampling rate and preprocessing mode [2].

4. Problem formulation

ESs' preprocessing mode and sensors' sampling rate can influence the computing accuracy, and the computing resources and bandwidth allocation of CC can influence the efficiency of computing and transmission. Significantly, these decisions are all closely associated. For example, if the wireless channel condition is poor or computation load of the system is large, ESs can select efficient preprocessing method and reduce the sampling rate. Hence, the CC may increase the computing and communication resources allocation ratios correspondingly. The advantage of the operations is to decrease the execution delay, transmission delay, and energy consumption. The disadvantage is that it will lose some processing accuracy. It shows that a trade-off exists in service delay, processing accuracy, and system energy consumption. For improving IIoT system's energy efficiency, we intend to minimize system energy consumption, which includes ESs' computing energy consumptions, ECs' offloading transmission energy consumption, and CC's energy consumption, with guaranteed processing accuracy and service delay. Every ES's computation task represents an application. We calculate time slot τ's energy consumption as

$$E_i(\tau) = e_i^{ES}(\tau) + e_i^{tra}(\tau) + e_i^c(\tau). \tag{12}$$

Because of the industrial environment's time-varying features, for minimizing long-term dynamic energy consumption, we need to manage the IIoT edge cloud collaboration system. Therefore, the EC computing system's average energy consumption is selected as performance measurement, i.e., $\frac{1}{T}\sum_{\tau=1}^{T}\sum_{i=1}^{N}E_i(\tau)$. Then we jointly optimize sampling rates of sensors, preprocessing method of ESs, and computing and communication resources of edge cloud, which denotes as $J_i(\tau) \triangleq \left[x_{i,k}^{\tau}, I_{i,y}^{\tau}, \alpha_i(\tau), c_i(\tau)\right], \forall i \in \mathcal{I}$, can be represented as

$$2\mathcal{P}_1: \min_{\{J_i(\tau), \forall i \in \mathcal{I}\}} \frac{1}{T}\sum_{\tau=1}^{T}\sum_{i=1}^{N}E_i(\tau) \tag{13}$$

$$\text{s.t.} 0 \le \alpha_i(\tau) \le 1, \sum_{i=1}^{N}\alpha_i(\tau) \le 1, \forall i \in \mathcal{I}, \tag{14}$$

$$0 \le c_i(\tau) \le 1, \sum_{i=1}^{N}c_i(\tau) \le 1, \forall i \in \mathcal{I}, \tag{15}$$

$$I_{i,y}^{\tau} \in \{0,1\}, \sum_{y \in \mathcal{Y}} I_{i,y}^{\tau} = 1, \forall i \in \mathcal{I}, \tag{16}$$

$$x_{i,k}^{\tau} \in \{0,1\}, \sum_{k=1}^{K} x_{i,k}^{\tau} = 1, \forall i \in \mathcal{I}, \tag{17}$$

$$\lim_{T \to +\infty} \frac{1}{T}\sum_{\tau=1}^{T} H_i(\tau) \le H_i^{th}, \forall i \in \mathcal{I}, \tag{18}$$

$$\lim_{T \to +\infty} \frac{1}{T}\sum_{\tau=1}^{T} A_i(\tau) \ge A_i^{th}, \forall i \in \mathcal{I}, \tag{19}$$

where (14)-(17) respectively represent the constraints of bandwidth allocation, cloud computing resource allocation, preprocessing method selection, and sampling rate.

Constraint (18) is average service delay in the long term. Constraint (19) is processing accuracy. They are the constraints of ES $i \in \mathcal{I}$ which have unique purposes, where H_i^{th} and A_i^{th} are requirements of application related threshold. $H_i(\tau)$ denotes the ES i's delay performance, so that $H_i(\tau) = F_i^{ES}(\tau) + F_i^{tra}(\tau) + F_i^{c}(\tau), \forall i \in \mathcal{I}$.

Remark *P*1 is a dynamic stochastic optimization problem and we must decide all these decisions in the time slot. The problem's objective is minimizing system energy consumption in a long-term way in dynamic network. Due to two reasons, solving the problem is challenging: (*i*) due to the number of previous information is extremely large, the statistics of data arrival rates and time-varying channel conditions may be hard to obtain in IIoT systems; and (*ii*) because of the quick growth of the ES and IIoT devices's number, traditional dynamic programming is difficult to handle its large state space and action space, which will result in high computational complexity [11]. Lyapunov optimization [15] is used to solve long-term stochastic optimization problem, but preprocessing mode selection $I_{i,y}^{\tau}$ and sampling rate adaption $x_{i,k}^{\tau}$ are discrete binary decision variable. Further, constraints (18) and (19) are nonlinear, making *P*1 be a mixed integer nonlinear programming problems. To handle the problem, heuristic algorithms are a low-complexity solution. However, the solution cannot guarantee algorithm performance, so in IIoT applications, it is not recommended. To address this issue, an online algorithm is designed to solve this question in the next section. In the first step, according to current network states, we use Lyapunov optimization method to decompose the long-term optimization problem into real-time optimization subproblems. In the second step, based on Markov approximation technology, we developed an approximation algorithm. We consider the future impact and introduce the continuous probability model, and obtain the asymptotic optimal solution of the subproblem within the verified analysis range.

5. Online resource management algorithm

5.1 Lyapunov-based online method

Dealing with the long-term accuracy and delay constraints are main challenges to solve problem P_1. Therefore, we use the Lyapunov optimization method. For IIoT applications, Lyapunov optimization method constructs overdue delay queues and accuracy deficit queues. The problem decomposition's detailed procedure is shown as follows.

First, we define the delay overflow queues and accuracy deficit queues of IIoT applications. For each ES i, the dynamic changes of the accuracy deficit queue are represented below:

$$Q_i(\tau+1) = \left[A_i^{th} - A_i(\tau)\right]^+ + Q_i(\tau). \tag{20}$$

Here, if $\mathcal{Z}$ is a non-negative value, $[\mathcal{Z}]^+ = \mathcal{Z}$. Otherwise, it is 0. $Q_i(\tau)$ indicates that there exists a deviation between the instantaneous accuracy and ESi's required long-term accuracy at time slot τ.

We represent overdue delay queue's dynamic change of ES i below:

$$M_i(\tau+1) = \left[H_i(\tau) - H_i^{th}\right]^+ + M_i(\tau), \tag{21}$$

where $M_i(\tau)$ represents the i-th ES's deviation between computation task's service delay and long-term required delay in time slot τ.

Then, Lyapunov function is defined according to [15] as

$$L(\Theta(\tau)) \triangleq \frac{1}{2}\sum_{i\in I}\left[Q_i(\tau)^2 + M_i(\tau)^2\right], \tag{22}$$

where $\Theta(\tau) \triangleq [Q_i(\tau), M_i(\tau)]$.

Thus, the Lyapunov drift can be represented as

$$\Delta(\Theta(\tau)) = \mathbb{E}[L(\Theta(\tau+1)) - L(\Theta(\tau))|\Theta(\tau)]. \tag{23}$$

Accordingly, we represent the Lyapunov drift-penalty function as

$$\Delta_V(\Theta(\tau)) = \Delta(\Theta(\tau)) + V\cdot\mathbb{E}[E_i(\tau)|\Theta(\tau)], \tag{24}$$

where $V \in (0, +\infty)$ is a control parameter. Next, the upper bound of $\Delta_V(\Theta(\tau))$ is derived for any feasible solution $J_i(\tau), \forall i \in \mathcal{I}$, which is written in Theorem 1.1.

Theorem 1.1 $\Delta_V(\mathcal{Q}(\tau))$ has an upper bounded for any $J_i(\tau), \forall i \in \mathcal{I}$, which can be written as

$$\begin{aligned}\Delta_V(\Theta(\tau)) \leq B + \mathbb{E}\sum_{i=1}^{N}\{Q_i(\tau)\left[A_i^{th} - A_i(\tau)\right] + M_i(\tau)\left[H_i(\tau) - H_i^{th}\right]|\Theta(\tau)\} \\ + V \cdot \mathbb{E}[E_i(\tau)|\Theta(\tau)],\end{aligned} \tag{25}$$

where B is a positive constant which can adjust the tradeoff between the satisfaction degree of the long-term accuracy and service delay constraints and the energy consumption cost.

Proof: We square two sides of accuracy deficit dynamics and we have

$$\begin{aligned}Q_i^2(\tau+1) &= \left[\left[A_i^{\text{th}} - A_i(\tau)\right]^+\right]^2 + Q_i^2(\tau) + 2Q_i(\tau)\left[A_i^{\text{th}} - A_i(\tau)\right]^+ \\ &\leq \left[A_i^{\text{th}} - A_i(\tau)\right]^2 + Q_i^2(\tau) + 2Q_i(\tau)\left[A_i^{\text{th}} - A_i(\tau)\right].\end{aligned} \tag{26}$$

We subtract $Q_i^2(\tau)$ from two sides and then multiply by 0.5. Then, for $i \in \mathcal{I} = \{1,2,3, \ldots ,N\}$, we sum up these inequalities. So, we have

$$\frac{1}{2}\sum_{i=1}^{N}\left[Q_i^2(\tau+1) - Q_i^2(\tau)\right] \leq \frac{1}{2}\sum_{i=1}^{N}\left[A_i^{th} - A_i(\tau)\right]^2 + \sum_{i=1}^{N}Q_i(\tau)\left[A_i^{th} - A_i(\tau)\right]. \tag{27}$$

Similarly, for delay overflow dynamics in (15), we can make such operations

$$\begin{aligned}M_i^2(\tau+1) &= \left[\left[H_i(\tau) - H_i^{th}\right]^+\right]^2 + M_i^2(\tau) + 2M_i(\tau)\left[H_i(\tau) - H_i^{th}\right]^+ \\ &\leq \left[H_i(\tau) - H_i^{th}\right]^2 + M_i^2(\tau) + 2M_i(\tau)\left[H_i(\tau) - H_i^{th}\right].\end{aligned} \tag{28}$$

We subtract $M_i^2(\tau)$ from two sides and multiply by 0.5. Then, for $i \in \mathcal{I}$, we sum up these inequalities:

$$\frac{1}{2}\sum_{i=1}^{N}\left[M_i^2(\tau+1) - M_i^2(\tau)\right] \leq \frac{1}{2}\sum_{i=1}^{N}\left[H_i(\tau) - H_i^{th}\right]^2 + \sum_{i=1}^{N}M_i(\tau)\left[H_i(\tau) - H_i^{th}\right]. \tag{29}$$

Combine (22) and (23), we can get

$$\begin{aligned}L(\Theta(\tau+1)) - L(\Theta(\tau)) \leq \frac{1}{2}\sum_{i=1}^{N}\left[A_i^{th} - A_i(\tau)\right]^2 + \frac{1}{2}\sum_{i=1}^{N}\left[H_i(\tau) - H_i^{th}\right]^2 \\ + Q_i(\tau)\left[A_i^{th} - A_i(\tau)\right] + M_i(\tau)\left[H_i(\tau) - H_i^{th}\right].\end{aligned} \tag{30}$$

Finally, $V \cdot E_i(\tau)$ is added to two sides of (30) and take expectation of two sides of $\Theta(\tau)$ as the condition. Then, desired result can be obtained in (25), where $\text{B} = \frac{1}{2}\sum_{i=1}^{N}\left[A_i^{th} - A_i(\tau)\right]^2 + \frac{1}{2}\sum_{i=1}^{N}\left[H_i(\tau) - H_i^{th}\right]^2$.

The online joint preprocessing method selection, sampling rate adaption. and resource management algorithm aims to minimize $\Delta_V(\Theta(\tau))$'s upper bound in Theoerm 1.1. The service delay and processing accuracy should be maintained at an expected level. At the same time, we can minimize the CC and ESs' system energy consumption. Algorithm 1 shows the details. Note that $P2$'s constraints and $P1$'s constraints are the same. The *P2*'s objective function corresponds to the right side of (25). In every time slot τ, we solve *P2* to obtain the optimal preprocessing method selection, sampling rate adaption, and resource management. Then, we update overdue delay queues and accuracy deficit queues.

Algorithm 1: Online Joint Sampling Rate Adaption, Preprocessing Mode and Resource Management Algorithm (OSPRA).

---

1. **Initialization:** At the beginning of slot τ, collect the status information of CC, ESs, and each sensors.

2. Observe the queue set $\Theta(\tau)$, channel gain $h_i(\tau)$, and data arrival rate $\lambda_n(\tau)$ of n-th device.

3. Determine $x_{i,k}^{\tau}$ for each sensor, $I_{i,y}^{\tau}$ for each ES, $\alpha_i(\tau)$ for each edge cloud link, and $c_i(\tau)$ for cloud computing by solving

$$\begin{aligned}\mathbf{P}_2: \min_{\{J_i(\tau)\}} U_i(\tau) &= B + \mathbb{E}\sum\nolimits_{i=1}^{N}\{Q_i(\tau)\left[A_i^{th} - A_i(\tau)\right] + M_i(\tau)\cdot\left[H_i(\tau) - H_i^{th}\right]|\Theta(\tau)\} \\ &+ V\mathbb{E}[E_i(\tau)|\Theta(\tau)] \\ \text{s.t.}\quad &(14) - (19).\end{aligned}$$

4. Update queue $Q_i(\tau)$ and $M_i(\tau)$ depending on (20) and (21).

5. Return the best value of $J_i(\tau)$.

6. $\tau = \tau + 1$.

Sampling rate adaption $x_{i,k}^{\tau}$ and preprocessing method selection $I_{i,y}^{\tau}$ are discrete binary decision variable. Meanwhile, the CC's bandwidth and computation resource allocation is nonlinear. Therefore, problem *P2* is mixed integer nonlinear programming (MINLP) problem.

Theorem 1.2 Problem *P2* is NP-hard.

Proof: Firstly, we discuss a specific problem case. In this case, we fix the CC's bandwidth and computation resource allocation. Therefore, sampling rate and preprocessing method are selected discretely in problem *P2*. We can easily reduce the case to a multiple knapsack problem and the problem is known as NP-hard [16].

To address this issue, network configurations are set up as a time-reversible continuous-time Markov chain's states. We can prove that after a finite number of iterations, the CC's preprocessing method selection, sampling rate adaption, and the bandwidth and computation resource allocation can achieve stable states.

5.2 Approximately optimal solution for *P2*

Denote feasible solutions's set as J, and the feasible solution of problem *P2* satisfy $j \in J$. Denote the probability of adopting solution j at time slot τ as q_j. Then, problem *P2* can be converted into the equivalent form:

$$\begin{aligned} \min_{q \geq 0} \quad & \sum_{j \in J} q_j \sum_{i \in \mathcal{I}} U_i(j, \tau) \\ \text{s.t.} \quad & \sum_{j \in J} q_j = 1, \end{aligned} \tag{31}$$

where $\sum_{i \in \mathcal{I}} U_i(j, \tau)$ is q_j's weight. The optimal solution of problem (31) results in minimum weight. We may transform the problem continuously by using log-sum-exp approximation [17].

First, convex log-sum-exp function $G_\delta(j, \tau)$ is used to approximate the optimization objective $U_i(j, \tau)$, which is represented below:

$$G_\delta(j, \tau) = \frac{1}{\delta} \log\left[\sum_{j \in J} \exp\left(\delta \sum_{i \in \mathcal{I}} U_i(j, \tau)\right)\right], \tag{32}$$

and we analytically show its approximation gap in Theorem 1.3.

Theorem 1.3 The convex log-sum-exp function $G_\delta(j, t)$ in (32) can approximate the optimization objective in (31) by

$$\min_{j \in J} \sum_{i \in \mathcal{I}} U_i(j, \tau) - \frac{1}{\delta} \log|J| \leq G_\delta(j, \tau) \leq \min_{j \in J} \sum_{i \in \mathcal{I}} U_i(j, \tau),$$

where δ is a positive constant and the approximation gap is upper-bounded by $\frac{1}{\delta} \log|J|$.

Proof: Given the constant δ, inequality holds:

$$\begin{aligned} \min_{j \in J} \sum_{i \in \mathcal{I}} U_i(j, \tau) &\geq \frac{1}{\delta} \log\left[\exp\left(\delta \min_{j \in J} \sum_{i \in I} U_i(j, \tau)\right)\right] \\ &\geq \min_{j \in J} \sum_{i \in \mathcal{I}} U_i(j, \tau) - \frac{1}{\delta} \log|J|. \end{aligned} \tag{33}$$

Convex log-sum-exp function's value precisely approximates min function's result, when δ approaches infinity, i.e.,

$$\min_{j \in J} \sum_{i \in \mathcal{I}} U_i(j, \tau) = \min_{\delta \to \infty} \frac{1}{\delta} \log\left[\sum_{j \in J} \exp\left(\delta \sum_{i \in \mathcal{I}} U_i(j, \tau)\right)\right]. \tag{34}$$

What's more, the value of the problem's optimal solution and log-sum-exp function $G_\delta(j, \tau)$ are equal according to Theorem 1.3, which is represented as follows:

$$\begin{aligned} \min_{q \geq 0} \quad & \sum\nolimits_{j \in J} q_j \sum\nolimits_{i \in \mathcal{I}} U_i(j, \tau) + \frac{1}{\delta} \sum\nolimits_{j \in J} q_j \log q_j, \\ \text{s.t.} \quad & \sum\nolimits_{j \in J} q_j = 1. \end{aligned} \tag{35}$$

Namely, we can convert problem (31) to problem (35).

By solving the KKT condition [17] of problem (35) can be represented as follows:

$$\begin{aligned} &\sum\nolimits_{i\in\mathcal{I}} U_i(j,\tau) - \frac{1}{\delta}\log q_j^* + \frac{1}{\delta} + \eta = 0 \\ &\sum\nolimits_{j\in J} q_j^* = 1, \\ &\eta \geq 0, \end{aligned} \tag{36}$$

We can obtain the probability distribution q_j^* of optimal solution as follows:

$$q_j^* = \frac{\exp\left(-\sum\nolimits_{i\in\mathcal{I}} \delta U_i(j,\tau)\right)}{\sum\nolimits_{j'\in J} \exp\left(-\sum\nolimits_{i\in\mathcal{I}} \delta U_i(j',\tau)\right)}, \forall j \in J. \tag{37}$$

We can see that the different solutions's probabilities have direct ratio with corresponding weights $U_i(j,\tau)$. Every solution $j \in J$ is paired with a specific state, we construct a time-reversible Markov sequential chain [18] which has a stationary distribution q_j^*. Switching one solution to another and transitioning between two states are equal. ES selecting new preprocessing mode and sampling rate and CC adopting new computation and communication resource allocation decision trigger it.

Algorithm 2: Markov Approximation-Based Algorithm for *P*2.

---

1. **Initialization:** Initialize $U_i(j,\tau)$ by initializing sampling rate $x_{i,k}^{\tau}$, preprocessing mode $I_{i,y}^{\tau}$, and resource allocation in ESs and cloud center.
2. **End initialization**
3. **Loop:**
4. Select a random solution and perform the following steps:
5. Compute all other feasible solutions for the bound $U_i(j,\tau)$.
6. Using the probability derived from (37), choose a feasible solution.
7. **Update** the feasible solution.
8. Record the optimal solution j^* when $U_i(j^*,\tau)$ is the smallest.
9. **End Loop**

We must guarantee that random two states can convert if we want to build a time-reversible Markov sequential chain. Therefore, we limit one preprocessing method selection and sampling rate in ES and CC's one communication and computation resource allocation in time slot. If we make a decision of preprocessing mode $I_i^y(\tau)$, sampling rate x_{k_i}, computation and communication resource allocation $\alpha_i(\tau)$, $c_i(\tau)$, previous solution j converts to new solution j' of transition rate $q_{j,j'}$ non-negatively. To satisfy the time-reversibility feature, we have designed a transition rate which can satisfy the equation which is written as follows:

$$q_j^* \cdot q_{j,j'} = q_{j'}^* \cdot q_{j',j}, \forall j, j' \in J, \tag{38}$$

The feasible solution's transition rate is represented as

$$q_{j,j'} = \vartheta \exp\left[-\frac{1}{2}\delta(U(j',\tau) - U(j,\tau))\right], \forall j, j' \in J \tag{39}$$

where ϑ is a positive constant. Transition rate $q_{j,j'}$ increases if weight gap $j' - j$ increases. It means that adopting a lower-weight solution has higher probability.

Algorithm 2 shows the algorithm based on Markov approximation which intends to solve problem $P2$. It can be executed on network platform. It can collect large amount of network state information to make real-time decisions. The algorithm combines in feasible solutions randomly to update time-reversible Markov sequential chain's state in update iterations. If $U_i(j^*, \tau)$ is minimized by a feasible solution j^*, it will be recorded and the algorithm explores the following combination in solutions until all combinations have been attempted.

6. Performance analysis

The algorithm combines Markov approximation and Lyapunov optimization and the performance of algorithm is analyzed theoretically.

6.1 Time complexity analysis

The introduced algorithm includes two algorithms (algorithms 1 and 2) mainly. In algorithm 1, Lyapunov optimization is used to resolve resource management, preprocessing method selection, and sampling rate adaption in dynamic environment. Therefore, algorithm 1 generates many feasible solutions. In solution update iteration, algorithm 2 records the optimal solution found up to now until it explores all feasible solutions. The Markov approximation algorithm converges with linear rate quickly, through adjusting appropriate parameters. Therefore, we can get the asymptotic optimal solution quickly. In the process of iteration, a solution is chosen by the system randomly for updating control information. Because long-term problem is decomposed into some instant subquestions by using Lyapunov optimization, we focus on solving approximate solutions' complexity. As we defined in Section III, Sampling rate adaptation has K feasible solutions at most, and preprocessing method has y feasible solutions at most. There are yK feasible solutions at most in set $U(j,\tau)$, because both are discrete. Each ES traverses all the solutions. Denote ρ as the ESs' average iteration number which aims to get the stationary Markov chain. Moreover, OSPRA algorithm's complexity of time can be represented as $O(Ky\rho)$.

6.2 Optimality analysis

Theorem 1.4 We set up coefficients δ and V, the optimality gap of initial problem's optimal solution and introduced algorithm's approximate solution theoretically is written as follows:

$$\sum_{\tau=0}^{T-1} \mathbb{E}[E_i(\tau)|\Theta(\tau)] \le p^* + B/V + \log|J|/(\delta V), \tag{40}$$

where p^* means the optimal solution theoretically.

Proof: Since executing drift-penalty algorithm can get accuracy strategies $H_i(\tau)$ and time delay $A_i(\tau)$ in time slot τ, we presume that accuracy actions $H_i^*(\tau)$ and time delay $A_i^*(\tau)$ are in the best decision.

Based on Theorem 1.1, the both sides' expectations can be represented as

$$\begin{aligned}
&\Delta_V(\Theta(\tau)) = \Delta(\Theta(\tau)) + V \cdot \mathbb{E}[E_i(\tau)|\Theta(\tau)] \\
&\le B + \mathbb{E}\sum_{i=1}^{N}\{Q_i(\tau)\left[A_i^{th} - A_i^*(\tau)\right] + M_i(\tau)\left[H_i^*(\tau) - H_i^{th}\right]\Theta(\tau)\} + V \cdot \mathbb{E}\left[E_i^*(\tau)|\Theta(\tau)\right] \\
&\le B + V \cdot p^*.
\end{aligned} \tag{41}$$

Then, by getting the summation of above derivation (41), we get

$$\begin{aligned}
(B + V \cdot p^*) \cdot T &\ge \sum_{\tau=0}^{T-1}\mathbb{E}[\Delta_V(\Theta(\tau))|\Theta(\tau)] \\
&= \mathbb{E}[L(\Theta(\tau))] + V \cdot \sum_{\tau=0}^{T-1}\mathbb{E}[E_i(\tau)|\Theta(\tau)] - \mathbb{E}[L(\Theta(0))].
\end{aligned} \tag{42}$$

Finally, we move $\mathbb{E}[L(\Theta(0))$ to the inequality's left side, and divide two sides by V. Since $\mathbb{E}[L(\Theta(0)) \ge 0$, we can find Theorem 1.4's conclusion.

From Theorem 1.4, if V(the control parameter) is sufficiently large, the algorithm can obtain the approximate solution which reaches the optimal solution p^* infinitely.

7. Simulation results

We carry on simulations to evaluate the proposed online algorithm's performance on joint preprocessing method selection, sampling rate adaption, and resource management in IIoT systems with the support of edge-cloud collaboration. Particularly, we show the performance of energy consumption, service delay, and processing accuracy, respectively.

7.1 Simulation setup

We setup an IIoT system with edge-cloud collaboration which has a remote CC and multiple distributed ESs on site. For example, in bearing vibration fault monitoring applications, each ES connects to 10 IIoT devices and is used to collect mechanical equipments's data of bearing vibration. Then, by one of the three preprocessing methods, the raw data can be preprocessed (which are WT [19], BiNOSP [20], CLPM [10]) and are offloaded to CC for further data analysis. We define that there are three candidate sampling rates for IIoT devices, which are initial sampling rates 33, 66, and 100%, and set the initial sampling rate φ_K=18 kHz [5]. Referring to [5], 0.59, 0.73, and 0.884 are respectively the three sampling rates' corresponding processing accuracies (**Table 2**).

Besides, we simulate the following benchmarks for comparison, aiming to show the advantage of the OSPRA algorithm.

Parameter	Value	Parameter	Value
$\lambda_{i,n}^{\tau}$	[0.5, 1] data/s	N	10
φ_K	18 kHz	A_i^{th}	0.8
h_c	0.9	f_i^y	1.2, 1.7, 2.2G cycles/s
W	[5, 25] MHz	$g_y(y)$	1.3, 1.5, 1.7
f_c	2.8 G cycles/s	P_i^{ES}	500 mW
m_y	[0.7, 0.95]	β_i, ε_c	550, 1200 cycles/bit
z_i^{ES}, z_c	10^{-7}, 10^{-27}	N_0	−174 dBm/Hz

Table 2.
Simulation parameters.

- **Accuracy-Guaranteed Resource Management Algorithm (AGRMA):** It does not preprocess data at edge servers and simply solves the joint sampling rate adaption, computing and communication resource allocation at the cloud. A deep reinforcement learning (DRL) method is used to address the random data arrival pattern and dynamic channel variation for guaranteeing long-term service accuracies [5].

- **Lagrangian-Based Offloading Scheduling Algorithm (LOSPA):** It applies the Lagrangian dual decomposition method in a definitive way to solve a resource

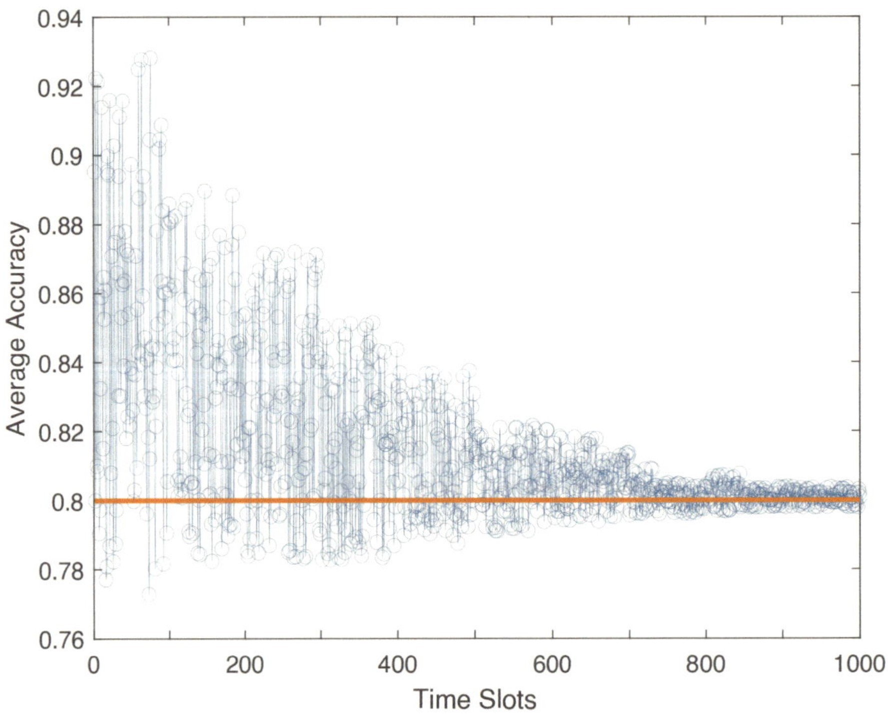

Figure 2.
Introduced algorithm's accuracy performance.

management problem and optimal offloading decision for an edge-cloud collaboration framework. However, it ignores the network uncertainties [21].

7.2 Performance evaluation

Here, we consider the computation tasks' average processing accuracy in ESs over a long run, and illustrate the algorithm's convergence performance in **Figure 2**. This figure shows that the initial average accuracy maintains in a high level, as the initial accuracy value is initially defined as zero. Furthermore, since the obtainable communication and computation resources are sufficient at the beginning, this algorithm tends to increase the average accuracy to the target value very rapidly. Moreover, despite the fluctuations, the computation tasks' average accuracy converges to the target value quickly after some time slots. Therefore, it can be concluded that the algorithm's stability is verified by the simulation.

Considering that the arrival rate of the end terminal's data traffic is an uncontrolled environmental variable while it directly affects each computation task's size, the impact of various data arrival rate on the final data processing accuracy can significantly affect the adaptability of OSPRA in such complicated and noisy environments. **Figure 3** demonstrates the box-plot distribution of the data processing accuracy under different rates of data arrivals. By increasing this rate, the distribution range of the accuracy only fluctuates very slightly. In particular, it shows that the maximum probability of error is smaller than 0.7. Moreover, the average value of the processing

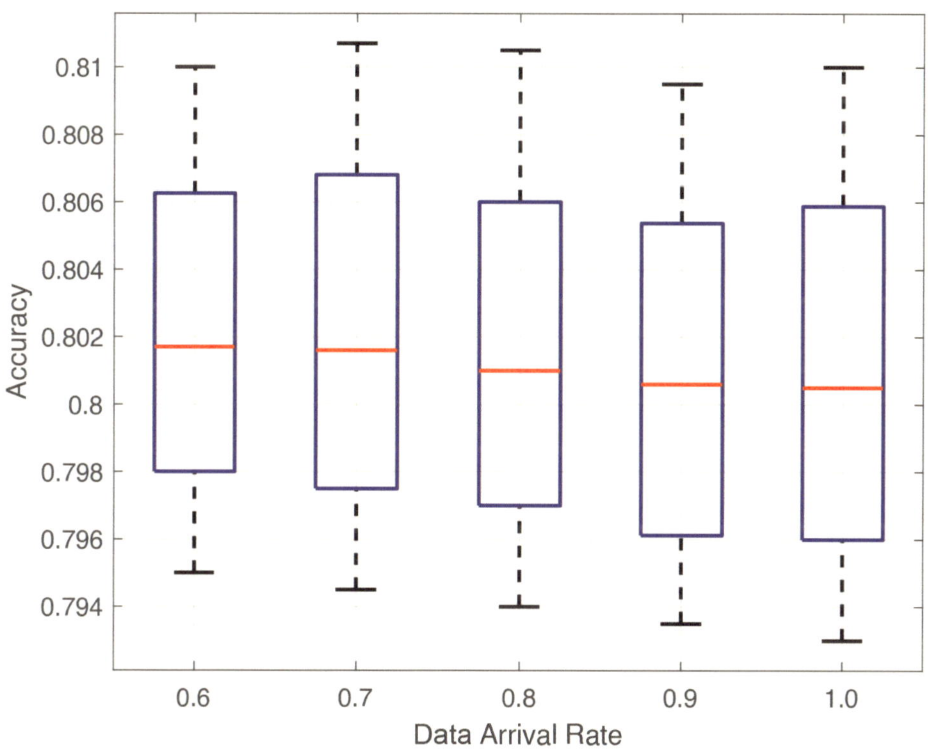

Figure 3.
Introduced algorithm's accuracy performance in terms of data arrival rates.

accuracy can be well controlled within a restricted range between 0.8 and 0.802, which indicates a good robustness of the proposed OSPRA to the instantaneous variations of the task size.

The average energy consumption of the proposed algorithm with various accuracy requirements is shown in **Figure 4**. It can be observed that if the accuracy requirement improves, the system has to in turn increase the sampling rate or choose a superior denoising performance in edge preprocessing method. As a result, the average energy consumption increases. LOSPA algorithm overlooks network uncertainties, so that the average energy consumption reduces smoothly. Changing processing accuracy does not have decisive performance impact. Oppositely, the average energy consumption increases for both OSPRA and AGRMA algorithms. However, in terms of minimizing the energy consumption, the proposed OSPRA obviously performs better. The reason is that AGRMA does not choose to preprocess at ESs, so that the sampling rate must increase when accuracy requirements increase. Oppositely, OSPRA can reach a trade-off between the preprocessing method selection and sampling rate, and therefore it can decrease the energy consumption and satisfy the accuracy requirements concurrently.

Figure 5 evaluates the energy consumption of the overall system with the increase of the Lyapunov control parameter V for different algorithms. When $V \leq 50$, the average energy consumption rapidly reduces as V increases. When $V \geq 100$, the average energy consumption prefers to be stable, because computing resources and channel capacity have an upper limit. The asymptotic optimality of the proposed algorithm can be seen as there exists a bounded deviation between the proposed algorithm's

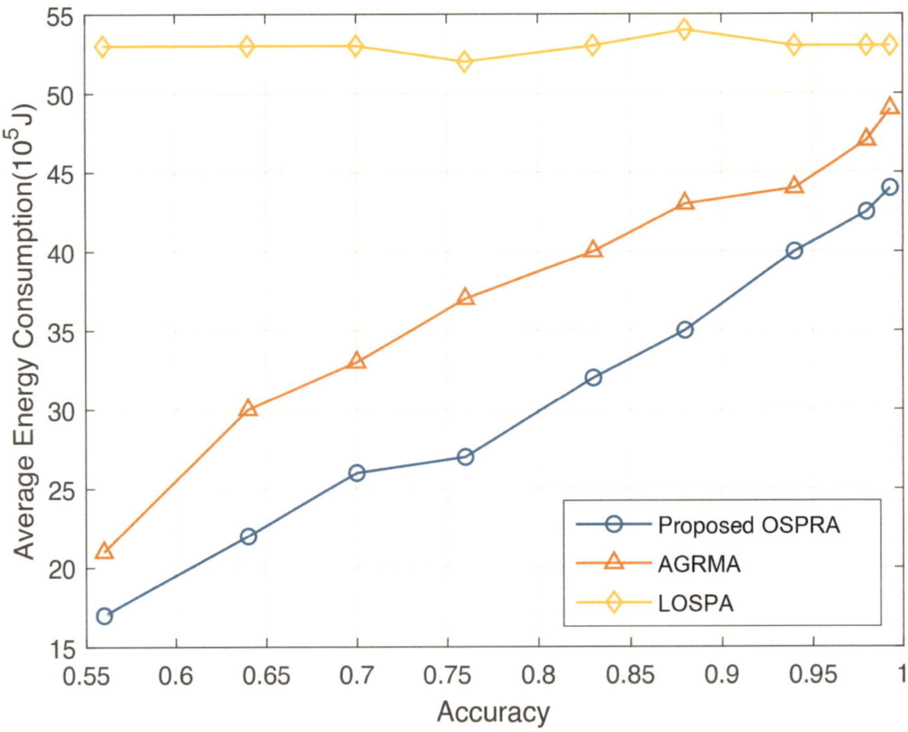

Figure 4.
Introduced algorithm's average energy consumption in terms of different accuracy requirements.

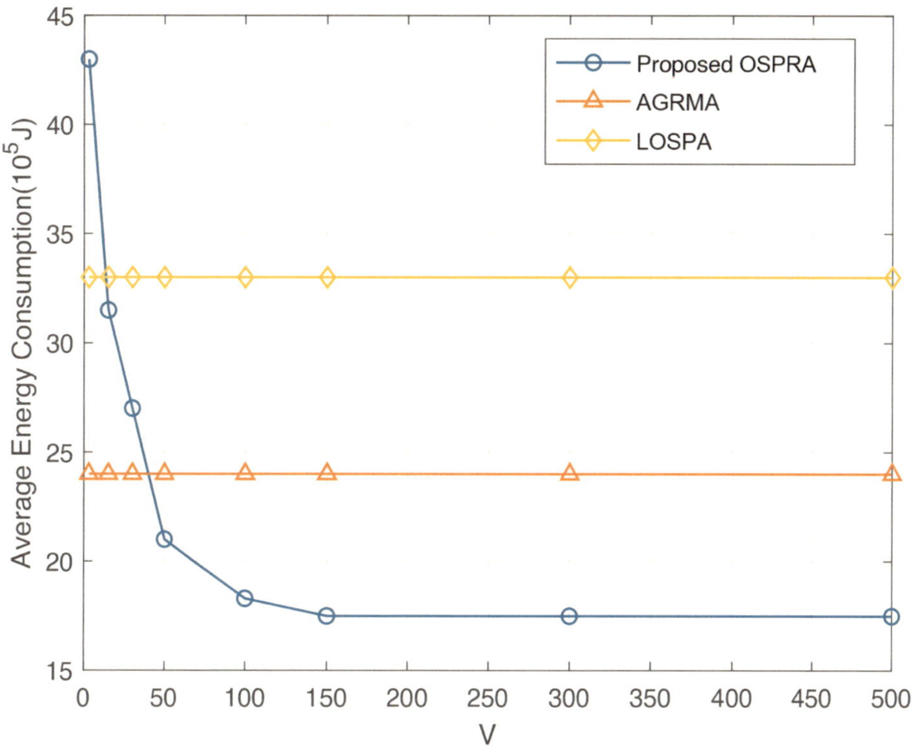

Figure 5.
Average energy with different parameter V.

average energy consumption and the optimal one, which numerically verifies Theorems 1.1 and 1.3. Besides, in this figure, we can find that the proposed OSPRA can control parameter V for adjusting the energy consumption weights of different users. That is to say, it guides us to select the parameter V according to various application requirements. It is worth noting that although we also draw the other two benchmark schemes' performances for comparison, both of them are independent of the control parameter V.

8. Conclusion

In this chapter, we have investigated a joint optimization problem of preprocessing method selection, sampling rate adaptation, and computing and communication resource allocation for IIoT systems with edge-cloud collaboration. With the objective of minimizing the energy consumption of the whole system while guaranteeing all applications' long-term service delay and data processing accuracy, a novel algorithm, called OSPRA, has been proposed. It has been proved that this proposed algorithm can solve the formulated problem in a dynamic way under network uncertainties. In addition, the feasibility and superiority of OSPRA have also been verified by extensive theoretical analysis and simulations.

Author details

You Shi[1], Yuye Yang[1], Changyan Yi[1], Bing Chen[1] and Jun Cai[2*]

1 Institution No. 1, The College of Computer Science and Technology, Nanjing University of Aeronautics and Astronautics (NUAA), Nanjing, China

2 Institution No. 2, The Department of Electrical and Computer Engineering, Concordia University, Montréal, Canada

*Address all correspondence to: jun.cai@concordia.ca

References

[1] Mach P, Becvar Z. Mobile edge computing: A survey on architecture and computation offloading. IEEE Communications Surveys & Tutorials. 2017;**19**(3):1628-1656

[2] Yi C, Cai J. A queueing game based management framework for fog computing with strategic computing speed control. IEEE Transactions on Mobile Computing. 2022;**21**(5):1537-1551

[3] Yi C, Cai J, Su Z. A multi-user mobile computation offloading and transmission scheduling mechanism for delay-sensitive applications. IEEE Transactions on Mobile Computing. 2019;**19**(1):29-43

[4] Yi C, Cai J. A truthful mechanism for scheduling delay-constrained wireless transmissions in IoT-based healthcare networks. IEEE Transactions on Wireless Communications. 2018;**18**(2): 912-925

[5] Wu W, Yang P, Zhang W, Zhou C, Shen S. Accuracy-guaranteed collaborative dnn inference in industrial IoT via deep reinforcement learning. IEEE Transactions on Industrial Informatics. 2020;**17**(7):4988-4998

[6] Yamaguchi M, Maruta K, Ono H. Operating mechanism for RF electromagnetic noise suppression sheets. IEEE Transactions on Magnetics. 2005;**41**(10):3565-3567

[7] Wang T, Ke H, Zheng X, Wang K, Liu A. Big data cleaning based on mobile edge computing in industrial sensor-cloud. IEEE Transactions on Industrial Informatics. 2019;**16**(2):1321-1329

[8] Mao W, Zhao Z, Chang Z, Min G, Gao W. Energy efficient industrial internet of things: Overview and open issues. IEEE Transactions on Industrial Informatics. 2021;**PP**(99):1-1

[9] Hariharakrishnan J, Mohanavalli S, Srividya, Kumar K. Survey of pre-processing techniques for mining big data. In: 2017 International Conference on Computer, Communication and Signal Processing (ICCCSP). Chennai, India: IEEE; 2017. pp. 1-5. https://ieeexplore.ieee.org/author/37086002878

[10] Rui L, Zhu Y, Gao Z, Qiu X. CLPM: A cooperative link prediction model for industrial internet of things using partitioned stacked denoising autoencoder. IEEE Transactions on Industrial Informatics. 2020;**17**(5): 3620-3629

[11] Guo K, Gao R, Xia W, Quek T. Online learning based computation offloading in MEC systems with communication and computation dynamics. IEEE Transactions on Communications. 2020;**69**(2): 1147-1162

[12] Zhang X, Mao Y, Zhang J, Letaief KB. Multi-objective resource allocation for mobile edge computing systems. In: 2017 IEEE 28th Annual International Symposium on Personal, Indoor, and Mobile Radio Communications (PIMRC). Montreal, Canada: PIMRC; 2017. pp. 1-5

[13] Lin R, Zhou Z, Luo S, Xiao Y, Zukerman M. Distributed optimization for computation offloading in edge computing. IEEE Transactions on Wireless Communications. 2020;**19**(12): 8179-8194

[14] Mao S, Leng S, Maharjan S, Zhang Y. Energy efficiency and delay tradeoff for wireless powered mobile-edge

computing systems with multi-access schemes. IEEE Transactions on Wireless Communications. 2019;**19**(3): 1855-1867

[15] Neely MJ. Stochastic network optimization with application to communication and queueing systems. Synthesis Lectures on Communication Networks. 2010;**3**(1):1-211

[16] Pisinger D. Where are the hard knapsack problems? Computers & Operations Research. 2005;**32**(9): 2271-2284

[17] Boyd S, Vandenberghe L. Convex Optimization. UK: Cambridge University Press; 2004

[18] Chen M, Liew SC, Shao Z, Kai C. Markov approximation for combinatorial network optimization. IEEE Transactions on Information Theory. 2013;**59**(10):6301-6327

[19] Xie ZJ, Song BY, Zhang Y, Zhang F. Application of an improved wavelet threshold denoising method for vibration signal processing. Advanced Materials Research. 2014;**889-890**: 799-806

[20] Zhang H, Chen X, Zhang X, Zhang X. A bi-level nested sparse optimization for adaptive mechanical fault feature detection. IEEE Access. 2020;**8**:19 767-19 782

[21] Kuang Z, Li L, Gao J, Zhao L, Liu A. Partial offloading scheduling and power allocation for mobile edge computing systems. IEEE Internet of Things Journal. 2019;**6**(4):6774-6785

SpringerBriefs in Complexity

Springer Complexity

Springer Complexity is an interdisciplinary program publishing the best research and academic-level teaching on both fundamental and applied aspects of complex systems—cutting across all traditional disciplines of the natural and life sciences, engineering, economics, medicine, neuroscience, social and computer science.

Complex Systems are systems that comprise many interacting parts with the ability to generate a new quality of macroscopic collective behavior the manifestations of which are the spontaneous formation of distinctive temporal, spatial or functional structures. Models of such systems can be successfully mapped onto quite diverse "real-life" situations like the climate, the coherent emission of light from lasers, chemical reaction-diffusion systems, biological cellular networks, the dynamics of stock markets and of the internet, earthquake statistics and prediction, freeway traffic, the human brain, or the formation of opinions in social systems, to name just some of the popular applications.

Although their scope and methodologies overlap somewhat, one can distinguish the following main concepts and tools: self-organization, nonlinear dynamics, synergetics, turbulence, dynamical systems, catastrophes, instabilities, stochastic processes, chaos, graphs and networks, cellular automata, adaptive systems, genetic algorithms and computational intelligence.

The three major book publication platforms of the Springer Complexity program are the monograph series "Understanding Complex Systems" focusing on the various applications of complexity, the "Springer Series in Synergetics", which is devoted to the quantitative theoretical and methodological foundations, and the "SpringerBriefs in Complexity" which are concise and topical working reports, case-studies, surveys, essays and lecture notes of relevance to the field. In addition to the books in these two core series, the program also incorporates individual titles ranging from textbooks to major reference works.

More information about this series at http://www.springer.com/series/8907

SPRINGER BRIEFS IN COMPLEXITY

Hermann Haken
Juval Portugali

Information Adaptation: The Interplay Between Shannon Information and Semantic Information in Cognition

Springer

Hermann Haken · Juval Portugali

Information Adaptation: The Interplay Between Shannon Information and Semantic Information in Cognition

Springer

Hermann Haken
Institute for Theoretical Physics
Center of Synergetics
University of Stuttgart
Stuttgart
Germany

Juval Portugali
Department of Geography
and the Human Environment
Tel Aviv University
Tel Aviv
Israel

ISSN 2191-5326 ISSN 2191-5334 (electronic)
ISBN 978-3-319-11169-8 ISBN 978-3-319-11170-4 (eBook)
DOI 10.1007/978-3-319-11170-4

Library of Congress Control Number: 2014948770

Springer Cham Heidelberg New York Dordrecht London

Printed on acid-free paper

Springer is part of Springer Science+Business Media (www.springer.com)

Prologue

Shannon's seminal information theory defines information as a quantity irrespective of the meaning it conveys. His theory was followed not only by studies that applied the theory to a variety of domains, but also by attempts to define notions of information with meaning, that is, *semantic information*. So far the two lines of thinking run in parallel; in that, they do not discuss the possible interaction between Shannon's and semantic notions of information. One exception was the chapter by Warren Weaver—Shannon's co-author in their seminal book from 1949: *The Mathematical Theory of Communication*. In that chapter, Weaver laid the foundations for incorporating semantic information within the overall framework of Shannon's theory of communication. Weaver's initiative was not followed, however.

Here, in this monograph, we follow Weaver's footsteps and show that Shannon's information acts as driving force for the formation of semantic information; and vice versa too, namely, that semantic information participates in the formation of Shannonian information. We further show that in cognition, Shannonian and semantic information are interrelated as two aspects of a cognitive process we term *information adaptation*. In the latter, the mind/brain adapts to the environment by the deflating and/or inflating of the information conveyed by the environment. In the process of information adaptation, quantitative variations in Shannon's information entail different meanings while different meanings affect the quantity of information. We illustrate the above conceptually and mathematically by reference to three cognitive processes: pattern recognition, face learning, and the recognition of a moving object.

We can trace the origin of this study to our collaborative paper some two decades ago (Haken and Portugali 1996) that introduced the notion of synergetic inter-representation networks (SIRN). The latter suggests that several cognitive processes that cannot be performed by a single cognitive act evolve as a sequential ongoing interaction between internal representations constructed in the mind/brain and external representations constructed in the world. In the above noted paper, the focus was mainly on cognitive mapping with some preliminary applications to collective cognitive processes; in subsequent studies (Haken 1996; Portugali 2000,

2002, 2011, 2014), the notion of SIRN was applied to art, human communication in general, urban dynamics, city planning, and design.

While the notion of SIRN added important insight to various cognitive phenomena, it still left us with a dilemma: how and by what means, do, internal and external representations interact? Inspired by Haken's (1998/2006) book *Information and Self-Organization*, our principle answer to this question was that internal and external representations interact by means of two forms of information they convey: the quantitative Shannonian information and the qualitative semantic information. This answer paved the way to our study (Haken and Portugali 2003), which started by applying information theory to "The face of the city …". In this study we showed, firstly, that different urban elements (buildings, roads, parks, etc., of various forms and uses) convey different quantities of information that can be measured by means of Shannon's bits. Secondly, that urban elements covey different meanings, (i.e., semantic information) to different urban agents (i.e., different receivers). But here came a somewhat surprising finding, namely, that "semantic information enters in disguise": We have realized that in order to determine the Shannonian quantities of urban elements, some kind of grouping is required. For example, grouping of buildings according to their architectural style, size, function, or combination thereof; or of roads according to their topology and so on; and grouping implies meaning. In other words, meaningful semantic information is a prerequisite to the determination of the Shannonian information bits of the various urban elements. This latter finding motivated us to dig deeper into the relations between Shannonian and semantic information. The outcome of this intellectual archaeological excavation is the present monograph with its notion of information adaptation.

Acknowledgments

We thank Mrs. Monika Bund and Mrs. Karin Hahn for their valuable assistance in the preparation of our manuscript, and Dr. Tomas Ditzinger of Springer Company for the excellent cooperation. We thank also Dr. Orna Zafrir-Reuven and Mr. Egbert Stolk for nicely drawing some of the figures.

Contents

Introduction

"Frequently", writes Shannon (1948, 1):

> the messages have meaning; that is, they refer to or are correlated according to some system with certain physical or conceptual entities. These semantic aspects of communication are irrelevant to the engineering problem. …

Shannon's notion of information was originally developed as means to measure the *channel capacity* of a communication system, when "channel capacity" is interpreted also as a measure of *choice*, *uncertainty*, *entropy* and *lack of knowledge* (Shannon 1948). The universal applicability of Shannon's notion of information, however, rests on Shannon's proof that it can be applied irrespective of meaning—"the semantic aspects of communication." As recently noted by Gleick (2011) and as we further discuss in Sect. 1.2 below, the appearance of Shannon's theory triggered some heated discussions regarding the absence of meaning in a theory of information. However, very soon two streams of studies could be observed: (1) Attempts to apply the theory to a variety of domains, ranging from engineering to psychology. (2) Attempts to develop notions of information with meaning, that is, *semantic information*. The above two streams run in parallel in the sense that they do not discuss the possible interaction between Shannonian and semantic information, namely, the extent to which variations in channel capacity, uncertainty, lack of knowledge, or entropy might entail different meanings and the extent to which meaning might affect channel capacity, choice, uncertainty, lack of knowledge, or entropy. This study attempts to show how such an interplay comes into existence in cognition by a process we term *information adaptation*. In the latter, the information conveyed by the environment entails a circular process: On one hand, the interaction between the incoming environmental data and the (task dependent) semantic information constructed by the mind-brain-body (MBB) gives rise to Shannon information in quantities *adapted* to the information processing capabilities of the MBB. On the other hand, however, quantitative variations (inflation or deflation) of Shannonian information give rise to different meanings (i.e., semantic information) that then determine the Shannonian channel capacity, uncertainty, lack of knowledge, or entropy, and so on in circular causality. We illustrate the above interplay between Shannonian and semantic information and the resultant information adaptation by reference to the processes of pattern recognition of static and moving objects and of pattern learning. We also indicate in brief how information adaptation participates in shaping the urban landscape.

The Structure of the Book

We develop our arguments in the following order: In Chap. 1, we introduce Shannon's theory of information, the attempts to define semantic information and the ways the two were applied to cognition. In Chap. 2, we clarify the relations between information and data, while in the next three chapters we lay the foundations for the notion of information adaptation: In Chap. 3. the empirical foundations, in Chap. 4 the theoretical foundations as derived from complexity theory, while in Chap. 5 the methodological foundations related as they are to notions of (conceptual) machines. Chap. 6 introduces the synergetic approach to pattern recognition as our basic paradigm in developing the notion of information adaptation, while Chap. 7 shows in details how, by means of the synergetic computer, the general principles of information adaptation developed in the foregoing chapters provide the basis for algorithms that can eventually be implemented on machines. Finally, Chap. 8 provides some further applications of information adaptation. We conclude the book with a short discussion regarding the main properties of information adaptation and their future potential.

Chapter 1
Shannonian Versus Semantic Information and Cognition

1.1 Shannonian Information

This is a well-known and widely used concept. We use the concepts of probability theory. Let us distinguish the different outcomes of "experiments" by an index k, e.g. when throwing a die its index k will distinguish between the numbers of eyes $k = 1, 2 \ldots, 6$ or when we read a text the different letters of an alphabet are distinguished by an index k. Now consider a series of experiments (including reading a text or sending a message), then the total number of experiments is N whereas the number with which a specific event with index k is occurring is given by N_k. Then

$$p_k = \frac{N_k}{N} \tag{1.1}$$

denotes the relative frequency of the occurrence of k. In a somewhat different interpretation p_k is interpreted as the probability for the occurrence of the event k. We assume as usual the normalization condition

$$\sum_k p_k = 1. \tag{1.2}$$

The Shannon entropy i is then defined by

$$i = -c \sum_k p_k \ln p_k \tag{1.3}$$

where the constant c must be chosen in such a way that in the case of two possible outcomes, e.g. $k = 1$ or 2, or "yes" or "no", etc. the information i just becomes 1 bit. In order to facilitate the notation we will drop the constant c in the following.

H. Haken and J. Portugali, *Information Adaptation: The Interplay Between Shannon Information and Semantic Information in Cognition*,
SpringerBriefs in Complexity, DOI 10.1007/978-3-319-11170-4_1

1.2 Semantic Information

The main reference to most studies on information theory is Shannon and Weaver's (1949) book *The Mathematical Theory of Communication*. Its publication, writes Gleick, (2011, p. 248), has left several people uncomfortable with a notion of information without meaning. Gleick quotes von Foerster who suggested calling Shannon's information theory "*signal theory*"

> ... because information was not yet there. There were '*beep beeps*' but that was all, no information. The moment one transforms that set of signals into other signals our brain can make an understanding of, *then* information is born—it is not in the beeps (ibid).

Such a reaction, as we'll immediately see, was like 'preaching to the converted'. In a short one page introduction to their book Shannon and Weaver indicate that this is a collaborative work in the sense that it is composed of two previously published papers: One is Shannon's paper from 1948 that appeared in *Bell System Technical Journal* and the other is an extended version of Weaver's (1949) paper that first appeared in *Scientific American*. Weaver's paper, which the authors recommend that it "may well be read first", gives a "panoramic view of the field" and "includes ideas [...] for broader application". These ideas refer to the possibility of incorporating semantic information within the overall framework of Shannon's theory of communication. "Relative to the broad subject of communication", writes Weaver (Shannon and Weaver 1949, p. 4), "there seem to be problems at three levels. Thus it seems reasonable to ask, serially:

Level A. How accurately can the symbols of communication be transmitted? (The technical problem.)
Level B. How precisely do the transmitted symbols convey the desired meaning? (The semantic problem.)
Level C. How effectively does the received meaning affect conduct in the desired way? (The effectiveness problem.)"

Weaver then suggests that "the theory of Level A is, at least to a significant degree, also a theory of levels B and C" and "that one's final conclusion may be that the separation into the three levels is really artificial and undesirable" (Shannon and Weaver 1949, p. 25). It is the generality of Shannon's theory at Level A, writes Weaver, that makes it applicable to all kind of symbols ("spoken words, or symphonic music, or pictures") as well as to Levels B and C. Note that the above relations between Levels A, B and C reminds one of the relations between syntax, semantics and pragmatics in linguistics and computer science. The fact that Shannon and Weaver decided to co-author (and not to edit) their book indicates that Weaver accepts Shannon's theory and that Shannon approves of Weaver's interpretation and suggestions.

In philosophy, following Shannon's theory, Bar-Hillel and Carnap (1953, pp. 147–148) suggested "An Outline of a Theory of Semantic Information" that "will serve as a better approximation for some future explanation of a psychological concept of information than the concept dealt with in communication theory" (ibid. 148). The need for such a theory followed their observation that "impatient scientists" applied Shannon's theory "to fields in which the term 'information' was used, pre-systematically, in a semantic sense, …" (ibid. 147). Subsequent studies on semantic information, mainly in philosophy (Floridi 2011, Fig. 1), centered on distinctions between instructional vs. factual information, which further was categorized into true and untrue information, further divided into intentional (disinformation) and unintentional (misinformation). As Floridi (ibid) writes, while in the past there have been attempts "to elaborate information theories *alternative* to" Shannon's, nowadays "few … follow these lines of research. The majority agrees that Shannon's theory "provides a rigorous constraint to any further theorising on all the semantic and pragmatic aspects of information."

The above "Weaver's optimistic interpretation of Shannon's work", as Floridi (ibid) refers to it, was thus not followed. The more common view today is to consider the relevance of Shannon's theory of communication to semantic information as a *weak constraint*—"as tennis is constrained by Newtonian physics, that is in the most uninteresting, inconsequential and hence disregardable sense" (Floridi, ibid).

The result as noted is two streams of studies: one that elaborates on Shannonian information and another, in philosophy, on semantic information with no or very little discussion regarding the possible interaction between the two.

1.3 Applications to Cognition

Shannon's theory was applied to cognition in several studies. Probably the most well known application is Miller's (1956) "The magic number seven, plus or minus two: some limits on our capacity for processing information". As the titles indicates, it pointed out that short-term memory is constrained in its capability to process one-dimensional information to about 2.5 bits of Shannonian information (Fig. 1.1). In a similar way, psychologist Jacobson showed that the information capacity of the human ear (Jacobson 1950) and eye (Jacobson 1951) can be quantified using Shannon's bits.

A second famous line of applications was initiated by psychologists Attneave (1954): Following Shannon's theory and in particular his paper on information and redundancy (Shannon 1951), Attneave suggested that visual perceptual information is highly redundant and as a consequence an important task of the process of perception is to reduce redundancy by "encode incoming information in a form more economical than that in which it impinges on the receptors". His most famous example for this is 'the sleeping cat' (Fig. 1.2). Attneave's view was supported and extended by Watanabe (1960), arguing that redundancy is important in inference and inductive reasoning and by Barlow (1961) who emphasized the significance of redundancy in neuro-physiological mechanisms of sensation and perception.

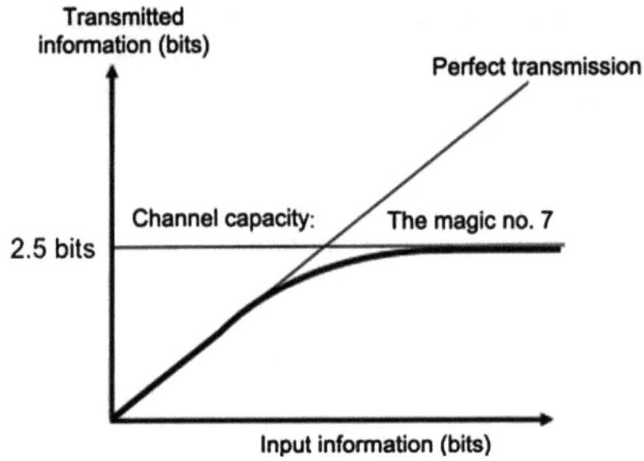

Fig. 1.1 The relations between input information and transmitted information according to Miller (1956): up to about 2.5 bits of information there is perfect transmission; beyond that threshold, transmitted information levels off

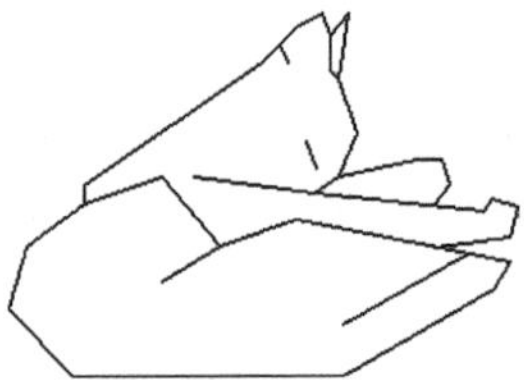

Fig. 1.2 Attneave's sleeping cat: "Drawing made by abstracting 38 points of maximum curvature from the contours of a sleeping cat, and connecting these points appropriately with a straightedge" (Attneave ibid Fig. 3)

However, in a more recent paper, and in light of mounting evidence, Barlow (2001) has changed his view on the information reduction issue suggesting that while Attneave and himself were "right in drawing attention to the importance of redundancy in sensory messages because this can often lead to crucially important knowledge of the environment" they were "wrong in emphasizing the main technical use for redundancy, which is compressive coding."

Attneave's studies were followed by applications of Shannon's theory to Gestalt psychology with the attempt to quantify the notion of 'figural goodness' (Attneave 1959). These studies have shown, first, that 'good Gestalts' are redundant, containing little information (that is, little uncertainty). Second, that "information is a function not of what the stimulus is, but rather of what it might have been" (Garner 1974, p. 194, quoted in Zabrodsky and Algom 1994, p. 463). This, according to Zabrodsky and Algom (1994) is the major contribution of information theory to psychology. It means that in perceiving a shape, one perceives not only the observed form, but also the potential or extra/alternative information enfolded in it.

The above applications of Shannonian information to cognition thus demonstrate that several technical-syntactic properties of various cognitive phenomena can be quantified by means of Shannon's information bits. They do not discuss the relations between these syntactic properties of cognition and semantic cognitive processes and the implications thereof to the use of information theory in the context of cognition. The same applies to the philosophical discussions on semantic information (Sect. 1.2)—they too had no influence on cognitive science. Neither was there an attempt to elaborate a cognitive science view on semantic information, nor was there an attempt to follow Weaver's (ibid) suggestion that Shannon's theory "is, at least to a significant degree, also a theory of" semantic information. This, despite the fact that the 'information processing approach' played a central role in the development of cognitive science, that cognition involves meaning, and that semantic memory is central to several cognitive processes. One exception is our above noted paper (Haken and Portugali, ibid).

Our own study "The face of the city is its information" starts in line with the above application by showing, in the first part of the paper, that different visible elements in the face of a city convey different amounts of information that can be quantified by means of Shannon's information bits (Haken and Portugali 2003). For example, when all buildings or roads of a city are identical to each other (Fig. 1.3 top) the Shanninian information they convey is very low; if they are all different (Fig. 1.3, 2nd line), information is very high and so on, as specified in Fig. 1.3. From the latter follows the "informational importance" of towers, piazzas, boulevards and other urban elements in making a city "legible"—as Lynch (1960, pp. 2–3) has termed the 'ease with which parts of a city can be recognized'.

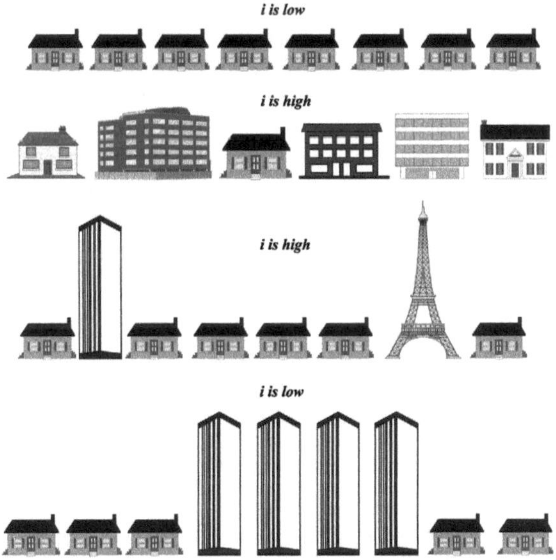

Fig. 1.3 Different configurations of buildings convey different quantities of Shannonian information: When all buildings of a city are identical to each other (*top*), the Shanninian information they convey is low; if they are all different (*2nd line*), information is very high; if high buildings are added to identical buildings (*3rd line*), information goes up; if the high buildings are spatially grouped, (*4th line*) information is low, and so on

1.4 Semantic Information Enters in Disguise

The second part of our paper (Haken and Portugali, ibid, Sect. 6.1) departs from the above applications of Shannonian information to cognition. It demonstrates that in the applications of Shannonian information to cognition "semantic information enters in disguise [...]. via the choice of the indices ... to which, implicitly, a specific meaning is attached" [e.g. indices k in Eq. (1.3) above]. A case in point is Fig. 1.4 that we have devised in the past to illustrate the above noted "figurative goodness" (Haken and Portugali 2003, Fig. 6): The pattern in Fig. 1.4, left, is taken from Solo (1994, Fig. 5.8) who introduced this pattern as an example for the effect of top-down processing in perceiving geometrical figures. We've added to it the pattern in Fig. 1.4, right, in which instead of triangles we drew circular dots. Due to collective effects, the pattern of triangles (Fig. 1.4, left) can be perceived in three different ways, i.e. it can be given three different meanings: all triangles pointing E, NW, or SW. Its Shannonian information is thus about 1.5 bits. In terms of complexity theory the perception of this pattern fluctuates between three attractors. On the other hand, however, the pattern of dots (Fig. 1.4 right) can be perceived in one way only; in other words, it can be given one meaning only. Its Shannonian information is thus zero bits. Figure 1.4 thus sheds light on the way "semantics enters in disguise", as well as on the way our pre-knowledge (or bias) enters the process.

Figure 1.4 sheds light also on the tendency of the human brain to give meaning to patterns. Thus, when Fig. 1.4 right is shown to people for the first time, the common response is that this is a structure-less pattern of dots. But when Fig. 1.4 left is shown to people for the first time, there are three typical responses: for some the first impression is a structure-less image; others see all the triangles pointing to the right, while still others to NW (very few have observed in the first glance the SW direction). But then, when the attention of the people was drawn to the other possibilities, they easily recognize the three structures enfolded in this figure.

The above findings can be further related to the work of visual neuroscientist and experimental psychologist Béla Julesz (1971/2006). Julesz constructed pairs of random dot patterns (stereograms) in which corresponding dots where in a precisely calculated way slightly shifted against each other so to take care of optical disparity which is the basis of *depth* perception (Fig. 1.5). When looking with only one eye, one perceives a completely *structure-less* ensemble of dots. However, if the left eye

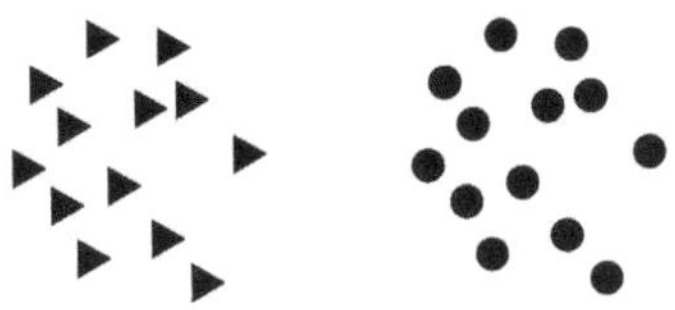

Fig. 1.4 *Left* A pattern of triangles that due to collective effects can be perceived in three different ways (E, NW, SW); in the language of complexity this pattern is dominated by three attractors. *Right* A pattern of circles that can be perceived in one way only

Fig. 1.5 A Julesz random dot stereogram. By putting a sheet of paper between the two stereograms, perpendicular to this figure, a square floating above a background will be recognized. The square on the right is the disparity map. *Source* Haken (1996), Fig. 16.29

glances at the left image and the right eye at the right image, after a few seconds a well-defined structure, e.g. a spiral is perceived. Generally speaking, our brain aims, all the time, at giving meaning to images even if the cues are weak. Haken and Reimann (see Haken 1996, pp. 260–273, Figs. 16.29 and 16.40) have modeled this effect by means of the synergetic computer (which we introduce in some length in Chap. 5). Figure 1.6 top and bottom represent the results from the synergetic computer simulation of this process.

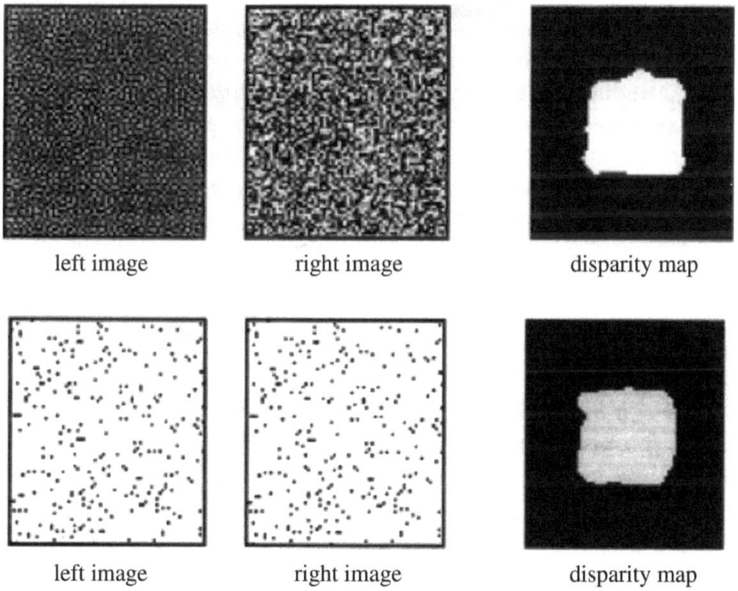

Fig. 1.6 Reimann and Haken's simulation of the Julesz recognition process using the synergetic computer model. *Top* The same, but with a differently coarse-grained random dot stereogram. *Bottom*, as above but with sparse random dots patterns. *Source* Haken 1996, Figs. 16.40, 16.41

Figurative goodness is a Gestalt psychologist's interpretation of Fig. 1.4. It means reduction of *complexity* or the subconscious search for *order*. But this interpretation raises a question: Where is the *original complexity* (which is then reduced)? A possible answer comes from a physicist's perspective. To see how let us start from a simpler picture than that of Fig. 1.4: While in Fig. 1.4, left, the triangles are perceived as pointing in *three* different directions, Fig. 1.7 shows an arrangement of elements with only two directions.

Such two-directional elements remind a physicist of *spins* (elementary magnets) arranged in a ferromagnet where two limiting cases are important: The *magnetic* states (*ordered*) as in Fig. 1.8 left or as in Fig. 1.8 right, with Shannon information $i = 1$ bits. This 2-directional example corresponds to the Gestalt psychologist's interpretation with respect to the triangles above (i is about 1.5 bits).

However, there is a totally different interpretation. The *nonmagnetic*, disordered state (above Curie temperature realized) as in Fig. 1.9 or any other random configuration. When there are N spins, Shannon information is

$$i = Log_2 2^N = N \text{ bits!}$$

This elaboration illustrates nicely both the way "semantics enters in disguise" and the way our pre-knowledge (or bias) enters the process; it also tells us 'where is the original complexity before being reduced'.

The mathematical expression for Shannon information is (beside a numerical factor, essentially Boltzmann's constant) identical with that for entropy in statistical mechanics, which forms the atomistic basis for the (phenomenological) thermodynamics. According to the latter, entropy is a *measurable* physical quantity. Thus, to be in accordance with measurements (or in other words, with physical reality), we *must* accept the "disorder" interpretation of entropy (or, equivalently, of information). Thus, we deal here with the mechanical ("syntactic") properties of the system, which is independent of meaning.

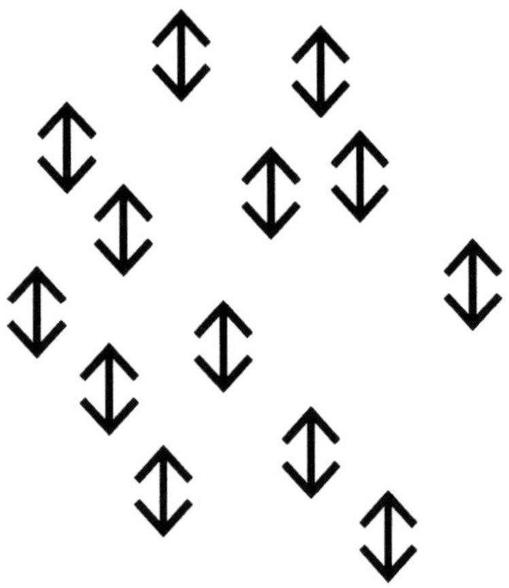

Fig. 1.7 An arrangement of elements pointing to two directions

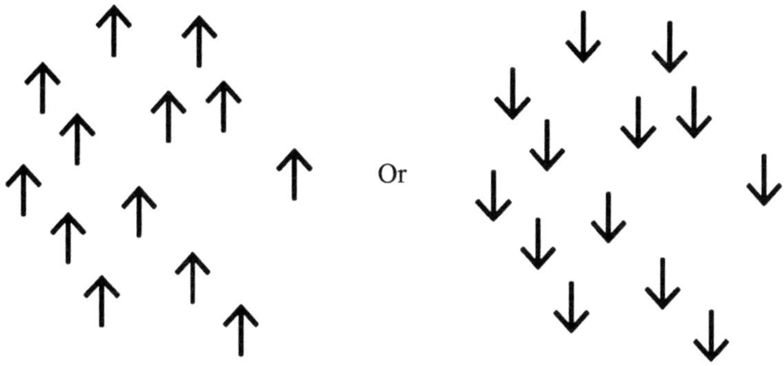

Fig. 1.8 Two states of *spins* arranged in a ferromagnet

Fig. 1.9 Random configuration

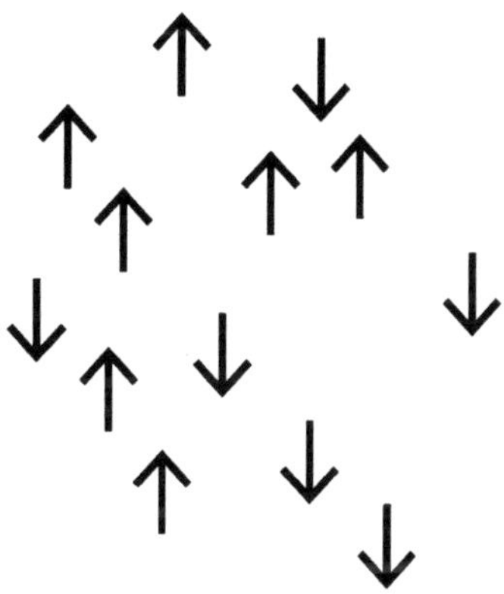

On the other hand, however, when it comes to cognition, semantic information is needed. That is, when we transfer our "insight" we have gained from the "spin" example to the "triangle" example we must say: In the disordered, structure-less case the directions of the N triangles are uncorrelated, so that there are 3^N possible arrangements (or possible interpretations) so that Shannon's

$$i \text{ about } N\, 1.5 \text{ bits}$$

When we recognize order, i.e. all triangles pointing to the same (but otherwise *unspecified*) direction

$$i \text{ about } 1.5 \text{ bits}$$

and when we "get stuck" on only one direction

$$i = 0 \text{ bits}$$

In both cases, $\mathrm{N} \to 1.5$ and $\mathrm{N} \to 0$, we thus deal with *complexity reduction*.

1.5 Toward Information Adaptation

Shannon was thus right in stressing that the "semantic aspects of communication are irrelevant to the engineering problem" but Weaver was also right is noting that Shannon's technical information theory "is, at least to a significant degree, also a theory of levels B and C", that is, of semantic information.

In the present study we go two steps further: We claim, firstly, that not only semantic considerations participate in the determination of Shannonian channel capacity (interpreted also as choice, uncertainty, lack of knowledge or entropy), but that several basic cognitive processes enable overcoming the "limits on our capacity for processing information" noted by Miller (ibid). That is, Miller showed that the "magic number 7" limits our information processing capacity but he also showed that the mind can overcome this innate limitation, for example, by increasing the dimensionality of the data, by re-arranging it in groups, "chunks" or a hierarchical structure; to which can be added: by processing it in a sequential order (Portugali 2002). In other words, by cognitive processes associated with semantics.

Secondly, we claim that Miller's is but a special case of a more general process we term *information adaptation*. In this process the mind-brain-body (MBB) adapts to changing environmental conditions and data by means of information inflation and or deflation (see definition below): Given a specific cognitive task in a specific environmental situation, if the incoming information is too low for the implementation of that task, the MBB adapts by inflating the information; if too high, it adapts by deflating the information. We exemplify this below in some details by reference to three cognitive processes—pattern recognition of stable and moving object and pattern learning. Each of these processes is associated with the generation of meaning, that is, of semantic information.

Chapter 2
Information Versus Data

2.1 General Discussion

Similarly to semantics, the relations between information and data are also counterintuitive and somewhat confusing: In the everyday usage the term 'information' is used interchangeably with 'data' and we tend to think that more data leads to more information; and yet, in the context of Shannon's information theory this is not necessarily the case. To see how, consider the Bull by Picasso (Fig. 2.1): From plate to plate there is less data but more Shannonian information (uncertainty) until the final plate which can be a bull, but also a buffalo, a mountain goat, or a gnou (Fig. 2.2). The process is irreversible. This process is called lossy data compression. We find here inverse relations between data and information: data compression is the opposite of information compression—it is information inflation.

2.1.1 On Knowledge

> The question how **knowledge** should be defined is perhaps the most important and difficult [...]. This may seem surprising: at first sight it might be thought that knowledge might be defined as belief which is in agreement with the facts. The trouble is that no one knows what a belief is, no one knows what a fact is, and no one knows what sort of agreement between them would make a belief true. (Bertrand Russell (1926), in "Theory of Knowledge")

The relation "less data → more information" is counterintuitive and might be seen as a result of the fact that Shannon's information is just a technical term with no relations to information as used in everyday language. But note that in some cases it does make intuitive sense as quite often more data leads to more uncertainty, that is, to more Shannonian information. For example, for a person who *knows*—that is, has in memory—one animal only—say, a bull—Picasso's Plate XI would be a bull (i is 0), while for a person who has more knowledge about animals (Fig. 2.2), Plate

H. Haken and J. Portugali, *Information Adaptation: The Interplay Between Shannon Information and Semantic Information in Cognition*,
SpringerBriefs in Complexity, DOI 10.1007/978-3-319-11170-4_2

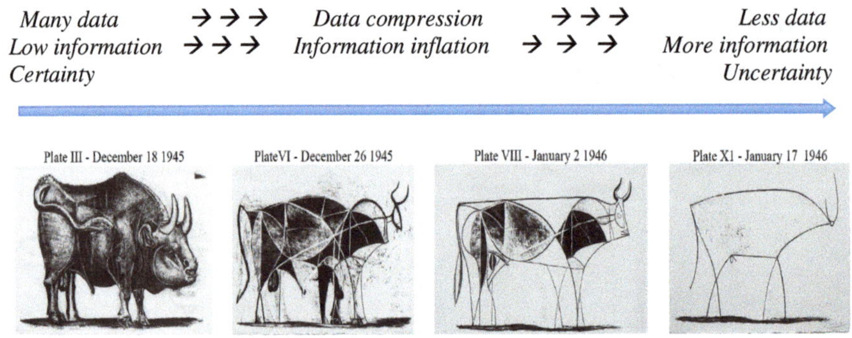

Fig. 2.1 Plates III, VI, VII and XI from the Bull by Picasso and the relations between the data, information and certainty they convey

Fig. 2.2 Is the painting at the center a bull?, a mountain goat?, a gnou?, a buffalo?

XI might be several things (i is high). Shannonian information is thus also a measure of more/less knowledge—the number of *meanings* one can attach to a given representation (e.g. Plate XI in Fig. 2.1). Weaver (ibid) suggested that Shannonian information is not only a measure of uncertainty but also of a 'freedom of choice'. To the latter we might add that it is also a measure of expectations, which in the present context mean attractors. So we are driven back to the issue of semantic information.

The antonym of lossy data compression is *lossless data compression* in which a given data representing a given entity can be compressed without loosing the specific meaning of that entity (e.g. Plates III–VII in Fig. 2.1). This is possible when

Fig. 2.3 Two caricatures of Einstein: Left by Stoyan L and right by E Myles

we deal with redundant data; the process is reversible—the original data can be recovered. Here too more data doesn't necessarily lead to more information. Lossless data compression can be exemplified by reference to caricatures that with few lines convey the face of a person (e.g. Einstein in Fig. 2.3, left).

This is also the idea behind the 'principle of parsimony' and famous phrases such as:

Less is more (Andreas del Sarto 1855)
It is futile to do with more things that which can be done with fewer. Occam's Razor (1288–1348)
I apologise for the length of this letter, but I didn't have time to write a shorter one. Blaise Pascale (1623–1662).
Everything should be made as simple as possible, but no simpler. Albert Einstein (1879–1955)

The notions 'information compression' and 'data compression' might often oppose each other, as we've just illustrated, and yet in the literature they often appear interchangeably. To avoid confusion we suggest leaving the term 'data compression' as it is, and instead of 'information compression', use *information deflation*. The antonym of the latter would be *information inflation*. Thus in the case of Picasso's Bull, each sequential drawing conveys less data but more information, more uncertainty and more possibilities. What we have here is thus a sequential process of information inflation implemented by means of data compression.

The discussions on lossy/lossless data compression refer to situations in which a given amount of data can or cannot be recovered. But the cognitive process of information adaptation by inflation/deflation goes beyond that. As we illustrate below in Chaps. 3 and 4, in some cases of information adaptation the brain adds data that doesn't exist in the stimulus, while in other cases the brain ignores data that does exist in the stimulus.

The above distinction between data and information feeds back to the discussion about the relations between Shannonian and semantic information, namely, it illustrates in a different way, how semantics enters in disguise into the definition of Shannonian information: Data in itself, that is, "pure data" with no meaning at all, has no Shannonian information. In order for data to become quantitative Shannonian information, semantic information is required in order to distinguish in a meaningful way between the different items that constitute the data, for example, to (pattern) recognize the items.

2.2 Mathematical Formulation. Some Basic General Concepts

Mathematically we start from the notion of "representation" as a set (or string) of symbols (or data), where we assume for clarity that these are numbers, e.g. in a binary system, 0 and 1. Thus a specific string, e.g. (0, 1, 1, 0, 1) is a representation. In this way, any picture can be encoded by a string of symbols: Introduce pixels and put: white <–>0, black <–>1.

This enables us, in a first step, to ignore "meaning", and deal with the processing of *representations*, e.g. by a human or some computer. How to interpret "processing"? It means in each actual case the transformation of a specific representation into another representation in one of the following manners:

(a) *one-to-one*
(b) *many-to-one (or fewer)*
(c) *one-to-many*

Compression of representation has only to do with (a).

A specific representation is replaced by a different shorter representation (string). "Lossless" is now defined as *reversible*: the original representation can be fully restored. (There are deep questions related to the Turing machine concerning the reversibility of this process, however!). "Lossy" compression is *irreversible*, the original representation cannot be fully restored or not at all.

Interestingly, these two different processes were discussed in computer theory: Rolf Landauer (1961) of IBM studied the "lossy" case which is realized in all computers and amounts to doing away bits, where pro bit one kT is produced (where k is Boltzmann's constant and T the absolute temperature), i.e. a heating up of the computer (which actually can be much larger than kT). Charles Bennett (1982), also of IBM, showed that a *lossless* computer is also feasible, at least in principle. Our brain produces heat!

Probably one may define redundancy in several ways, e.g. in the context of engineering. In the present context we would suggest: A specific representation is redundant if it can be *reversibly* compressed. (Redundancy may also mean that a set of representations can be replaced by a single representation provided the latter serves the same purpose(s) as the original set.)

We can now refer to information in the Shannon sense. Here we are dealing with a *whole set* of representations. Let P_j be the probability of the "event": occurrence of a representation labeled by j, then

$$i_j = -\log_2 P_j$$

is the information of that representation.

If $P_j = 1$ (centainty!)
$i_j = 0$
If $P_j \approx 0$ (great improbability because of the possibility of other representations)
i_j very large.

Information i is defined as average

$$i = \sum_j P_j i_j = -\sum_j P_j \log_2 P_j.$$

In this case, it will be better to speak of information entropy to make a distinction with respect to the information of a single representation.

Now we can define information *deflation* as lowering the (numerical) value of i, and information *inflation* as increase of i. This can be directly related to data processing.

2.2.1 Information Deflation

The number of representations is reduced (case (b) above). For illustration: When there are originally N representations with $P_j = 1/N$, then $i = \ln N$ means large uncertainty for large N, whereas reduction to 1 representation: $P_k = 1$, all other $P_j = 0, j \neq k$ implies information $i = 0$

i.e. complete certainty.

Or, more generally, reduction of high information (entropy) to zero information, means a move from uncertainty –> certainty. This process is irreversible because the final representation has several originators.

2.2.1.1 Information Inflation

Here one representation is replaced by many representations (case (c) above). This clearly means increase of information (entropy). Whether this process is reversible depends on additional knowledge: If there is only one original representation, the process is reversible. On the other hand, one or several representations could also stem from the transformation of different representations: then (c) is irreversible.

2.3 Data, Information and Meaning. How Are These Related?

We will try to formalize this problem on the basis of our former interpretation of meaning. Meaning does not result from data per se but only in the context of a receiver, which is a complex system in the sense noted above, namely, that it has memory. Such a receiver has in its memory $N + 1$ states, $k = 0, 1, \ldots, N$, which in a task of pattern recognition of faces, for instance, "mean" "face 1" or "face 2" etc., while $k = 0$ means no effect on the receiver.

The reader will note that here we do not distinguish between semantic and pragmatic information. This implies that we adopt a strictly operational point of view. We leave it open, however, how to observe the effect on the receiver. (This effect could be a specific reaction of the receiver (person/machine) or the storage in memory.)

We distinguish the representations by a label j. The length of the corresponding j is denoted by Lj In the context of our contribution we consider the case that a representation represents a "pattern" (e.g. a picture, see below, or a string of letters etc.).

Then *pattern recognition* is formalized by

> Pattern j represented by representation j
> causes receiver to acquire state k with the conditional probability $p(k|j)$ for $k = 1, \ldots, N$ or $p(0|j)$, i.e. no pattern is recognized.

The probabilities are normalized so that $\sum_k p(k|j) = 1$.

Here, we do not discuss how to determine the probability distribution experimentally.

Lossless compression of a representation is now defined by $p(k|j) = p(k|j')$ for the case of two different representations j and j' with respective lengths $L_{j'} < L_j$.

Equivalently, we may speak of *meaning conservation*, if the same meaning k is conveyed by compressed representations or in view of our above statements, by reduced redundancy.

A special case and of particular interest is $p(k|j) = 1$, where a specific state k (a specific meaning!) is attached to the given representation j with certainty. Or in other words, pattern j has been "recognized".

Lossy compression of a representation means $p(k|j') < p(k|j)$for the case of j, j' with $L_{j'} < L_j$.

An example is

$$
\begin{aligned}
p(k|j) &= 1 \quad \text{for a fixed}\, k\, \text{and}\, j,\ \text{but} \\
p(k|j') &= \tfrac{1}{2} \quad j' \neq j \\
p(k'|j') &= \tfrac{1}{2} \quad \text{for a fixed}\, k, k'\, \text{and}\, j'
\end{aligned}
$$

The transition from j to j' increases the number of possible interpretations: i.e. information inflation.

Application to Picasso's bull: To bring out the essentials: take the number of black pixels as measure of length L_j. The index j = 1, 2, 3, 4 corresponds to the plates III, VI, VII, XI. Then L_j decreases from left to right in the picture sequence.

Left picture, $j = 1$, if $k = k_0$ means "bull", then $p(k_0|1) = 1$

Right picture, $j = 4$.

Lossless compression of representation: if

$$p(k_0|4 = 1)$$

This is the required feature of a caricature!

Lossy compression of representation: if (for instance)

$p(k_0|4) = \frac{1}{2}$ and $p(k_1|4) = \frac{1}{2}$, where k_1 means deer.

In this case we deal with increased uncertainty, information inflation, partial loss of meaning of representation 4. Complete loss of meaning of representation j' happens, if for

$$p(k|j') = 0 \quad \text{for}\, k = 1, .., \text{ N, and}$$
$$p(k|j') = 1 \quad \text{for}\, k = 0, \text{ i.e. no effect on receiver.}$$

Categorization can now be formalized along these lines as well as the process of improving pattern recognition (e.g. by increasing the length L_j, i.e. by providing more and more details of a picture).

Chapter 3
The Empirical Basis of Information Adaptation

3.1 Introduction

As noted above, as a result of mounting empirical evidences, Barlow (2001) has changed his view on the information reduction issue originally suggested in the 1960s by Attneave, himself and Watanabe. In this 2001 paper Barlow mentions that his and Attneave's views are still valuable in that they shed light on the significance of redundancy; however, he doesn't specify how these mounting evidences must change our view about the way Shannonian information applies to cognition. In fact, to the best of our knowledge there was no attempt yet to re-consider information theory in light of the more recent empirical findings. In what follows we suggest a first attempt in this direction. Similarly to previous attempts to apply Shannon to cognition, we'll concentrate on visual information processing.

In neuroscience, the eyes are considered as part of the brain. Accordingly, the brain's processing of optical information starts in the retina by discrete, locally arranged receptor cells. In the retina the cells process information, in particular by lateral inhibition. The optical fiber then transports the signal (which is encoded by electrical pulses) via the lateral geniculate body to the neurons of the visual cortex (Fig. 3.1) with its Areas V1–V4. In the first layer, the neurons (cor)respond to their receptive fields. Then, at higher levels, neurons getting inputs from lower areas, react to specific orientations of lines, and to corners. The discovery of these bottom-up information-processing effects is due to Hubel and Wiesel (1959, 1962, 1965).

3.2 Deconstruction–Reconstruction

In his recent book Kandel (2012) terms this bottom-up process as *deconstruction* and suggests that it is implemented by the brain's syntactic capabilities. He further suggests that the process of deconstruction is a first stage of perception. The second

H. Haken and J. Portugali, *Information Adaptation: The Interplay Between Shannon Information and Semantic Information in Cognition*,
SpringerBriefs in Complexity, DOI 10.1007/978-3-319-11170-4_3

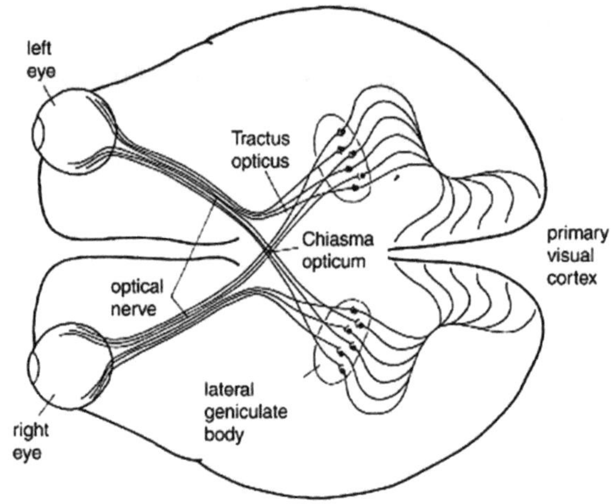

Fig. 3.1 Schematic representation of the visual pathway of a human

stage is a top-down process Kandel terms *reconstruction*. The latter is implemented by the brain's semantic (meaning giving) capabilities. The empirical evidences for this top-down process come from studies by Margaret Livingstone, Doris Tsao and Winrich Freiwald (Livingstone 2002; Tsao and Livingstone 2008; Freiwald et al. 2009; Freiwald and Tsao 2010), who have localized six areas in the lower temporal lobe of a monkey, which react only to faces. These areas—called *face patches*—form a network that processes different aspects of the considered face, e.g. its form (i.e. geometry) and its orientation with respect to the vertical. Drawing on an analogy with "computer directed face recognition", Kandel further suggests that the process of reconstruction too evolves in two steps: For example, in a face/pattern recognition task Step one would be discovery of a face (an object is a face) while Step two, recognition (it belongs to a specific person).

3.3 Analysis–Synthesis

The above process of deconstruction–reconstruction is similar in several ways to the literal meaning of the notions of 'analysis–synthesis': In both cases uncertainty is reduced (information deflation) at the local (microscopic) level and at the global level. In analysis we try to understand a (suspected) system by scrutinizing the properties of its parts (local pixel arrangements), while in synthesis—in a way—we study the correlations between the system's elements. Clearly, by disregarding the (putatively!) existing correlations we increase the uncertainty—allowing for many configurations. But this raises a delicate question on the role of our subjective judgment: In cases, analysis and synthesis, in the beginning there will be many possible outcomes—whose number we (our brains) narrow down in the course of analysis/synthesis.

In light of the above, we suggest that Kandel's use of the words "deconstruction" and "reconstruction" is somewhat misleading and that the wording analysis–synthesis are more appropriate. To see how, let us start with the notion of "retinotopy", which means that the output from *neighboring* sensory cells of the retina serves as input to *neighboring* cells of the visual cortex starting with area V1. Thus, this projection from the retina to the visual cortex conserves the *topology*. The areas V1–V4 now analyze the input locally but do not destroy the somewhat more global topology. Thus this process does not deconstruct (like a watchmaker decomposing a watch into its parts). Rather this action is similar to a geographer who analyses (and possibly rearranges, for reasons of clarity) fine details, but retains the topology of the map. This cartographer thus *analyses* (rather than deconstructs). Eventually, the brain has to draw its conclusions from the *correlations* starting from a somewhat larger scale up to the size of the original image. At this stage it *synthesises* (but it does not reconstruct).

But in between analysis and synthesis, there is a fundamental problem: How can it be that we recognize objects independent of their size, orientation and position? This problem is solved by the synergetic computer (see below) using a suitable preprograming of data by means of specific transformations (which in our opinion are rather elegant) and by the HMAX model (see below).

Analysis and synthesis will take different forms and outcomes when dealing with simple and complex systems (For their definition cf. below Chap. 5): In the case of simple systems—e.g. clockwork—analysis means deconstructing/dismantling the global system to its elementary local parts. Such a system can be fully reconstructed by synthesis, that is, by putting together the parts in the proper way. By dismantling the system we increase the information (uncertainty), namely, there might be many ways to put them back together, while by putting them back properly we reduce information and reach certainty.

The situation is different when dealing with complex systems, which due to emergent properties, are not the sum of their parts: here the process of analysis/deconstruction entails loss of properties (information) that exist only at the global system. It is here that the specific personal information accumulated in a person's memory has a role to play—to add the global properties that do not exist in the parts. In the case of the mind/brain this is implemented by the process of synthesis—Kandel's reconstruction—by an interaction between the (bottom-up) locally deconstructed parts and the (top-down) globally memorized elements. We suggest that this also applies to the differences between Shannonian and semantic information: Shannon deals with simple, closed, clockwork like systems—e.g. a telephone—while we are dealing with a complex system—the mind/brain.

3.4 Hybrid Images and the Meaning of the Deconstruction/Analysis Process

From the above follows a somewhat philosophical question that concerns the exact meaning of the decomposition ("deconstruction" or rather "analysis") process and the implied reconstruction process (synthesis): Does the process of deconstruction *destroy* the correlations between larger areas of the visual fields as implied by Kandel? In this case, data are irreversibly destroyed, uncertainty and thus Shannon information inflated, with the implication that the process of reconstruction is solely implemented by means of information stored in, or generated by, the MBB. If the deconstruction process does not destroy the correlations, then one can think of several possibilities. One is that the data in the correlations are not yet used, the corresponding part of Shannon information remains unaltered (i.e. not inflated) and reconstruction is implemented by means of the correlation of data that was ignored and not used in the deconstruction phase. A second possibility is that the process of deconstruction is also a learning process—learning the relations between the parts. As if the brain is a watchmaker that decomposes a clock and in the process reveals the specific correlations between the parts (i.e. the code).

3.4.1 Hybrid Images

And there is a third possibility, which is, that the human brain acts along two parallel pathways. To see how consider the case of hybrid images that were introduced by Oliva and Schyns (1997) as experimental tools for studying multi-scale perception processes during scene recognition. Building on the finding that the human visual system analyses images by several band-pass filters, hybrid images are constructed by blending a low-pass filtered image with a high-pass filtered image. The result is a counterintuitive experience in which lowering the resolution by blurring an image, or by looking at it from a distance, enables its recognition. Take a look, first, at Fig. 3.2 *left*. As can be seen, one immediately recognizes Marilyn Monroe. Now look at Fig. 3.2 *middle* and you will recognize Einstein. In Fig. 3.2 *right* the picture is even "more Einstein". This was achieved by

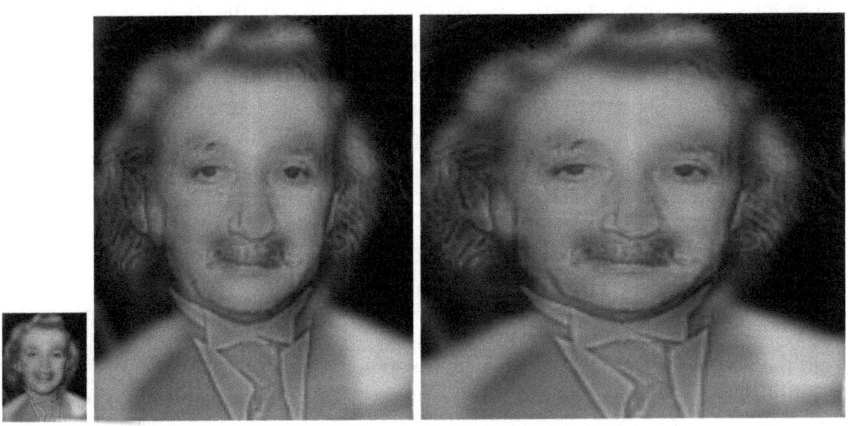

Fig. 3.2 The same picture is interpreted in two different ways (cf. text)

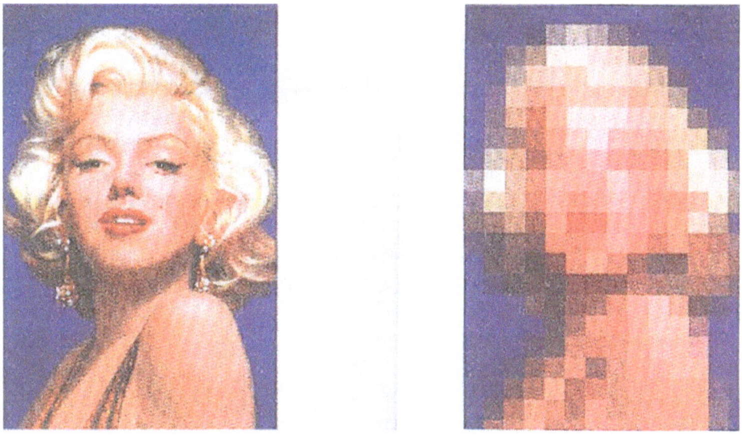

Fig. 3.3 How resolution affects visual recognition

changing the proportions of the picture as can be seen. Actually, as a detailed analysis has revealed (cf. Sect. 3.4.2 below), this effect rests on the degree of local resolution.

A second example is Fig. 3.3. In Fig. 3.3 *left* you see the face of Marilyn Monroe, while in Fig. 3.3 *right*: you see a configuration of rectangular squares. Now, if you use glasses, just take them off; or, if you don't, try half-close your eyes, or simply distance yourself from the picture and look again. What do you see? You see Marilyn Monroe.

The Fig. 3.3 experiment thus suggests that the Monroe picture that was encoded by large square pixels becomes recognizable if the hard contours are "softened" by half-closing eyes, the effect of which is equivalent to a (spatial) low frequency filter.

A third example is Fig. 3.4. In Fig. 3.4 *middle* you see an arrangement of "symbols" with no legible meaning—some are Latin letters, while others are Arabic numbers. But if you look at this arrangement from a distance, or half close your eyes, or take off your glasses, so that the symbols will get blurred, suddenly the text is legible; in fact it is identical to the text in Fig. 3.4 *left*.

And there is a second way to "play" with Fig. 3.4 which is in close analogy to the Monroe example in Fig. 3.3 above: Look, first, at the text of Fig. 3.4 left and read it. Now look closely at Fig. 3.4, center; what do you see? You see an arrangement of "symbols" with no legible meaning: some are Latin letters, while others are Arabic numbers. Now, look at this text from a distance, or half-close your eyes (or take off your glasses) so that the individual symbols become less sharp, i.e. blurred; suddenly you can read and understand the text. Fig. 3.4 right is a somewhat more difficult version of Fig. 3.4 center in that there are two more numbers (0 and 6) replacing the letters "O" and "B".

How to interpret the "double recognition" process in the above three examples? As is known from 3D-vision Haken (1991/2004), our brain uses different methods and cues (simultaneously). Thus, one possibility is that the above "double

THIS MESSAGE	TH15 M3554G3	TH15 M3554G3
SERVES AS PROOF	53RVE5 45 PROOF	53RVE5 45 PR0OF
FOR WHAT	FOR WH47	F0R WH47
ASTOUNDING THINGS	457OUND1NG 7H1NG5	4570UND1NG 7H1NG5
OUR MIND	OUR M1ND	0UR M1ND
CAN PRODUCE!	C4N PRODUC3!	C4N PR0DUC3!
IMPRESSIVE!	1MPR3551V3!	1MPR3551V3!
IN THE BEGINNING IT WAS	1N 7H3 B3G1NN1NG 17 W45	1N 7H3 63G1NN1NG 17 W45
DIFFICULT, BUT	D1FF1CUL7, BU7	D1FF1CUL7, 6U7
NOW, IN THIS	NOW, 1N 7H15	N0W, 1N 7H15
LINE, YOUR MIND READS	L1N3, YOUR M1ND R34D5	L1N3, Y0UR M1ND R34D5
IT AUTOMATICALLY	17 4UTOM471C4LLY	17 4UT0M471C4LLY
WITHOUT THINKING	W17HOU7 7H1NK1NG	W17H0U7 7H1NK1NG
ON IT	ON 17	0N 17
BE PROUD OF IT!	B3 PROUD OF 17!	63 PR0UD 0F 17!
ONLY CERTAIN	ONLY C3R741N	0NLY C3R741N
PEOPLE CAN READ IT.	P3OPL3 C4N R34D 17.	P30PL3 C4N R34D 17.
IF YOU BELONG	1F YOU B3LONG	1F Y0U 63L0NG
TO THOSE, THEN	7O 7HOS3, 7H3N	70 7H0S3, 7H3N
SHARE THIS PLEASE	5H4R3 7H15 PL34S3	5H4R3 7H15 PL34S3

Fig. 3.4 How resolution affects legibility, that is, textual recognition. *Left*–text only. *Center* –letter and numbers replacing some letters: I → 1, E → 3, S → 5, T → 7, A → 4. *Right* two more numbers replacing letters: O → 0, B → 6

recognition" processes indicate that the human visual recognition system acts along (at least) two different pathways:

Path 1 is based on low pass spatial frequency filter—it stresses soft variations of grey values (also more female features) we recognize Monroe in Fig. 3.2.

Path 2 is based on high pass spatial frequency filter—the extreme case is lines (contours), When these basic features are given more value we recognize Einstein in Fig. 3.2.

Two interrelated questions arise here: First, where and how are these pathways realized by the neural substance? Clearly this question can be answered only by experiments that measure the correlations in spike patterns of *many neurons*. In our opinion this difficult task has hardly been accomplished.

Second, in what circumstances and how, our MBB employs, sequentially or simultaneously in parallel, these two pathways? As a working hypothesis we might suggest an answer that follows from our above noted study (Sect. 1.3) "The face of the city" (Haken and Portugali 2003). This study commences with Yarbus' (1967) famous eye movement experiment (Fig. 3.5) demonstrating that some elements in the face of a person (eyes and mouth in Yarbus's Fig. 3.5) or a city (landmarks in Fig. 1.3 above) attract more attentions than other element.

In Chap. 5 below we introduce the synergetic computer (SC) as means to model, simulate and thus interpret empirical data, including the interplay between order parameters. In order to incorporate the above "Yarbus oriented interpretation" into the SC approach, several steps are required. This is so because in the formalism of

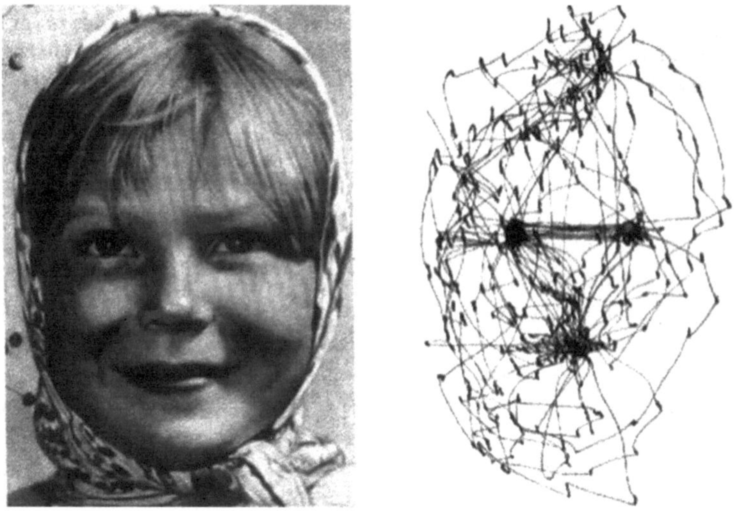

Fig. 3.5 Yarbus' (1967, Fig. 115) record of eye movement during free examination of a photographed face. The eyes and mouth attract most of the attention

SC, a specific pixel arrangement does not act directly as an attention parameter and is merely replaced by it. That is, attention parameters act (both in the vulgar and mathematical sense) as multipliers of, in each case, specific (pixel) configurations. This enhancement effect can be achieved in at least two ways: Firstly, by frequency filtering as described in some details below in Chaps. 5 and 7. Secondly, in line with the above interpretation, by means of a scanning process discovered by Yarbus's eye movement studies, where the following mathematical model applies: In one or several steps our eyes "scan" an image and observe "*boring*" areas with *weak* pixel change and "*interesting*, important" strong local pixel changes, i.e. locally high spatial frequencies. Mathematically, we have a measure at hand which local pixel configurations must be enhanced by attention parameters. In the brain, these localizations trigger attention which in turn reinforces specific features, makes them dominant so to give rise to recognize Einstein or Monroe. As specified in Sect. 3.4.2 below, this suggestion requires a non-linear, at least two-steps, approach.

Applying the above interpretation to Fig. 3.3, *right*: when we look at this picture, the pixels trigger and are reinforced by attention parameters, our attention is captured by the straight lines of the pixels and we see just pixels. But when we half-close our eyes, the straight lines loose their prominence and our attention is reinforced by the colors/tones of the picture and we see Monroe. Finally with the text of Fig. 3.4: when we look at Fig. 3.4 *center*, the letters and numbers capture our attention in equal strength. But when we half close our eyes, the numbers become less prominent compared to the letters, the letters attract more attention, and dominate the interpretation. This is so also since the forms of the numbers resemble their corresponding letters (1 = I, 5 = S etc.) so that when we half close our eyes the differences between 1 and I, or 5 and S become blurred and the word THIS replaces the configuration TH15 and so on.

Note that in all the above cases the first step is a process of learning, but with two important differences: The first difference concerns the time of learning (or recapitulation of) Monroe face and the text: In the first "play" of Fig. 3.4, the recognition process of Figs. 3.4 *center* and *right* was based on knowledge learned some *time* ago; in the second "play" (which is analogous to Fig. 3.4), the recognition was based on information learned *immediately before* the task: reading the text in Fig. 3.4 *left* first, acted as a cue for the recognition task that followed.

The second difference concerns the difference between the recognition processes of an image versus that of a text. In the *Monroe case* our brain is concerned with *vision only*, i.e. the "spontaneous" recognition of a (learned) pattern in an image. In our example the original pattern has been manipulated in a specific way by "approximating" it by means of colored rectangles, i.e. by *fewer* data/features. In the text example where letters have been distorted by replacing them by numbers, i.e. by *false* data/features, our brain is concerned with *language understanding*, i.e. a more difficult intellectual task than pattern recognition. But in both cases *blurring is crucial* for recognition.

Finally, note that in all the above cases (Figs. 3.2 to 3.4), "blurring", means: low spatial frequency band pass filtering or, equivalently, *doing away* high spatial frequency *data*. In the present context this means *information inflation*, i.e. giving room to more interpretations, or, mathematically in terms of the synergetic computer model (Chaps. 5 and 7) it means opening access to the relevant attractor, that is, order parameter (Fig. 7.2). Clearly, while reading the "puzzle" of Fig. 3.4 we are simultaneously learning how to adapt the numbers.

3.4.2 A Model of Hybrid Images

Following our information adaptation model (Chap. 7 below), we have been able to cast our qualitative discussion of the Einstein/Monroe hybrid image into a detailed mathematical model that takes the band-pass filters into account (Haken and Portugali, submitted). The profile of the fine lines representing Einstein's face is represented by narrow Gaussians, whereas the smooth variations of Monroe's face are represented by a finite superposition of sine waves. We show quantitatively that blurring affects the sharp Gaussians which are now broadened, strongly, but the soft sine-waves only weakly. We introduce an appropriately defined Shannon information of these different images and show that blurring increases that of Einstein's image strongly, but that of Monroe's only little. As a consequence, in the SC-formalism the relative weight of Einstein's image in the superposition of the hybrid image becomes smaller so that in the SC–competition the "Monroe" interpretation wins. This mechanism is strongly enhanced by the "Yarbus effect" discussed above.

Our approach allows us to make contact with previous work by Ditzinger and Haken (1986) who developed a quantitative model on the recognition of bistable images, based on attention parameter dynamics (cf. Chap. 7). According to this work, there are two different kinds of visual perception:

(1) If the relative weights of the two percepts differ strongly, there is only one stable interpretation. This is the case of the above analyzed hybrid image.
(2) If the weights are nearly equal, oscillations between the two percepts occur. Our prediction is that this phenomenon should be observable also in the case of hybrid images if the degree of blurring is gradually changed.

The above detailed mathematical analysis can be directly applied also to Figs. 3.3 and 3.4. With respect to Fig. 3.3 *right*, blurring enhances its Shannon information and thus lowers its relative weight as compared to the percept of Fig. 3.3 *left*. With respect to Fig. 3.4, its interpretation requires a two-step process.

(1) By blurring, the Shannon information of all "characters" represented by lines is enhanced.
(2) This facilitates the *error-correction* used in language-understanding. By blurring the wrong characters (i.e. the numbers) become less "false".

In terms of synergetics, error correction is based on the interplay between order parameters and enslaved parts. The parts (characters) call upon their order parameters ("meaning") which in turn enslave the parts, in this case by correcting the false characters. [This approach has been realized in China in the frame of language understanding by the SC. (Private communication)]

3.5 Computational Models: Link Between Bottom-Up and Top-Down

There are several computational models that attempt to simulate the above deconstruction–reconstruction, or analysis–synthesis, processes (Poggio and Serre 2013) of which the HMAX hierarchical model is probably a typical one. We'll discuss this model in some details in Sect. 7.10 below; here we examine it as an extension to the empirical findings discussed above. As can be seen in Fig. 3.6, the model is in line with Kandel's scheme, that is, it suggests that the process of deconstruction starts bottom-up from a scene in the world up to areas V1–V4, reconstruction starts top-down with visual routines and AIT, and they meet half-way at the complex units of AIT and the simple units of PIT.

The bottom-up process of deconstruction in the HMAX model (as in Kandel's scheme), is based on Hubel and Wiesel's (1959, 1962, 1965) findings, while the top-down process of reconstruction commences, as indicated by Fig. 3.6, with the notion of *visual routines*. The latter notion was introduced by Shimon Ullman

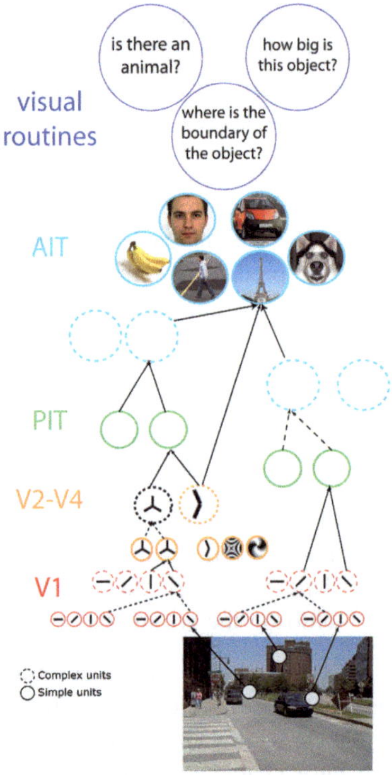

Fig. 3.6 Poggio and Serra's (ibid) sketch "of the *HMAX* hierarchical computational model of the visual cortex (tentative mapping with areas of the visual cortex shown in color, some areas of the *parietal cortex* and dorsal streams not shown). Acronyms: *V*1, *V*2 and *V*4 correspond to primary, secondary and quaternary visual areas, *PIT* and *AIT* to posterior and anterior inferotemporal areas, respectively."

(1984, 1996)[1] as part of his attempt to model information processing in the cortex as a bi-directional search procedure: bottom-up and top-down processes that eventually meet halfway. As in the HMAX model, the aim of the bottom-up process is to identify the relevant parts of the scene, while the top-down process aims at identifying (or defining) the correlations, that is, the relations between the parts—the syntactic relations (is a given part inside or outside another part?) and the semantic relations (is this is a person or animal?). But here arises once again the issue of the correlation discussed above: In order for the top-down brain process to identify the correlations, they must first exist at the bottom, that is, they must first emerge, or be identified, by the bottom-up process.

An alternative modeling approach is offered by the *synergetic computer* (SC) that we introduce below in Chap. 5 and further discuss in Chap. 7 in relation to the HMAX model. As we show below, while the SC does not explicitly model the process of deconstruction, its inner logic (associated as it is with the synergetic paradigm of pattern recognition), offers a process that remedies the absence of correlations in the HMAX model: According to the SC, the process of (visual) pattern recognition evolves bottom-up in two parallel pathways as discussed above:

---

[1] Ullman has further suggested the notion of "Sequence seeking".

one that identifies the parts (Hubel and Wiesel's lines, corners etc.) and another that identifies the correlations and/or the topology, that is, the rules of the interaction between the parts. Next, the interactions between the parts according to the above rules give rise to several order parameters that compete until one or a few order parameters win the completion. Finally, once the order parameter(s) comes into being it (they) enslaves the other parts of the system in a top-down process that is implemented by means of visual routines, sequence seeking and possibly other top-down processes. (For more details see Chap. 4 below).

Comparing the Kandel-HMAX model with that suggested by the synergetic computer (SC) we see that in both cases the two pathways could be realized by different systems of neurons or by the same system enabling two different kinds of operation (mode). When we follow Kandel we must assume that these (virtual or real) pathways start after areas V1–V4, but still have to be explained by a further development of, e.g. the HMAX approach of Riesenhuber and Poggio (1999). Concerning the (SC) in its invariant form we may suggest two options:

(1) Its preprocessing (in its present or somewhat modified form) is performed in area V1–V4. There is no experimental evidence, however. At this early stage, the local correlations between pixels (the "construction plan of the object") is saved ("Retinotopy").
(2) Its preprocessing is performed after areas V1–V4, assuming the output of these areas as "raw data". This approach might be alternative to a (further developed, see above) HMAX model including a complementary top-down procedure (Which is not needed by SC).

Chapter 4
A Complexity Theory Approach to Information

4.1 Complexity Theory

Complexity theory is an umbrella name for several theories that deal with systems that are open, complex and in far from equilibrium condition. Such systems it was found tend to achieve their order by means of self-organization in a bottom up manner and to exhibit phenomena such as chaos and fractal structure. Some of the leading theories are Haken's (1977) Synergetics, Prigogine's (1980) dissipative structures, Mandelbrot's (1983) fractal geometry, chaos theory (Lorentz 1963; Feigenbaum 1978) and more recently the new network theory as developed by Barabasi (2002), Watts (2004) and others. Of the latter, Haken's synergetics is the complexity theory that was most intensively applied to information theory (Haken 1988/2000/2006) as well as to cognition and psychology (Haken 1991/2004, 1996).

Relevant to the present discussion is the notion of *complex adaptive system* (CAS) that is due to Gell-Man (1994) and Holland (1992). In *The Quark and the Jaguar* Nobel Laureate in physics Gell-Mann (1994, p. 17) characterizes a complex adaptive system as follows:

> … a complex adaptive system acquires information about its environment and its own interaction with that environment, identifying regularities in that information, condensing these regularities into a kind of 'schema' or model, and acting in the real world on the basis of that schema. In each case there are various competing schemata, and the results of the actions in the real world feed back to influence the competition among those schemata.

The notion of CAS thus highlights the property that complex systems are capable of adapting their structure and behavior to their environment. This adaptability of complex systems results from their openness and ability to self-organize in face of changing environmental conditions. Nonadaptive systems, per contra, maintain their structure irrespective of the environment. Nonadaptability is thus a property of closed, simple and mechanistic systems.

H. Haken and J. Portugali, *Information Adaptation: The Interplay Between Shannon Information and Semantic Information in Cognition*,
SpringerBriefs in Complexity, DOI 10.1007/978-3-319-11170-4_4

4.2 Complexity and Information

The link between the theories of complexity and information follows directly from the very definition of Shannon's information as entropy. Shannon has used the notion entropy in the sense given to it in thermodynamics. In the latter entropy is a property of *closed* systems that tend to evolve from order to maximum entropy (disorder); as such Shannon information refers to nonadaptive communication systems. Complexity theories are about *open* systems in far from equilibrium conditions that tend to evolve from disorder to order, that is to say, to communication systems that are CASs. As just noted, such a system "acquires information about its environment [...] identifying regularities [...] [constructing] 'schema' or model, and acting in the real world on the basis of that schema" (ibid). One challenge here is to find "the information entropy under the constraints of an *open* system" (Haken 2000, p. 95); a second and related challenge is to reformulate Shannon's information in the context of open, complex and self-organizing system.

To this end let us re-examine Shannon's (1948, Fig. 1) general communication system as described by him in his original paper from 1948 (reproduced here as Fig. 4.1). As can be seen it is built of two symmetric parts: information source and transmitter on the left, receiver and destination on the right, and in between a channel (perturbed by a noise source) that connects the two sides. According to Shannon, the transmitter and receivers are technical 'syntactic' devices, such as a telephone, that transmits/receives the signals coming from the source without attaching to them meaning. This system is closed and nonadaptive in the sense that the transmitter and receiver are essentially machines and as such passive syntactic devices, they have no connection to, do not interact with, and are not influenced by, other information sources (in the environment) but the one that appears in Fig. 4.1 left—they just transmit or receive the data but do not feedback/interact.

Shannon devotes long discussions to the various stations in this communication chain except for one—the destination. "The *destination*", he writes (ibid, p. 2), "is the person (or thing) for whom the message is intended", and this is it. How does

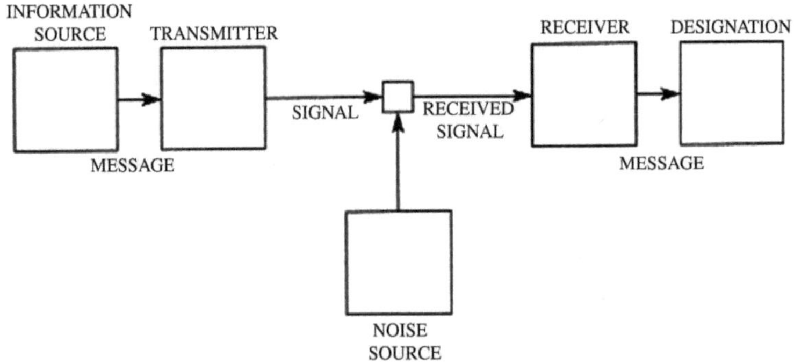

Fig. 4.1 Shannon's (1948, Fig. 1) general communication system

the person (or thing) extract the information out of the message it gets from the receiver? How does that person (or thing) interpret the signals in the message and create information? Shannon is silent about such semantic questions for the simple reason that they "are irrelevant to the engineering problem". His main focus of interest was the inner square of Fig. 4.2, that is, the quantity of information in the message that leaves the information source (S) and reaches the transmitter (T), from which through the channel it goes to the receiver (R) that transfers the message to the destination (D).

The symmetric counterpart of the destination is the information source S that generates the message. Shannon discusses the information source in some length—the types of messages it may produce (messages that are used in telegraph, or radio, or television and so on—ibid, p. 2), the various ways to describe the message mathematically (ibid, p. 4); but he says nothing about who *is* the information source—who is the entity that created the message and the way it or s/he produced it in the first place. From his short reference to the destination we can assume that the information source 'is the person (or thing) that creates or generates the message.' How? Once again, Shannon is silent apparently because such a question is "irrelevant to the engineering problem".

By isolating and focusing on the communication machinery—"the engineering problem"—Shannon's theory implies a distinction between two aspects of communication/information: (1) *The engineering/syntactic problem of communication*, referring to the flow of information (however created by the information source) through the transmitter to the receiver and from the latter to the destination. From this perspective the meaning of the message is irrelevant, as emphasized by Shannon. (2) *The semantic/cognitive problem of communication*, referring to the way the information source S created the information, and the way the destination

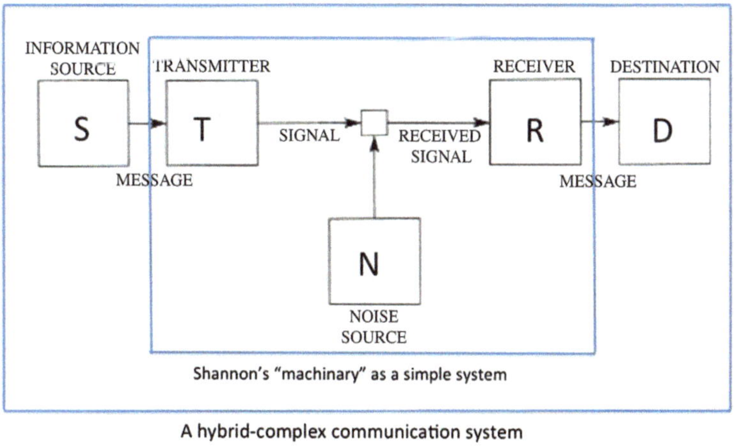

Fig. 4.2 Shannon's communication machinery as a hybrid system, composed of a mechanical/syntactic system (*inner square*) and a complex, adaptive system (*outer square*)

D extracts/interprets the message that comes from the receiver. That is to say, to *information formation* or *production,* on the one hand, and *information recognition* or *interpretation,* on the other. Here, the meaning of the message *is* relevant. The first is a problem of a closed, simple, mechanical system (Fig. 4.2 inner square), while the second of an open, complex, adaptive system (Fig. 4.2 outer square). The overall system of communication is thus a *hybrid complex system*—a notion recently suggested with respect to cities (Portugali 2013). In the present case (Fig. 4.2) this is a hybrid complex communication system composed of two complex subsystems—person S at the information source and person D at the destination, connected by means of two simple subsystems—the transmitting (T) and receiving (R) machines, themselves connected by a channel (C), interrupted by a noise source (N).

4.3 Forms of Communication

Given the above hybrid and complex communication system (Fig. 4.2), we can now examine different forms of communication ranging from face-to-face communication to communication mediated by various machines. To be concrete, let us assume that we are dealing with communication between two persons, that is, between S and D in Fig. 4.2.

(1) **Face to face**. The most direct form of communication is face-to-face interaction with no intervention of mediating mechanical devices. The basic medium of interaction here is spoken language. However, as is well recorded (Goffman 1959; Kendon et al. 1975; Demeulenaere 2011), *face-to-face* interaction does not only communicate words but also pitch, intonation, speed, conscious or subconscious gestures, facial expressions, nodding, and possibly breathe, odor as well as dressing. Thus there is a large amount of exchanged data.
(2) **Skype**. This form of communication (Wright and Webb 2011) is based on acoustic and visual signals, that cover most of the features in (1), but neglecting more basic senses such as e.g. odor or context.
(3) **Hand written text**. The latter not only conveys words, but also the kind of handwriting, the choice of paper, arrangement of text etc. On the other hand, printed/typed text conveys only the words (similarly to No. 5 below).
(4) **Telephone**. Transfers only the vocal features of spoken language.
(5) **Computers, telegraph, telex**. Transfer only language with its words but without any other features (See Wright and Webb ibid).
(6) **Virtual reality**. These new developments try to convey more sensations, e.g. tactile.

Several notes are in place here: First, as can be seen, different forms of communication convey different amounts of data; in the above list, the amount of data decreases from 1 to 5. This is in line with Shannon's theory. Second, the various applications of information theory to cognition (Chap. 1 above) were referring to form No. (1). In the latter, the mechanical devices of the Shannonian system (the inner square of Fig. 4.2) are not machines—rather they are embodied in the two persons: T is embodied in S, while R in D. Third and as a consequence of the above, while in forms (2) to (6) we have a clear boundary between information production/formation and recognition, on the one hand, and information flow, on the other, in (1) the two are embodied and as such inseparable. In other words, here Shannonian and semantic information are inseparable. Finally, it must be emphasized that the above six forms of communication provide only a partial list whose aim is illustrative. There are, of course, other forms of communication not discussed here, some referring to direct (person to person) communication between individuals as above, while others to indirect interaction via collective media of communication such as a language or a city (e.g. Chap. 8, Sect. 8.3).

Semantic information thus refers to processes of information production/formation and to their mirror image, processes of information extraction/recognition, while Shannonian information to information transfer and flow. This "division of labor" reminds one of the similarities and differences between Shannon's mathematical theory that we are discussing here, and another conception of communication developed in the domain of media studies by McLuhan (1964/2003) in his *Understanding Media: The Extensions of Man* with his famous aphorism "The medium is the message" (Strate and Wachtel 2005). Both Shannon and McLuhan treat the message and the communication technological devices as two distinct entities, as in Fig. 4.2, and both focus their attention on the inner box of Fig. 4.2—the communication machinery in Shannon's theory and the 'medium' in McLuhan's language. They differ in their view on the relations between the message and the communication device. According to Shannon, message and medium are fully independent of each other so that the messages with their "semantic aspects [...] are irrelevant to the engineering problem" with the implication that the communication machinery is irrelevant to the semantic problem. For McLuhan, per contra, the medium determines the message—it is *the* message. When using the notion 'message', Shannon refers to the literal meaning of this word whereas McLuhan to its sociological and cultural dimensions; for example, the messages determined by the invention of media such as movie, or the electric light bulb, are their effect on social and cultural life.

McLuhan does not specify, however, exactly how the medium determines the message. Such a specification entails, in fact, our present discussion: From the first half of the present section we learn that each medium, or form of communication, implies different quantities of data; from Chap. 2 we know that different quantities of data are associated with different levels of Shannonian information, that is, with different levels of certainties, uncertainties and possibilities; while from the discussion below we'll learn how humans, by means of their cognition, behavior, action and the media they are using, adapt to different configurations of Shannonian and semantic information.

4.3.1 Complexity, Cognition and Information Adaptation

The human brain and its associated cognitive capabilities and processes are often described as the ultimate known examples of complex systems. However, while in the domain of brain studies the view that the MBB is a complex system has become commonplace, in mainstream cognitive psychology and cognitive science this view is only recently starting to be recognized and appreciated—for example in Spivey's (2007) recent book. Thus, in the foreword to that book Ulrich Neisser writes: "Until now dynamical systems have had little to say about genuinely cognitive achievements such as language, categorization, or thought" (ibid, p. 7). And, in his introduction Spivey (ibid, p. 4) writes that his dynamical approach "draws much of its inspiration from related theoretical frameworks that preceded it …" including Kelso (1995), Thelen and Smith (1996) and others that were, in fact, inspired by Haken's theory of synergetics.

The MBB is a complex system of a special kind, however—it has memory! And it is this memory that makes the MBB not only complex, but also *adaptive* system, that is to say, a complex adaptive system as described above. This is so since as we specify in Chap. 3 above, information processing by the MBB is influenced, on the one hand, by its "syntactic" processing capabilities, while on the other, by the semantic information generated by/from its memory. By means of an interaction between the latter, and the data from the environment, the MBB enters a process of self-organization that enables it to *adapt* to its environment.

The information processing as described in Chap. 3 above with respect to vision, can serve as a prototypical case study of information adaptation. According to Kandel (2012) the process evolves as an interaction between a bottom-up syntactic process of deconstruction and a top-down semantic process of reconstruction. In Chap. 3 we've suggested that a better way to describe this process is in terms of interaction between a bottom-up process of *analysis* and a top-down *synthesis*. Both interpretations imply a play between two worlds: internal and external—in Kandel's (2012, p. 284) words:

> Thus, we live in two worlds at once, and our ongoing visual experience is a dialogue between the two: the outside world that enters through the fovea and is elaborated in a bottom-up manner, and the internal world of the brain's perceptual, cognitive and emotional models that influences information from the fovea in a top-down manner.

This description of Kandel corresponds directly to our (Haken and Portugali 1996) notion of SIRN (synergetic inter-representation network) that models a complex-cognitive agent as being subject to two information sources: *external* that comes from the environment and *internal* that is generated by the agent's memory (Fig. 4.3). The output message transmitted by that agent emerges out of the interaction between these two information sources. See Chap. 5, Sect. 5.3.4 for further details.

Taken in conjunction with the above noted processes of information analysis and synthesis (*deconstruction* and *reconstruction* in Kandel's conceptualization) we can say that the data/information that enters from the external world through the fovea undergoes a two stages process: In stage one the MBB does two operations in parallel: In pathway 1, which is based on low-pass spatial frequency filter, it

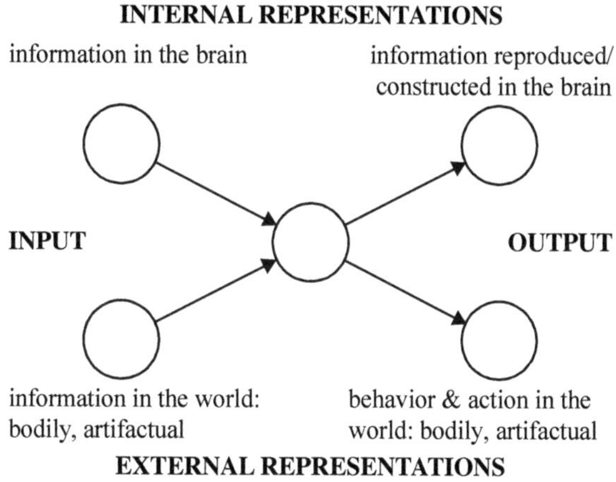

Fig. 4.3 The basic SIRN model, as derived from Haken's synergetic computer. It symbolizes a self-organizing agent that is subject to two forms of information; intern and external, and is actively constructing two forms of information, again internal and external. *Source* Haken and Portugali (1996)

stresses soft variations of the incoming data values; in pathway 2, which is based on high pass spatial frequency filter, it analyses and rearranges the incoming data into smaller classes of segments (of lines, corners and so on) and distributes them in the brain's layers/areas V1–V4. This twofold process as we've seen above evolves bottom-up and is implemented by the brain's syntactic capabilities.

One may ask why the brain does this kind of "preprograming" (from the retina to areas V1–V4)? A possible answer is that by so doing it gives (locally!) some kind of "meaning" to arrangements of, say, pixels. This arrangement of pixels represents ("means") a line, a corner, a specific orientation of the line. Thus locally this process reduces the uncertainty, in a way, it reduces the amount of information of these pixel arrangements. It thus enhances contrasts and contributes to the fundamental foreground-background issue. *But*, at the same time, the whole decomposition ("deconstruction") (probably) produces a large uncertainty ("information") as to what these newly constructed elements (lines, etc.) belong. (Which is, of course, the ultimate goal of pattern recognition).

The first stage of analysis ("deconstruction") thus produces, on the one hand, *local* information deflation, that is, certainty regarding the meaning of the parts, while on the other, *global* information inflation, that is, uncertainty regarding the interrelations between the parts. The second stage of synthesis ("reconstruction") is a top-down process that is implemented by the brain's semantic (meaning giving) capabilities, such as pattern recognition, abstraction or categorization. Here, once the data/information from the external world is distributed in the brain as above, the brain synthesizes or recreates the pattern by giving it meaning (e.g. recognizes, categorizes, …). This is implemented by means of interaction between the local information created in stage one and global information (gestalt principles/models, categories, memorized patterns) stored in/generated by memory. The result is a

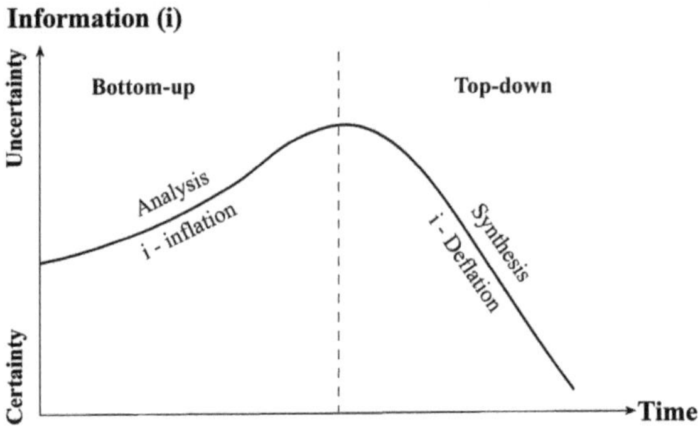

Fig. 4.4 The 2-stages process of information adaptation: It starts with a *bottom-up* process of information inflation and continues with a *top-down* process of information deflation until the appropriate quantity of information is adapted to the required task

process of global information inflation by which the low quantity of local Shannonian information with its high local certainty and high global uncertainty, is being transformed into low quantity of global Shannonian information with high global certainty. To the latter one may add that the possibility of this transformation rests on the specific correlations between the data. One might even say: meaning is implicit in (or encoded by) the correlations. (Actually, pattern recognition algorithms including the synergetic computer, rest on the use of correlations).

What we thus have here is a distinction between local and global meaning, that is, *local* and *global semantic information*: In the first bottom-up stage, the global information in the outside world that enters through the fovea is being analyzed and rearranged into locally meaningful elements (lines, corners, etc.); by means of this process the MBB "loses" ("trades of") global meaning in order to "gain" the locally meaningful information elements that will become the parts of the subsequent process of synthesis. In the second top-down stage, the MBB, by means of interaction between its memorized global information and the local semantic informational elements (created in the first stage), reconstruct back the global meaning/semantic information.

We propose seeing the above two stages of analysis and synthesis and the shifts between information inflation and deflation as two aspects of a single *information adaptation* process (Fig. 4.4): The process starts with information inflation, proceeds with information deflation in order to adapt, that is, to synthesize and reconstruct the information to the specific task (e.g. pattern recognition).

4.4 A Communication System of a Complex Adaptive Cognitive System

Our basic proposition then is that the cognitive process of information adaptation takes place in, or corresponds to, the two stages of analysis-synthesis described above, and is implemented by information inflation or deflation. That is, in some

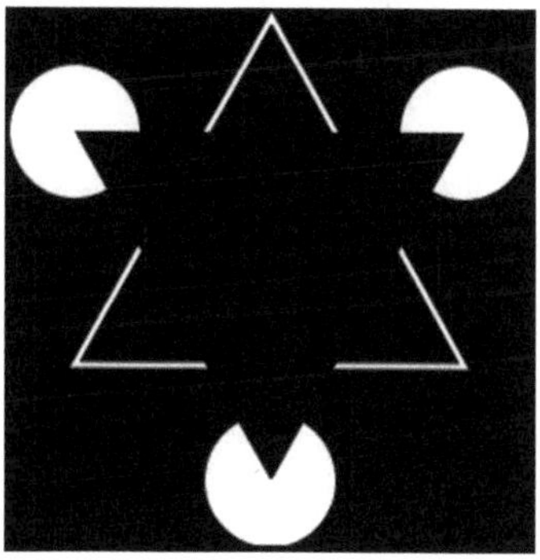

Fig. 4.5 The Kaniza *triangle* illusion

information adaptation cases the brain adds data that doesn't exist in the row data/information, while in other cases the brain implements adaptation by the exact opposite—by ignoring data/information that exists in the row information. These two cases can be illustrated by reference to some well-known visual illusions. For example, in the case of the Kaniza triangle illusion (Fig. 4.5), information adaptation is implemented by information deflation (increase of certainty), that is, the MBB adds data with the implication that we see lines where there are no lines. On the other hand, the "Monkey Business" illusion as originally described by Simons and Chabris (1999), Fig. 3 and in Chabris and Simons' (2010) *The Invisible Gorilla* (Fig. 4.6), illustrates the exact opposite: The process of information adaptation is implemented by overlooking (i.e. compressing) a lot of data that is not relevant to the task. The notion of *attention parameter* as formulated by Haken's (1996) Synergetics (and further discussed in Chap. 7 below) is of specific significance here.

In the context of our interpretation of Shannon's communication system as a complex adaptive system (Fig. 4.2), the process of information adaptation can be described as follows: Two persons, S at the information source and D at the destination, are communicating by means of a certain information communication machinery T and R (interrupted by N). For simplicity, assume that we are dealing with a one-way communication by which S produces a message (e.g. a pattern) and then transmits it to D. In terms of synergetics, S's task is thus *pattern formation* while D's task is *pattern recognition* Haken (1991/2004). Since we are dealing with communication between two persons, person's S task is to produce the information so that person D will be able to understand it, that is, S attempts to adapt the information to D. Given Shannon's information entropy, this is implemented by means of semantic information that determines the index k in Eq. 1.3 (that serves as label of the probabilities p_k fixing Shannon information) and as a consequence the quantity of information (i in Eq. 1.3 above) that goes from S to T. At the destination there is person D whose main task is to pattern recognize the message, that is, to give meaning to the signals/data coming from R and thus adapt the signal to the information "stored" in her/his memory.

As can be seen, the above complexity-cognitive information setup differs from the Shannonian one also in its basic question and focus: Shannon's main interest

Fig. 4.6 The gorilla illusion: when the observers' attention is directed to the ball and players, 50 % of them do not see the gorilla. *Source* Simons and Chabris (1999), Fig. 3. Figure provided by Daniel Simons (www.dansimons.com)

was in channel capacity; the focus of interest of the various cognitive applications is on the relations between the information source and the cognitive agent, be it the encoder (the left side of Fig. 4.1) or the decoder (right side). Thus, in Miller's application (above) the focus of interest is the information processing limitations of a person facing an information source; in Attneave's on the way the mind/brain encodes data from the environment and so on.

Appling the SIRN processes of information inflation, deflation, adaptation (Fig. 4.3, above) to this setup, a complex, adaptive, cognitive, communication system would appear as in Fig. 4.7: On the left side there is a cognitive agent S that by means of the interaction between the data coming from an external information/data source and the information coming from its memory, encodes, interprets and then transmits the information to the channel. On the right side there is agent D that by means of the interaction between the information coming from the channel and the information coming from its own memory, encodes, interprets and then externalizes the information. As emphasized above, most cognitive applications of information theory focus on the left or right sides of Fig. 4.7 while the complete information setup of Fig. 4.7 thus refers to a special case of interaction between two agents.

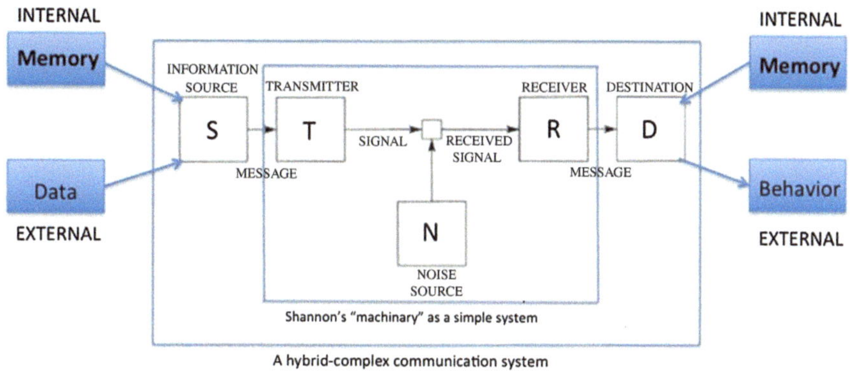

Fig. 4.7 A communication system of a complex adaptive cognitive system

It is interesting to note that the above conceptualization was anticipated by Weaver (Shannon and Weaver 1949, p. 26) when he wrote:

> One can imagine, as an addition to the diagram [e.g. Fig. 4.1 above], another box labeled "Semantic Receiver" interposed between the engineering receiver (which changes signals to messages) and the destination. [...] Similarly one can imagine another box in the diagram which, inserted between the information source and the transmitter, would be labeled "semantic noise," [...] And the problem of semantic decoding must take this semantic noise into account.

From the conjunctive perspective of complexity and cognition both Shannonian information and semantic information are *emergent properties* of the cognitive system—an outcome of the interaction between an external information source and internal information source that originates in the cognitive system (mind/brain) of a dynamical system. By means of this interaction the dynamical system *constructs* these two forms of information. The process of information adaptation we suggest refers to the interaction between the Shannonian and semantic information that leads to adaptation, that is, to the appropriate balance between Shannonian and semantic information required for the implementation of a specific task. As we'll see below, the process of information adaptation resembles the process of circular causality as conceptualized by synergetics: Facing a certain task (e.g. pattern recognition of data coming from an information source) the cognitive system by means of its memorized semantic information determines the Shannonian quantity of the information coming from that source; if the latter is below the information quantity required by the task, the cognitive system by means of semantic information generated by its memory inflates the information; if above, it deflates it and so on in circular causality until adaptation. In Chaps. 6–8 below we exemplify this process at it takes place in actual cognitive processes.

Chapter 5
On Synergetic Computers and Other Machines

In this study we make an intensive use of the concept *synergetic computer* (SC). We've referred to it above as means to interpret empirical findings (Chap. 3) and as means to reformulate Shannon's communication system in terms of a complex system (Chap. 4), and we'll further use it below (Chaps. 6–8) to develop our notion of information adaptation. In this chapter we shortly introduce the SC and relate it to some philosophical and technical issues associated with its usage. In a way of introduction we can say that the SC is a kind of conceptual machine similar in several ways to the Turing machine, on the one hand and to Shannon's machinery (his communication system), on the other; hence the title of this chapter—"on synergetic computers and other machines".

5.1 Can Machines Think?

Employing the SC as means to study information processing as it takes place in the human mind/brain raises the question of the extent to which computer models can truly model such processes—a question that attracted, and is still attracting, a lot of attention since Turing (1937, 1950) has introduced his famous notion of a (conceptual) "machine" known as the *Turing Machine* and the associated *Turing test*. Turing opens his 1950 paper on "Computing machinery and intelligence" in which he introduced the "Turing test", with the following sentence:

> I propose to consider the question, "Can machines think?"

In the first part of the paper he develops the test, while in the second (Sect. 6) he discusses in some length contrary views on the main question and then dismiss them one by one. Before doing so, however, he states clearly his own view on the question:

> Nevertheless I believe that at the end of the century the use of words and general educated opinion will have altered so much that one will be able to speak of machines thinking without expecting to be contradicted. I believe further that no useful purpose is served by concealing these beliefs. The popular view that scientists proceed inexorably from well-

H. Haken and J. Portugali, *Information Adaptation: The Interplay Between Shannon Information and Semantic Information in Cognition*,
SpringerBriefs in Complexity, DOI 10.1007/978-3-319-11170-4_5

> established fact to well-established fact, never being influenced by any improved conjecture, is quite mistaken. Provided it is made clear which are proved facts and which are conjectures, no harm can result. Conjectures are of great importance since they suggest useful lines of research (Turing ibid, 442).

Finally he concludes by stating:

> We may hope that machines will eventually compete with men in all purely intellectual fields. But which are the best ones to start with? Even this is a difficult decision. Many people think that a very abstract activity, like the playing of chess, would be best. It can also be maintained that it is best to provide the machine with the best sense organs that money can buy, and then teach it to understand and speak English. This process could follow the normal teaching of a child. Things would be pointed out and named, etc. Again I do not know what the right answer is, but I think both approaches should be tried.
>
> We can only see a short distance ahead, but we can see plenty there that needs to be done (Turing ibid, 460).

According to Hodges (1992) and (Gleick 2011) Shannon and Turing met each other in the year 1945 and for several months the two men were communicating. Shannon, according to Hodges, was impressed by Turing's machine—as can be testified explicitly by Shannon's (1956) paper on "A Universal Turing machine …" and implicitly by the fact Shannon's communication system (Fig. 4.1 in Chap. 4 above) is in a way a kind of conceptual machine. Shannon was fully aware, as we've seen above, to Weaver's view that his machinery can be extended to include semantic information, but insisted that his communication system is essentially an "engineering" entity. Thus, similar questions that entailed the Turing Machine ('in what way a Turing machine is related to human reasoning?') are relevant also to Shannon's theory ('can Shannon's machinery (Fig. 4.1 above) be applied to human cognition?'), as well as to the SC that we employ here.

5.2 Trivial Versus Non-Trivial Machines in Relation to Simple Versus Complex Systems

The famous "cyberneticist" Heinz von Foerster's (2003) responded to such questions by a distinction between *trivial* versus *non-trivial machines*: He defined a trivial machine (Fig. 5.1 top) "by the fact that it always bravely does the very same thing that it originally did." (ibid 309). Such a system/machine is thus: "(i) **synthetically determined;** (ii) **independent of the past;** (iii) **analytically determinable;** (iv) **predictable.**" On the other hand, a non-trivial machine is: "(i) **synthetically determined;** (ii) **dependent on the past;** (iii) **analytically determinable;** (iv) **unpredictable**." This is so because "Non-trivial machines have "inner" states (Fig. 5.1 bottom). In each operation, this inner state changes, so that when the next operation takes place, the previous operation is not repeated, but rather another operation can take place." (Ibid 312).

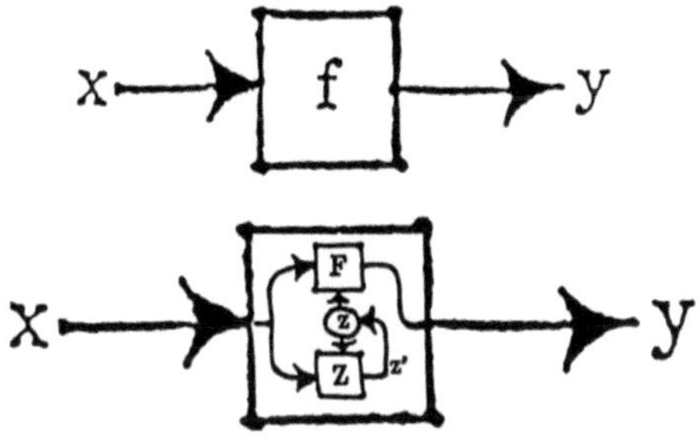

Fig. 5.1 *Top* trivial machine. *Bottom* Non-trivial machine. Drawings by Heinz von Foerster

How is the above distinction between trivial versus non-trivial machines referring to complex versus simple systems and then to information? Several observations can be made in response to this question:

(1) Von Foerster assumes that his two machines are completely deterministic, i.e. any chance events ("stochastics") are excluded. In contrast, as we know from synergetics, in all complex and *self-organizing* systems, stochastic influences are crucial for triggering a process of self-organization.
(2) Von Foerster explicitly excludes memory beyond a "holding" time Δt of states z. This could be remedied, however, by the assumption of, e.g., limit cycles so that a specific state Z_0 reappears again and again. In our opinion such kind of processes are (besides stochastic influences) responsible for the complexity of nontrivial machines. If the limit cycles etc. are unstable, even chaotic states might occur.
(3) He assumes reversibility. In all cases, present days' computing processes are irreversible, and Rolf Landauer (1961), some 50 years ago, calculated the amount of heat due to this mechanism.

But leaving aside (1) and (3) we may follow von Foerster's insight into a nontrivial machine (or perhaps in our language) into a complex system by saying that its specific properties stem from the internal states z. Or in other words: the output of a nontrivial machine is (surely within limits) unpredictable because of our lack of knowledge of the internal states z. It is precisely here where Shannon information (entropy) comes in as a measure of our lack of knowledge, or to turn things into the positive, as a means to make guesses (probabilistic predictions) on a system's output ("behavior").

This argument is reinforced when (1) and (3) are taken into account in addition to (2). Actually, even the output (behavior) of a trivial machine is not completely predictable (think of a failure of a clock—von Foerster's example of a trivial machine), so strictly speaking, the difference between trivial and non-trivial machines is—eventually—only of a quantitative nature.

While at the time of its publication von Foerstr's distinction was very useful, over the past decades our understanding of the behavior of "machines" has changed dramatically. In the field of *deterministic chaos* it was discovered that even "trivial" machines may exhibit complex behavior. An example is the pendulum, a prototypical example of a clock! Its complex behavior appears when the pendulum may turn over. Still more pronounced "complex" behavior is shown by the still simple system of a double pendulum. On the mathematical side, even very simple algorithms such as the "logistic map" lead to complicated time series. Furthermore, our expectations on what machines are able to do proceed from utopia to reality: Self-repairing machines, self-organizing machines etc.

Thus our experience necessitates a redefinition of "trivial" versus "nontrivial" machines. Along the general lines of thought of complexity theory we suggest the following distinction between *simple machines* (or dynamical systems) and *complex machines* (or dynamical systems):

Simple systems. These are systems whose structure and functions can be formalized by algorithms of finite length, including random generators. An algorithm may be supplemented by diagrams, graphs (e.g. of networks) but must not be substituted by them. (The role of random generators might require an in-depth discussion). An important question is on which material substrates (machines!) and how an algorithm can be implemented.

Complex Systems. It is not determined whether such a system is simple or not. It may not be determined for practical reasons (e.g. insufficient data) or "in principle". At least in general we may assume that such a system can be approximated by a sequence of simple systems (machines) in the hope to capture (the) relevant (or essential) features. (An example is the synergetic computers for pattern recognition introduced above). Convergence of such an approach is hoped for, but incompleteness is still possible (i.e. "surprises"). A truly complex system is thus inexhaustible; it cannot be represented by a formalism. The fundamental question in cognitive (or brain) science is, of course, whether the human brain is a truly complex system.

Von Foerster's distinction between trivial versus non-trivial machines reminds one of the distinction between Behaviorism versus cognitivism and thus takes us back to the domain of complexity, cognition and information. It is common to describe behaviorism and its basic stimulus-response model by reference to the notion of *black box* (BB). Now, the BB concept in itself leaves it open as to what kind of machine that box is. If the response (behavior) is uniquely determined by the (sensory) input, it is surely von Foerster's trivial machine,—but if not, we have to deal with some kind of non-trivial machine. However, behaviorism's main proposition was that 'the response is uniquely determined by the input' and that as a consequence the inner states of the mind/brain can be ignored—hence the view that the mind/brain can be treated as a BB. In fact, the "cognitive revolution" of the 1950s that gave rise to the cognitive science—*The Mind's New Science* as Gardner (1987) termed it—was exactly on this issue: people such as Chomsky and others criticized behaviorism suggesting that in order to fully understand the relations between stimulus and response, the inner state of the mind/brain must be taken into consideration.

5.3 The Synergetic Computer

5.3.1 Motivation

Probably since centuries, the motivation behind the development of a "thinking machine" has been the desire to study and understand the functioning of a human being: That is, to build a robot or a machine that imitates a human being, in other words, that senses, thinks, acts, feels like a human. A nowadays generally preferred way to this goal is based on concepts that are formalized and even quantified in the frame of mathematics by means of *algorithms*. Any material realization must obey the laws of physics. (A requirement that has led "robotics" to the need of "embodiment" and "situatedness"—see Brooks 1999). But there is besides the required physical pillars "energy" and "matter" a third one, namely, information—be it in the popular sense of message or instruction or in the strictly scientific sense of Shannon information (entropy). It is the latter interpretation we are using throughout in the present study.

Concerning "algorithms" it is worthwhile to have a look at the development of mathematics in the course of—even millennia. We think it is fair to say, that many of the concepts and their corresponding formalisms were inspired by the interplay between (our observation of) physical phenomena and the attempts at their appropriate "modeling", i.e. formalization at an abstract level. And to make such formalization operational, algorithms, i.e., concrete mathematical instructions are needed. This remark may shed some light on the hard core of what is called "artificial intelligence" that started from "symbol manipulation" but then has proceeded along different lines. All of them can be characterized as "algorithmic", nearly all of them being based on specific physical models of (highly simplified) neurons (thus the field of neurocomputers), or the—in particular by physicist highly acclaimed—spinglass-model of a neural net by Hopfield.

5.3.2 Self-organization

However, there is still a further source of inspiration that has led Haken to develop concepts for the SCs, namely the large class of self organizing systems that appear in many fields, ranging from physics over to say, economy and sociology. "Self-organization" means that a system composed of many individual parts acquires its highly ordered spatial, temporal or functional structure without any specific interference from the outside. The development of a theory of self-organization is the central topic of the interdisciplinary field of synergetics. An outline of it would be far beyond the scope of our study here.

We've already referred to synergetics in Chap. 4 above in connection with our complexity approach to information. Here, however, we add a few remarks that will clarify the concept of the SC within the general context of synergetics' specific interpretation of processes of self-organization. Consider the spontaneous formation of an ordered structure (a "pattern") in a physical system out of equilibrium. A prototypical example is a liquid layer in a vessel heated from below and cooled from above. While for a small temperature gradient no macroscopic pattern appears, above a critical gradient a roll pattern appears. According to synergetics, the ordering mechanism can be mathematically described by the concepts instability, order parameters, slaving principle.

Instability means "readiness" for pattern formation. In the beginning, many different patterns are virtually possible. Each pattern has a specific strength (amplitude) characterized by its order parameter. These order parameters compete among each other until one on them—the initially strongest order parameter—wins (at least in general) the competition. The winner then *enslaves* all the individual parts and forces the total system (here the liquid) into the ordered state. Figure 5.2 illustrates the process by means of three examples a, b, c, that represent three initially dominant "virtual" patterns.

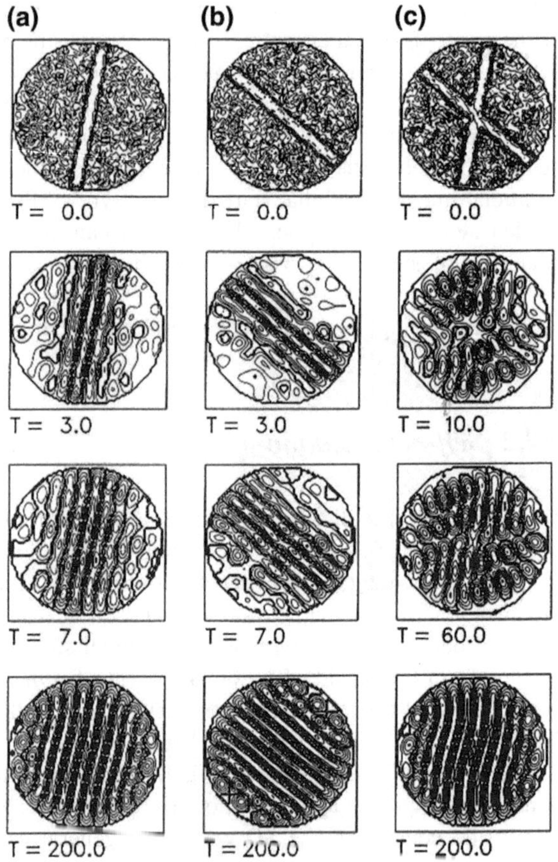

Fig. 5.2 Computer simulation of the developments of rolls in a liquid heated from below (*top view* of the vessel). **a** The first frame (t = 0) shows the initial orientation of the upwelling, which develops in the course of time into a specific final roll state. **b** Same as (**a**) but with a different orientation of the initially prescribed upwelling of the fluid. **c** The initial state consists of superposition of two lines of upwelling fluid with different strength. Eventually only one pattern survives to win the completion. From Haken (1988/2000/2006) p. 22, Fig. 4.3

5.3.3 From Pattern Formation to Pattern Recognition

The synergetic approach to pattern recognition commences with an analogy between the above process of pattern formation in matter (liquid) and the cognitive process of pattern recognition (Fig. 5.3). More specifically, in *pattern recognition by the synergetic computer*, advantage is taken of the same mechanism described above with respect to liquid: Once a set of features is given, they form their order parameters that will compete with other order parameters (governing other feature-configurations). Eventually the order parameter with the strongest support will win and will force the system to exhibit the complete set of features belonging to that order parameter.

Thus there is a complete correspondence between the complementation process during pattern formation and the *associative memory* during pattern recognition. What we just described can be, and has been, cast into an algorithm that defines the SC. In the next two chapters we will describe the final outcome being formulated by means of the feature "vectors" and their dynamics. Note that the corresponding equations can be transformed into such for the *order parameters* alone. This opens new views on the brain processes. They can be studied at the level of features detectors materially realized by localized neurons, or at the level of order parameters which refer to the whole neural net and represent "ideas". This interpretation may elucidate the intimate interplay between ideas, i.e. percepts, and their material substrate.

The basic concept of the SC has been extended in several ways: Firstly, the recognition process has been made invariant against the translation, rotation and size of an object in an image by means of a preprocessing which is based on Fourier transformations and a logarithmic map (Fuchs and Haken 1988). Though there are some indications that the brain might use such processes, a final verification is lacking. (Fourier transforms are involved in processes of neural phase-locking, discovered by Gray and Singer (1989), and suggested by them as a solution to the "binding problem"; a logarithmic map was suggested in brain models by Wilson and Cowan (1973) (map from retina to visual cortex).

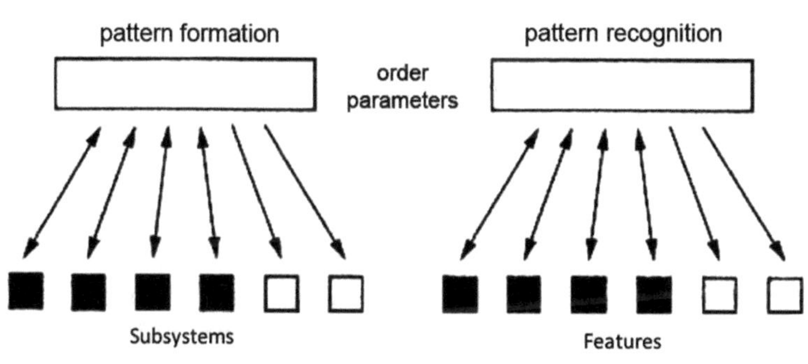

Fig. 5.3 Analogy between pattern formation (*left*) and pattern recognition (*right*). In pattern formation the subsystems are enslaved by the order parameter; in the case of pattern recognition it is the features that are enslaved by order parameters. Based on Haken (1991/2004) p. 37, Fig. 5.2

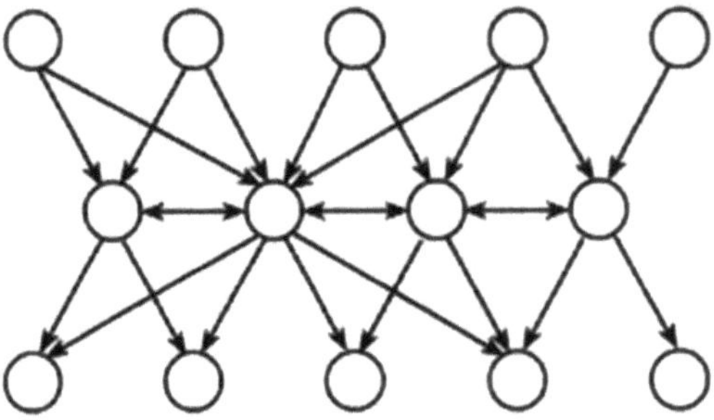

Fig. 5.4 Haken's SC (1991/2004) implemented on a three-layer network. For details, see text

Secondly, the dynamics of "attention parameters" was included in the SC algorithm. This addition allows the analysis of *complex scenes* (Fuchs and Haken 1988) (cf. Chap. 6 below) and the modeling of the recognition of ambiguous figures (Ditzinger and Haken 1986).

Thirdly, the SC has been realized as a *parallel computer* based on a three layers network. The latter was a consequence of Haken's (1991/2004) demonstration that the synergetic algorithm of pattern recognition by means of associative memory can be also implemented on a network which acts in a highly parallel manner. As illustrated in Fig. 5.4, the SC envisions a complex cognitive system (e.g. mind/brain) as a three-layers network in which the input layer with its model neurons represents the initially given input activity; the middle layer represents the order parameters of the system, while the output layer with its neurons represents the final activity of each neuron. This SC was suggested as an alternative to the conventional neural network model in that the elements of its inner layer are order parameters as defined by synergetics. The discussion in the Chaps. 6–8 that follow and in particular the mathematical sections in them, are based on this second generation SC.

5.3.4 SIRN—Synergetic Inter-Representation Networks

In a paper from 1996 we've developed a variation of the SC in order to capture and model the process of SIRN—synergetic inter-representation networks (Haken and Portugali 1996). As already noted above (Chap. 4), SIRN refers to cognitive processes that cannot be implemented by a single cognitive act and are thus being executed by a sequential interaction between internal representations constructed in the mind and external representations constructed in the world. Our derivation of the SIRN model started by looking at the net of Fig. 5.4 in enfilade way from the side. The result is shown at Fig. 5.5, bottom, left. Adding to the latter external inputs and outputs, we arrive at our basic SIRN model (Fig. 5.5 bottom, right). As can be seen, this is the above SC composed of two kinds of inputs, internal and external and two kinds of outputs, again internal and external. As in the above SC,

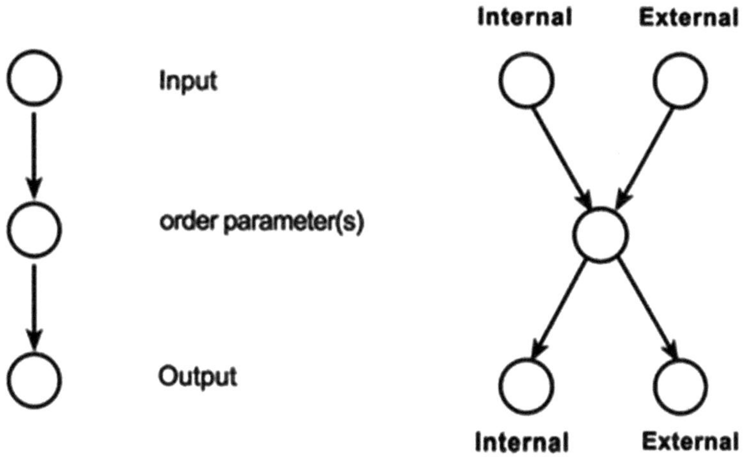

Fig. 5.5 The derivation of the SIRN model. *Left,* the result of looking at the network of Fig. 5.4 in enfilade way from the side. *Right*, the result of adding internal and external inputs and outputs

the middle node symbolizes the order parameters that emerge out of the dynamic interaction between internal and external representations (Haken and Portugali 1996, Figs. 2–4). Our interpretation of Shannon's communication system in terms of a complex adaptive system (Chap. 4, Fig. 4.7) is based on this model, rotated to the left.

Chapter 6
Pattern Recognition as a Paradigm for Information Adaptation

6.1 Pattern Recognition

Information wise, a pattern recognition task starts when a person (or computer) is offered partial information/data about a pattern and is asked to produce the whole information about it. According to Synergetics' pattern recognition paradigm (Haken 1996), as well as to others (Steinbuch 1961), such a task is implemented by means of *associative memory*: The partial information/data offered triggers a process of self-organization that gives rise to a competition between several order states represented by "order parameters". This competition is resolved when one of the order parameters wins. The process by which it forces the many parts to its specific dynamics, is termed *the slaving principle* (Haken 1983). In what follows we want to show that pattern recognition is essentially a process of information adaptation: in certain circumstances, when the incoming information is too high, it is implemented by information deflation, while in others, when the incoming information is too low, by information inflation.

6.2 Pattern Recognition of Faces as Information Adaptation by Means of Deflation

A case in point is the synergetics' paradigm of pattern recognition of faces (Haken 1991): A test person/computer is shown a small part a pattern of a face (Fig. 6.2, left) and is asked to recognize it out of several patterns stored in/generated by, its memory (Fig. 6.1).

In terms of the above (Chap. 2) discussion regarding data versus information, the process (Fig. 6.2 upper part) is the symmetric reverse of The Bull (Fig. 2.1): The shown pattern (e.g. Fig. 6.2, left) has little data and high Shannonian information (that is, uncertainly). The task of pattern recognition is to give meaning, that is,

H. Haken and J. Portugali, *Information Adaptation: The Interplay Between Shannon Information and Semantic Information in Cognition*,
SpringerBriefs in Complexity, DOI 10.1007/978-3-319-11170-4_6

Fig. 6.1 Examples of prototypes stored in the SC

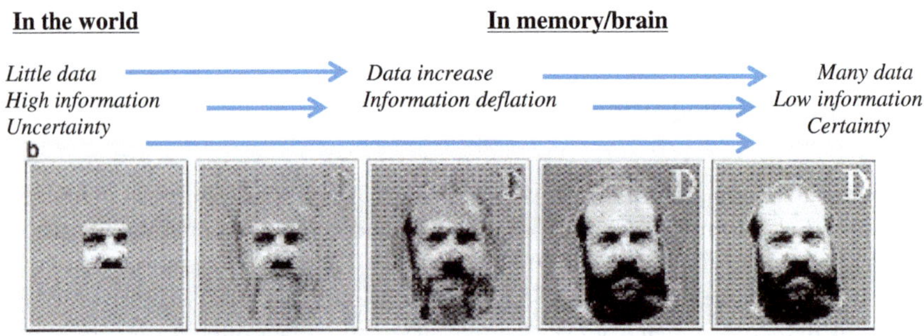

Fig. 6.2 Example of a pattern recognized by the SC

semantic information, to the pattern. The mind/brain implements this task by adding data, deflating the Shannonian information and reducing uncertainty (Fig. 6.2 right). The process implies adaptation because the MBB continues with this process (of adding data/deflating information) up to the stage where recognition/meaning is achieved.

Mathematically, we may distinguish different patterns by the label G, where G may stand for a set of features, i.e. the grey values of the pixels into which the pattern is decomposed. We decompose G into J (essential) and T (unessential) features, e.g. J may characterize a face at a specific position in space with a specific orientation, a specific size and in a standard form, i.e. without deformations, e.g. showing no facial expressions. A typical example is the photo in our passport! T then may represent transformations such as translation in space, rotations, scaling or deformations. Shannon information is given as usual by

$$i = -c \sum_{G} P(G) \ln P(G) \tag{6.1}$$

where P is the probability to observe a pattern characterized by the label G.

We want to show that by means of the decomposition of G into J and T, which is achieved by the recognizing system, i.e. our brain or an advanced computer, Shannon information (6.1) can be deflated. To this end we write $P(G)$ as

$$P(G) = P(J,T) \tag{6.2}$$

so that (6.1) reads

$$i = -\sum_{J,T} P(J,T)\ln P(J,T). \tag{6.3}$$

(we have dropped the factor c)

According to general rules of probability theory we may decompose the joint probability $P(J,T)$ according to

$$P(J,T) = P(J|T)f(T), \tag{6.4}$$

where the first factor represents the conditional probability and the second factor the probability to observe the object at a specific location, etc. before the transformation T has been made. The usual normalization conditions

$$\sum_J P(J|T) = 1 \tag{6.5}$$

and

$$\sum_T f(T) = 1 \tag{6.6}$$

must be observed. Inserting (6.4) into (6.3) and using (6.5) allows us to cast i into the form

$$i = -\sum_{\mathrm{T}} f(T)\sum_J P(J|T)\ln P(J|T) - \sum_T f(T)\ln f(T), \tag{6.7}$$

where the first term is a sum over the different transformations T of the conditional information $i(\cdot|T)$

$$i(\cdot|T) = -\sum_I P(I|T)\ln P(I|T), \tag{6.8}$$

averaged over the distribution $f(T)$ The second term in (6.7) represents the information of the transformation T alone. When T is irrelevant for the recognition, we may drop this term and thus deflate information to the first term in (6.7). In a final step we may simplify the first sum in (6.7) by estimating (6.8) taking the most probable $i(\cdot|T)$ for a $T = T_0$

$$\max_{\mathrm{T}} i(\cdot|T) = i(\cdot|T_0). \tag{6.9}$$

Taking into account the normalization condition (6.6) we then obtain an estimate for the deflated information according to

$$i_{deflated} = \sum_T f(T) i(\cdot|T) \leq i(\cdot|T_0) \sum_T f(T) = i(\cdot|T_0). \tag{6.10}$$

Why are these rather straightforward considerations fundamental for the understanding of human cognition as well as for devising computers with recognition capabilities? The issue is that Shannon information gives us a measure for the number of bits that can or must be stored and then further processed. Clearly, since the number of transformations T can be enormous the reduction of information according to

$$i_{deflated} < i(\cdot|T_0) \tag{6.11}$$

is quite appreciable. A central point is, of course, in how far a cognitive system can extract the transformations T so that only the normal "pattern" is stored. In computer science a number of algorithms have been developed that allow such compressions. At least to our knowledge this question has not yet been studied in detail with respect to the human brain and it will be a challenging task to study which neural mechanisms allow the processing of transformations, which in other words make the recognition process independent of transformations T. Below we will discuss the work by Riesenhuber and Poggio (1999) which deals with the invariance problem in a new way.

6.3 Pattern Recognition of Caricatures as Information Adaptation

A similar process takes place in the case of the caricatures such as that of Einstein (Fig. 2.2 above) or that of Fig. 6.3: A test person is shown a caricature and is asked to recognize it. Let us assume that the person has seen, and thus can construct in memory, several images of Einstein (e.g. Fig. 6.3). In such a case the process evolves as above. However, if the task is: "who is this person?", then, the information adaptation process will end when the answer is Einstein!; if the question is: "who is this person and what is the source of this drawing?", the information adaptation process will end when and if the person identifies Fig. 6.3, right.

A similar process of information adaptation by means of deflation takes place with respect to Fig. 6.4, but with one important difference: Here the task might be "what is this?" and an appropriate answer: "A face!", that is, a category which is a construction of the mind.

Fig. 6.3 Images of Einstein

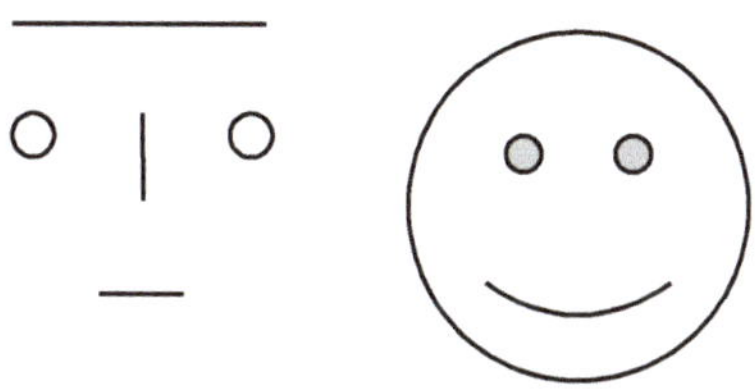

Fig. 6.4 Information adaptation by means of deflation with respect to a caricature

6.4 Pattern Recognition as Information Adaptation by Means of Inflation

There is, however, another way to look at caricatures and sketches, namely, from the perspective of the caricaturist. His/her task here would be to convey the category "face" (Fig. 6.4) or the face of Einstein (Fig. 6.3) with little data, without loosing meaning, that is, sematic information. This task is achieved by means of a process of information adaptation that involves lossless data compression and information inflation (Fig. 6.5).

Let us consider the process of information inflation and its mathematical description in some detail. To be as concrete as possible we take as a starting point Fig. 6.4. In order to be able to introduce the concept of information, we need to consider an ensemble of figures. To introduce this ensemble we imagine a two-dimensional grid with its pixels, which may contain empty pixels, dots or dashes

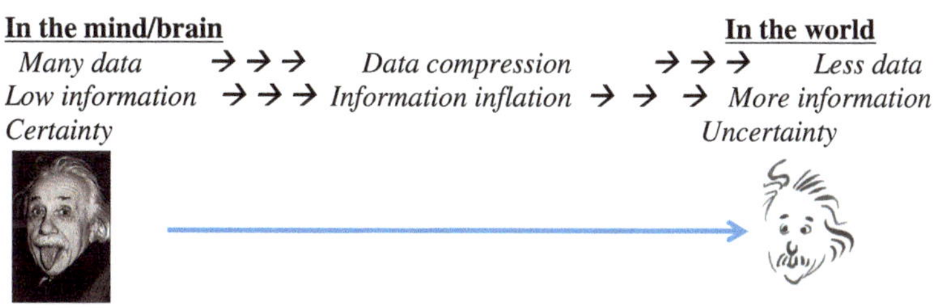

Fig. 6.5 Information adaptation involving lossless data compression and information inflation

(bars). We may imagine, to be still more concrete and in accordance with the findings by Hubel and Wiesel (ibid), that only bars are admitted. Depending on the various realizations of arrangements of bars we may introduce a distribution function.

$$f_0(\mathbf{q}_0). \tag{6.12}$$

The corresponding Shannon information is then given by the by now well-known formula. Now consider the action of semantics. According to it we want to attribute meaning to the individual pattern. Most probably, this process requires several stages in which hypotheses are made. First indicators may suggest: look for a face as long as this is compatible with the specific arrangement. There are very many possible realizations of faces that come to our mind so that the bars are no more sufficient but must be replaced by grey values of the various pixels. For a connection of this approach with the HMAX approach see below. We denote these grey values by $\mathbf{q}$. Because of the plethora of faces induced by the original pattern $\mathbf{q}_0$ we have to introduce the joint probability distribution $F(\mathbf{q},\mathbf{q}_0)$. The corresponding information is given by

$$i = -\sum_{\mathbf{q}\mathbf{q}_0} F(\mathbf{q},\mathbf{q}_0)\ln F(\mathbf{q},\mathbf{q}_0). \tag{6.13}$$

According to probability theory we may decompose F according to

$$F(\mathbf{q},\mathbf{q}_0) = f(\mathbf{q}|\mathbf{q}_0)f(\mathbf{q}_0) \tag{6.14}$$

where $f(\mathbf{q}|\mathbf{q}_0)$ is the conditional probability. Inserting (6.14) into (6.13) yields

$$i = -\sum_{\mathbf{q}_0,\mathbf{q}} f_0(\mathbf{q}_0)f(\mathbf{q}|\mathbf{q}_0)\ln F(f_0 f) \tag{6.15}$$

or

$$i = -\sum_{q_0,q} f_0 f \ln f_0 - \sum_{q_0,q} f_0 f \ln f. \tag{6.16}$$

Because of the normalization condition

$$\sum_{q} f(q|q_0) = 1 \tag{6.17}$$

(6.16) can be cast into the form

$$i = -\sum_{\mathbf{q}_0} f_0 \ln f_0 + \sum_{\mathbf{q}_0} f_0(\mathbf{q}_0)i(.|\mathbf{q}_0) \tag{6.18}$$

where i in the last term is given by

$$i(.|\mathbf{q}_0) = -\sum_{\mathbf{q}} f(\mathbf{q}|\mathbf{q}_0)\ \ln f(\mathbf{q}|\mathbf{q}_0). \tag{6.19}$$

Quite clearly the original information determined by f_0 alone is enhanced by the second term in (6.18) where (6.19) can be interpreted as the additional information under the condition that a pattern q_0 is present. The whole term is then averaged by the original distribution function f_0. Clearly these considerations can be generalized in a variety of ways, e.g. we may interpret the pattern vector q as having components that do not stand for grey values but that may denote objects. Then q describes a specific spatial arrangement of objects.

In the beginning of this section we spoke of a "caricature". But in the context of pattern recognition we must scrutinize the problem further. In fact, a "caricature" may convey the meaning: this is an arbitrary face, or this is a specific face, e.g. that of Einstein (Fig. 6.3). In this latter case information deflation must follow the just described inflation. In how far our brain follows this "roundabout" or manages a short cut must be left open.

Chapter 7
From General Principles of Information Adaptation to Concrete Specific Models

7.1 Introductory Remarks

In the foregoing chapters we have developed some general principles of information adaptation. What is lacking is an approach that shows how to derive algorithms that can, eventually, be implemented on machines (computers) and that may serve as models of (visual) pattern recognition by the human brain.

There is, in fact, a huge body of theories and specific models on brain functions. A discussion of these approaches is far beyond the scope of our article so that we refer the reader to relevant reviews, e.g. Cisak Drew and Kalaska (2007), Grossberg (1988), Ullman (1996), Poggio and Serre (2013). The later article is from Scholarpedia (http://www.scholarpedia.org/article/Main_Page) in which further bibliography can be found in the following domains: Computational neuroscience, in particular: Experimental neuroscience (vision). Theoretical neuroscience (network dynamics, brain models, dynamical systems/pattern formation). Computational intelligence (brain theory, recurrent networks, information theory, pattern recognition).

Our discussion is largely based on the synergetic computer (SC). As we've seen in Chap. 5 above, the SC is based on fundamental concepts of synergetics (in particular order parameters and slaving principle) and as such it differs—to the best of our knowledge—from all other computer algorithms known so far. As we will see, it goes beyond the well-known principle of "winner takes all" which will allow us to shed light on the Einstein/Monroe puzzle mentioned above (Chap. 3).

Quite clearly, in view of the enormous complexity of the brain's organization and function, with its various areas, hierarchical and columnar structures, its networks of billions of neurons with their intricate spiking patterns, the SC—like other neural network models—is very simple. But it will help us to elucidate the fundamental role of *information adaptation*. As we will show, *Shannon information* is much more than a measure of channel capacity; *it is a driving force for the formation of meaning*, i.e. of semantic information. We first deal with the task of defining probability of patterns.

H. Haken and J. Portugali, *Information Adaptation: The Interplay Between Shannon Information and Semantic Information in Cognition*,
SpringerBriefs in Complexity, DOI 10.1007/978-3-319-11170-4_7

7.2 Task: Define Probability of Patterns

We characterize a pattern by a set of data (e.g. features) a_k

$$G = (a_1, a_2, \ldots\ldots a_l)$$

We assume that all $\boldsymbol{a_k}$ can be quantified, $\boldsymbol{a_j} \rightarrow \boldsymbol{q_k}$, real numbers

Example 1 Picture with pixels $\boldsymbol{k}$, pixel $\boldsymbol{k}$: white $q_k = 0$, black $q_k = 1$

Example 2 Animal with specific features, e.g. a_l feather: it has none $q_l = 0$, it has $q_l = 1$.

Thus a pattern is characterized by a set of numbers

$$G \rightarrow Q = (q_1, q_2 \ldots q_l)$$

This implies that we replace j by the explicit form of Q in the expression of Shannon information

$$S = -\sum_j p_j \ln p_j, \quad \sum_j p_j = 1 \tag{7.1}$$

Shannon information S thus becomes formally

$$S = -\sum_{q_1,\ldots,q_l} p(q_1, \ldots, q_l) \ln p(q_1, \ldots, q_l) \tag{7.2}$$

(Note that already here semantic information enters in "disguise").

7.3 Information Deflation via Correlation Functions. Jaynes' Maximum (Information) Entropy Principle

S in (7.2) contains all cases of $G \Rightarrow Q$. In practice, only specific realizations $G \Rightarrow Q$ are met. Thus S must be reduced by (experimentally) given constraints. Here we follow the line that correlations between data G are measured (on large samples). Thus we treat correlation functions of data such as

$C_2(a_l, a_k)$, $C_3(a_l, a_k, a_m)$ etc.

Which, because of $G \rightarrow Q$ are defined as

$$C_2 \rightarrow f_{l,k}^{(2)} \ldots = \sum\nolimits_Q p(Q) f^{(2)}(q_1, q_2) \tag{7.3}$$

and higher order correlations correspondingly.

Note that the explicit form of $f^{(2)}(q_l, q_k)$ is given by the measurement apparatus (or our senses), and $f_{kl}^{(2)}$ is determined by the average over the performed measurements. But $p(Q)$ in (7.3) is unknown! This is an inverse problem. It is solved by an unbiased guess in $p(Q)$ based on Jaynes' maximum (information) entropy principle. Its solution is

$$p(Q) = e^{\lambda}\exp\left(-\Sigma\lambda_{kl}f^{(2)}(q_l, q_k) - \Sigma\lambda_{klm}f^{(3)}(q_l, q_k, q_m) - \cdots\right) \quad (7.4)$$

λ serves for normalization of $p(Q)$, i.e. $N = e^{\lambda} = (\Sigma p(Q))^{-1}$

$\lambda_{kl}, \lambda_{klm}\ldots$ are Lagrange parameters. Their determination is a difficult task, and in addition, they are very numerous.

To get some insight into the meaning of $p(Q)$ we write it in the form

$$p(Q) = N\,exp(-V(Q)) \quad (7.5)$$

and call $V(Q)$ a potential (for reasons see below). Where $V(Q)$ has a minimum at some $Q = Q_l$, $p(Q)$ has its maximum, i.e. the specific pattern Q_l has a high probability of occurrence, i.e. it is a pattern that must be learned.

In general, there are numerous minima with patterns Q_l to be learned, $l = 1, \ldots$.

So far, our discussion has been quite general, but to proceed further, we must make explicit assumptions on $f^{(2)}$, $f^{(3)}$ etc., calculate the Lagrange parameters λ_{lk}, determine the minima of $V(Q)$, and characterize the minima further. From this general approach, not much can be said about the nature of these minima: are they well separated, deep or flat etc.

7.4 Need for Models: Prototype Patterns

To cut this Gordian knot, we have to introduce suitable models for $V(Q)$ (we may suspect that nature has done it in a specific way by a neural net (the brain!), which neuroscience tries to explore).

[Readers not interested in the mathematical details of our specific model can skip this section and proceed to 7.5].

A generic model that reflects the hilly landscape of $V(Q)$ can be based on low-dimensional polynomials

$$V(Q) = \sum_{kl} C_{kl}q_kq_l + \sum_{klm} C_{klm}q_kq_lq_m + \cdots . \quad (7.6)$$

which fixes the measurement functions f in (5.4) and where C_{kl} are constant coefficients. But how to relate the Lagrange multipliers $\lambda, \lambda_1, \lambda_2, \ldots$ to the minima of $V(Q)$? This is solved by the concept of the synergetic computer. Let Q_l, $l = 1,\ldots L$ be the positions of the minima of $V(\boldsymbol{Q})$ and the vector $\boldsymbol{v}_l = N_l\boldsymbol{Q}_l$ be normalized.

For illustration we assume that the v's are orthogonal, k

$$v_i v_k = \delta_{lk}$$

The potential of the synergetic computer is

$$V(Q) = -\frac{1}{2}\sum_k \mu_k (v_k Q)^2 - \frac{1}{4}B\sum_{kk^1} (v_k Q)^2 (v_{k'} Q)^2 - \frac{1}{4}C\sum_k (v_k Q)^4, B, C > 0 \tag{7.7}$$

We call μ_k attention parameter, which we may choose > 0 (attention is paid to prototype v_k), or $\mu_k = 0$ (no attention paid).

A comparison between $V(\boldsymbol{Q})$ defined via Lagrange parameters λ_{jk} etc. in (7.4) and V defined by prototypes $\boldsymbol{v}_k$ shows that the $\lambda' s$ can be uniquely expressed by $\boldsymbol{v}_k$. Since the number of prototypes is much smaller than that of the λ_s, an enormous reduction of e.g. computer time is reached.

7.5 Learning

As we have seen above in (7.3) (and more detail in (7.4)) the potential $V(Q)$ depends on parameters λ_{jk} (or more directly, on prototype patterns $\boldsymbol{v}_k$). i.e

$$V(Q) = V(Q, v).$$

These parameters can be fixed by the requirement, that the average over the experimentally determined distribution $f(Q)$

$$\langle V(Q,\, \lambda)\rangle \; = \text{Min}.$$

This problem can be solved by suitable algorithms or—in neural nets—by Hebb's rule on synapses. What is more relevant in the present context is the following: Once $V(Q)$ is fixed, its minima at specific positions in Q space are fixed.

We label these minima that define the prototypes by an index l, but the crucial point is this: A specific l now denotes a specific concept, e.g. "mother" (see below, Sect. 8.1). Thus calling upon a specific l (<-> concept) means calling upon a specific whole configuration (set of data), $\boldsymbol{Q}_l$. We may attribute to l a variable ξ_l which in terms of synergetics is an order parameter.

To make contact with psychological experience, our approach to the formation of a concept must be generalized. In fact, when recalling l (e.g. "mother") we recall

(1) not precisely all data contained in $\boldsymbol{Q}_l$—some are distorted or missing
(2) but we may recall additional data (e.g. circumstances)

These concepts can be taken care of by mathematics—at least in principle.

(1) The so-called fixed point $\boldsymbol{Q}_l$ is replaced by its basin of attraction
(2) The "memory space" spanned by $\boldsymbol{Q}$ must be supplemented by a new space C ("circumstances") so that $\boldsymbol{Q}$ is embedded in $Q \cup C$

A final remark on "learning" or on the determination of $\boldsymbol{V(Q)}$: As we have seen above, there is a choice on the "constraint" functions $f_{kl}^{(2)}$ etc.

We must assume that in psychological praxis, specific data (features) must be taken care of with greater weights than others (e.g. in the baby example below: the smell of the mother).

Another example is: two different views, front and profile belong to the *same* person. What is the "binding feature"? His or her name or other properties?

7.6 Recognition

So far, we have discussed learning in a more or less abstract manner which nevertheless can be made operational. Now we discuss recognition: A test pattern $\boldsymbol{Q}$ is offered—is it identical or close enough to an already learned prototype?

To find an answer we interpret $\boldsymbol{p(Q)}$ as the stationary solution of a Fokker-Planck equation which in turn belongs to a (nonlinear) Langevine equation (in vector form)

$$\frac{dQ}{dt} = -gradV(Q) + F \tag{7.8}$$

where F are so-called fluctuating forces. This equation describes a dynamical process which can be easily visualized. $\boldsymbol{V(Q)}$ is a hilly landscape in which a stone or ball is gliding downhill into its closest valley (Fig. 7.1). The whole valley including the slopes surrounding it, defines the basin of attraction. In terms of pattern

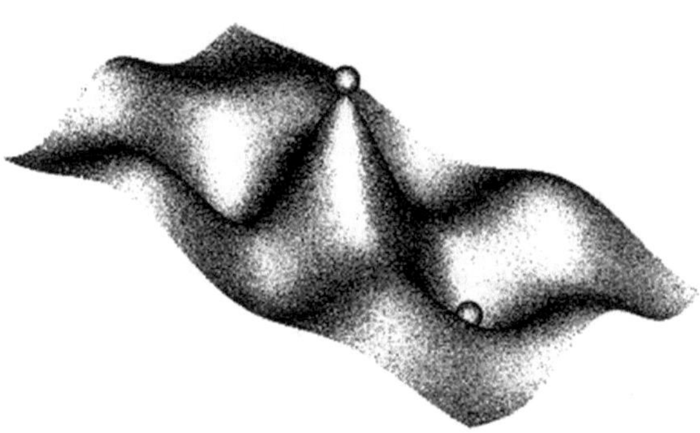

Fig. 7.1 Visualization of $V(Q)$ as a hilly landscape. *Source* Haken (2004), Fig. 4.7. Compare to Fig. 7.2 below

recognition: an offered test-pattern $\boldsymbol{Q}_t$ being close enough to prototype pattern $\boldsymbol{Q}_l$ is pulled into that state—the pattern is ultimately recognized. A more explicit example of the above equation for $\boldsymbol{Q}$ will be discussed below. In our discussion we have ignored some problems of great practical interest. In life, we recognize a pattern irrespective of his/her position and orientation in space, facial expression, illumination etc.

Must a recognition system store all these highly numerous instantiations (e.g. space is continuous!)? Will it then be possible to find appropriate prototype patterns via a search for original minima of $V(Q)$ in an immense search space? A way out of this dilemma is via suitable transformations of the original data. After such transformations, in the light of Shannon information, we may state the following: Because of the identification of a comparatively small number M of prototypes, Shannon information is deflated to:

$$S = M\, ln\, M.$$

When a basin of attraction must be taken into account, S must be *inflated* accordingly. Its exact amount depends on the size and structure of the basin of attraction.

In view of what we've stated above ("basic concepts" and "conceptual tools") we may base pattern recognition on two principles:

(1) Associative memory, i.e. completion of incomplete data (formerly learned).
(2) Minimization of a potential $V(Q)$

This potential depends sensitively on transformations (cf above section) as Shannon information does (from which $V(Q)$ is derived). The basic problem both in the development of (pattern recognition) computers and in our understanding of the function of the human brain consists in answering the question: which transformations and at which stages of the recognition stages are they used? The same holds true for the role of attention. We will discuss these questions in the section "Machinery" that follows.

Finally, while the concept of minimization of a potential $V(Q)$ is quite striking, some caution is needed. As we know from Hopfield nets (which exploits an analogy with the theory of Spinglasses) there may be numerous unwanted minima related to "ghost states". To let the computer escape from such states, fluctuations must be applied to drive the system out of such a trap ("simulated annealing"). In the parlance of our paper, we would state that Shannon information is inflated. While the problem of ghost states does not arise in the synergetic computer, it is by no means clear that in a real brain states analogous to those unwanted states may be reached and must be overcome. We will discuss all these questions in the Sect. 7.9 "Machinery".

7.7 Some More Properties of the SC

The basic pattern recognition equation reads

$$\frac{dQ}{dt} = \sum_{k} \mu_k v_k (v_k Q) - B \sum_{k \neq k} (v_k, Q)^2 (v_k Q) v_k - C(QQ)Q \tag{7.9}$$

where $Q = Q(t)$ time dependent. In Eq. (7.9), the brackets (.) denote scalar products.

As we believe, the great advantage of the synergetic computer rests on its explicit formulation of the potential landscape $V(Q)$ so that the recognition dynamics can be visualized by a ball sliding down on a slope to a valley closest to the ball's starting point (i.e. the initial value of $\boldsymbol{Q}(t)$). As a detailed analysis shows:

> $Q(t) \to v_k$ for $t \to \infty$ for a specific k (meaning!) depending on initially presented
> $\boldsymbol{Q}(t = 0)$, i.e. pattern k is "recognized".

This process works, only, however, if the pattern vector $\boldsymbol{Q}$ contains sufficient data. Actually, mathematically the dynamics happens in a high-dimensional space. But to bring out the essential aspect, consider a two-dimensional cross-section through $V(\boldsymbol{Q})$ (Fig. 7.2). If the pixel size is too large the initial position of our "fictitious" ball is not well defined and the ball might slide down to several valleys belonging to different prototypes.

In this situation the dynamics of the synergetic computer implies a superposition of the prototype vectors belonging to the corresponding valleys $v_{k1}, v_{k2}, \ldots, v_{kn}$ so that the process ends up with a certain superposition:

$$Q(t) \to v_{k_1} + v_{k_2} + \cdots + v_{k_n} \tag{7.10}$$

(Case of degeneracy also discussed in Haken (ibid); case of a saddle point or edge).

In a number of cases such a superposition may define a category. When there are no more clues, this uncertainty remains. In a number of cases, depending on the relative position between the "center of gravity" of the initial state (uncertainty of

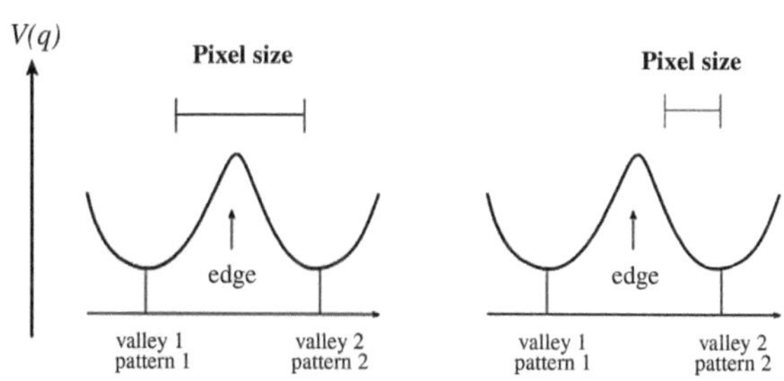

Fig. 7.2 Visualization of impact of pixel size on initial position of "ball"

the ball's position) and the position of the potential's edge a slight propensity towards a specific valley may be present. If more data become available by a smaller pixel size this propensity may become enhanced. (see below Sect. 8.2). There is, however, another possibility: When more pixels (data) become available other features may become dominant which means that under the new initial condition a different valley is reached. This mechanism may explain the transition from "Monroe" to "Einstein" (cf. Sect. 3.3 in Chap. 3, Fig. 3.2) as well as the process in Sect. 8.2 below. Note the relation between pixel size and spatial frequency band pass filter! Generally speaking, the degeneracy is resolved when more data are available: more precise initial value $\boldsymbol{Q}(0)$. To calculate the wanted probability distribution and the information i we use the transformation

$$Q(t) = \xi_l(t)v_1 + \cdots + \xi_M(t)v_M + rest \tag{7.11}$$

where $(v_k \; rest) = 0$.

Because of (7.11), we may determine the *order parameter* $\xi_k(t)$ at each moment t by

$$\xi_l(t) = (v_k Q(t))$$

A typical diagram is presented in Fig. 7.3 below from which the order parameter can be read off.

To obtain the probability for object k, p_k we must form

$$p_k = \xi_k^2 \left(\sum \xi_k^2 \right)^{-1} \tag{7.12}$$

which obeys the normalization condition.

Fig. 7.3 A complex scene to be recognized by the SC. From Fuchs and Haken (1988)

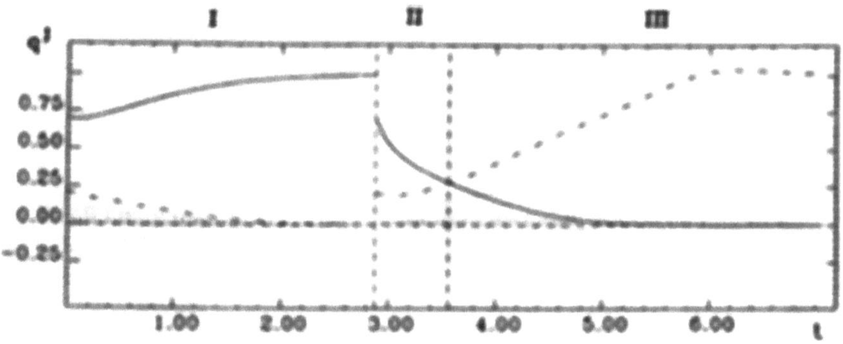

Fig. 7.4 Time evolution of the order parameters for woman and man corresponding to Fig. 7.3. When the order parameter for a woman has come close to unity, it is switched to zero and then a new time evolution sets in as shown, eventually indicating that the man has been recognized. From Fuchs and Haken (ibid)

This allows us to calculate a diagram corresponding to Fig. 7.4, and then the information i. Its qualitative behavior can be deduced by means of the relations

$$(Q(t)Q(t)) = \sum_k \xi_k^2(t) + \text{negligible rest.} \tag{7.13}$$

With "diffuse" data, many $\xi_k \neq 0$, so that, $p_k \neq 0$ which implies information is large. Finally, only a single $p_k = 0$, all others = 0, which means $i = 0$, i.e. minimal.

7.8 On Attention Parameters

The important role of the attention parameters μ_k is demonstrated by the following computer experiment made with the SC in its invariant version. Figs. 7.3 or 7.5 with their scenes of partly hidden faces of different sizes served as input. Then the SC "recognized" the lady. Then the corresponding attention parameter μ was put to zero, Fig. 7.3 served again as input, and the SC "recognized" the second face of Fig. 7.3. This procedure could be continued up to several faces (Fig. 7.5) so that the SC was able to analyse the whole scene. The required manipulation can be done "by hand" or by an algorithm developed by Ditzinger and Haken (1986) to deal with ambiguous figures, where the attention parameters were treated as dynamic variables.

The just described analysis of a complex scene is an impressive example for the interplay between information deflation and inflation, (and as such for information adaptation). First step: recognition of the lady—information deflation. Second step: preparation for recognition of second face—information inflation. Recognition of that face: information deflation and so on.

Fig. 7.5 A scene composed of five faces recognized by the SC using the procedure described in the text. From Fuchs and Haken (1988)

7.9 Time Dependent Data Set

At each instance of time we are given a representation Q (i.e. a set of data) to which, based on our memory (previous experience) we attach different meanings m_k, $k = 1, 2, \ldots, M$, to which we may attach probabilities $p_1 p_2, \ldots, p_M$. This allows us to calculate the information i_k according to

$$i_k = -\ln p_k$$

(up to a constant factor) and the total information

$$i = -\sum_k p_k \ln p_k.$$

Thus we have the scheme I:

Scheme I

Representation	Meaning	Probability	Information
	m_1 → →	p_1	i_1
	m_2 → →	p_2	i_2
q	$m.$ → →	$p.$	$i.$
	$m.$	$p.$	$i.$
	m_M → →	p_M	i_M
		Total $\sum_k = 1$	$i = \sum_k i_k$

If a data set becomes more precise in the course of time, the representation $\boldsymbol{Q}$(t) changes also and thus the probabilities p_k and, in our context most important, the information i. This leads us to the scheme II:

Scheme II

$t =$	$t_1 < t_2$	$\dots$	$< t_L$	time sequence
$q(t)$:	$q(t_1)$	$q(t_2)\ \dots$	$q(t_L)$	pattern sequence
	$p_1(t_1)$	$p_1(t_2)\ \dots$	$p_1(t_L)$	change of probability distribution
	.	.	.	
	.	.	.	
	$p_M(t_1)$	$p_M(t_2)\ \dots$	$p_M(t_L)$	
	$i(t_1)$	$i(t_2)\ \dots$	$i(t_L)$	information sequence

In view of our foregoing qualitative discussion, we expect—more or less—the following picture (for the example of $M = 3$), that is, Fig. 7.6:

In this representation we assume that the recognition process is fast compared to the temporal change of data. Actually, qualitatively, Fig. 7.6 applies to the recognition process itself representing the time-dependence of the solutions of the SC.

A final remark may be in order. The following concepts are equivalent (though their use depends on the theoretical frame):

$$\textbf{Prototype (pattern)} \longleftrightarrow \textbf{meaning} \longleftrightarrow \textbf{hypothesis}$$
$$v_k \qquad\qquad m_k \qquad\qquad h_k$$

For $k = 1, 2, 3, \dots$, M

To each label k we attach an *order parameter* ξ_k, i.e. also to v_k, m_k, h_k.

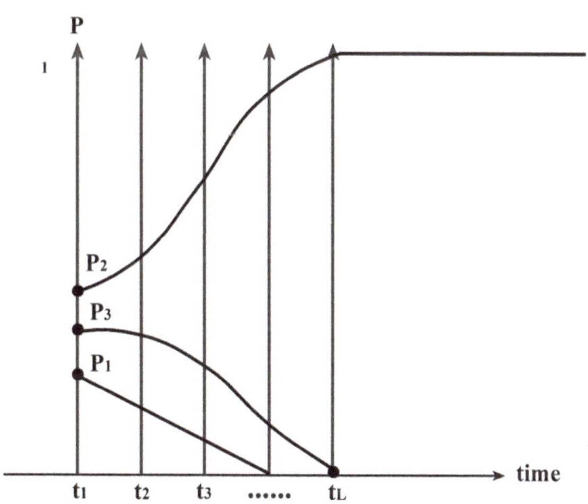

Fig. 7.6 p_k, $k = 1, 2, 3$, versus time t, p_2 wins → "pattern 2" (representation) is recognized

Above we have shown how we can realize scheme III by an explicit mathematical approach.

Scheme III

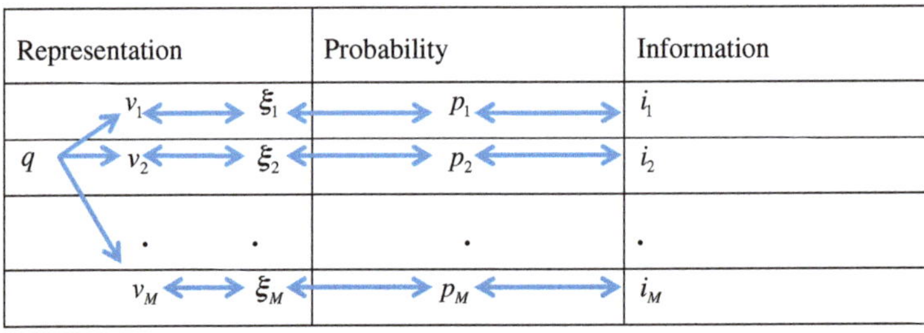

7.10 Machinery

In the context of our paper the problem of making pattern recognition operational may serve as a nice illustration of Heinz von Foerster's concept of trivial/nontrivial machines or our generalization to "simple/complex" systems. We discuss them at the conceptual level—not on the "hardware" level, the latter being outside our aim.

1. We start with the concept of the *synergetic computer* mainly for two reasons. It is, as we will see, a "*simple*" system, and we are familiar with it because one of us (Haken 1991/2004) developed the corresponding algorithms and implemented them on serial computers.

The patterns treated are faces or city maps represented by discrete gray values of pixels on a discrete grid.

7.10.1 First Step: Preprocessing

Both learning of prototypes and recognition are made invariant against position in space, size and orientation (for the expert: Fourier transformations and logarithmic map). This preprocess is performed without any pre knowledge or pre assumption. In other words, the patterns are encoded in a specific way. The process is that of a trivial machine: each pattern is uniquely transformed into another one.

7.10.2 Second Step: Learning

Central to the synergetic computer is its explicit potential function $V(Q)$. (For example, it contains second and fourth order products of (transformed) gray values.

Their average values are fixed by a sequence of inputs. The structure of $V(Q)$ allows us to calculate the prototypes by minimization of $\langle V(Q) \rangle$).

$V(Q)$ can be calculated in a straight forward way from "experimental" data and the prototype patterns determined—again a straight forward procedure.

$V(Q)$ describes a potential landscape, where valleys are related to the specific attractor states of the synergetic computer model, just at the position of the prototype patterns.

7.10.3 Third Step: Recognition

A given pre processed "picture", i.e. a specific set of data, serves as initial value for the solution of a set of differential equations, that determine the "trajectory" (in the transformed Q-space) from the initial state to the final state ("fixed point") thereby identifying the offered ("test") pattern with a specific prototype.

There is one exception: if the test pattern lies on the border between valleys, edges or saddle points.

There are some more potentialities of the synergetic computer, e.g. the sequential analysis of scenes by an appropriate choice of attention parameters.

This does not put our conclusions in question: All processes are uniquely determined and run in each case in a specific direction like clockwork:

The synergetic computer—as a specific example—is a trivial machine and surely a simple system.

In both cases—learning and recognition—it deflates Shannon information by each step until S = min is reached, which is

$$S = MlnM,$$

when learning of M prototypes, and

$$S = 0$$

in the case of pattern recognition.

7.11 The HMAX Model: Outline—Relation to Information Adaptation

7.11.1 The Invariance Problem

While the concept of the synergetic computer is based on theoretical grounds (rooted in synergetics) and its realization by a neural network is considered only subsequently, the HMAX model has its origin in a concrete neural network design.

(Just a note for the expert: The SC network is a three-layer network where the hidden variables are just the order parameters). The motivation for the development of the HMAX model is the brain's astonishing capability of recognizing objects (e.g., faces, geographic items) irrespective of their position and orientation in space, their size, deformation etc. In other words, human recognition is *invariant* against a variety of object *transformations*, in particular *displacements*, *rotations*, and *scaling*. How does a human brain solve this problem?

A probable answer, which lies also at the bottom of the HMAX model, lies in the pioneering work of Hubel and Wiesel (1959, 1962, 1965). When experimentally studying the lower layers of the visual cortex (called V1–V4) they discovered specified neurons that react ("fire") most strongly when a bar of an image (registered by the retina) showed in *specific direction*. Such a cell is a very simple example of a *feature* detector. But how can the brain (1) discover such a *directed* bar that can be situated at any position in the image and (2) nevertheless, can abstract from dealing with the position? This is, of course, just a slightly different formulation of "translation invariance".

7.11.2 The HMAX Model

Question (1) was answered experimentally by Hubel and Wiesel: Such specific cells (for a bar oriented in a specific direction) are *distributed* all over the lowest layer(s) of the visual cortex!

As for question (2), here the HMAX model (and some of its precursors) adapts a proposal of Hubel and Wiesel (invariance properties of hyper-complex cells) to the problem of translation invariance: The corresponding model postulates that above the layer with its bar-specific cells ("simple cells", S-cells) there is a second layer with one cell (or unit) that is responding (sending out signals ("spikes")) if in the image there is a *specifically oriented bar irrespective of its position*. This cell ("complex cell", C-cell) receives inputs from all other locally distributed cells via nerve fibers (Fig. 7.7). Whenever a localized feature detector for a specific bar direction r registers such a bar, this S-cell sends its signal to the C-cell, which *does not register* from where it receives its input. It just sends its own signal to the next layer of the "model brain" saying there is a *specific bar direction irrespective of position*.

Let us distinguish the localized neurons S by an index j. Then the input i (or correspondingly the output) of the C-cell is taken as a sum over the signals S_j stemming from the neurons j.

$$i = \sum_j S_j \tag{7.14}$$

Clearly, if any $S_j \neq 0$, then also $i \neq 0$, i.e. the bar is recognized. There is, however, a serious drawback: Generally, $S_j \neq 0$ due to clutter, noise etc., even if

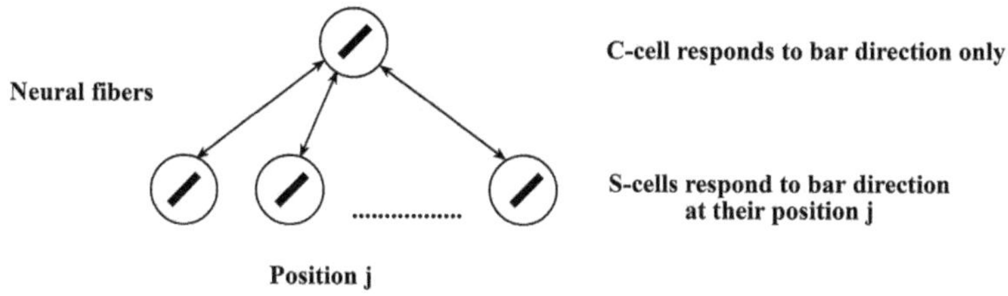

Fig. 7.7 Two layers network with S-cells and one C-cell. In principle, the C-layer contains cell specific for a set of bar-directions. C-cells respond to bar direction only. S-cells respond to bar direction at their position *j*

there is no specific bar direction in the image. Though the S_j are small, their sum *i* may be significant which may ruin the whole approach.

This dilemma is solved by the HMAX model: Replace the whole sum over *j* by the biggest maximal (!) signal S_j. Then all the disturbances stemming from the other detectors are eliminated.

For the sake of illustration, we have based our brief outline of the HMAX model on the example of a bar with a specific direction. In the HMAX model, one may use any other (localized) feature(s), up to (perhaps) complex patterns. Furthermore the summation index *j* that in (7.14) referred to the location of the feature detectors, can be replaced by rotation angles α. In each case it must be assumed that all the values of j, ϕ, α etc., are realized by neural units. (In the Hubel-Wiesel experiments it was shown that at the individual "locations" there is a whole set of "orientation-tuned" S-cells).

A nice interpolation formula between the purely linear relation (1) and the maximum principle is due to Edelman and Poggio (1990). According to them the output C of the "invariant" cell is

$$C = \sum_j \frac{\exp(p|Sj|)}{\sum_k \exp(p|S_k|)} S_j \tag{7.15}$$

where p is an adjustable parameter. If p = 0, we recover a linear relationship (1), while for p $\to \infty$, the prefactor of S_j is strongly peaked around a term with index j with maximal $|S_j|$.

We may state, that HMAX is based on a winner-takes-all strategy. (Our remark might help to develop HMAX further). This brief outline may suffice here to prepare the ground for relating HMAX with the central issue of our paper: information adaptation. Needless to say that we ignored a number of "technical" details such as the use of filter functions (Gauss, Gabor), the effects of interpolation between discretely registered features etc. Furthermore, the HMAX model may be generalized to a whole hierarchy of layers, where the C-cells of one layer serve as S-cells giving input to the next layer:

$$S_1 \rightarrow C_1(= \boldsymbol{S}_1) \rightarrow C_2(= \boldsymbol{S}_2) \rightarrow \text{etc.}$$

While it may be tempting to compare the SC approach with the HMAX approach, this task is beyond the scope of our article. On the theoretical side it would require benchmark studies, and on the experimental side multi-electrode recording etc.

At any rate, both SC and HMAX can be subsumed under the concept of information adaptation.

7.11.3 Information Adaptation

Now we interpret the HMAX model in terms of information adaptation. Our starting point is Sect. 6.1.1 with its formula (6.3), which we write somewhat more explicitly as

$$i = -\sum_{J,T} P(J,T)\log_2 P(J,T) \tag{7.16}$$

We consider the example of S-cells for only two bars, horizontal and vertical with angel $\vartheta = \vartheta_1 = 0, \vartheta_2 = 90°$, respectively, and positioned at sites $j = 1,2, \ldots,$ N. In (7.16), we identify T: position j, J: rotation angle ϑ.

The decomposition (6.4) reads

$$P(\vartheta,j) = P(\vartheta|j)f(j) \tag{7.17}$$

Because the orientation angles ϑ are independent of position j,

$$P(\vartheta|j) = p(\vartheta) \tag{7.18}$$

Since all positions j in the image are equally probable, because of (6.6)

$$f(j) = N^{-1} \tag{7.19}$$

and assuming the direction ϑ equally probable, because of (6.5)

$$p(\vartheta) = \frac{1}{2} \tag{7.20}$$

After these simple identifications, we can insert (7.17) with (7.18–7.20) into Eq. (6.7) of Sect. 6.1.1. The sums over j and ϑ can be simply done. We obtain: first sum in (6.7): deflated information

$$i_d = -\sum_{\vartheta} p(\vartheta) log_2 p(\vartheta) = 1\,\text{bit} \tag{7.21}$$

Second sum in (6.7) information of transformation $T \rightarrow j$.

$$i_T = log_2 N \text{ bits.} \tag{7.22}$$

Because of the numerous S-cells taking care of the number of possible positions of a bar in the image,

$$i_d \ll log_2 N, \tag{7.23}$$

i.e. an enormous amount of information deflation. We have seen above how the network design of the HMAX model achieves this effect.

Clearly, our analysis can be generalized to other transformations and $S \rightarrow C$ projections used by the HMAX model.

Chapter 8
Some Further Applications and Discussions of Information Adaptation

8.1 A Baby Learning the Concept "Mother"

Consider the case of a baby learning the face of his/her mother by seeing it again and again from different positions. Fig. 8.1 may serve as a guide for our discussion. In the upper left corner, the various kinds of external stimuli and their effects on the sensory organs are listed. The upper part on the r.h.s. symbolizes the "registration" of stimuli by the baby's brain at a sequence of instances. We call each corresponding set of sensations a representation. Some of them may be (more or less) the same ("learning by repetition").

Because there will be, nevertheless, *many* different representations, the corresponding information is large. We may assume that the baby may recall a specific representation with a certain "strength" (or, more precisely speaking, probability). This is also indicated by our Fig. 8.1 (middle part). By means of a *higher abstract* level the baby may *deflate* information by forming the concept "mother". (Which at an early stage, need not be linked to the word "*mother*", which is anyway absent in the animal world). Or, in other words, the concept "mother" emerges.

Synergetics allows us to deal both conceptually and mathematically with the emergence of a new concept that acts as "order parameter (Haken 1988, 2000, 2006). An open question remains, however: does the order parameter have a material, i.e., neural, counterpart, corresponding to the classical idea of a "grandmother cell"?

The abstract concept mother becomes observable, at least indirectly, to an observer (3rd person) by the baby's activities: movement, sound production, articulation, or facial expression. [By means of the concept "mother", the individual representations acquire a specific *meaning* to the baby (1st person).]

But the baby does not only deflate information, s/he can also inflate it when triggered by specific cues, e.g. a smell, the baby may recall a variety of representations which contain this specific smell. This process can also be considered as action of associative memory (AM). If, in the present case, only a smell is given,

H. Haken and J. Portugali, *Information Adaptation: The Interplay Between Shannon Information and Semantic Information in Cognition*,
SpringerBriefs in Complexity, DOI 10.1007/978-3-319-11170-4_8

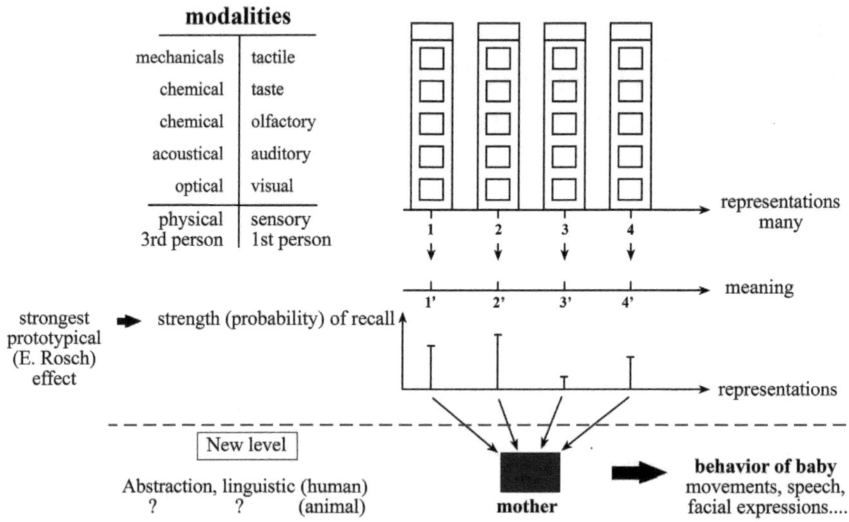

Fig. 8.1 *Upper left*: Various kinds of external stimuli and their effects on the sensory organs. *Upper right*: "Registration" of stimuli by the baby's brain at a sequence of instances. *Middle*: "Strength" or probability of recall. *Bottom*: By means of information deflation the concept "mother" emerges

(i.e. not sufficient data) AM inflates information. If sufficient data are given, AM deflates information ("pattern recognition"), see also below: "the approaching object".

Besides the concept "mother", the baby will learn (or develop) related ones, such as "father", etc. Clearly, one has to deal with hierarchies that serve information adaptation which, depending on the task, may be deflation or inflation.

8.2 Information Adaptation to an Approaching Object

Imagine the following scenario: You stand in an open area and you observe at the horizon an object moving towards you. At this stage there is little data and the object can be anything and thus the information (uncertainty) is high. As the object gets closer, more data are added and you realize that it is a person, that is, your MBB adapts to the incoming data by deflating the information (uncertainty) and by pattern recognizing the moving object as a the category 'person'. As this person gets still closer and more data are added, you realize that it is a woman—your MBB once again adapts to the added data by further deflating the information; as before this is implemented by means of pattern recognizing the advancing person as the category woman. Finally as this woman gets even closer you realize that this is Eve —a good friend of yours. Your MBB finally adapts to the added data by deflating

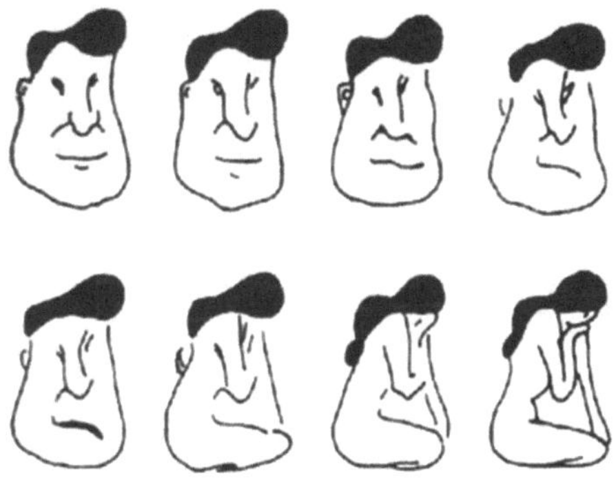

Fig. 8.2 Hysteresis in perception. When you look at this sequence of patterns starting from the *upper left*, look then to the *right*, switch to the *lower left*, your percept of a man's face will switch to a "woman" only at the end of second line. When you proceed in the reverse direction, the percept switching from "woman" to "face" occurs in the first line

the information to zero (complete certainty). Now imagine that Eve says Hi to you and continues her walk. As she gets further away you will continue to pattern recognize her as Eve despite the fact that a process of lossy data compression is taking place here.

Note that the time evolution of the process of information adaptation as described above is not linear and smooth but rather it evolves in punctuations. That is, while the increase of data is continuous, the pattern recognition process of information adaptation is abrupt and thus discrete: a moving object, person, woman, Eve. This property of "punctuated recognition" might become even more pronounced due to hysteresis effects that operate here. Namely, that the recognition of a given pattern is influenced by a previously recognized pattern—a phenomenon that is typical of sequential pattern recognition processes like the one illustrated in Fig. 8.2.

Note the interrelations between pattern recognition and categorization: in certain circumstances the MBB pattern recognizes a category (e.g. a person).

8.3 Adapting the Face of the City to Humans' Information Processing Capabilities

In the various examples of information adaptation discussed so far, the process was implemented by the MBB, which mentally inflated and/or deflated the incoming data/information. The latter—the source of the incoming data or information—was given and thus remained fixed and not altered in the process. Here we direct attention to a process of information adaptation that is implemented by acting on the information source. (The following is based on Chap. 9 by Haken and Portugali in Portugali 2011, Figs. 9.8, 9.9). As noted in Chap. 1 and in Fig. 1.3, in our previous study (Haken and Portugali 2003) we showed that different urban elements convey

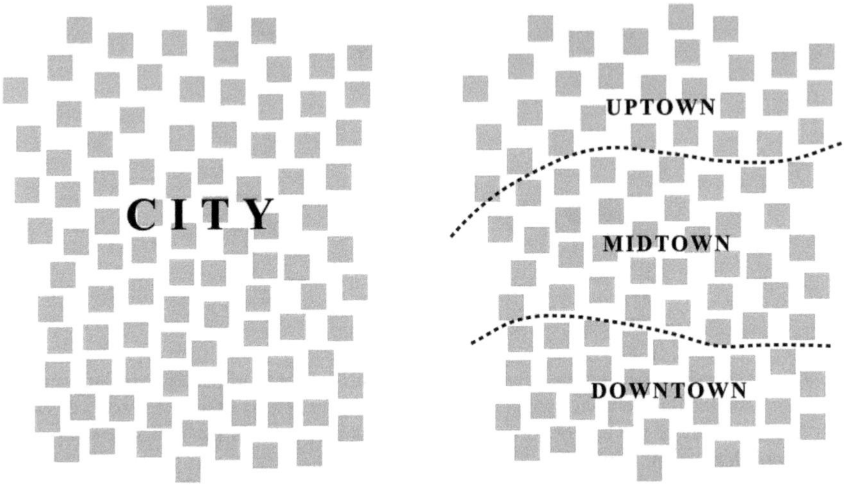

Fig. 8.3 If all building in a city (*left*) are identical to each other, information is zero and categorization (*right*) will entail information inflation. On the other hand, if all buildings in a city (*left*) are different form each other, information is too high and categorization (*right*) will entail information deflation

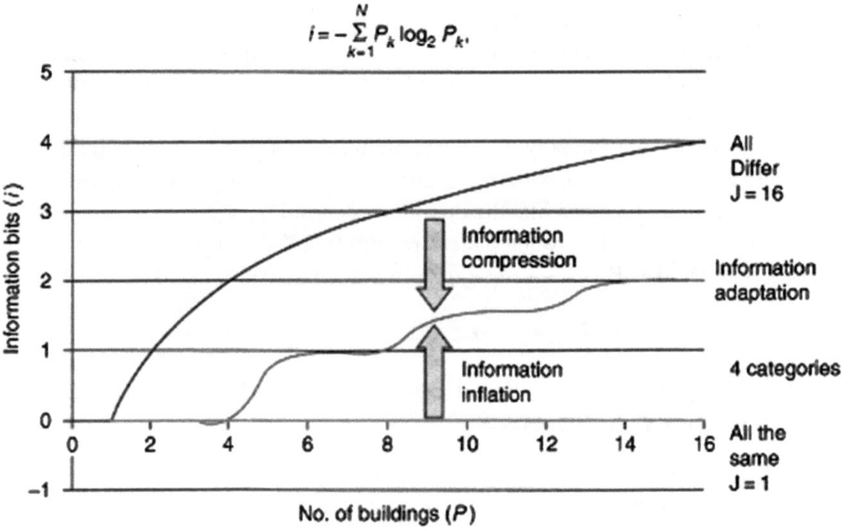

Fig. 8.4 The interplay between information deflation and inflation entails information adaptation

different amounts of information that can be quantified by means of Shannon's information bits. Thus, if all buildings in a city are identical to each other, as in the imaginary city of Fig. 8.3 left, for instance, then the information such a city will convey to each of its inhabitants and users will be zero. In such a situation dividing/categorizing the city into uptown, midtown, downtown, as in NYC (Fig. 8.3, *right*), will entail information inflation. On the other hand, however, if in the imaginary city of Fig 8.3, *left* each building is unique and different, the information this city will convey to each person is very high—much beyond a person's information processing capabilities. In such a reality, dividing/categorizing the city into uptown, midtown, downtown (Fig. 8.3, *right*), will entail information deflation. From this perspective, a "good city form" (the title of Lynch's book from 1981), is one which (among other things) adapts its form and structure to the information processing capabilities of its inhabitants and users. Indeed, one of the major tasks of urban planning and design is to find this information adaptation balancing point (Fig. 8.4) and thus make the city legible, that is, cognitively adaptable to its inhabitants and users.

Concluding Notes

As we have just seen, the processes of pattern recognition and categorization may involve, in certain circumstances, information deflation, while in others information inflation. Both processes start when the human sensory system is subject to incoming information of various forms and quantities. In some cases the amount of incoming information is beyond the receiver's information processing capability, while in others the incoming information is quantitatively insufficient. As illustrated above, the mind/brain responds, or *adapts*, to such circumstances by deflating or inflating the information to a Shannonian quantity it can conveniently handle and to its existing semantic structures. We've termed this process 'information adaptation'. Its essence, as we've seen, is a circular causality play between Shannonian and semantic information: On the one hand, semantic information conditions and thus allows Shannonian information; while on the other hand, it comes into being by deflating or inflating Shannonian information. From this follows a new meaning to the notion of *information processing* in connection with cognition: not the manipulation of symbols on the hardware of the brain, but an interplay between Shannonian and semantic information.

Looked upon from the perspective of information adaptation, Shannon information is much more than a mere measure of channel capacity. In fact, it acts as a *driving force* for the brain's formation of concepts (meaning). Thus it causes the generation of *semantic* information. On the other hand, by the process of *information adaptation* the latter regulates Shannon information. More specifically, the process of information adaptation comprises information inflation and deflation as well as an interplay between Shannonian and semantic information:

1. *Information inflation* can be achieved in several ways as we have shown above. Firstly, by the *omission of data*. An example was provided by Picasso's bull. Secondly, by static or dynamic *blurring*. One example for the static case is the action of low spatial frequency band pass filter (Monroe picture, illegible/legible text); another one supplementing grey values to caricatures. Dynamic blurring, on the other hand, is achieved by the action of noise, e.g. simulated annealing in Hopfield nets. Thirdly, by the *Change* of weights of *correlation function*, e.g. by attention parameters.

H. Haken and J. Portugali, *Information Adaptation: The Interplay Between Shannon Information and Semantic Information in Cognition*,
SpringerBriefs in Complexity, DOI 10.1007/978-3-319-11170-4

2. *Information deflation* can be achieved by the *elimination* of (situation dependent) *irrelevant features* of objects such as their position, orientation, size, deformations via suitable transformations as in the HMAX model. In the SC-approach, information deflation is achieved by the *reduction* of the high-dimensional feature space to the low-dimensional *order parameter*-space by means of a specific dynamics. The order parameters in turn represent *meaning*.
3. *The interplay between Shannonian and semantic information.* Information inflation and deflation lead to the formation of semantic information, which in turn steers information adaptation.

From a wider perspective, it is our opinion that information adaptation is a general principle that underlies processes of pattern recognition, sensory-motor control as well as brain processes associated with the formation of new concepts and ideas. In the latter connection, our elaboration of the concept of information adaptation sheds new light also on the "creativity problem" from the point of view of cognitive science in combination with operational, computational approach.

Scientists and practitioners of various disciplines, including economics, management and sociology, surely will notice analogies between our concepts and their own, e.g. between "information inflation" and "brain storming", just to use a popular catchword. Finally, as shortly illustrated in Sect. 8.3, the process of information adaptation sheds new light on the dynamic of cities and on urban planning and design.

In developing our arguments, we've briefly presented two rather different models for pattern recognition (the HMAX and the SC) both of which have their advantages, disadvantages and limitations (not discussed here). But what is important, both models can be subsumed under an overarching general concept: Information adaptation.

In conclusion we may quote the final remarks made by two pioneers in the field –Poggio and Serra (2013):

> As noted by Chuck Stevens, "Models are common; good theories are scarce". Progress in the field of computational vision will thus require synergies between multiple fields from mathematics and statistics to computer and brain sciences.

Possibly, the concept of information adaptation is a good starting point for such a theory.

References

Attneave, F. (1954). Some informational aspects of visual perception. *Psychological Review*, 61 (3),183–193.

Attneave F (1959) Applications of Information Theory to Psychology. New York: Holt, Rinehart and Winston

Barabasi AL (2002) *Linked: How Everything Is Connected to Everything Else*. New York: Plume

Bar-Hillel Y. and Carnap, R. (1953). Semantic Information. *The British Journal for the Philosophy of Science,* 4, 14. (Aug.), pp.147–157.

Barlow, H. B. (1961). The coding of sensory messages *Current Problems in Animal Behaviour* ed W H Thorpe and O L Zangwill (Cambridge: Cambridge University Press) pp 331–60.

Barlow, H.B. (2001). Redundancy reduction revisited. *Network: Computation in Neural Systems* 12, 241–253.

Bennett, C. H. (1982). "The thermodynamics of computation—a review". *International Journal of Theoretical Physics* 21 (12): 905–940.

Brooks R.A. (1999) *Cambrian Intelligence: The Early History of the New AI*. MIT press.

Chabris, C and Simons, D (2010). *The Invisible Gorilla: And other ways our intuitions deceive us.* Crown, NY.

Cisak, P., Drew, T., Kalaska, J., Eds. (2007). *Computational Neuroscience: From neurons to theory and back again*. Elsevier, Amsterdam.

Demeulenaere P. (2011). *Analytical sociology and Social Machanism*. Cambridge University Press.

Ditzinger T. (2014). Illusionen des Sehens: Eine Reise In die Welt der Visuellen Wahrnehmung. Springer, Berlin

Ditzinger T. & Haken H. (1986). Oscillations in the perception of ambiguous figures, *Biological Cybernetics* 61, 279–287

Feigenbaum M (1978) Quantitative universality for a class of nonlinear transformations. J Stat Phys 19(1): 25–52

Floridi, L. (2011). Semantic conceptions of information. *Stanford Encyclopedia of Philosophy*.

Foerster von H. (2003). *Understanding Understanding: Essays on Cybernetics and Cognition*, Springer

Freiwald WA and Tsao DY (2010). Functional Compartmentalization and Viewpoint Generalization Within the Macaque Face-Processing System. *Science 5 November 2010: Vol. 330 no. 6005 pp. 845–851*

Freiwald WA*, Tsao DY*, Livingstone MS. 2009. A face feature space in the macaque temporal lobe. *Nature Neuroscience*, 12: 1187–1196.

Fuchs, A. and Haken, H. (1988) *Biol. Cybern*. 60, 17–22

Gardner H (1987) *The Mind's New Science*. New York: Basic

Gell-Mann M (1994) *The Quark and the Jaguar: Adventures in the Simple and the Complex*. New York: Freeman

Gleick, J. (2011) *The Information: A History, a Theory, a Flood.* Fourth Estate. London

H. Haken and J. Portugali, *Information Adaptation: The Interplay Between Shannon Information and Semantic Information in Cognition*,
SpringerBriefs in Complexity, DOI 10.1007/978-3-319-11170-4

Goffman, E. (1959) *The Presentation of Self in Everyday Life.* Anchor Books, US

Gray, C. M. and Singer, W. (1989) Stimulus-specific neuronal oscillations in orientation columns of cat visual cortex. *Proc. Natl. Acad. Sci.* USA. 86: 1698–1702.

Grossberg, S. (1988). Nonlinear neural networks: Principles, mechanism and architecture. *Neural Net.* 1 17–61.

Haken, H. (1977) *Advanced Synergetics: An Introduction*, 2nd print. Berlin/Heidelberg/ New York: Springer

Haken, H. (1988/2000/2006). *Information and Self-Organization: A Macroscopic Approach to Complex Systems.* Springer.

Haken, H. (1991/2004). *Synergetic computers and cognition*, 2nd ed. Springer.

Haken, H. (2003). *Synergetics. Introduction and Advanced Topics.* Springer.

Haken, H. (1996) *Principles of Brain Functioning.* Springer.

Haken, H. (1983) *Synergetics, An Introduction.* Springer.

Haken H. and Portugali J. (1996). Synergetics, Inter-representation networks and cognitive maps, in *The Construction of Cognitive Maps*, J. Portugali (Ed.), Kluwer Academic Publishers, Dordrecht, 1996, 45–67.

Haken, H. & Portugali, J. (2003). The face of the city is its information. *Journal of Environmental Psychology*, 23, 382–405 (2003).

Haken, H. and Portugali, J. Hybrid Images and Information Adaptation (submitted). ICPRAM 2015 conference. Lisbon.

Hodges, A. (1992), *Alan Turing: The Enigma*, London: Vintage, pp. 243–252

Holland J.H. (1992) Complex Adaptive Systems—A New Era in Computation (Winter) *Daedalus* 121(1): 17–30

Hubel, D.H. and Wiesel T.N. (1959). Receptive fields of single neurons in the cat's striate cortex, *Journal of Physiology* 148, 574–591, 1959

Hubel, D. H. and Wiesel, T. N. (1962). Receptive fields, binocular interaction and functional architecture in the cat's visual cortex. *Journal of Physiology*, 160:106-154

Hubel D. and T.Wiesel (1965). Receptive fields and functional architecture in two nonstriate visual areas (18 and 19) of the cat. *J. Neurophysiol.*, 28:229–89, 1965.

Jacobson, Homer (1950). *Science 4 August 1950: Vol. 112 no. 2901 pp. 143–144*

Jacobson, Homer (1951). The Informational Capacity of the Human Eye. *Science 16 March 1951: 292–293.*

Julesz B. (1971/2006). *Foundations of Cyclopean Perception.* Originaly published in Chicago by The University of Chicago Press; in 2006 it was published by the MIT press.

Kandel E. (2012). *The Age of Insight: The Quest to Understand the Unconscious in Art, Mind, and Brain, from Vienna 1900 to the Present.* Random House, NY.

Kelso, S. (1995) *Dynamic Patterns: The Self-Organization of Brain and Behavior.* Cambridge, MA: MIT Press

Kendon, A, Harris, R.M. Key M.R. Eds. (1975). *Organization of Behavior in Face-To-Face interaction.* Mouton, The Hagues

Kohonen, T. (1987). *Associative Memory and Self-Organization*, 2nd ed. Springer.

Landauer, R. (1961) Irreversibility and Heat Generation in the Computing Process. IBM Journal Of Research And Development, Vol. 5, No. 3, 261–269

Livingstone, M. S. (2002) *Vision and Art: the Biology of Seeing.* New York: Harry N Abrams

Lorenz EN (1963) Deterministic non-periodic flow. *J Atm Sci* 20: 130–141

Lynch, K. (1960) *The Image of the City.* Cambridge, MA: MIT Press

Lynch K. (1981). *Good city form.* MIT Press, Cambridge

McCulloch, W., Pitts, W., (1943). A logical calculus for the ideas immanent in nervous activity. *Bull. Math. Bio.* 7 115–133.

McLuhan, M. (1964/2003). *Understanding media: The extensions of man.* Corte Madera, CA: Gingko Press.

Mandelbrot, B.B. (1983) *The Fractal Geometry of Nature.* San Francisco: Freeman

Miller, G. A. (1956). The magic number seven, plus or minus two: some limits on our capacity for processing information. *Psychological Review* 63(2), 81–97.

Oliva, A., and Schyns, P.F., (1997). Coarse Blobs or Fine Edges? Evidence That Information Diagnosticity Changes the Perception of Complex Visual Stimuli. *Cognitive Psychology* 34, 72–107, 1997.

Poggio, T., Edelman, S. (1990). A network that learns to recognize 3D objects. *Nature* 343 263–266.

Poggio T. and Serre T. (2013), Models of Visual Cortex. *Scholarpedia,* 8(4): 3516.

Portugali, J. (2000). *Self-Organization and the City*. Springer.

Portugali, J. (2002). The seven basic propositions of SIRN (Synergetic Inter-Representation Networks) *Nonlinear Phenomena in Complex Systems* 5(4): 428–444.

Portugali, J. (2011) *Complexity, Cognition and the City*, Springer

Portugali J. (2014) What makes cities complex? In Portugali J. and Stolk E Eds. *Complexity, Cognition, Urban Planning And Design*. Springer

Portugali, J. and Stolk E. (2014) A SIRN view on design thinking—An urban design perspective. *Environment and Planning b: Planning and Design* (Forthcoming)

Prigogine I (1980) *From Being to Becoming*. San Francisco, CA: Freeman

Riesenhuber, M. and T. Poggio (1999). Hierarchical models of object recognition in cortex. *Nature Neuroscience* 12:1019–1025.

Rosch, E., Mervis, C., Gray, W., Johnson, D. and Boyes-Braem, P. (1976). Basic objects in natural categories. *Cognitive Psychology* 8: 382–439.

Russell B. (1926). Theory of Knowledge. *The Encyclopaedia Britannica*

Simons, D. J., & Chabris, C. F. (1999). Gorillas in our midst: Sustained inattentional blindness for dynamic events. Perception, 28, 1059-1074.

Shannon, C. E. (1948). A Mathematical Theory of Communication. Reprinted with corrections from *The Bell System Technical Journal* 27, 379–423, 623–656 (July, October, 19).

Shannon, C. E. (1951). Prediction and entropy of printed English. *Bell Syst. Tech. J.***30** 50–64.

Shannon (1956), "A Universal Turing Machine with Two Internal States", *Automata Studies*, Princeton, NJ: Princeton University Press, pp. 157–165

Shannon and Weaver's (1949) *The Mathematical Theory of Communication*. Illinois: Univ of Illinois Press

Spivey, M. (2007) *The Continuity of Mind*, Oxford Univ. Press NY

Solo, R.L. (1994), *Cognition and the Visual Arts*. MIT press, Cambridge, Mass.

Steinbuch, K. Die Lernmatrix. (1961). *Biological Cybernetics* 1 (1), 36–45.

Strate, L. and Wachtel, E. (Eds.). (2005). *The legacy of McLuhan*. Cresskill, NJ: Hampton Press

Thelen E, Smith LB (1994) A Dynamic Systems Approach to the Development of Cognition and Action. Cambridge, MA: MIT Press

Turing, A.M. (1936), "On Computable Numbers, with an Application to the Entscheidungsproblem", *Proceedings of the London Mathematical Society*, 2 (1937) 42: 230–65,

Tsao DY and Livingstone MS 2008 Mechanisms of face perception. *Ann Review of Neuroscience* 31: 411–37

Turing, A.M. (1937), "On Computable Numbers, with an Application to the Entscheidungsproblem: A correction", *Proceedings of the London Mathematical Society*, 2 (1937) **43** (6): 544–6

Turing, A.M. (1950). Computing machinery and intelligence. Mind, 59, 433–460

Ullman, S. (1984) Visual Routines, *Cognition*, 18, 97–157.

Ullman, S. (1996) *High-level Vision: Object Recognition and Visual Cognition*. M.I.T. Press, Cambridge, MA

Watanabe, S. (1960). Information-theoretical aspects of inductive and deductive inference *IBM J. Res. Dev.* 4 208–31

Watts, D.J. (2004) The "new" science of networks. *Ann. Rev Sociol* 30: 243–70

Weaver, W. (1949). The mathematics of communication. *Scientific American* 181, 1, 11–15.

Wilson, H.R., Cowan, J.D. (1973) A mathematical theory of the functional dynamics of cortical and thalamic nervous tissue. *Kybernetik* 13, 55–80

Wright, K. and Webb, L.M. Eds. (2011). *Computer-Mediated Communication in Personal Relationships*. Peter Lang, NY.

Yarbus AL (1967) Eye Movements and Vision. New York: Plenum Press

Zabrodsky H, Algom D (1994) Continuous symmetry: A model for human figural perception. *Spatial Vision* 8(4): 455–467

MIX
Papier aus verantwortungsvollen Quellen
Paper from responsible sources
FSC® C105338

If you have any concerns about our products,
you can contact us on
ProductSafety@springernature.com

In case Publisher is established outside the EU,
the EU authorized representative is:
Springer Nature Customer Service Center GmbH
Europaplatz 3, 69115 Heidelberg, Germany

Printed by Libri Plureos GmbH
in Hamburg, Germany

SPRINGER BRIEFS IN COMPLEXITY

Hermann Haken · Juval Portugali

Information Adaptation: The Interplay Between Shannon Information and Semantic Information in Cognition

Engineering

ISBN 978-3-319-11169-8

9 783319 111698

▸ springer.com